T0220894

Smart Systems for Industrial Applications

Scrivener Publishing
100 Cummings Center, Suite 541J
Beverly, MA 01915-6106

Artificial Intelligence and Soft Computing for Industrial Transformation

Series Editor: Dr S. Balamurugan (sbnbala@gmail.com)

Scope: Artificial Intelligence and Soft Computing Techniques play an impeccable role in industrial transformation. The topics to be covered in this book series include Artificial Intelligence, Machine Learning, Deep Learning, Neural Networks, Fuzzy Logic, Genetic Algorithms, Particle Swarm Optimization, Evolutionary Algorithms, Nature Inspired Algorithms, Simulated Annealing, Metaheuristics, Cuckoo Search, Firefly Optimization, Bio-inspired Algorithms, Ant Colony Optimization, Heuristic Search Techniques, Reinforcement Learning, Inductive Learning, Statistical Learning, Supervised and Unsupervised Learning, Association Learning and Clustering, Reasoning, Support Vector Machine, Differential Evolution Algorithms, Expert Systems, Neuro Fuzzy Hybrid Systems, Genetic Neuro Hybrid Systems, Genetic Fuzzy Hybrid Systems and other Hybridized Soft Computing Techniques and their applications for Industrial Transformation. The book series is aimed to provide comprehensive handbooks and reference books for the benefit of scientists, research scholars, students and industry professional working towards next generation industrial transformation.

Publishers at Scrivener
Martin Scrivener (martin@scrivenerpublishing.com)
Phillip Carmical (pcarmical@scrivenerpublishing.com)

Smart Systems for Industrial Applications

Edited by

C. Venkatesh, N. Rengarajan, P. Ponmurugan

and

S. Balamurugan

Scrivener
Publishing

This edition first published 2022 by John Wiley & Sons, Inc., 111 River Street, Hoboken, NJ 07030, USA and Scrivener Publishing LLC, 100 Cummings Center, Suite 541J, Beverly, MA 01915, USA
© 2022 Scrivener Publishing LLC
For more information about Scrivener publications please visit www.scrivenerpublishing.com.

Wiley Global Headquarters
111 River Street, Hoboken, NJ 07030, USA

For details of our global editorial offices, customer services, and more information about Wiley products visit us at www.wiley.com.

Limit of Liability/Disclaimer of Warranty
While the publisher and authors have used their best efforts in preparing this work, they make no representations or warranties with respect to the accuracy or completeness of the contents of this work and specifically disclaim all warranties, including without limitation any implied warranties of merchantability or fitness for a particular purpose. No warranty may be created or extended by sales representatives, written sales materials, or promotional statements for this work. The fact that an organization, website, or product is referred to in this work as a citation and/or potential source of further information does not mean that the publisher and authors endorse the information or services the organization, website, or product may provide or recommendations it may make. This work is sold with the understanding that the publisher is not engaged in rendering professional services. The advice and strategies contained herein may not be suitable for your situation. You should consult with a specialist where appropriate. Neither the publisher nor authors shall be liable for any loss of profit or any other commercial damages, including but not limited to special, incidental, consequential, or other damages. Further, readers should be aware that websites listed in this work may have changed or disappeared between when this work was written and when it is read.

Library of Congress Cataloging-in-Publication Data

ISBN 978-1-119-76200-3

Cover image: Pixabay.Com
Cover design by Russell Richardson

Set in size of 11pt and Minion Pro by Manila Typesetting Company, Makati, Philippines

10 9 8 7 6 5 4 3 2 1

Contents

Preface

In this digital era, the towering intellectual abilities demonstrated by machines, known as artificial intelligence (AI), continue to advance innovations with the goal of improving the world. Artificial intelligence broadens horizons in the field of science, which will help change essential things and modulate eternal facts. This advancement in AI miraculously continues to retain an inspired vision in regards to emerging technologies. Hence, this book provides readers with the tools to fill in the AI-related knowledge gaps yet to be conquered through the use of smart intelligent systems for industrial applications.

Today, due to our subjugation to technology, there is much more to reckon within our quest for knowledge. Therefore, the knowledge included in the chapters of this book, which covers AI topics related to smart homes, smart cities, and smart towns, the industrial Internet of things, and smart earth and smart metering, will be helpful when confronting the most recent technological challenges in a timely manner.

In order to help the reader thrive in an AI world, the book covers a broad range of topics about AI from a multidisciplinary point of view, starting with its history and continuing on to theories about artificial vs. human intelligence, concepts and regulations concerning AI, human–machine distribution of power and control, delegation of decisions, the social and economic impact of AI, etc. The prominent role that AI plays in society by connecting people through technologies is highlighted in this book. It also covers key aspects of various AI applications in electrical systems in order to enable growth in electrical engineering. The impact that AI has on social and economic factors is also examined from various perspectives. Moreover, many intriguing aspects of AI techniques in different domains are covered such as e-learning, healthcare, smart grid, virtual assistance, etc. The contents of this book will be useful for students, teachers, and researchers who would like to know more about AI, which is a new technology that broadens the boundaries of learning in this contemporary world. Reading this book will be like taking a voyage through the land of AI.

Our sincere gratitude goes to all those who contributed to the valuable chapters of this book. Also, thanks go to the editorial director and the production editor at Scrivener Publishing, whose ardent support made the completion of this book possible.

Dr. C. Venkatesh
Namakkal, India
Dr. N. Rengarajan
Erode, India
Dr. P. Ponmurugan
Namakkal, India
Dr. S. Balamurugan
Coimbatore, India
October 2021

AI-Driven Information and Communication Technologies, Services, and Applications for Next-Generation Healthcare System

Vijayakumar Ponnusamy[1*], A. Vasuki[2], J. Christopher Clement[3] and P. Eswaran[4]

[1]ECE Department, SRM IST, Kattankulathur, Chennai, India
[2]Department of Electronics and Communication Engineering, SRM Institute of Science and Technology, Vadapalani, Chennai, Tamil Nadu, India
[3]School of Electronics Engineering, VIT, Vellore, India
[4]ECE Department, SRM IST, Chennai, India

Abstract

Today, the introduction of communication technology has turned out an immense influence on healthcare. Communication technology enables real-time monitoring of a patient remotely to detect the health metrics and disease symptoms at an affordable price. Community-level health monitoring is also possible through these communication technologies, which saves time and enables us to serve more patients. Artificial Intelligence (AI)–based communication ensures reliable communication, which is a vital factor in the healthcare industry. AI with the Internet of Things (IoT) in healthcare makes self-diagnosing capability via wireless body area networks (WBANs), which uses wearable sensing devices. The wearable WBAN is a challenging one because it involves radiation of EM waves on the human body. mHealth is another technology that enables one to reach healthcare services anywhere at any time through the mobile application using specialized communication protocols. Augmented and virtual reality allows efficient diagnosis and does surgery using real-time digital visual aids with more precision. All those technologies require specialized wireless communication. Thus, this chapter intended to cover challenges, methodology, communication protocols, and

Corresponding author: vijayakp@srmist.edu.in

C. Venkatesh, N. Rengarajan, P. Ponmurugan and S. Balamurugan (eds.) Smart Systems for Industrial Applications, (1–32) © 2022 Scrivener Publishing LLC

applications of IoT-based healthcare, mHealth healthcare, body area networks, and augmented and virtual reality.

Keywords: Augmented reality, AI-driven communication, healthcare, Internet of Things, mHealth, wireless body area networks, virtual reality

1.1   Introduction: Overview of Communication Technology and Services for Healthcare

In recent days, communication technologies play a vital role in upcoming healthcare solutions. The drastic improvement in communication technologies, especially in the areas of wireless communication, offer anytime-anywhere connectivity to support advanced services for healthcare.

In our globe, the population is one of the main aspects to develop the most modernized technologies to reach the information as much as simple and easier to other people; most of the technologies have achieved its higher level to this advanced method by adopting those features. Uncertainly, some sectors are not utilizing the technology properly even though it helps mankind; the medical healthcare system is one of those. In the more regions of the world, the population is in denser growth and its impossible for a doctor or a specialized one to take care of every person they are examining and vice versa for patients also not able to reach doctors at a certain time [1], in these kinds of situations, eHealth is used to take care of these responsibilities. Together with the development of the internet, eHealth is one of the widely accepted healthcare services. It encompasses the applications of communication technologies for the support of healthcare activities. Telemedicine, telecare, clinical information networks, and analysis of heterogeneous data sources are the various branches of eHealth [2]. eHealthcare system design is illustrated in Figure 1.1.

This technology refers to Information and Communication Technologies (ICTs); these are the tools used by the healthcare professionals and also by the patients to diagnosis the health condition by themselves or with their relatives. It is a digitalized technology that supports capturing, storing, processing, and exchanging the information to provide the best healthcare support. The base principle of the ICT is to prevent and diagnosis the problem in an efficient way through digital technology; the ICT technology transformation in medical sectors are varied according to the platform. The wireless technology has emerged as a drastic one that can be unavoidable, so the smartphone technologies enable remote monitoring systems. These are used to avoid the condition of an emergency condition by detecting in

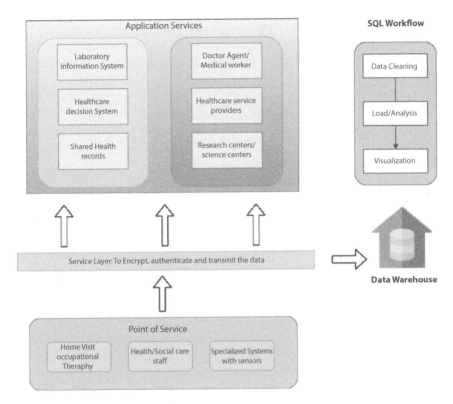

Figure 1.1 eHealthcare system design.

initial conditions [1], so it is highly adopted. It refers to projects that allow the telehealth to promote patient-centered healthcare at a lower cost; the quality of the healthcare system is also more reliable in the technology. It enables a new way of communication between the doctors and the patients, to reduce the time for the patient to reach the doctor's place.

Even though it has many advantages, the implementation of the ICT in practice is quite a complex one and requires a different level of changes by the healthcare providers and the healthcare organizations. It facilitates the sharing of data across the continuum of care across healthcare delivery organizations and different geographical areas. It mainly avoids unnecessary therapeutic interventions through the healthcare establishment and patient involvement.

This system involves the diagnosis of the patient from the point of the service area to initialize the method; the **required** devices are included into the eHealthcare system that will provide the service that has the real-time conferencing with the data between a doctor and a patient; it consists of the session that enables the prototype to client service media application. The data generated through the conferencing are recorded and sent through the service layer to attain a level of security and authenticity of the service and then to store the data in the data warehouse; it contains a collection of data that are used by the medical professionals [3]; the storing data vary for the same user for different readings; for those purposes, the structured query language is used because of the complexity of data in database relational database is more sophisticated. However, it might have an issue of managing larger database complexity. It has more advanced security features of data handling before inserting the data into the data server; it cleans the data, loads it and analyzes it for any vulnerabilities. Finally, it visualizes the loaded data for the analytical purpose [1–3]; the SQL structure handles data handling works.

The acquired data sources are accessed by the authorized healthcare member where the entire medical healthcare statistics of the patient are all displayed to the specialized person. It has also maintained a healthcare decision system that is more emerging features that will provide the solutions for the already existing diagnosis. This eliminates the repetitive task of producing the same results. It is also connected with the health records system and the research centers, so the data will serve as a tool for the modern medical development process. The regular steps carried in the day-to-day medical procedures are all automated in the eHealthcare system and the accuracy is one of the prominent features in this method. The laboratory information system provides the ease of access to the records and manages and stores the data for clinical laboratories [4], tracking of the test orders and sending those data in the digitalized form through a searchable database.

Mobile health is another critical paradigm, which overcomes the geographical, organizational, and temporal barriers in healthcare services. The idea has evolved in accordance with the technological changes in communication protocols that have changed from GSM, GPRS, wireless LAN to 4G and, more recently, 5G communication technologies [5]. The wireless ECG transmissions, wireless ambulance services, video images and teleradiology, and other integrated mobile telemedical monitoring systems are some examples of applications of 2G and 3G technologies. The evolution of mHealth for personalized medical systems with flexible functionalities is possible because of the development of 4G networks. Moreover, the reduced latency and good media services in healthcare are achieved with the advent of 5G communication technologies in mobile healthcare.

Personalized health is user-specific, and it is targeted toward taking patient-specific decisions. It is also called otherwise as adaptive health. In personalized health, the sources of data include wearable devices and sensors with implementable micro- or nanotechnologies. The data collected from these devices are combined at the decision center for making up any decision [6]. The idea can be enhanced to P4 medicine, in which the data sources could be the genetic information from each individual.

Table 1.1 Role of communication technologies in healthcare.

Source	Technology	Applications in healthcare
[1, 2]	eHealth	• Health information networks • Electronic health records • Telemedicine services • Wearable and portable devices • Health portals
[3]	Digital Healthcare	• Digital health information software • Digital health strategy
[4]	Impact of eHealth Technology	• eHealth measure • 51% of people with multiple chronic conditions use eHealth for self-management on a daily basis
[5]	e-med	• Wireless internet telemedicine • Wireless ECG transmission • Wireless ambulance services • Tele-radiology • Mobile tele-medical monitoring system
[6]	Ubiquitous and personalized eHealth	• Intelligent mobile agents • Wearable devices • Sensors with implementable micro or nanotechnologies
[7]	Smart health	• Remote ECG monitoring • Mobile Picture Archiving and Communications System (PACS)-X-ray services
[8]	mHealth	• Machine-to-machine (M2M) communication • M2M processes health records like blood pressure, body temperature and heart rate

The collective insight on one's biology can address the source of disease and the condition of health, which can impact screening and diagnosis. Smart health is supported by smart devices like mobile phones and likely devices for the practicing of public and individual healthcare. Other than mobile phones, the devices used for smart health include sensors, robots, smart cards, and the internet with a pay-according to user basis [7].

Mobile broadband connectivity alleviates the issues caused by limited coverage of healthcare services in remote areas. Along with the existing 4G, the advent of 5G networks revolutionized healthcare communication technologies in terms of increased data rate, reduced latency, and improved capacity to support many challenging applications [8]. Machine-to-machine communication in the current era enables day-to-day objects and the surrounding atmosphere managed and connected through extensive devices, communication protocols, and clouds or servers. IEEE standards, namely, IEEE 802.15, the wireless personal area network, and wireless body area network (WBAN), are adopted in many healthcare systems. The summary on applications of communication technologies in healthcare is given in Table 1.1.

1.2   AI-Driven Communication Technology in Healthcare

The development of communication technologies plays a significant role in the growth of healthcare as an industry. To quote a few advancements in healthcare are rapid growth in the number of patient records that are converted into electronic health record. The health record is a document that covers historical information about the patients. Technology in healthcare is not only introducing digital transformation; it becomes a trend in controlling in every aspect of healthcare. In recent trends, Artificial Intelligence (AI) also gains attention in the enhancement of various system modeling, processes, and ease of prediction [9]. Most of the human illness are identified and diagnosed through image processing and pattern recognition algorithms. In recent times, AI is used to enhance the accuracy of imaging tools. In this chapter, we provide a detailed discussion of the impact of AI and various communication technologies in healthcare.

1.2.1   Technologies Empowering in Healthcare

In this section, we provide an overview of recent AI technologies that are responsible for recent shifts in healthcare, as shown in Figure 1.2.

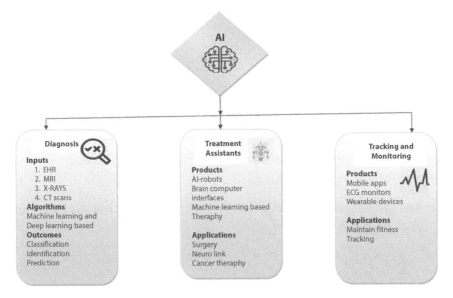

Figure 1.2 Impact of AI in different domains of healthcare.

1.2.2   AI in Diagnosis

In this section, we present the effect of AI in healthcare for diagnosis application with examples. A simple process of AI transformation is shown in Figure 1.3. Online-based application has been developed to ease the process and increases real-time availability and accessibility of health-related information. Online healthcare has set a new channel for data transfer between the patient and the health unit. Extracting and analyzing the health record is a challenging task, which is achieved by reliable AI algorithms. These algorithms can predict the disease by understanding the nature of the patient's record. Deep learning–based risk scoring and stratification tools are successfully developed to identify probable correlation from an unknown dataset within the patient's record.

Application of AI in healthcare is utilized for acquiring a huge amount of data, processing the complex inheritance in them, and supporting decisions in case of the limited human intervention [10]. AI's processing capabilities overcome the limitations mentioned above in healthcare and new methods to help doctors. AI is mainly used in diagnosing the illness compared with prognosis and therapy. Diagnosis is the process of observing and testing the patient, collecting information, analyzing the data, and finally providing a treatment plan. Diagnosis in AI is achieved by feeding patient information to the computing system, which produces diagnosis output.

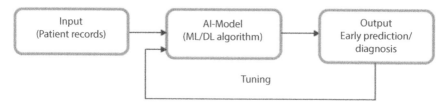

Figure 1.3 AI-based diagnosis process.

1.2.3 Conversion Protocols

In this section, we discuss two basic protocols used for transforming the process into AI-based [11].

(i) Expert system
(ii) ANN-based model

The expert system is a technique that is followed for transforming the conventional diagnosis process into an AI-assisted. It outlines the step by step process involved from input to output by framing conditional protocols. The protocols are developed in domain wise by the clinician's experience and knowledge. Artificial Neural Networks (ANNs) are a parallel processing technique or model which consists of neurons as processing elements, wherein neurons are linked and arranged layer-wise. Layers are also connected. The neurons are assigned with a functional unit and weight value based on the type of application. Weights of the processing could be varied to reach the specified result by applying a backpropagation algorithm. The parallel processing capability of ANN makes it more convenient method for medical applications. ANN-based model is illustrated in Figure 1.4.

Other than a medical diagnosis, ANN is used for analyzing the radiographs in radiology. Gamma, CT, ultrasound, and MRI images are manipulated using ANN. The digitized inputs are given to ANN, processed by inner layers of ANN, and produce appropriate outputs. Orthopedic injuries are successfully identified by trained ANN. In cytology, ANN is used to classify or group the abnormal cells from the specimen cell. It has also been utilized for interpreting EEG and ECG signals. Accuracy of performance on waveform analysis, identification of abnormalities, and data interpretation by ANN is very much useful and reduces the human intervention.

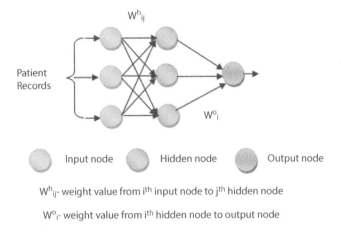

Figure 1.4 ANN-based diagnosis model.

1.2.4 AI in Treatment Assistant

Surgeries are performed by robotic machines, which are controlled by doctors. Robotic surgery is preferred with less invasive techniques, which allow them to perform tasks with better accuracy and control. Mobile ECG monitors and wide usage of smart health watches are utilized for keeping track of and after the surgery. Robotic assistants are employed in elderly care for assisting them in daily routines.

Interfacing the human mind and technology has significant applications in healthcare. Brain-computer interfaces assisted by AI enable patients with neurological diseases to talk, move, and communicate with others. In this scenario, a combination of AI and interfaces decode the neural activities related to the movement of limbs, which further stimulate the indented action.

Immunotherapy is one of the promising cancer treatments. In this therapy, tumors are treated naturally with the human immune system. But a lesser number of patients are responding to these kinds of treatments. Currently, a precise machine learning algorithm is developed to classify and identify the capability of the natural body immune system to treat cancer. AI is also supporting to enable virtual biopsies in the field of radiology, which achieves harnessing image-based algorithms to characterize the patterns and genetic structures of tumors.

AI could reduce the impact on shortages of well-trained healthcare providers by handling over some diagnostic tasks which are allocated to humans. An AI imaging tool take X-rays for tuberculosis symptoms with better accuracy compared to the human. This algorithm is diversified, which considers the environmental factors influencing the disease.

1.2.5   AI in the Monitoring Process

Smartphones have provided numerous tools for patients, which are extremely useful for extracting, transferring, and processing health information. Machine learning algorithms develop mobile applications for analyzing child facial diseases. These algorithms detect unique features such as the child's jawline, eye, and nose placement to identify the craniofacial abnormalities.

Tracking health information is extended away from hospitals through wearable devices to maintain the fitness of the patients. Wearable devices are made up of internal sensors to measure and save health parameters. AI is used for extracting and analyzing the vast data from the devices and generates useful insights.

1.2.6   Challenges of AI in Healthcare

The potential of AI to increase access to healthcare is tremendous. However, sensible information of the patients is used for processing, which must be protected with restricted access. AI is a system developed by humans; it should have the capability of discriminating features to secure the information. Now, the technology exists everywhere, which causes an impact on human health. It is also required to maintain the balance in using techniques in healthcare.

The essential applications of AI in healthcare are summarized in Table 1.2.

1.3   AI-Driven mHealth Communication System and Services

AI aims to mimic human cognitive functions. It is bringing a paradigm shift to healthcare, powered by the increasing availability of healthcare data and the rapid progress of analytics techniques [12–14]. Recently, AI techniques are applied in mHealth services and systems. There are various health-oriented smartphone applications available. There are around 160,000 of them, which are downloaded about 660 million times [15]. Moreover, blood pressure and heart rhythm are a few smartphone-connected devices

Table 1.2 Applications of AI in healthcare.

Source	Subject matter	Parameter analyzed/considered	Related performance measures
[9]	AI in Healthcare	• Brain Computer Interfaces (BCI) • Next generation radiology tools • Expansion of AI-healthcare network • Electronic Health Record (EHR) • Antibiotic Resistance • Pathology analysis • Intelligent medical machines • Immunotherapy • Risk predictor • Health monitoring system • Diagnostic tools • Clinical decision-making	• BCI improves quality of life for patients with ALS, strokes and 5 lakhs people with spinal card injuries with every year • Virtual biopsies characterize the phenotypes and genetic properties of tumors • Voice recognition and dictation help in Clinical documentation. • 75% EHR use as a tool for right diagnosis • AI-based Risk scoring and stratification tools • DL identifies novel connections between seemingly unrelated data sets
[10]	Natural language processing	• Virtual Assistant • MelaFind • Robotics Assisted Therapy	• Helps the patients with Alzheimer's disease • Diagnose tool to analyze irregular moles melanoma skin cancer • Assists the patients during stroke recovery
[11]	Biological intelligence	• Medical data mining • ANN-based prediction • AI-Clinical decision-making	• Diagnoses orthopedic trauma from radiographs • 10% more accurate than conventional decision

that enable remote assessment of health conditions [15]. Identifying atrial fibrillation is one of the hottest topics in the field. The detection of atrial fibrillation was carried by comparing smartwatch data with around normal ECG data of 9,750 patients [16]. A deep learning algorithm combined with smartwatch applications exhibited excellent forecasting of atrial fibrillation with a specificity of 90.2% and a sensitivity of 98%.

1.3.1   Embedding of Handheld Imaging Platforms With mHealth Devices

Authors Bhavani *et al.* organized the integration of pocket-size ultrasound (POCUS) with mHealth devices to deal with heart diseases. In the reporting, there were around a total of 253 patients with heart diseases, which are randomized into two groups of mHealth clinics and standard healthcare. The pocket-size echocardiography was used from remote on medical decision-making with patients who have valvular heart diseases. The mHealth devices are associated with minimum referral time for intervention and improved probability of intervention in comparison with standard healthcare. mHealth also decreases the death rate and hospitalization. In work, the authors have embedded POCUS with mHealth devices and verified that the embedding could be performed in previous medical clinics with the required clinical outcome.

1.3.2   The Adaptability of POCUS in Telemedicine

Thus, POCUS has enabled point-of-care screening to resource-limited communities. The screening is associated with cardiovascular diseases. Moreover, the scanning of 1,023 studies was done in a remote place whose images were sent to the physicians for review through internet-based platforms. The sending and reviewing process was completed with the median time of 11:44 h. This study has proved that the remote assessment of echocardiographic has an added value of using internet-based assessment for cardiac illnesses.

The interpretation of images from remote was tested in a smartphone. Around 83 patients images were sent to remote locations and tested in smartphone applications. It is observed that the non-expert diagnosis was revised by remote experts.

It is also possible to apply deep learning and machine learning in the analysis of echocardiography. It is shown that the algorithms like random forests and support vector machines could distinguish between hypertrophic cardiomyopathy and athlete heart more precisely than any traditional measures. Moreover, supervised learning approaches with the required number of ECG variables verified the superiority of machine learning algorithms by distinguishing between restrictive cardiomyopathy and constrictive pericarditis [17].

The usage of deep learning algorithms for image classification is very obvious. These kinds of applications are useful in computer vision. The algorithms can recognize the patterns in heterogeneous syndromes and cardiovascular images. The deep learning methods can improve the accuracy of 2D STE and other modalities of imaging [18, 19]. The idea can be extended to other imaging modalities, namely, 3D STE and cardiac image of magnetic resonance imaging kind. The deep learning algorithms work well even in noisy data, namely, strain imaging. The diseases like Takotsubo cardiomyopathy, hypertension, Brugada syndrome, heart failure, and atrial fibrillation can also be diagnosed with deep learning algorithms. An autonomous interpretation of echocardiography was successfully implemented through a deep learning algorithm by Zhang *et al.* [20]. Using the data collection of 14,000 samples, the algorithm could successfully distinguish between broad echocardiographic view classes (e.g., short axis and parasternal long axis) with an accuracy of 96%.

Automated quantification of cardiac structure with the help of Convolutional Neural Networks (CNNs) was superior to manual measurements. Moreover, authors have trained the CNN to detect pulmonary artery hypertension, cardiac amyloidosis, and hypertrophic cardiomyopathy with high accuracy. These evolutions prove that the idea of embedding AI techniques in mHealth devices has become a reality. Machine learning and deep learning techniques are an effective means of handling the sheer complexity of the data. While comparing with other disciplines, cardiologists have numerous amounts of data at their disposal. Since the data complexity grows, it is important for an AI technique to be embedded in the clinical practice. So, it is expected in the future that all cardiologists to be data scientists and physicians simultaneously.

The summary of the above discussed articles on AI-driven mHealth communication is listed in Table 1.3.

1.4   AI-Driven Body Area Network Communication Technologies and Applications

The development and growth of wireless sensor networks play a vital role in the field of medical and health servicing sectors. In modern technology, wireless communication provides a lot of possibilities for the sharing of

Table 1.3 Impact of AI-mHealth communication system in healthcare.

Source	Subject matter	Role of AI-Driven mHealth devices	Related performance measures
[12–14]	Medical big data analysis	• Personalized clinical decision-making	• A complex diagnosis process in multiple chronic illnesses became simpler • Similarities in illness patterns are analyzed effectively
[15]	Digital healthcare	• Health Monitoring - Continuous Glucose Monitoring (CGM) • CardioMEMS Heart Sensor with Wireless implantable Hemodynamic Monitoring (W-HM) • Automated diagnostic algorithm	• POCUS uses in heart diseases • CGM early detects hypoglycemic episodes • W-HM results in 30% reduction in heart failure readmissions (hazard ratio 0.70, 95% confidence interval 0.60–0.84)
[16]	Atrial fibrillation detection	• C statistic–based trained ANN using smart watch data	• ANN predicts AF with 90.2% specificity and 98% sensitivity
[17]	Echocardiographic evaluation	• Machine learning–based Associative memory classifier	• Achieves 22% more accuracy in prediction than SVM.
[18, 19]	Transthoracic 3D Echocardiography (TTE) Left Heart Chamber Quantification	• Automated Adaptive Analytics Algorithm	• Achieves better correlation (r = 0.87 to 0.96) with manual 3D TTE
[20]	Echocardiogram Interpretation	• CNN-based detection trained with 14 035 Echocardiogram images	• CNN detects hypertrophic cardiomyopathy, cardiac amyloidosis, and pulmonary arterial hypertension with 95% accuracy.

information at anytime and anywhere. The main objective of this chapter is to explore body area network communication technologies driven by AI. Medical AI mainly utilizes computer network topologies to perform monitoring, recording, diagnoses, and treatment process [21].

A body area network has wide applications in medical and non-medical fields. In the medical field, they are either used as wearable devices or implanted in a patient's body or as a remote monitoring system to keep track of patient's health based on the sensory nodes positioned in their bodies. This is very sensitive to older adults or patients with chronic diseases. Through biomedical sensors, motion detectors, and wireless communication, monitoring of every activity like glucose, blood pressure, and pulse rate is done. Figure 1.5 shows a typical body area network with wearable devices for health monitoring. All the required information is collected through the central hub and processed wirelessly to the healthcare provider or medical staff during emergencies. The end devices can also be wearable [22–24], which act as transducers to display human activities, temperature, and pressure.

Communication in the body sensor network is of two types.

(i)   In-body communication uses RF signals between sensory nodes, which are implanted in our human body. The frequency at which the communication has to take place is

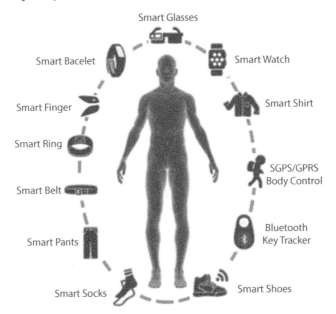

Figure 1.5 Wearable devices in the health monitoring system (Adopted from [21]).

defined by Medical Implantable Communication Service (MICS), and the range of frequency is 402–405 MHz
(ii) On-body communication is the communication between wearable sensory nodes, which consists of biosensors. Ultra-wideband (UWB) can be used for on-body communication. IMS based, which is mainly used for industrial, medical, and scientific applications having a range of 2.4–2.485 GHz. Many electronic applications operate on this band.

1.4.1 Features

Since the nodes are placed inside and outside the human body, it requires less power consumption as the devices are battery operated. So, it is essential that for the battery to work longer, power consumption should be less. As communication deals with bio-signals in the medical field, the Quality of Service (QoS) plays an important role. So, the user can detect proper information and treat accordingly.

As the network deals with information transmission related to vital parameters of human beings, the security of data is critical to avoid unauthorized accessibility. In the case of biosensors, the threshold value is set. So, if any parameter increases or decreases below the threshold value, then it generates an alarm, so fewer false alarms are required. Wireless Medical Telemetry Service (WMTS) and UWB are technologies that are used for body monitoring systems because of their low transmission power.

1.4.2 Communication Architecture of Wireless Body Area Networks

In this section, we discuss the architecture of WBAN, which is divided into the three-stage process to depict the working mechanism of WBAN as shown in Figure 1.6 [25].

Stage 1: Intra sensor communication
The communication among the sensors around the human body is considered in this stage. A personal server acts as a gateway, which is used by communication signals within the human body. Gateway transfers the data to the next stage of architecture.

Stage 2: Medium
This stage enables the data transfer between the personal server and user through an access point, which is considered as a central unit of the network, which can make decisions in case of emergencies.

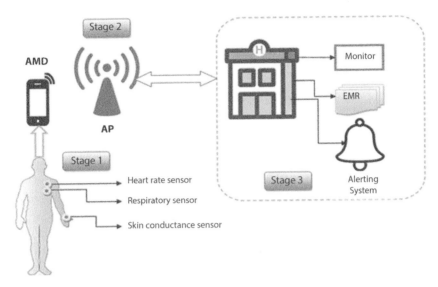

Figure 1.6 Architecture of WBAN communication.

Stage 3: Beyond WBAN

Smartphones are used to interlink between the access point and medical server, in which patient historical data could be stored. The medical environment database is a very sensitive part of stage 3. Security against this stage is fulfilled to protect the personal history of the patients.

1.4.3 Role of AI in WBAN Architecture

Internal communication among the sensors and measured parameters from the human body are processed using deep learning algorithms. AI-based data processing models analyze massive amounts of data from the sensors and extract useful information from them. Figure 1.7 shows the role of AI in WBAN. The extracted features are used to diagnosis the

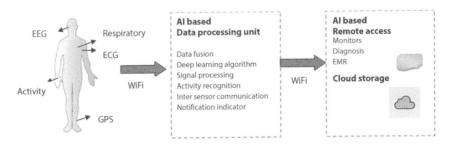

Figure 1.7 AI-enabled WBAN architecture.

disease, wherein the proposed model is trained with related data. CNNs are used for feature extraction; based on the inputs, CNN generates the possible, reliable outputs.

1.4.4   Medical Applications

WBAN technology improves the efficiency of the activities from patient to doctor, like monitoring the patient's health regularly and notifications or emergency calling in a flexible way. It offers automatic medical services through remote monitoring of the patient's vital parameters. All the information is stored from the control unit. It helps the patient to stay at home and get continuous support remotely. In case of any emergency, the sensors implanted in the patient's body raises the alarm of urgent notification, which will be notified by nearby healthcare provides healthcare services over a distance with the help of communication technology. This can be done by online video consultation with doctors, the transmission of reports and images, and remote medical diagnosis. E-prescription is provided after monitoring the patient's health conditions. Pulse oximeters are used to measure the amount of oxygen level in the blood bypassing the beam of red and infrared into the human body. Color differentiation is the fundamental concept of oximeters; oxygenated blood is more red, where deoxygenated is purple-blue.

1.4.5   Nonmedical Applications

In non-medical applications, WBAN is used in sports where devices can be wearable. It is effective to monitor the physiological activities of the wearer like heart rate, temperature, blood pressure, and posture of any attitude in sports. Navigation, timer, and distance can also be measured with the help of WBAN sensors.

1.4.6   Challenges

Medical sensors are used to monitor a patient's body continually and collect information so they should be active all the time; hence energy consumption is high. In body communication, sensors are implanted in vital areas of the body, so if the batteries are consumed fully, the patient has to undergo body surgery to replace a new one. Since the collection of data requires more energy than sending data through wireless time out Mac protocol, which is used in WBAN. Transmission of data is affected by jamming, bit error rate, and link quality. This can be minimized by using

Table 1.4 Role of AI in wireless body area networks.

Source	Subject matter	Applications	Role of WBAN
[21]	Impact of MEMS in WBAN	• Personal health monitoring	• Wearable WBAN ○ Assessing soldier fatigue and battle readiness ○ Aiding professional and amateur sport training • Implant WBAN • Cardiovascular diseases ○ Cancer detection
[22–24]	Wireless Healthcare	• Health monitoring devices • Wearable devices (computer)	• Collects multi-physiological information for diagnosing, monitoring the health
[25]	Privacy and security in remote health monitoring	• TinySec • Biometrics • Bluetooth and Zigbee security services • Wireless security protocols	• Link layer encryption and authentication of data in biomedical sensor networks • Employs self-body as a way to manage cryptographic keys for sensors • Logical Link Control and Adaptation (*L2CAP*) provide improved QoS.

Cooperate Network Coding (CNC) since it does not require any retransmission when there is any failure in any of the nodes.

The major challenge is the security and privacy of the patient's medical information. Data confidentiality should be maintained to avoid unauthorized access. So, to make sure that the data is sent by appropriate user authentication is necessary. It is also essential to see that received data is not manipulated so that data must be protected for proper medical diagnosis.

The applications and impact of WBAN in healthcare are summarized in Table 1.4.

1.5 AI-Driven IoT Device Communication Technologies and Healthcare Applications

Healthcare providers around the world are a huge source of data, starting from patient history to drug trials. With digitization as a backdrop, many of these records are converted into electronic forms enhancing its utility and enabling vital care decisions. This data has innumerable applications like reviewing the past, understanding the current, and helping predict future trends in the healthcare of patients. AI algorithms, when paired with healthcare data, can drive remarkable insights into intelligent reasoning, quicker analysis of data, provide informed acumen into patient's healthcare and even extend into decisions on investments in healthcare infrastructure.

1.5.1 AI's and IoT's Role in Healthcare

The rise in the Internet of Things (IoT) has enabled two things—monitoring and broader reach of patient healthcare. Devices are interconnected while they remotely manage healthcare equipment. They not only update the individual patient record but also act as a source for AI-driven healthcare analytics at large. Wearable healthcare devices have seen a rise in recent years owing to the popularity of healthier living. Automated at home healthcare management and monitoring chronic conditions have been the other key drivers in the surge of IoT. In a way, it aids practitioners in making well-informed decisions resulting in quicker diagnosis for effective treatment. Thus, increasing innovations in wearable devices like insulin monitors to portable blood pressure monitors, and it is ever-expanding. Advances in healthcare have made it feasible for an emerging field like Remote Healthcare Management [26]. Key attributes to the possible success of Remote Healthcare Management are as follows.

1.5.2   Creating Efficient Communication Framework for Remote Healthcare Management

Patients to rehabilitate at home are a common condition post-treatments or part of a few during which there is a possibility of relapse due to inadequate care. In today's scenario, patients are provided with AI-powered wearable technology that enables remote monitoring once they have been discharged or in cases where equipment supports is required for treating them. It brings about significant benefits like early warnings of deterioration in patients to allow targeted interventions, also minimize administrative ordeal of hospitalization and readmission. A quick response to any fluctuation in health conditions is made feasible with IoT. Therefore, remote monitoring services become dependable round the clock.

Sensors used in IoT devices are linked together yet separately identified over a communication infrastructure [27]. IoT has three layers of communication: sensors that have the physical interface. This system provides connectivity and server where all the sensory data is stored and processed, as shown in Figure 1.8. The first two layers are simple and can be very cost-effective and predominately setup at the patient's end. The third layer is traditionally a cloud where an array of services is provided with the help of AI algorithms performance big data analytics. The cloud layer is interconnected with local layers through the multi-hop network, making it susceptible to challenges of reliability, availability, and soundness. With varying latency and bandwidth, traditional cloud computing architecture needs to be reviewed as the patient is the end-user, and in emergencies, establishing connections could have adverse effects. In remote healthcare monitoring, there is always an increase in the number of connected

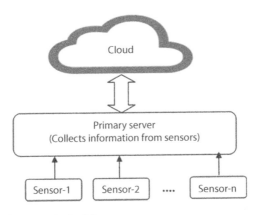

Figure 1.8 IoT architecture for healthcare.

devices, and with it comes the sensory data, which could cause potential overload on the communication infrastructure. Currently, many types of research are underway to make this architecture effective, enabling layer two to pre-process using computational capabilities and close loop architecture. Allowing this layer creates a system where essential and critical services can be locally controlled and, in turn, reducing the load on IoT communication infrastructure through effective task and resource management.

The overall objective was to minimize the effects of varying latency and bandwidth between gateways and servers here; it is the traditional cloud computing. It is tested with hierarchical computing architecture where existing machine learning methods can help in a fog-enabled IoT system. At a local level, it explores the feasibility of delivering adaptive transmission of data inside a closed-loop environment [27].

1.5.3   Developing Autonomous Capability is Key for Remote Healthcare Management

Remote monitoring is a robust model of healthcare. The advent of wearable devices aided in the smart healthcare application, in turn, enabling quicker clinical diagnosis and ease of disease prediction. The host of sensors is deployed in healthcare, uniquely placed inside the body either as implants or sensing devices over the physical body. Many of these can also communicate with small handheld devices such as smartphones or digital assistants. Dynamic and Interoperable Communication Framework (DICF) is primarily designed [28] to improve efficiency and enhance the decision-making capabilities of these wearable sensors. It optimizes various constraints of a sensor, namely, lifetime, storage capacity, handling multiple communication channels, and decision-making. The radio transmitter is used by sensors to interact with Aggregator Mobile Device (AMD); it can be a mobile platform. Information received is distinguished by the physiological source or based on sensor types. Periodic sensing for the collection of data varies with the kind of sensor and the human body. This periodic sensing is called a session. A session is, in turn, capable of sensing both periodic and event while monitoring is in progress. Pattern and range are clearly defined for transmitting data from AMD to service provider or clinic. So, when their data which does not fall within this range, an abnormality detected. AMD quickly generates an emergency notification and prioritizes transmission. In such events of AMD transmits completed sensed data to the clinic or the service provider without requesting the permission of end-users or patients.

Before the trigger of emergency is actuated, local machine learning algorithm checks for early diagnosis and first aid suggestions. Machine learning starts to establish causes and conditions using sensory data with varied conditions of patients and different patient data. Data collected and analyses at a local level significantly increase as different learning algorithms are applied to the results for further analysis. AMD performs the role of the hub by collecting data and relaying it to the clinic of the service provider, data accumulation at periodic intervals, and data gathering post applying algorithms. With the capacity of AMD, there is a significant improvement in processing capability at the local level. Data is stored as an Electronic Medical Record (EMR), which is interconnected with the notification system and monitoring unit. This enables a process of classification and decisions based on regression models. This decision-making model improves the performances of wearable devices in terms of event detection and emergency interval identification in a remote monitoring system. DICF aids in building a robust sensor dependent personal healthcare system. It also facilitates data collection, event detection, analysis, and communication with interconnected wearable sensors. AI-based remote healthcare system is shown in Figure 1.9.

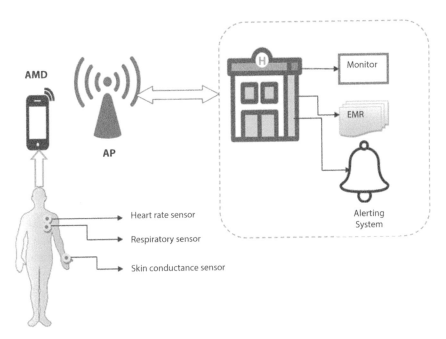

Figure 1.9 AI-based remote healthcare management.

1.5.4   Enabling Data Privacy and Security in the Field of Remote Healthcare Management

Internet of Medical Things (IoM) has gained specialization in recent years with growing applications. Both embedded and wearable sensors gather comprehensive information about patients. It is shared with medical professionals for diagnosis. The sensitive nature of this data gives rise to protection and privacy, which is currently a significant challenge of the IoM. It uses anonymity-based authentication to mitigate privacy issues. To ensure the session is secure, upon mutual authentication, both medical professionals and medical sensors utilize private session keys. Research in this area of authenticity and privacy of data is still at the nascent stage. Currently, available authentication features are not suitable to achieve the privacy goals in terms of its features. At this juncture, there is not a credible and efficient authentication program in this segment. One of the key issues in achieving the goal is two-factor security in the event of loss or tampered smart card. Research is deplored to investigate the adversarial model, which is expected to mitigate various redundancies and ambiguities. This paper explores a methodology with 12 independent criteria analyzed using an adversary model for practical use. Broadly, it enables a better understanding of privacy requirements if not successful. In [28], the authors explore the feasibility of smart revocation/reissue and improve security efficiencies using a formal model. Secure-Anonymous Biometric-Based User Authentication Scheme (SAB-UAS) is tested for efficiency and meeting security goals.

In [29], the authors present SAB-UAS using a smart card with three entities in the healthcare communication chain, medical practitioners, wireless gateways, and wearable sensors. Moment SAB-UAS scheme starts process, two master keys are generated along with a long-term secret key by Wireless gateways, which is then transmitted to wearable sensors. Gateways quickly try to use one of the master keys, establishing it as a public key. This system is simulated at three stages, mainly user name registration, system login and authentication, and any case of revocations. After simulating SAB-UAS at three stages, the formal security analysis is also simulated. Random Oracle model is used to prove the security efficiency of SAB-UAS. The simulation clearly shows SAB-UAS scheme can securely protect sensitive information from various retrieval mechanisms. An informal security attack is also simulated with different 12 independent conditions, and it can meet the security goals setup. It is essential to understand whether SAB-UAS is also efficient because the electronic healthcare system comprises lightweight resources with very many limitations like storage capacity, bandwidth, and processing capabilities. Resource efficiency analysis is computed to understand storage, communication, and computation capabilities observed under the following conditions:

(i) Analysis of Packet Delivery Ratio (PDR): With a large number of sensors, efficiency in a PDR of SAB-UAS deteriorates.

(ii) Analysis of End-to-End (ETE) delay: There is a lesser delay compared to other methods. But with the increasing number of communication nodes, the delay in ETE is proportional.

(iii) Analysis of Throughput Transmission Rate (TTE): SAB-UAS has a better throughput rate compared to other authentication systems, and there are negligible deviations in TTE even when there were increased communication nodes.

(iv) Analysis of Routing Overhead (RTO): SAB-UAS seems to have tactful management of packet routing enhancing network performance and bandwidth usage.

The above simulations are essential in an environment of Remote Healthcare because the speed and efficiency of resources play a critical role in patient health. Response time should not be lost at the cost of security as well. SAB-UAS performs well compared to other authentication systems. Maybe with increasing communication nodes, it has lower efficiency in PDR and ETE. This proposed SAB-UAS scheme can substantially improve performance at the storage, computation, and communication level at the same time, keeping costs at lower. This, in turn, makes Remote Healthcare Management a real-time application. SAB-UAS has robust security when it comes to both formal and informal security threats and potential attacks. The essential of IoT and security of collected information are summarized in Table 1.5.

1.6   AI-Driven Augmented and Virtual Reality–Based Communication Technologies and Healthcare Applications

Technology is getting better, smaller, and faster. Virtual reality (VR) is a highly interactive, computer-based multimedia environment in which

Table 1.5 Role of AI-driven IoT in healthcare services.

Source	Subject matter	Applications	Related performance measures
[26]	Digital transformation	• Automated management and monitoring chronic conditions	• Sensor devices usage increases up to 23.8% Compound Annual Growth Rate (CAGR)
[27]	Hierarchical computing Architecture for Healthcare IoT	• Machine learning–based data analytics • Closed-loop autonomous system	• Employed in arrhythmia detection for patients suffering from cardiovascular diseases • Achieves 93.6 accuracy using k-fold cross validation method.
[28]	Regulation of wireless devices operation	• Dynamic and interoperable communication framework	• Enhances the decision-making capabilities of wearable sensors. • Optimizes device lifetime, storage capacity and handling multiple communication channel
[29]	Security parameters	• Secure-Anonymous Biometric-based User Authentication Scheme (SAB-UAS)	• Achieves delay up to 0.02 seconds in a network with 160 sensor nodes. • Also achieves throughput of 2500bps with a same network

the user becomes the participant in a computer-generated world. VR and augmented reality (AR) are having an impact on most aspects of modern life. AR is an integration of the real world and the virtual world, with the aim of providing additional information about something in the real world with information displayed in the virtual world. In recent times, the scope of AR applications has expanded to include innovation for the domains of Research, Science, Medicine, Telecommunications, etc. For instance, a person could look at a painting or a machine in the real world, hold up their smartphones or tablet in front of the painting or machine, and see on the screen the painting or machine with additional useful information, thus augmenting reality. It is becoming ever more in demand in every segment of the economy, particularly in healthcare. With the technological advancements in AI, their demand is also increasing progressively in healthcare applications. Not just in healthcare, VR is helping organizations in different sectors to train their workforce as a good communicator. In reference to Healthcare and Medical Clinics, simulations are developed with a pre-defined script and one or more avatars with whom the player can interact. This article describes the impact of VR and AR in communication technologies and healthcare applications.

1.6.1 Clinical Applications of Communication-Based AI and Augmented Reality

AI, together with AR, has vast clinical and surgical applications in healthcare. The unsupervised models allow the system to recognize the patterns followed by the initiation of the algorithm based on previous patterns. In addition, reinforcement learning algorithms use positive and negative rewards or punishments in their learning methodologies [30]. Whether the relationship between input and output is linear or not, the programs go through more decision-making layers to deduce a mathematical rule to create outputs based on specific inputs. The disciplines of medicine that rely on deep learning that include radiology and pattern recognition have become more precise than human intervention methods [31]. Deep learning algorithms are applied in finding out malignancy and improving neonatal imaging and neurologic imaging qualities.

The AI models are used to forecast the readmission and delayed discharge [32]. There are various lung cancer models used to aid in the prediction, diagnosis, and planning of treatments [33]. The prediction of survival rate after surgery is modeled for cervical cancer patients [34]. From applications like simple prognostic tools to big and complex models,

AI is used. There is also a saying that AI models are superior to traditional regression models for outcome prediction [34]. All the way, virtual AI is yet to reach its high potential in gynecology. There are various opportunities that exist to improve the treatment and diagnosis, especially in gynecologic oncology.

1.6.2   Surgical Applications of Communication-Based on Artificial Intelligence and Augmented Reality

There are developments in the new paradigm that enhance human abilities more than AI to support, along with decision-making and surgery. The development of AI-based AR communication systems can reduce natural limitations, improve awareness so that it can minimize error, and improve the efficiency of movement. The AR-based AI communication has already proved to reduce surgery time and they verify the improved accuracy [35]. The communication assisted AR is applied in gynecologic surgery in the way of robotic tools to overcome the drawback in surgical skills. The communication-based and robotic-assisted tools reduce the human tremor so that the accuracy can be maximized.

The anatomical relationship that exists between healthy organs and pathologic was well understood by surgeons by exhibiting the preoperative available images. Particularly if the organs of interest are immobile, then AR-based surgeries are successfully implemented. The recent application of AR in improved myoma detection and fibroid mapping are very good examples [36]. Some other similar techniques are used in gynecologic oncology for the identification of sentinel lymph nodes that have reduced the morbidity incorporated with group lymphadenectomy [37]. The communication technologies associated with three-dimensional printing to create physical models for better visualization of organ configuration offers an AR, which is unrealizable through other traditional imaging techniques. With recent techniques, advanced communication-enabled 3D printers can emulate various tissue types [38]. Given the changes in myoma size, position, and length within a uterus, 3D printing of a uterus can help the surgeon come up with good prior operative planning. In this manner, communication technologies associated with AI and AR offer a great deal in helping gynecological surgeons.

We concluded that further research and application of VR and AR in the healthcare and communication technologies are necessary. The summary of above discussed article is given in Table 1.6.

Table 1.6 Impact of AI-driven augmented and virtual reality in healthcare.

Source	Subject matter	Methods proposed	Performance analysis
[30]	Clinical applications	• Deep learning–based diagnosis	• Detects metastases in hematoxylin and eosin–stained tissue sections of lymph nodes of women with breast cancer • Achieves 95% CI using 3-layer CNN
[31]	Clinical applications -Radiology	• Clinical decision-making using CNN	• Achieves 20% improvement over sonographer readings after training with ultrasound images of left and right carotid artery from 203 patients.
[32–34]	Clinical applications - survival prediction	• Probabilistic Neural Network • Multi-layer Perceptron • Gene expression classifier • Support Vector Machine • Radial Basis Neural Network • K-means algorithm	• Trained with 23 demographic, tumor-related parameters and selected perioperative data from 102 patients. • PNN achieves high prediction ability with an accuracy of 0.892 and sensitivity of 0.975
[35]	Surgical Applications	• Rotational matrix and translation vector algorithm to reduce the geometric error	• Improves the video accuracy by 0.30–0.40 mm (in terms of overlay error) • Enhances processing rate to 10–13 frames/s • Depth perception is increased by 90–100 mm
[36–38]	Surgical Applications	• Feasibility of laparoscopic Sentinel Lymph Node (SLN) staging	• 245 SLN nodes were removed out of 370 lymph nodes from 87 patients.

References

1. Gaddi, A., Capello, F., Manca, M., *eHealthcare and Quality of Life*, Springer, Verlag Italia, 2014.
2. Oh, H., Rizo, C., Enkin, M., Jadad, A., What is ehealth (3): a systematic review of published definitions. *J. Med. Internet Res.*, 7, 1, e1, 2005.
3. Gurung, M.S., Dorji, G., Khetrapal, S., Ra, S., Babu, G.R., and S Krishnamurthy, R.S., Transforming healthcare through Bhutan's digital health strategy: progress to date. WHO South-East Asia Journal of Public Health, pp. 77–82, doi: 10.4103/2224-3151.264850.
4. Zulman, D.M., Jenchura, E.C., Cohen, D.M., Lewis, E.T., Houston, T.K., Asch, S.M., How Can eHealth Technology Address Challenges Related to Multimorbidity Perspectives from Patients with Multiple Chronic Conditions. *J. Gen. Intern. Med.*, 30, 8, 1063–70, 2015.
5. Laxminarayan, S. and Istepanian, R.S.H., Unwired e-med: the next generation of wireless and internet telemedicine systems. *IEEE Trans. Inf. Technol. Biomed.*, 4, 3, 189–193, Sept 2000, https://doi.org/10.1109/TITB.2000.5956074.
6. Germanakos, P., Mourlas, C., Samaras, G., A mobile agent approach for ubiquitous and personalized ehealth information systems, in: *Proceedings of the Workshop on 'Personalization for e-Health' of the 10th International Conference on User Modeling (UM'05)*, Edinburgh, pp. 67–70, 2005.
7. Lee, J., Smart health: concepts and status of ubiquitous health with smartphones, in: *ICTC 2011*, pp. 388–389, Sept 2011, https://doi.org/10.1109/ICTC.2011.6082623.
8. Wu, G., Talwar, S., Johnsson, K., Himayat, N., Johnson, K.D., M2M: from mobile to embedded internet. *IEEE Commun. Mag.*, 49, 4, 36–43, April 2011, https://doi.org/10.1109/MCOM.2011.5741144.
9. Jennifer Bresnick, J., Top 12 Ways Artificial Intelligence Will Impact Healthcare, World medical Innovation Forum, 2018, accessed 30 April 2018, https://healthitanalytics.com/news/top-12-ways-artificial-intelligence-will-impact-healthcare.
10. Micah Castelo, M., The Future of Artificial Intelligence in Healthcare, Healthtech Magazine, 2020, accessed 26 Feb 2020, https://healthtechmagazine.net/article/2020/02/future-artificial-intelligence-healthcare .
11. Sandeep Reddy (November 5th 2018). Use of Artificial Intelligence in Healthcare Delivery, eHealth - Making Healthcare Smarter, Thomas F. Heston, IntechOpen, DOI: 10.5772/intechopen.74714. Available from: https://www.intechopen.com/books/ehealth-making-health-care-smarter/use-of-artificial-intelligence-in-healthcare-delivery.
12. Murdoch, T.B. and Detsky, A.S., The inevitable application of big data to healthcare. *JAMA*, 309, 1351–2, 2013.

13. Kolker, E., Özdemir, V., Kolker, E., How Healthcare can refocus on its Super-Customers (Patients, n=1) and Customers (Doctors and Nurses) by Leveraging Lessons from Amazon, Uber, and Watson. *OMICS*, 20, 329–33, 2016.

14. Dilsizian, S.E. and Siegel, E.L., Artificial intelligence in medicine and cardiac imaging: harnessing big data and advanced computing to provide personalized medical diagnosis and treatment. *Curr. Cardiol. Rep.*, 16, 441, 2014.

15. Bhavnani, S.P., Narula, J., Sengupta, P.P., Mobile technology and the digitization of healthcare. *Eur. Heart J.*, 37, 1428–1438, 2016, https://doi.org/10.1093/eurheartj/ehv770.

16. Tison, G.H., Sanchez, J.M., Ballinger, B., Singh, A., Olgin, J.E., Pletcher, M.J., Vittinghoff, E., Lee, E.S., Fan, S.M., Gladstone, R.A. *et al.*, Passive detection of atrial fibrillation using a commercially available smartwatch. *JAMA Cardiol.*, 3, 409–416, 2018, https://doi.org/10.1001/jamacardio.2018.0136.

17. Sengupta, P.P., Huang, Y.M., Bansal, M., Ashrafi, A., Fisher, M., Shameer, K., Gall, W., Dudley, J.T., Cognitive machine-learning algorithm for cardiac imaging: a pilot study for differentiating constrictive pericarditis from restrictive cardiomyopathy. *Circ. Cardiovasc. Imaging*, 9, e004330, 2016, https://doi.org/10.1161/CIRCIMAGING.115.004330.

18. Tsang, W., Salgo, I.S., Medvedofsky, D., Takeuchi, M., Prater, D., Weinert, L., Yamat, M., Mor-Avi, V., Patel, A.R., Lang, R.M., Transthoracic 3D echocardiographic left heart chamber quantification using an automated adaptive analytics algorithm. *JACC: Cardiovasc. Imaging*, 9, 769–782, 2016, https://doi.org/10.1016/j.jcmg.2015.12.020.

19. Lancaster, M.C., Salem Omar, A.M., Narula, S., Kulkarni, H., Narula, J., Sengupta, P.P., Phenotypic clustering of left ventricular diastolic function parameters: patterns and prognostic relevance. *JACC: Cardiovasc. Imaging*, 12, 7, 1149–1161, 2018, https://doi.org/10.1016/j.jcmg.2018.02.005. [epub].

20. Zhang, J., Gajjala, S., Agrawal, P., Tison, G.H., Hallock, L.A., Beussink-Nelson, L., Lassen, M.H., Fan, E., Aras, M.A., Jordan, C. *et al.*, Fully automated echocardiogram interpretation in clinical practice. *Circulation*, 138, 1623–1635, 2018, (https://doi.org/10.1161/CIRCULATIONAHA.118.034338).

21. Movassaghi, S., Abolhasan, M., Lipman, J., Smith, D., Jamalipour, A., Wireless Body Area Networks: A Survey. *IEEE Commun. Surv. Tutor.*, 16, 3, 1658–1686, 2014.

22. Rodrigues, J.J.P.C. *et al.*, Enabling Technologies for the Internet of Health Things. *IEEE Access*, 6, 13129–13141, 2018.

23. Ooi, P., Culjak, G., Lawrence, E., Wireless and wearable overview: stages of growth theory in medical technology applications. *International Conference on Mobile Business (ICMB'05)*, IEEE, 2005.

24. Khalid, H. *et al.*, A comprehensive review of wireless body area network. *J. Netw. Comput. Appl.*, 143, 178–198, 2019.

25. Al-Janabi, S. *et al.*, Survey of main challenges (security and privacy) in wireless body area networks for healthcare applications. *Egypt. Inform. J.*, 18, 2, 113–122, July 2017.

26. Sangita Singh, S., Artificial Intelligence and the Internet of Things in Healthcare, Healthcare and Life Sciences, 2018, accessed 6 April 2018, https://thejournalofmhealth.com/artificial-intelligence-and-the-internet-of-things-in-healthcare.

27. Azimi, I. *et al.*, HiCH: Hierarchical Fog-Assisted Computing Architecture for Healthcare IoT. *ACM Trans. Embed. Comput. Syst.*, 16, 5s, 1–20, Sept. 2017.

28. Baskar, S., A dynamic and interoperable communication framework for controlling the operations of wearable sensors in smart healthcare applications. *Comput. Commun.*, 149, 17–26, Jan. 2020.

29. Deepak, B.D., Al-Turjman, F., Aloqaily, M., Alfandi, O., An Authentic-Based Privacy Preservation Protocol for Smart e-Healthcare Systems in IoT. *IEEE Access*, 7, 135632–135649, 2019.

30. Bejnordi, B.E., Veta, M., van Diest, P.J. *et al.*, Diagnostic Assessment of deep learning algorithms for detection of lymph node metas-tases in women with breast cancer. *JAMA*, 318, 2199–2210, 2017.

31. Saba, L., Biswas, M., Kuppili, V. *et al.*, The present and future of deep learning in radiology. *Eur. J. Radiol.*, 114, 14–24, 2019.

32. Francis, N.K., Luther, A., Salib, E. *et al.*, The use of artificial neural networks to predict delayed discharge and readmission in enhanced recovery following laparoscopic colorectal cancer surgery. *Tech. Coloproctol.*, 19, 419–428, 2015.

33. Rabbani, M., Kanevsky, J., Kafi, K. *et al.*, Role of artificial intelligence in the care of patients with non small cell lung cancer. *Eur. J. Clin. Invest.*, 48, 1–7, 2018.

34. Obrzut, B., Kusy, M., Semczuk, A. *et al.*, Prediction of 5-year overall survival in cervical cancer patients treated with radical hysterectomy using computational intelligence methods. *BMC Cancer*, 17, 840, 2017.

35. Murugesan, Y.P., Alsadoon, A., Manoranjan, P., Prasad, P.W.C., A novel rotational matrix and translation vector algorithm: geometric accuracy for augmented reality in oral and maxillofacial surgeries. *Int. J. Med. Robot.*, 14, e1889, 2018.

36. Bourdel, N., Collins, T., Pizarro, D. *et al.*, Augmented reality in gynecologic surgery: evaluation of potential benefits for myomectomy in an experimental uterine model. *Surg. Endosc.*, 31, 456–461, 2017.

37. Mendivil, A.A., Abaid, L.N., Brown, J.V. *et al.*, The safety and feasibility of minimally invasive sentinel lymph node staging using indocyanine green in the manage-ment of endometrial cancer. *Eur. J. Obstet. Gynecol. Reprod. Biol.*, 224, 29–32, 2018.

38. Waran, V., Narayanan, V., Karuppiah, R. *et al.*, Utility of multi material 3D printers in creating models with pathological entities to enhance the training experience of neurosurgeons. *J. Neurosurg.*, 120, 489–492, 2014.

2

Pneumatic Position Servo System Using Multi-Variable Multi-Objective Genetic Algorithm–Based Fractional-Order PID Controller

D.Magdalin Mary[1]*, V.Vanitha[2] and G.Sophia Jasmine[1]

[1]Department of Electrical and Electronics Engineering Sri Krishna College of Technology, Coimbatore, Tamilnadu, India
[2]Department of Electrical and Electronics Engineering, VSB College of Engineering Technical Campus, Coimbatore, Tamilnadu, India

Abstract

In the last few decades, pneumatic servo systems are gaining popularity in numerous industrial applications because of numerous benefits such as high power to volume ratio, high rapidity, less economic, and easy maintenance plus long life. Servo pneumatic positioning systems have proven to be more cost effective than hydraulic systems because of the availability of air in abundance. In the pneumatic system, mid-air pump is consumed to supply the compressed air by regulating the proportional valve slots and drive the piston connected to the payload. Proportional integral differential (PID) controller is able to compensate the nonlinearity, and its performance becomes unsatisfactory when the system conditions change. The fractional-order PID (FOPID) controllers are robust and accurate than conventional PID controllers as they have two additional parameters for tuning. In this work, the fractional order of pneumatic servo system is used in the model of air pump and FOPID is propositioned to control the position of valve. The way to progress its performance, the controller parameters are optimized using genetic algorithm (GA). Proposed algorithm is validated for different reference positions and various values of evolution parameters define the system performances and give the optimized solutions in all aspects.

Keywords: Pneumatic position servo system, FOPID, GA, MATLAB, PIC microcontroller

---

*Corresponding author: magdalinmary4@gmail.com

C. Venkatesh, N. Rengarajan, P. Ponmurugan and S. Balamurugan (eds.) Smart Systems for Industrial Applications, (33–62) © 2022 Scrivener Publishing LLC

2.1 Introduction

The flexibility of proportional integral differential (PID) controller is less, when the reference and other conditions of the system change considerably. The system has the following advantages as easy of maintenance, spotlessness, PWR, and modest assembly which has been used broadly in automation application as food industries, medical, mechatronics, and bio-engineering. Due to essential compressibility of airflow through orifice valve in cylinder, movement of piston based on the position, variation of system parameters yields a nonlinear system with uncertainties. In nonlinear PID (NPID) controllers, the variation of nonlinear gain is exploited for greater accuracy. Literatures show that fractional-order PID (FOPID) controller, which combines the concept of fractional system theory and integer-type PID (IPID) controller gives better response than standard PID controller. But the tuning of controller parameters in FOPID is tougher than IPID. If these parameters are not tuned accurately, then the system performance will be poor [2, 10]. Many optimization techniques such as GA, MFA, and PSO are used to tune the parameters of FOPID to improve the system response [11, 12]. The numerous governing techniques are proposed for pneumatic control system as PID controller, robust control, sliding mode control. Due to its reliability and control mechanism, FOPID control is commonly used in industries [18]. The implementation of PID are widely used in ON/OFF solenoid valve position which includes constrained integral term, forward loop position, compensation of friction element, and the performance indices of the function compare with the solenoid valve. The flexibility in PID controller is reduces due to its nonlinearity. In NPID controller, the variation of nonlinear gain is exploited for greater accuracy. In recent days, the numbers of intelligent control techniques are developed to progress the accuracy of the system with trajectory tracking. Neural control–based PID has the proposed compensation under various load operating conditions used to get optimized design in PID controllers.

The sliding mode adaptive control provides the stability in system parameters to achieve desire performance [5]. In pneumatic system with back stepping adaptive sliding control, the parameters are not essential to its design. This makes the superior control than other supplementary techniques. In many systems, the gain control is not specified, while controlling the system would not give a proper approach. Adaptive back stepping approach is used to control the performance of the system with positioning. This approaches need not requires related information about the parameters of the system and gain control. Most of the control techniques are adaptive control, intelligent control, and sliding mode control results to improved system performance, even though the controller gives better response they have high value of computational cost related to PID. Nowadays, FOPID controllers have attracted more with its collective performance with the Podlubny's work in which the concept being demonstrated with improved performance than conventional PID controllers. Based on effort of Podlunby, FOPID would give enhanced results based on their control mechanism in pneumatic servo system. Combined fractional position system and integer-order proportional integral differential (IPID) controller are constructed as FOPID. Additionally, two parameters are available in FOPID compared with IPID. The tuning of controlled parameters remains difficult in this type. Though the parameters are not optimized, FOPID is used to control the pneumatic position system whose tracking accuracy decreases. The literature work gives this problem in integer order model. Intelligent controller is used to get optimized solution in FOPID.

In order to get the improved gain value and superior control, MATLAB/Simulink is developed to estimate the working of the converter. Next, the fitness function and objective functions are used to control the stable position of transient state and steady state performance for different reference signals. The fitness functions are selected based on the different objectives and reference signals [13]. Finally, least distance for minimum points is suggested as the best non-dominate solution from the non-dominate individual to reach complete optimal parameters. The fractional-order system is specified as proposed work by replacing the integer order control. The FOC has the better response than classical PID controllers [3, 6]. The FOPID controller is established by system with fractional-order control and IPID [1]. The tuning of control parameters is more tough in FOPID than IPID. In FOPID whose parameters are not optimized accurately, it will give poor performance of the system [1, 2]. In NPID controllers, the variation of nonlinear gain is exploited for greater accuracy [8].

Genetic algorithm (GA) is used to optimize fractional-order system with evolutionary control [11, 12]. GA allows to tune all the parameters and get balance of different objectives to overcome the problems caused by the physical arrangement of the weight [9]. The proposed work insists the following for controlling the system with FOPID. GA searches the optimal factors of FOPID online for better performance than conventional method. In order to get the improved gain value and superior control, MATLAB/Simulink is developed to estimate the working of the converter. The fitness and objective functions are aids to control the stable position of system response with various references [13]. Smallest distance for minimum points is suggested as the best non-dominate solution from the non-dominate individual to reach complete optimal parameters. The fractional-order system is specified as proposed work by replacing the integer order control. The objective and fitness functions are aids to control the stable position of system response with various references [13]. An advanced algorithm such as GA allows to tune five control parameters of FOPID online to get balance of different objectives and hence overcomes the problems produced by the physical arrangements of the weights to multi-objectives [9, 16]. In this work, GA-based FOPID controller is implemented for pneumatic control positioning system, which gives satisfactory solution during uncertain conditions. Fractional-order model of the system is used for MATLAB simulation, where the tuning of proportional, integral, and derivative, λ and μ, are done using GA [14, 15]. The proposed algorithm is validated by implementing the optimized values of the controller in the hardware using microcontroller. Results shows that FOPID offers superior control over IPID for different conditions and the changes in throttle control.

2.2   Pneumatic Servo System

Pneumatic system has numerous advantages, such as smooth construction, consistency, ruggedness, and easy maintenance [3]. They are commonly used in automated industries. Due to essential compressible gas, there is a difficulty in controlling the gas out flow using valve, chamber friction, and inconstancy in system parameters. They are fundamentally nonlinear time-varying systems [3, 10]. In practical, PID controller is used to modify the acceleration feedback and compensate the nonlinearity. The flexibility of PID control is weak, when the reference and other conditions of the system changes considerably [6]. The proposed method will give satisfactory solution about uncertain conditions. Error changes due to the different conditions and the changes in throttle control. For other intelligent control techniques, it provides better result, but high cost, related to PID control [19]. The FOC has the better response than classical PID controllers [3, 6]. The FOPID controller is established by system with fractional-order control and IPID [1]. The tuning of control parameters is more tough in FOPID than IPID. In FOPID whose parameters are not optimized accurately, it will give poor performance of the system [1, 2]. In NPID controllers, the variation of nonlinear gain is exploited for greater accuracy [8].

In conventional pneumatic servo systems have been used in many fields [14, 17], such as the active suspension system on the Shinkansen bullet train, moulding machines for glass lenses, and amusement robots, because of the numerous advantages of high power, compliant property, and good force controllability. However, the characteristic of a pneumatic servo is nonlinear, which make control difficult [21, 22]. Therefore, control methods of a pneumatic servo, applying advanced control theories such as fuzzy control or robust control, have been investigated.

Pneumatic position servo system comprises of cylinder (Figure 2.1), variable resistor, solenoid valves, air pump, and piston. The compressed air is pumped through air pump and passed through the chamber A or B in the cylinder, where the valve is regulating the flow level. The incoming valve regulates the mass flow in each chamber to get pressure difference among two chambers [15]. The difference in pressure will drive the piston and payload and the velocity of the system load is controlled by rheostat with the piston [1, 4]. The aim of the controller is to track the position of the piston and payload through a desired path [2] and its dynamic characteristics are represented by a fractional-order model. A 230-V supply is stepped down to 5 V using step down transformer and rectified using bridge rectifier and then given to variable resistor. The PIC microcontroller receives the position of the piston and converts it from analog to digital form before it is given to PC using serial bus. A 12-V relay board is used for tripping the supply when the position of the load is not at zero in initial position.

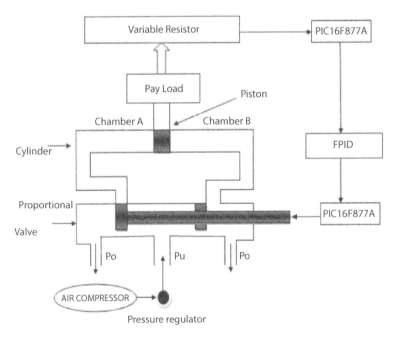

Figure 2.1 Pneumatic position servo system.

2.3   Existing System Analysis

The pneumatic position is controlled using self-regulation of NPID (SNPID) controller. The performance of the system is developed with the specific changes of nonlinear gain in NPID. The various test has taken and the error signal is reprocessed continuously for different values by self-regulation non-linear function. The controller is applied with changing of loading of pressure, compared with NPID and classical PID evaluation. Simulation and various experimental studies have been implemented using SNID. The initial performance of the system has been examined through simulation. Test has been conducted for various level of displacement to find out the consistency of the system performance. Different benchmark experiments and different load condition are conducted for system validation and slight differences can found them in transient state. The system using SNPID specifies excellent performance in accuracy, robust control, and fast response compared with other types. Also, SNPID provides minimum value of steady state error with minimal of peak overshoot. The servo system has the performance characteristics of time-variant, nonlinear, disturbances, and variation in parameters that will make the system is very difficult to control. Classical PID control does not provide the better accuracy of the system for various external disturbances.

Next, the neural network control combined with PID for pneumatic system was analyzed. Based on the learning rule, the system results are compared with the classical PID controller. Survey on neural network gives improved performances than PID control. It has fast response, adaptability, robustness, and reliability. Neural network + PID control performs better based on optimization of system response compare with conventional PID. It comprises inherent aspects as neurons, topological structure, and knowledge-based learning rule for improving system operation. Due to lack of control in pneumatic servo system, it is tough to adopt with conventional method. Literature research shows neural network control of pneumatic servo system has fast response, suitable static and dynamic control, robustness, and good adaptability. Neural network control can be used a system with complex, nonlinear, and uncertainty that has extensive challenging applications. It is used to tuning of FOPID control with particle swarm optimization (PSO) technique which gives strong stochastic optimizing output. It depicts the movement of swarm particles around search space to solve the problem. Comparison of SNPID, neural + PID, and optimization of FOPID using PSO techniques was analyzed.

The proposed approach defines the position control of pneumatic system using FOPID optimized with GA. The following parameters to be tuned up for optimum response. It consists of proportional, integral, and derivative gain, fractional-order integrator, and fractional-order differentiator. The approach defines the implementation of the system with fast tuning optimum parameters. Optimized FOPID-based [20] pneumatic servo system influences the improved performance of the system. In last decades, fractional-order dynamic system and various types of controllers have been studied in engineering. FOPID techniques were enhanced by Podulbny. He demonstrated the system output which compared with the classical PID controllers. PSO uses number of swarm particles that searching the optimal solution. Using fitness function, the system parameters can be optimized with fewer numbers of iterations. In PSO simulation, results show the better results than other methods. The proposed method can apply in practical system for their précised control of high power to weight ratio. The techniques give efficient results in optimal design controllers. Pneumatic servo system is used in automatic control industries. It requires high accuracy of control due to their compressibility of gas and friction. The rods less cylinder with two chambers are used. The controllers are not required any pressure sensors and reference value before connecting with the system. It has no preceding idea and uncertainty of the system. Based on the results, the proposed method achieves superior mechanism over sliding mode controllers (SMCs). The controllers track three reference signals with better précised output compare with SMCs.

Proposed linear model pneumatic system controller has main topologies: first, designing of adaptive back stepping controller without having any knowledge about actual model of the system; second, the model can able to design a controller without having previous model information of reference signal; and third, system can design a controller without expensive of pressure sensors and it has better practical application prospects. The control parameters of power factor correction (PFC) is designed by a small signal model. The output of PFC converter gives nonlinear response. GA is used to optimize the parameters of PFC converter for desired operation. From the assigned fitness function the quasi optimal control parameters are obtained. The fitness function of individual parameters of PFC converter is executed in MATLAB M-file. GA is used to get optimal parameters around search space through numbers of iteration. Simulation results shows the transient response of the system by optimizing the parameters. The control parameters of PFC converter are optimized using GA. MATLAB coding is established to calculate the performance of the PFC converter for various control parameters. After optimizing, the response of the system has reduced overshoot, settling time, better transient and steady state response. The proposed method is used to optimize the even topology of the converter and provides suitable approach for evaluating power electronic circuits.

Drawbacks:

- The accuracy of integer order PID controller is low.
- The existing system using integer order PID controller requires high power consumption.
- The control performance of IPID controller with improved control parameters derived by GA can is poor in the sensor accuracy and energy consumption.
- The robustness of the system is poor.

2.4   Proposed Controller and Its Modeling

The system we proposed uses FOPID controller instead of IPID controller for position control of pneumatic position servo system. It provides a better efficiency of the system by using FOPID controller. This system provides more accurate output compare to that of IPID controller. The power consumption of this system using FOPID controller is much lesser than the previously existing system. The robustness of this system is better than previously existing system using traditional IPID controller.

2.4.1   Modeling of Fractional-Order PID Controller

2.4.1.1   Fractional-Order Calculus

Fractional-order operator, $t_o D_t^{\lambda e}$, is defined

$$t_o D_t^{\lambda e} \triangleq \begin{cases} \dfrac{d^{\lambda e}}{dt^{\lambda e}}, & \text{Real}(\lambda e) > 0 \\ 1, & \text{Real}(\lambda e) = 0 \\ \displaystyle\int_{t1}^{t2} (dt)^{-\lambda e}, & \text{Real}(\lambda e) < 0 \end{cases} \qquad (2.1)$$

where t_1 and t_2 are the upper and lower time limits for the operator.

The term λe is the fractional order. It is an arbitrary complex number. Real(λe) is the real part of λe.

The Grnwald-Letniknov (GL) fractional-order derivative $t_0 D_t^{\lambda e}$ of the function f(t) is defined

$$t_0 D_t^{\lambda e} f(t1) = \lim_{c \to 0} (c)^{-\lambda e} \sum_{k=0}^{\frac{t1-t2}{c}} -1^k \left(\begin{array}{c} \lambda e \\ K \end{array} \right) f(t - kc) \qquad (2.2)$$

where -1 is the rounding operation, c is the calculation step, and $\left(\begin{array}{c} \lambda e \\ K \end{array} \right)$ is the binomial coefficients defined as e^0.

Integration and differential denoted by a uniform expression.

$$\left(\begin{array}{c} \lambda e \\ K \end{array} \right) = \frac{\lambda e(\lambda e - 1)(\lambda e - 2)\ldots\ldots\ldots(\lambda e - k + 1)}{k!} \qquad (2.3)$$

The fractional-order operator can be done by using the following equation [8]:

$$t_0 D_t^{\lambda e} f(t) \approx \frac{1}{c^{\lambda e}} \sum_{k=0}^{n} q_{\lambda 2,k} f(t - kc) \qquad (2.4)$$

where $n = \dfrac{t1 - t2}{c}$

$$q_{\lambda e,k} = (-1)^k \left(\begin{array}{c} \lambda e \\ k \end{array} \right) \qquad (2.5)$$

$$q\_(\lambda e, 0) = 1$$

$$q_{\lambda e,k} = \left(1 - \frac{1 - \lambda e}{k} \right) q_{\lambda e,k-1} \qquad (2.6)$$

By ignoring the very old data, an approximate fractional-order approximation is obtained by

$$t_o d_t^{\lambda e} f(t) \approx (t - L) D_t^{\lambda e} f(t) \approx \frac{1}{c} \sum_{k=0}^{n} q_{\lambda e, k} f(t - kc) \qquad (2.7)$$

where $n = \left[\dfrac{L}{C} \right]$, and L is the memory length.

2.4.1.2 Fractional-Order PID Controller

The equation of the IPID controller is

$$u(t) = K_{pi} e(t) + K_{ii} \int_0^t e(t) dt + K_{di} \frac{de(t)}{dt} \qquad (2.8)$$

where K_{pi}, K_{ij} and K_{di} and are the proportional, integral, and differential coefficient, respectively, where $e(t) = y_d(t) - y(t)$ is the system error, $y_d(t)$ is the reference input, $y(t)$ is system response, and $u(t)$ is controlled output [6, 9]. The FOPID controller is an extension of the conventional IPID controller with the integral and the differential orders as fractional one [7].

FOPID controller is represented as

$$u(t) = K_{pf} u(t) + K_{ift_o} D_t^{-\lambda e} e(t) + K_{dft_o} D_t^{\mu} e(t) \qquad (2.9)$$

λe indicates integral order.
μ indicates the differential order.
K_{pf}, K_{if}, and K_{df} are fractional-order controller gains.
Laplace transfer function of the controller is given as

$$G(s) = K_{pf} + K_{if} S^{-\lambda e} + K_{df} S^{\mu} \qquad (2.10)$$

The FOPID has additionally more adjustable parameters, λ and μ, than IPID controller and have five control parameters (K_{pf}, K_{if}, K_{df}, λe, and μ) to find a better control performance [9]. For optimization, the GA has a possibility to come with five optimum parameter space to achieve best control performance.

2.5   Genetic Algorithm

GA is an adaptive empirical search algorithm depends on the mutative concepts of natural selection and genetics. It emphasizes the intellectual manipulation in finding solution to the optimization problems. Based on the historical information, GA searches for random variables through the best performance region of the search space. GA technique resembles the survival of the fittest principle proposed by Charles Darwin. In view of nature's law, competition or struggle among the individuals results in the fittest predominating the inferior ones.

Alike chromosomes in DNA, the population in every generation has certain character strings impinged from the parent. In the search space each one of the individual signifies a point and has a feasible solution. The next stage through which the individuals undergo is the evolution process. Every individual in the population strives for the best position and mates. The fittest individual competes and yields offspring, whereas the inferior individuals will not proceed to the successive process. In every generation, the offspring thus produced from the fittest parent will be more suitable for the environment.

2.5.1   GA Optimization Methodology

GA optimization has for four major phases and requires a fitness function for optimization. The four steps are summarized as follows (Figure 2.2):

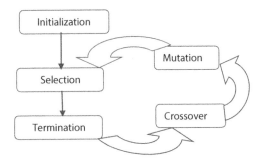

Figure 2.2 Phases in genetic algorithm.

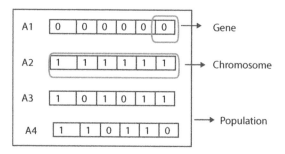

Figure 2.3 GA initialization process.

1. Initialization: population of chromosomes are initialized
2. Selection: reproduce chromosomes
3. Crossover: produce next generation of chromosomes
4. Mutation: random mutation of chromosomes in new generation

2.5.1.1 Initialization

This is the initial phase in which a set of individuals are produced. Every individual is a solution to the problem and they are characterized by set of parameters called as genes. They are combined to form chromosome (Figure 2.3).

2.5.1.2 Fitness Function

Fitness function is the most crucial part of the algorithm. The capability of an individual entity to race with other entities is determined using fitness function. Fitness score is bestowed to every individual and the possibility for the selection of an individual for reproduction is entirely based on this score. It is the function that the algorithm optimizes. The word fitness is taken from evolutionary theory. Fitness is the word coined from evolutionary theory.

2.5.1.3 Evaluation and Selection

Population generation is followed by evaluation. It is the process in which the fitness level of the newly generated off springs is estimated using a fitness function. The inferior individuals are eradicated during selection and the best individual proceeds to the next generation.

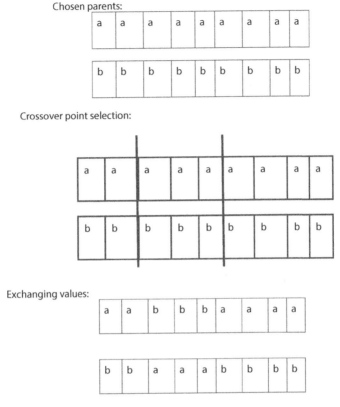

Figure 2.4 Crossover procedure.

2.5.1.4   Crossover

The most important phase of GA is crossover. For every mating parent, a crossover point is randomly selected from the genes. Figure 2.4 illustrates the crossover procedure. The procedure has three steps. First step is the selection of parents from the population. Crossover points are further selected. In Figure 2.4, the crossover points are shown as dotted lines. After the crossover points are selected, their values are exchanged to obtain a new offspring.

2.5.1.5   Mutation

Mutation is the process in which the values of gene are altered. The gene to be mutated are curtained by the mutation parameter. Mutation results

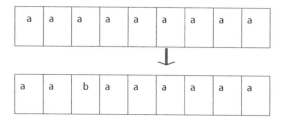

Figure 2.5 Mutation.

in the generation of novel features in the offspring. Occasionally, the feature may lead the offspring to be poor or superior. Figure 2.5 exhibits the mutation phase.

2.5.2 GA Parameter Tuning

GA execution involves tuning of three parameters, namely, crossover probability, mutation probability, and the number of optimal generations. The population evolution depends on crossover and mutation whereas number of generations are chosen such that the solution is an optimal one. Studies had been carried out with crossover probability ranging between 0.2 and 0.1. Its corresponding mutation probability is taken as 0.4, and hence, maximum fitness is reached. Figures 2.6 and 2.7 show the results of GA tuning.

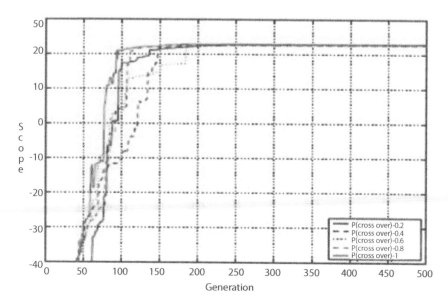

Figure 2.6 Fitness with crossover probabilities.

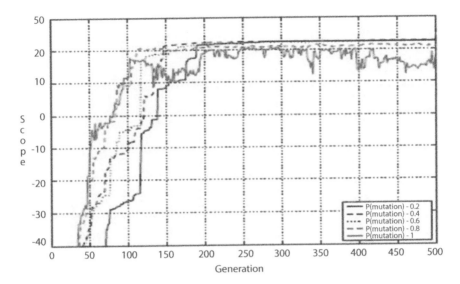

Figure 2.7 Fitness with mutation probabilities.

2.6   Simulation Results and Discussion

2.6.1   MATLAB Genetic Algorithm Tool Box

MPLAB established by Microchip Technology is an exclusive integrated software setting for the improvement of applications in PIC microcontrollers. MPLABX is the state-of-the art edition of MPLAB, developed on the Net Beans platform. They support project management, code editing, debugging, and programming of Microchip 8-bit PIC and AVR (including ATMEGA) microcontrollers, 16-bit PIC24 and dsPIC microcontrollers, as well as 32-bit SAM (ARM) and PIC32 (MIPS) microcontroller (Figure 2.8).

GA finds its extensive application in control engineering. MATLAB has an integrated GA toolbox which helps the control engineers to apply genetic search methods effectively. Figure 2.9 is the GA toolbox in finding solution to control system design problems.

2.6.2   Simulation Results

A high level matrix language containing M file with MATLAB code is developed to set the five parameters for position control of the piston. The software is analyzed for different values of reference input and the characteristics graph are taken down with the gain of Kp, Ki, and Kd.

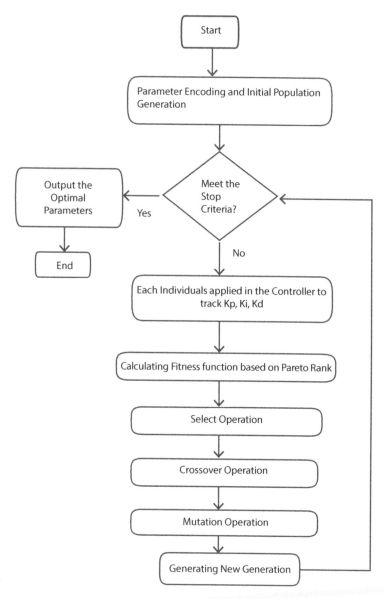

Figure 2.8 Flowchart of genetic algorithm.

2.6.2.1   Reference = 500 (Error)

When the reference value is set as 500 and the Kp, Ki, and Kd values are taken manually (10, 0.5, and 3) without using GA, then the output will be coming as follows. Figures 2.10, 2.11 and 2.12 shows the control error, control action and system output.

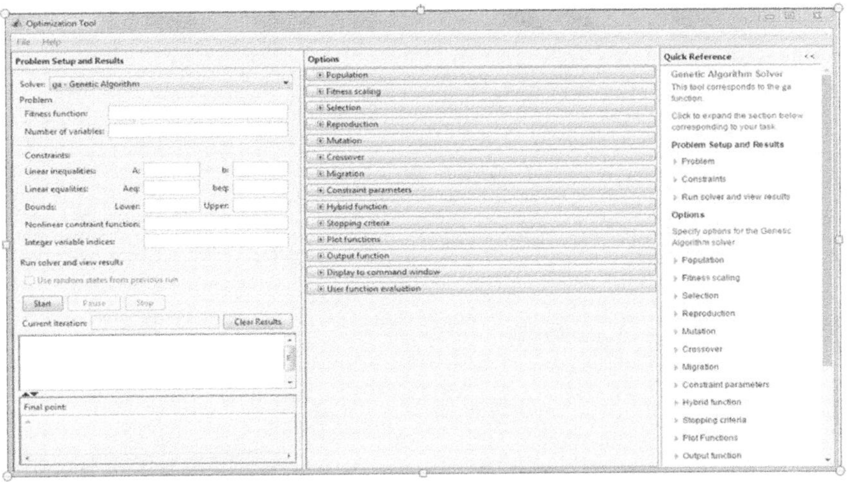

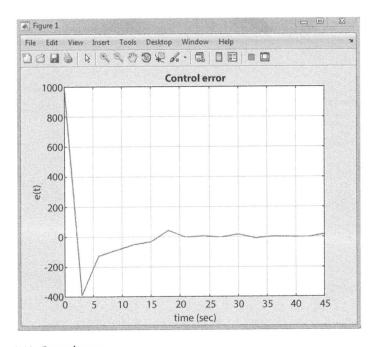

Figure 2.9 Genetic algorithm tool box.

Figure 2.10 Control error.

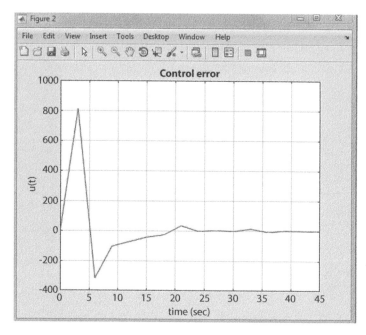

Figure 2.11 Control action.

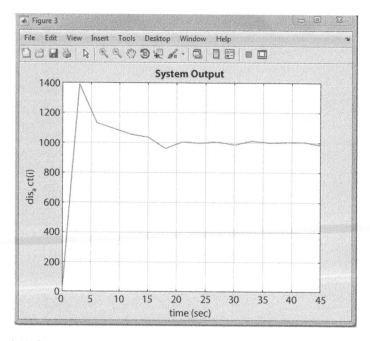

Figure 2.12 System output.

Figures 2.13 a, b and c shows the piston displacement at a reference = 500 (error) using Kp = 10, Ki = 0.5 and Kd = 3 without GA.

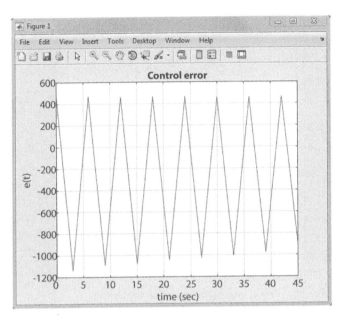

Figure 2.13 (a) Control error for reference value 500 (error).

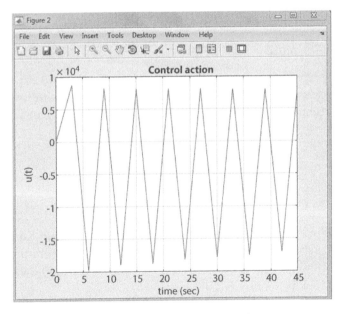

Figure 2.13 (b) Control action for reference value 500 (error).

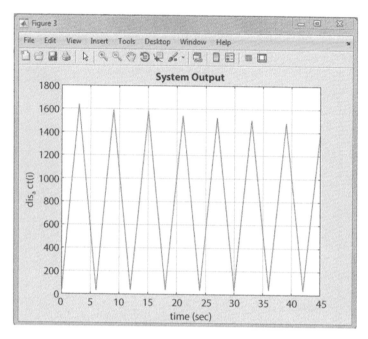

Figure 2.13 (c) System output for reference value 500 (error).

Here, the displacement of the piston is not settled at a reference value. Hence, this output is considered as error. To rectify this, we use GA.

2.6.2.2   Reference = 500

When the reference value is set as 500 and the Kp, Ki, and Kd values are taken by execution of iterations in GA, then the error is minimized and the displacement is settled at the reference value in the output as shown in Figures 2.14a, b and c.

The Kp, Ki, and Kd values obtained by GA are 0.221923828125,1.32339 6901967211, and 0.12735267270242523.

2.6.2.3   Reference = 1,500

When the reference value is set as 1,500 and the Kp, Ki, and Kd values are taken by execution of iterations in GA, then the error is minimized and the displacement is settled at the reference value in the output as shown in Figures 2.15 a, b and c.

The Kp, Ki, and Kd values obtained by GA are 0. 38281, 0.19672, and 0.24252.

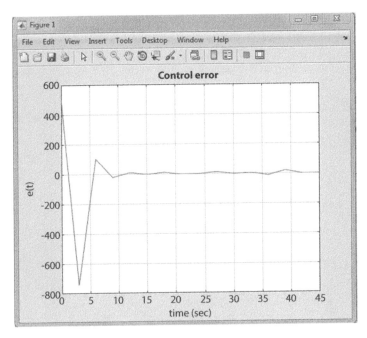

Figure 2.14 (a) Control error for reference value 500.

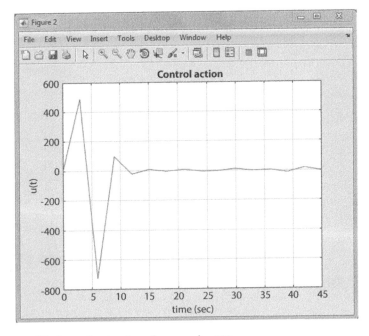

Figure 2.14 (b) Control action for reference value 500.

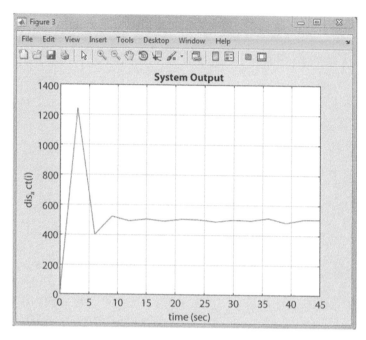

Figure 2.14 (c) System output for reference value 500 (error).

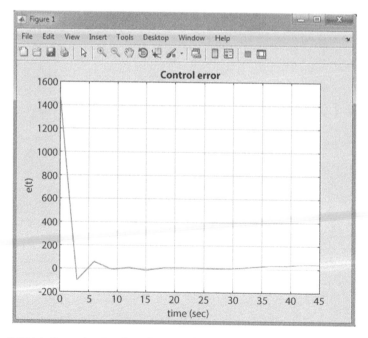

Figure 2.15 (a) Control action for reference value 1,500.

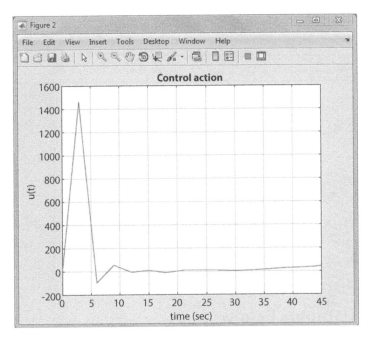

Figure 2.15 (b) Control action for reference value 1,500.

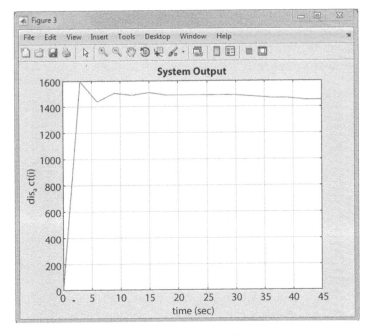

Figure 2.15 (c) System output for reference value 1,500.

Table 2.1 Analysis report.

Distance	Kp	Ki	Kd	Settling time
Error 500	10	0.5	5	NIL
500	0.22192	1.32339	0.12735	11 seconds
1,000	0.93028	0.31099	0.75421	8 seconds
1,500	0. 38281	0.19672	0.24252	9 seconds

2.6.2.4   Analysis Report

The MATLAB software has been analyzed for different values of reference. Kp, Ki, and Kd and settling time have monitored across each references (Table 2.1).

2.7   Hardware Results

The displacement of the piston is measured and converted to digital signal and then given to the System. The FOPID using GA generates the most accurate value using successive iterations. This value is given to the controller, which moves the piston to that value. Thus, the position is controlled using FOPID controller. Figure 2.16 shows the hardware setup of the position servo system.

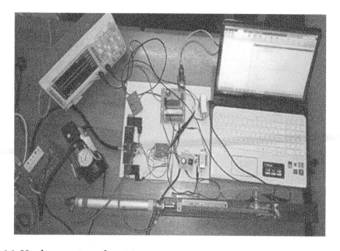

Figure 2.16 Hardware setup of position servo system.

Figure 2.17 illustrate the average output voltage of piston using hardware module.

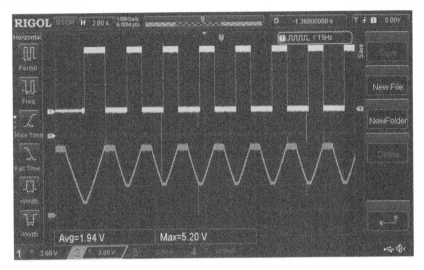

Figure 2.17 CRO output waveform.

CRO output consist of average output voltage of piston based on displacement.

The displacement of the piston is not settled at a reference value. Hence, this CRO output waveform is considered as error. To rectify this, we use GA. Figure 2.18 shows average output waveform of 500 reference (error).

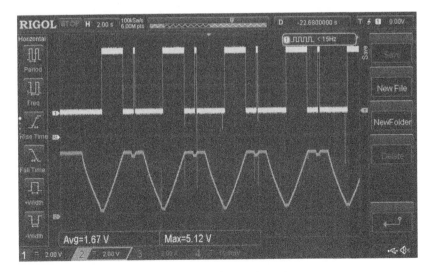

Figure 2.18 CRO output waveform of 500 reference (Error).

Figure 2.19 a shows the average output waveform for reference value of 500 with GA.

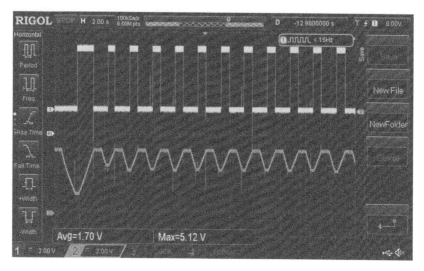

Figure 2.19 (a) CRO output waveform of 500 reference.

2.7.1   Reference = 500

When the reference value is set as 500 and the Kp, Ki, and Kd values are taken by execution of iterations in GA, then the error is minimized and the displacement is settled at the reference value. The Kp, Ki, and

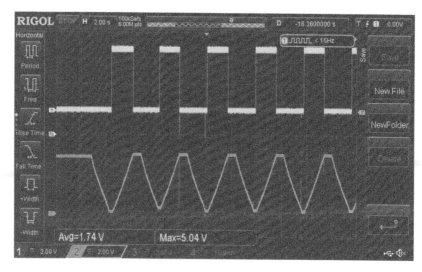

Figure 2.19 (b) CRO output waveform of 1,500 reference.

Kd values obtained by GA are 0.221923828125,1.323396901967211, and 0.12735267270242523.

2.7.2   Reference = 1,500

When the reference value is set as 1,500 and the Kp, Ki, and Kd values are taken by execution of iterations in GA, then the error is minimized and the displacement is settled at the reference value. The Kp, Ki, and Kd values obtained by GA are 0.38281, 0.19672, and 0.24252. Figure 2.19 b shows the average output waveform for reference value of 1500 with GA.

2.8   Conclusion

Resembling the fractional-order dynamics of gas flow, the pneumatic system also has similar dynamics. Based on the analysis from the literature survey, it has been found that the fractional-order controllers provide enhanced control for the systems that possess fractional-order dynamics. Hence, in this work, FOPID controllers are used to control pneumatic position servo system. One of the challenging issues while applying FOPID controller is the tuning of parameters. In this paper, MMGA method based on Pareto rank is proposed for tuning FOPID parameters. It is evident from the results that FOPID is exceeding IPID in terms of greater accuracy and less energy consumption. It is worthwhile to point out that the dynamic behavior of FOPID controllers are superior to PID controllers. The efficacy of the proposed method is also exhibited by comparing its performance with six methods proposed in the literature. The pneumatic position control system using FOPID gives the best performance than IPID controller. GA is used to find the optimized values of FOPID controller. This paper discussed about the implementation of optimized FOPID controller using GA to find the maximum fitness solution. Simulation results in MATLAB and hardware results from PIC microcontroller validated the proposed algorithm thereby showing the superior performance of FOPID over IPID controller in a pneumatic position servo system.

References

1. Ren, H.-P., Wang, X., Fan, J.-T., Kaynak, O., Adaptive backstepping Control of a Pneumatic System with unknown Model Parameters and Control Direction. *IEEE Access*, 7, 64471–64482, 2019.
2. Salim, S.S.N., Rahmat, M.F., Faudzi, M., Ismail, Z.H., Sunar, N., Position control of pneumatic actuator using self-regulation nonlinear PID. *Math. Probl. Eng.*, 2014, Article ID 957041, 12, 181–195, 2014.

3. Gong, Q.H., Control of pneumatic servo system based on neural network PID algorithm. *Appl. Mech. Mater.*, 457, 1344–1347, 2014.
4. Ren, H.-P. and Chao, H., Experimental tracking control for pneumatic system. *IECON 2013-39th Annual Conference of the IEEE Industrial Electronics Society*, pp. 4126–4130, 2013.
5. Taheri, B., Case, D., Richer, E., Force and stiffness backstepping-sliding mode controller for pneumatic cylinders. *IEEE/ASME Trans. Mechatron.*, 19, 6, 1799–1809, 2014.
6. Garmsiri, N. and Sepehri, N., Emotional learning based position control of pneumatic actuators. *Intell. Autom. Soft Comput.*, 20, 3, 433–450, 2014.
7. Essa, ME-SM., Aboelela, M.A.S., Hassan, M.A.M., Abdraboo, S.M., Fractional Order Fuzzy Logic Position and Force Control of Experimental Electro-Hydraulic Servo System, in: *2019 8th International Conference on Modern Circuits and Systems Technologies (MOCAST)*, IEEE, pp. 1–4, 2019.
8. Ren, H.-P., Wang, X., Fan, J.-T., Kaynak, O., Fractional order sliding mode control of a pneumatic position servo system. *J. Franklin Inst.*, 356, 12, 6160–6174, 2019.
9. Al-Dhaifallah, M., Kanagaraj, N., Nisar, K.S., Fuzzy fractional-order PID controller for fractional model of pneumatic pressure system. *Math. Probl. Eng.*, 2018, 9, 2018.
10. Liu, L. and Zhang, S., Robust fractional-order PID controller tuning based on Bode's optimal loop shaping. *Complexity*, 2018, 14, 2018.
11. Dastjerdi, A.A., Saikumar, N., HosseinNia, S.H., Tuning guidelines for fractional order PID controllers: Rules of thumb. *Mechatronics*, 56, 26–36, 2018.
12. Kumar, P., Chatterjee, S., Shah, D., Saha, U.K., Chatterjee, S., On comparison of tuning method of FOPID controller for controlling field controlled DC servo motor. *Cogent Eng.*, 1, 1357875, 2017.
13. Machado, J.A.T., Optimal tuning of fractional controllers using genetic algorithms. *Nonlinear Dyn.*, 1–2, 447–452, 2010.
14. Ren, H.-P., Fan, J.-T., Kaynak, O., Optimal design of a fractional-order proportional-integer-differential controller for a pneumatic position servo system. *IEEE Trans. Ind. Electron.*, 66, 8, 6220–6229, 2018.
15. Ramezanian, H. and Balochian, S., Optimal design a fractional-order PID controller using particle swarm optimization algorithm. *Int. J. Control Autom.*, 4, 55–68, 2013.
16. Ren, H.P. and Zheng, T., Optimization design of power factor correction converter based on genetic algorithm, in: *2010 Fourth International Conference on Genetic and Evolutionary Computing*, 2010.
17. Estrada, A. and Plestan, F., Second order sliding mode output feedback control with switching gains—Application to the control of a pneumatic actuator. *J. Franklin Inst.*, 351, 4, 2335–2355, 2014.
18. Efe, M.O., Fractional order systems in industrial automation—a survey. *IEEE Trans. Ind. Inform.*, 7, 4, 582–591, 2011.

19. Junyi, C. and Binggang, C., Fractional-order control of pneumatic position servosystems. *Math. Probl. Eng.*, 2011, 2011.
20. Tepljakov, A., Alagoz, B.B., Yeroglu, C., Gonzalez, E., HosseinNia, S.H., Petlenkov, E., FOPID controllers and their industrial applications: a survey of recent results. *IFAC-Papers Online*, 51, 4, 25–30, 2018.
21. Meng, D., Tao, G., Zhu, X., Integrated direct/indirect adaptive robust motion trajectory tracking control of pneumatic cylinders. *Int. J. Control*, 86, 9, 1620–1633, May 2013.
22. Zhang, X., Wang, Y., Wang, C., Su, C.-Y., Li, Z., Chen, X., Adaptive Estimated Inverse Output-Feedback Quantized Control for Piezoelectric Positioning Stage. *IEEE Trans. Cybern.*, 99, 1–13, Apr. 2018.

3

Improved Weighted Distance Hop Hyperbolic Prediction–Based Reliable Data Dissemination (IWDH-HP-RDD) Mechanism for Smart Vehicular Environments

Sengathir Janakiraman[1], M. Deva Priya[2]* and A. Christy Jeba Malar[3]

[1]*Department of Information Technology, CVR College of Engineering, Mangalpally, Vastunagar, Hyderabad, Telangana, India*
[2]*Department of Computer Science & Engineering, Sri Krishna College of Technology, Kovaipudur, Coimbatore, Tamil Nadu, India*
[3]*Department of Information Technology, Sri Krishna College of Technology, Kovaipudur, Coimbatore, Tamil Nadu, India*

Abstract

Vehicular Ad hoc NETwork (VANET) is determined to be the most indispensable technology for facilitating Intelligent Transportation Systems (ITSs). ITS plays an anchor role in enhancing traffic efficiency, comfort and convenience to passengers and drivers, and vehicle road safety. In this context, Global Positing System (GPS) is generally used for estimating the position of the vehicles with the view to guide the drivers and passengers during travel. Majority of the existing schemes proposed in the literature are determined to still possess a room for improvement in terms of accuracy in localization. The degree of prediction is also not to the expected level. In this chapter, an Improved Weighted Distance Hop Hyperbolic Prediction-based Reliable Data Dissemination (IWDH-HP-RDD) mechanism is proposed as a cooperative vehicle localization enhancement scheme for smart vehicular environments. This proposed IWDH-HP-RDD utilizes an improved version of weighted distance hop hyperbolic prediction technique that forecasts the position of the nearby vehicles using GPS positions. It is determined to reduce errors by fusing data that is determined based on the derivation of accurate distance and

Corresponding author: m.devapriya@skct.edu.in

C. Venkatesh, N. Rengarajan, P. Ponmurugan and S. Balamurugan (eds.) Smart Systems for Industrial Applications, (63–92) © 2022 Scrivener Publishing LLC

GPS information. This proposed IWDH-HP-RDD scheme uses vehicle trajectory, number of vehicles and distance information error for assessing the accuracy of localization through distance information. The simulation experiments of the proposed IWDH-HP-RDD scheme is conducted using EstiNet network simulator for identifying its potential toward the improvement of percentage increase in localization accuracy and warning data dissemination rate and percentage decrease in localization error and latency. It is seen that the localization error of the proposed IWDH-HP-RDD scheme for varying number of anchor nodes SVs decreases on an average by 5.12%, 6.62% and 7.82% in contrast to the baseline PDRLS, CVPLS, and RCIC-CS approaches, respectively.

Keywords: Vehicular ad hoc network (VANET), Global Positing System (GPS), Intelligent Transportation Systems (ITSs), Improved Weighted Distance Hop Hyperbolic Prediction (IWDHP), warning message delivery, localization error

3.1   Introduction

In the recent past, Vehicular Ad hoc NETwork (VANET) is evolving as a promising research area due to the significant incorporation of wireless communication technology into the vehicular network. They belong to a category of Mobile Ad hoc NETworks (MANETs), wherein vehicles act as mobile nodes so as to facilitate trusted communication among nearby Road Side Units (RSUs) and neighboring vehicles. Nevertheless, VANETs are actually dissimilar to other networks with distinctive features involved in the process of data dissemination. In specific, the vehicles in VANETs are limited to road topology during motion such that the data concerning roads need to be accessible so as to envisage the probable locations of the vehicular nodes in the network. These vehicular nodes enable substantial sensing, communication and computing potentialities with incessant transmission competences to support the intrinsic functionalities.

However, VANETs face numerous challenges that are related to network sizes and mobility factors. These nodes in the network are found to be more dynamic, as most of the vehicles alter their positions while moving at a greater speed. Indoor parking lots and urban street canyons, green foliage like trees and buildings may introduce unwanted errors. These errors in vehicle communication can influence the performance of critical safety applications and may provide inaccurate information to its users leading to huge degree of misguidance. These errors are mainly due to Non–Line-of-Sight (NLOS) nodes in the network that increase the packet latency with unreliable data dissemination. The increased mobility rate of vehicular nodes in the network leads to a highly dynamic topology, while the links between vehicular nodes connect and disconnect often. Furthermore, VANETs are possibly huge enough to contain varied participants that allow the choice of expanding the road network effectually and proficiently. These networks have drawn maximum attention from the academia and industry due to their inherent unique characteristic features and challenges.

Emergency situations on road demand attention. Vehicle drivers in a VANET should promptly respond to these situations so as to save lives and losses [1]. If the drivers delay to respond, then the likelihoods of collision among Emergency Vehicles (EVs) and Non-Emergency Vehicles increase, leading to destruction of human lives and roads [2]. Imprecise observation and insufficient data updates of a situation or event demanding immediate action are the predominant causes for the deferred response of drivers. If the drivers are not provided with latest information, then they cannot make decisions under life-threatening situations. Accurate information and right perception of emergency events are mandatory for controlling vehicles on roads and guaranteeing ideal choices that direct vehicle motion during disasters [3]. It is necessary for averting erroneous assumptions that end in crashes and devastating accidents. Collisions and disasters on roads hinder the timely arrival of police patrol and ambulances and also impede recovery actions. This maximizes the chances of vehicle collision among vehicles as the time needed by the EVs to travel toward the endpoint is restricted [4]. The accidents induced by EVs on road are known to be approximately 25% more than those caused by non-EVs. It is also established that more number of accidents instigated by both categories of vehicles are at the road crossings. At these road junctures, the perceptibility or reportage of vehicles is observed to be less [5].

Vehicle-to-Vehicle (V2V) and Vehicle-to-Infrastructure (V2I) communications among vehicles are made possible depending on the positioning of Intelligent Transportation Systems (ITSs). ITS-supported V2I and V2V communications are principally accountable for distributing and keeping informed about the values of velocities, frequencies and positions of vehicles in a short duration [6]. The accurate data associated with vehicles is essential to direct the drivers to take prompt and responsive actions that eradicate the likelihood of crashes among vehicles [7]. In addition, the time taken for data propagation is affected by high foliage, buildings or parameters including vehicle mass. Likewise, planned or unplanned behavior of NLOS nodes can also lead to enormous delay as the vehicles are of variable composition, speeds, shapes and densities [8]. NLOS nodes are primarily accountable for improved delay as they hamper the messages sent from the source to the destination. Lack of latest information from NLOS nodes lead to fatal accidents [9, 10]. The nodes should be restricted at a quick and specific degree so as to reduce delay. Furthermore, a complete protocol that is proficient in lessening the latency in conveying emergency messages is indispensable for VANETs [11]. Therefore, the principal challenge in VANET is the formation and conservation of maximum coverage among the vehicles such that the delays between the arrival and reception of emergency messages are ideally minimized. Meta-heuristic algorithms are capable of localizing NLOS nodes in VANETs. Further, the challenges in NLOS are mainly based on communication, security and location. In case of communication, features like signal strength, signal blockage, communication range, signal interference and sender authentication contribute to NLOS conditions. Further, malicious intrusions, intentional attacks, un-intentional attacks, fake position attacks, physical objects, stationary obstacles, moving obstacles, trees, building and vehicles may also lead to NLOS conditions. Related to security, NLOS nodes are open to wormhole attacks, privacy invading, reply message attacks, message forwarding and messages tampering. Finally, NLOS conditions are determined to emerge when the availability, message sender reliability and issues related to the integrity of services and quality degrade during vehicular nodes' location verification process.

The major contributions of the proposed Improved Weighted Distance Hop Hyperbolic Prediction–based Reliable Data Dissemination (IWDH-HP-RDD) mechanism are listed as follows.

(i) It is proposed as a cooperative vehicle localization enhancement scheme for smart vehicular environments. This proposed IWDH-HP-RDD utilizes an improved version of weighted distance hop hyperbolic prediction technique that forecasts the position of the nearby vehicles using Global Positing System (GPS) positions.

(ii) It is determined to reduce errors by fusing data that is computed based on the derivation of accurate distance and GPS information.

(iii) It uses vehicle trajectory, number of vehicles and distance information error for assessing the accuracy of localization through distance information.

(iv) The simulation experiments of the proposed IWDH-HP-RDD scheme is conducted using EstiNet network simulator for identifying its potential toward the improvement of percentage increase in localization accuracy and warning data dissemination rate and percentage decrease in localization error and latency.

3.2   Related Work

Few potential works on efficient localization of NLOS nodes in VANET are proposed in the literature. Nevertheless, only few significant works are propounded to deal with delay minimisation as it is mandatory for delivering emergency messages. The most noteworthy research works are systematically studied and detailed for finding their merits and demerits.

A scheme to segregate intentional and malevolent NLOS nodes affected by Sybil attack based on signal strength is proposed by Xiao et al. [12]. In this scheme of localization, the signal strength is regularly updated among the cooperating nodes in the network. The neighboring NLOS vehicular nodes are found by updating the signal strength of nodes. In this distributed scheme, every node is proficient in determining its own signal strength and sharing it among the cooperating nodes in VANET for qualifying their specific locations. Computation and communication overheads experienced in deploying the algorithm are high as determining the signal strength consumes energy and demands more number of packet re-transmissions. Capkun et al. [13] have designed a GRANT protocol–Based Localization Mechanism (GRANTBLM) for reducing processing at the destination while receiving emergency messages. This NLOS detection approach involves a Base Station (BS) denoted as Covert node that is specifically designed for localization. This scheme is capable of performing localization even under reduced Received Signal Strength Index (RSSI) conditions. The presence of Covert node helps in averting the malevolent nodes from determining the precise location of nodes. The main limitation is the passive nature of this scheme that involves secret key generation without examining the need for generation.

Song et al. [14] have proposed a cooperative mechanism to circumvent identical and false statements from nodes during the process of localization. This scheme uses Time-of-Flight (ToF) metric for assessing the distance of a node from the reference nodes for efficient localization. Foci-based Elliptical computation is executed to assist the reference nodes in dealing with imprecise localization of NLOS nodes. The main limitation of this approach is the increase in computation overhead with increase in number of nodes in VANET. Leinmüller et al. [15] have propounded a trust model for measuring and determining the reliability of the adjoining vehicles during transmission of emergency messages. The trust of each vehicular node is determined using multi-purpose sensors for enumerating the trustworthiness. This sensor-based NLOS node identification scheme consumes huge amount of energy and involves more number of packet re-transmissions in the sensing phase. Ros *et al.* [16] have designed Acknowledged Broadcast from Static to highly Mobile (ABSM) protocol that is wholly distributed and dynamic. It adapts to the scenario by not maintaining the degree of mobility recognized by vehicles. The decision to forward messages lying with the vehicular node is dependent on the information obtained from the neighborhood through periodic beacon messages. The scheme seems to be scalable involving less number of parameters.

Abumansoor and Boukerche [17] have propounded Position Verification Secure Message Based Localization Mechanism (PVSMBLM) for safeguarding vehicle identification based on hash indexing. This scheme is proficient in localizing the NLOS nodes in contrast to the ToF and echo packet based detection schemes. This unique hash-based secret key aids in precisely identifying NLOS nodes in the extended area. The main drawback of this method is the demand for producing a unique secret key for every session as it increases the communication overhead. Bai *et al.* [18] have proposed a reliable and effective data dissemination technique. The positions of vehicles at proximity are anticipated to improve reliability and circumvent redundant traffic in the network. The dynamic topology and connectivity problems are considered and the forwarder details are added to the packet header, and two vehicles are chosen in different directions to transmit data. Each forwarder selects a vehicle from among its neighbors and sends it to the next forwarder. It is seen that the scheme offers improved data dissemination rate and less delay.

Zemouri *et al.* [19] have designed Road-Casting Protocol (RCP), a dissemination protocol for security messages in urban areas. It is based on a cooperative forwarding scheme with appropriate Region of Interest (RoI) defined to guarantee efficient management of network load. They have analyzed and shown better performance based on propagation loss model for urban VANET communications, and packet delivery ratio, end-to-end delay and network load. Pramuanyat *et al.* [20] have propounded Location-Aware Reliable Broadcasting protocol (LARB) that employs maximum hop count instead of GPS that is based on the number of hops based on the number of vehicles within a particular distance. The protocol is based on DECA. The protocol uses one-hop information to choose neighbors. The area of rebroadcasting is limited based on the number of hops. The source sets the maximum number of hops to the hop counter to send data messages. The nodes decide whether they will forward data by taking the hop count. If it is zero, then the message is beyond the area of transmission. The performance is analyzed based on coverage, outlier ratio and transmission speed.

Alodadi *et al.* [21] have proposed Cooperative Volunteer Election-Based Localization Mechanism (CVEBLM) for context sensitive components that support the embedding of On-Board Units (OBUs). The OBUs are accountable for gathering, examining and decision-making during emergency message transfer. It seems to be better in contrast to GRANTBLM and echo packet-based localization schemes as they elect a node from among the cooperating nodes as volunteers for efficient obstacle detection during data distribution. It involves less response time and communication overhead and provides enhanced channel utilization rate as it rapidly detects the NLOS nodes. The only shortcoming of this approach is that the process of volunteer node election consumes more time and it is relied without assessing its legitimacy. Dua *et al.* [22] have proposed a scheme Reliability-aware Intelligent Data Dissemination (ReIDD) protocol to handle the broadcast storm problem in VANETs. They have used game theory, wherein players, strategy space and decisions are employed. To deal with the message overhead, messages are forwarded to the ensuing destination by choosing a consistent path. In the coalition game, the vehicles are treated as players, wherein every vehicle has a primary payoff value based on the communication range, storage demands and computation power. Clusters are formed based on the payoff value of players and they send messages to other players within the same association thereby offering better reliability. The performance is analyzed in terms of service time, throughput and packet delivery ratio. Oliveira *et al.* [23] have dealt with transmitting in parallel leading to frequent contention and broadcast storms. In sparse density areas, vehicles fail in message delivery. The proposed Adaptive Data Dissemination Protocol (ADDP) deals with providing reliable message dissemination. The protocol updates the beacon's periodicity and decreases the number of messages and beacons. Hazard messages are disseminated through suitable nodes called candidate nodes dealing with redundant messages and channel conflicts. The number of warning message retransmissions are avoided by using a network coding theory-based data aggregation scheme.

Sattar *et al.* [24] have designed a reliability model for time-critical safety messages for multi-hop VANET. The reliability drops exponentially below a particular value of packet loss probability. Energy-based protocols are the demand of Internet of Vehicles (IoV). Restrictive flooding is energy-efficient for ensuring reliability. The V2V network is modeled as a set of nodes linked through WAVE links thus establishing a backbone. The vehicles broadcast emergency messages which are consequently flooded in a multi-hop fashion. The probability that the message is delivered before the expiry of lifetime gives the reliability. The performance of the system is evaluated based on hop count and packet loss probability. A hybrid localization scheme stimulated by the advantages of Pedestrian Dead Reckoning (PDR) for finding RSS is propounded by Ciabattoni *et al.* [25]. It deals with the issues seen in NLOS situations by heading and step length estimation and beacon information integration. It enhances locality awareness which sequentially improves the degree of data propagation. Amuthan and Kaviarasan [26] have propounded Weighted Inertia-based Dynamic Virtual Bat Algorithm (WIDVBA) for improving the features of the outmoded virtual bat method that incorporates the advantages of Simulated Annealing (SA) and Particle Swarm Optimization (PSO). This scheme overcomes the issue of early convergence by including the advantages of weighted inertial factor in contrast to the existing virtual binary bat-based schemes. The area and degree of exploration are increased and decreased dynamically based on the positions of NLOS nodes. WIDVBA shows an increase in the number of NLOS nodes. The time involved in identifying the NLOS nodes increases with increase in the neighbor awareness rate. Amuthan and Kaviarasan [27] have designed a Rank Criteria Improved Confidence-based Centroid Scheme (RCICCS) which involves a combined cost found using the primitive and penalty costs so as to improve the efficiency in positioning NLOS nodes. Effective localization of NLOS nodes is found based on rank criterion dependent neighbor confidence measure that is enhanced during perturbation involving gradients. The proposed scheme offers better delivery rate of emergency messages and neighborhood awareness.

3.2.1   Extract of the Literature

The exhaustive literature review conducted over the existing works of the literature aided in identifying the following shortcomings.

(i)   Majority of the proposed NLOS localization schemes still possess a room for improvement in improving their accuracies toward location prediction.

(ii)   Most of the localization algorithms are both range-based and range-free approaches and majority use the benefits of anchor nodes for detecting the positions which may not be possible in all the real time scenarios.

(iii)   The mean absolute error achieved by the existing NLOS localization schemes are not up to the expected level of performance.

3.3 Proposed Improved Weighted Distance Hop Hyperbolic Prediction–Based Reliable Data Dissemination (IWDH-HP-RDD) Mechanism for Smart Vehicular Environments

The nodes in NLOS condition are to be predicted such that the EVs can distribute the essential data to these nodes in limited time, thus involving minimized overhead and delay with improved channel utilization. In this chapter, IWDH-HP-RDD mechanism is propounded as an effectual scheme that predicts the NLOS nodes in a dynamic environment based on the advantages of the algorithm with dynamic hyperbolic properties and independent of range.

IWDH-HP-RDD is an enriched NLOS node identification scheme propounded for guaranteeing effectual message distribution involving multiple hops among vehicles and enabling position identification using weighted distance hyperbolic prediction. The accurate identification of Line-Of-Sight (LOS) circumstances is not dependent on both RSUs and cellular networks for transferring data. The self-directed nature of IWDH-HP-RDD over infrastructure services is the prime benefit when compared to the present schemes available for NLOS node identification. The challenge involved in multi-hop message distribution which is involved in recognizing vehicles in immediacy without any infrastructure-service is made possible in IWDH-HP-RDD based on the following:

- Enabling effective data distribution within the communication range and utilizing special nodes called anchor nodes to perform the same among the vehicles that are not within the range of communication.
- Lessening the delay involved in the transmission of emergency messages which is the main aim of this work.

Initially, IWDH-HP-RDD employs a relay model based on Distance Vector (DV) hop for distributing the information necessary for finding the distances among the nodes in the vehicular network, which comprises of visible reference nodes and non-visible NLOS nodes. The relay model based on hop count enables the NLOS nodes to compute and save the distances with respect to the reference nodes (r_j). Every node in the network has an active table to store the information related to the hop count between the NLOS nodes and the reference nodes (HC_i^j), and coordinates of the reference nodes (x_j, y_j) correspondingly. The table is updated periodically depending on the data gathered from the neighbors of the non-visible nodes to enumerate the factor of improvement. The factor of improvement gives the mean of single hop distances to every "r_i" as shown in Equation (3.1). Table 3.1 gives the Nomenclature.

$$MD_i^j = \frac{\sum_{k=1}^{n} ED_i^j}{\sum_{k=1}^{n} HC_i^j} = \frac{\sum_{k=1}^{n} \sqrt{(p_i - p_j)^2 + (q_i - q_j)^2}}{\sum_{k=1}^{n} HC_i^j}, i \neq j \qquad (3.1)$$

where "E_i^j" and "HC_i^j" signify the Euclidean distance and least hop count existing between "r_i" and "r_j" correspondingly.

The distance ($\widehat{D}_N$) that exists between NLOS and anchor (reference) nodes is given by,

$$\widehat{D}_N^i = MD_i^j * HC_N^i \qquad (3.2)$$

where "HC_N^i" refers to the least hop count between the non-visible nodes and "r_j", and "MD_i^j" is the mean distance to the adjoining "r_i".

The main drawback of the relay model based on DV hops used in the proposed mechanism is the computation of improvement factor which is wholly dependent on the increase in the node count. This rise leads to an increase in the hop count between the anchor and non-visible nodes resulting in accumulative error. The upsurge in total hop count also raises the error of NLOS node detection. This relay model is improved using mean factor of improvement "$\widehat{MD}_i^j$" inclined by the number of nodes "n" as shown in Equation (3.3).

Table 3.1 Nomenclature.

Notation	Description
$\widehat{D}_N^i$	Distance between NLOS and anchor nodes
HC_i^j	Hop count from reference node r_i to r_j
HC_N^i	Hop count between the NLOS nodes
r_i and r_j	Reference nodes
(x_i, y_i)	Coordinates of the reference nodes and r_i

(Continued)

Table 3.1 Nomenclature. (*Continued*)

Notation	Description
ED_i^J	Euclidean distance
MD_i^J	Mean distance in single hop
n	Node count
$\widehat{MD}_i^J$	Factor of improvement
φ	Mean hop distance error metric
ω	United location factor
$\hat{P}_{NLOS}(x_i, y_i)$	Column vector with (x_i, y_i) coordinates of NLOS nodes
H_P^T, H_p, and CM^{-1}	Hyperbolic matrices
SV_k, SV_{k+1}	Localization estimate of an unknown smart vehicle in successive iterations
$H_{P(k)}^T$, $H_{P(k)}$, $H_{P(k+1)}$, $H_{P(k+1)}^T$ CM_k, CM_{k+1}	Hyperbolic matrices at successive iterations
k	Individual recursion
N_{AN}	Collection of anchor nodes
IM	Identity matrix
$\left(SV_{x_i},\ SV_{y_j}\right)$	Coordinates of anchor nodes
$G_{p(k)}$, $G_{p(k)}^{-1}$, $G_{p(k+1)}$, $G_{p(k+1)}^{-1}$	Hyperbolic matrices used for estimating the value of SV_{k+1} from SV_k
$L_{p(k+1)}$, $L_{p(k)}^{-1}$, $L_{p(k+1)}^{-1}$	Intermediate hyperbolic matrices used for estimating the value of SV_{k+1} from SV_k
n	Number of smart vehicles
α	Very large integer value used in multilateration

$$\widehat{MD}_i^j = \frac{\sum_{k=1}^n MD_i^j}{n} \tag{3.3}$$

This computation of mean factor of improvement leads to either decreasing or increasing of mean hop distance of every hop in contrast to the mean distance of the present hops. The distance between the NLOS and anchor nodes is computed as shown in Equation (3.4).

$$\widehat{D}_N^i = \widehat{MD}_i^j * HC_i^j \tag{3.4}$$

Similarly, detection based on weighted DV hop reduces the error rate during non-visible node identification by computing the mean hop distance error metric as shown in Equation (3.5).

$$\varphi = \frac{\sum_{k=1}^n \dfrac{\left| E_i^j - E\widehat{D}_i^j \right|}{HC_i^j}}{\sum_{k=1}^n HC_i^j} \tag{3.5}$$

Thus, the mean hop distance is computed using Equation (3.6).

$$\widehat{MD}_i^j = \widehat{MD}_i^j * \kappa\varphi \tag{3.6}$$

where the environment dependent "κ" varies from -1 and 1 for balancing the mean distance between the non-visible NLOS and visible reference nodes. The distance between them is computed as shown in Equation (3.7).

$$\widehat{D}_N^i = \widehat{MD}_i^j * HC_i^j \tag{3.7}$$

In addition to the enhancement that is to be integrated into the proposed IWDH-HP-RDD, hyperbolic positioning is incorporated to find a location that decreases the sum of the squared error in the comprehensive collection of calculated distances. This is attained by altering linear optimization parameter into a non-linear optimization parameter depending on the united location factor (ω) using Equation (3.8).

$$\omega = \sum_{i=1}^n \left(\sqrt{(p - p_i)^2 + (q - q_i)^2} - \widehat{D}_N^i \right)^2 \tag{3.8}$$

Based on "ω", the hyperbolic transformation scheme achieves positioning of non-visible NLOS nodes based on the least square computation. The united location factor "ω" enables contracting the locations of the NLOS node that repeatedly diminishes the area of positioning of the non-visible NLOS nodes depending on the maximum and the minimum Euclidean distances " $ED_1^j, ED_2^j, \ldots, ED_n^j$ " between the visible reference and the non-visible NLOS nodes. The distance between them as estimated in Equation (3.7) is modified based on the mean Euclidean distance as shown in Equation (3.9).

$$\widehat{D}_N^i{}^2 = (p - p_i)^2 + (q - q_i)^2 \tag{3.9}$$

The above Equation is extended and modified into a matrix as shown in Equation (3.10)

$$H_p \widehat{P}_{NLOS}(x_i, y_i) = \widehat{D}_N^i \tag{3.10}$$

where the value of "H_p" varies from $2p_1$, $2p_2$ to $2p_N$, $2q_N$.

Similarly, " $\widehat{P}_{NLOS}(x_i, y_i)$ " signifies the column vector with (x_i, y_i) coordinates of non-visible NLOS nodes, and " $\widehat{D}_N^i$ " varies from $p_2^2 + q_2^2 - d_{N-2}^2 + d_{N-1}^2$ to $p_2^2 + q_2^2 - d_{N-(n)}^2 + d_{N-(n-1)}^2$ with "N" neighbors connected to visible reference nodes.

The matrices " H_P^T ", "H_p", and "CM^{-1}" are column vectors of "N" which reduce to a column vector with two values when non-visible NLOS nodes are identified. Lastly, the positions of the NLOS nodes are calculated as shown in Equation (3.11) using hyperbolic matrices.

$$\widehat{P}_{NLOS}(x_i, y_i) = (H_P^T CM^{-1} H_p)^{-1} H_P^T CM^{-1} \widehat{D}_N^i \tag{3.11}$$

where " H_P^T ", "H_p", and "CM^{-1}" are the hyperbolic matrices involved in the reduction of the distance between the known visible nodes and the unknown non-visible nodes. The proposed scheme extremely reduces the sum of the distances between the NLOS nodes and the observed anchor nodes. The steps of the proposed IWDH-HP-RDD scheme are illustrated in Figure 3.1.

This proposed IWDH-HP-RDD scheme is an improved version of the aforementioned localization algorithm attained by the application of recursive least squares. This improved version of localization is implemented

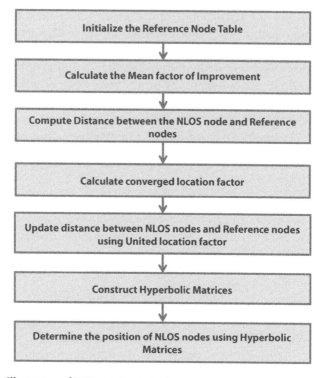

Figure 3.1 Illustration of IWDH-HP-RDD scheme.

through the utilization of finite number of reference nodes that are selected from available anchor population. In order to implement the proposed IWDH-HP-RDD scheme, a collection of anchor node population is chosen from the nodes of the network. Suppose, "SV_k" is the localization estimate of an unknown Smart Vehicle (SV) at an individual recursion "k", then "SV_k" is defined based on Equation (3.12).

$$SV_k = (H_{p(k)}^T H_{p(k)})^{-1} H_{p(k)} CM_k \qquad (3.12)$$

In this context, the collection of Anchor Nodes (N_{AN}) in every iteration is randomly selected from the population for attaining localization. The localization of position associated with the unknown SV using a recursive formula with recursive index "k+1" is achieved through the method of multi-lateration. If a new collection of anchor nodes is considered in the network, then an updation of "SV_{k+1}" need not be done with the help of recursive index "k". This process of position estimation of the unknown SVs can be achieved based on the method of recursive least squares as presented in Equation (3.13).

$$\begin{bmatrix} H_{p(k)} \\ H_{p(k+1)} \end{bmatrix} SV_k = \begin{bmatrix} CM_k \\ CM_{k+1} \end{bmatrix} \tag{3.13}$$

At this juncture, if the initial position of SV is "$SV_k = 0$", then the least square solution associated with the "SV_k" with the recursive index "k+1" is determined based on Equation (3.14).

$$H_{P(k)} = G_{P(k)}^{-1} H_{P(k)}^{T} CM_k \tag{3.14}$$

where the value of "$G_{P(k)}^{-1}$" is determined based on Equation (3.15).

$$G_{P(k)}^{-1} = H_{P(k)}^{T} H_{p(k)} \tag{3.15}$$

The position estimate of "SV_{k+1}" is updated based on the recursive least square through the inclusion of function corresponding to "SV_k", "$G_{p(k+1)}$", "$H_{p(k+1)}$", and "CM_{k+1}", respectively. This representation of "SV_{k+1}" is presented in Equations (3.16) and (3.17).

$$G_{p(k+1)} = G_{p(k)} + H_{p(k+1)}^{T} H_{p(k+1)} \tag{3.16}$$

$$H_{P(k)}^{T} CM_k = \begin{bmatrix} H_{p(k)} \\ H_{p(k+1)} \end{bmatrix}^{T} \begin{bmatrix} CM_k \\ CM_{k+1} \end{bmatrix} = G_{p(k+1)} \, SV_k - H_{p(k+1)}^{T} H_{p(k+1)} \, SV_k + H_{p(k+1)}^{T} CM_{k+1} \tag{3.17}$$

where the value of is "$G_{p(k)}$" is determined based on Equation (3.18).

$$G_{p(k)} = G_{p(k+1)} - H_{p(k+1)}^{T} H_{p(k+1)} \tag{3.18}$$

Then, the estimated position of the unknown "SV_{K+1}" is determined based on Equation (3.19).

$$SV_{K+1} = SV_k + G_{p(k+1)}^{-1} H_{p(k+1)}^T (CM_{k+1} - H_{p(k+1)} SV_k) \qquad (3.19)$$

where the value of "$G_{p(k+1)}$" is obtained based on Equation (3.20).

$$G_{p(k+1)} = G_{p(k)} - H_{p(k+1)}^T H_{p(k+1)} \qquad (3.20)$$

In this context, "SV_{k+1}" is computed from "SV_k" based on "$G_{p(k+1)}^{-1}$" rather than "$G_{p(k+1)}$". Furthermore, the recursive function of "$G_{p(k+1)}^{-1}$" is derived using Woodburg formula as presented in Equation (3.21).

$$G_{p(k+1)}^{-1} = G_{p(k)}^{-1} - G_{p(k)}^{-1} H_{p(k+1)}^T (I_M + H_{p(k+1)} H_{p(k+1)}^T G_{p(k)}^{-1}) H_{p(k+1)}^T G_{p(k)}^{-1}$$
$$(3.21)$$

where "I_M" refers to the identity matrix.

If $L_{p(k+1)} = G_{p(k+1)}^{-1}$ is the second recursive update, then the value of "$L_{p(k+1)}^{-1}$" is updated based on Equation (3.22).

$$L_{p(k+1)}^{-1} = L_{p(k)}^{-1} - L_{p(k)}^{-1} H_{p(k+1)}^T (I_M + H_{p(k+1)} H_{p(k+1)}^T L_{p(k)}^{-1}) H_{p(k+1)}^T L_{p(k)}^{-1} \quad (3.22)$$

Then, the value of "SV_{k+1}" (position of SV) is updated based on Equation (3.23).

$$SV_{K+1} = SV_k + L_{p(k+1)} H_{p(k+1)}^T (CM_{k+1} - H_{p(k+1)} SV_k) \qquad (3.23)$$

This value of "SV_{k+1}" represents the actual position of the unknown SV in the network.

In addition, Algorithm 3.1 presents the complete view of the proposed IWDH-HP-RDD scheme used for localizing SVs in order to enhance the degree of data dissemination.

Algorithm 3.1 Proposed IWDH-HP-RDD scheme.
Input: SVs are deployed randomly in a 200 × 200 meters sensing area which includes a set of anchor nodes with coordinate (SV_{x_i}, SV_{y_j}) with $1 \leq i \leq n$, where "n" is the number of SVs that need to be localized in the network.
Output: Estimated position "SV_k" of "n" unknown vehicle.

Step 1:   Begin

Step 2:   Initialize the position of the unknown SV "$SV_k = 0$"

Step 3:   Also initialize the covariance matrix "$L_{p(k)}$" based on the formula $L_{p(k)} = \alpha * I_M$, where "I_M" and "α" refer to the identity matrix and very large positive integer value

Step 4:   Select an anchor node set randomly for accomplishing the task of localization process

While (termination criteria are not satisfied) do

Step 5:   Step 5.1:   Apply the process of trilateration and determine the minimum hop count between the chosen anchor nodes

Step 5.2:   Perform optimization of mean distance of hops determined between the candidate anchor nodes based on the distance hop function transformation using Equation (3.7)

Step 5.3:   Estimate the minimal hop count between the unknown SVs and selected anchor nodes

Step 5.4:   Determine the distance between the unknown SVs and the nearest proximity selected anchor nodes

Step 5.5:   Estimate the position of unknown node "SV_k" based on the method of least squares as shown in Equation (3.23)

Step 6:   End while

Step 7:   The estimated coordinates (SV_{x_i} , SV_{y_j} of unknown SVs

Step 8:   End

3.4   Simulation Results and Analysis of the Proposed IWDH-HP-RDD Scheme

The potential of the proposed IWDH-HP-RDD scheme and the benchmarked Position Dead Reckoning-based Localization Scheme (PDRLS) [28], Cooperative Volunteer Protocol-based localization scheme (CVPLS) [21] and Rank Criterion Improved Centroid Confidence Scheme (RCIC-CS) [27] are explored using EstiNet simulator. The simulation environment considered for implementing the proposed IWDH-HP-RDD scheme and the benchmarked PDRLS, CVPLS and RCIC-CS schemes comprise of 300 SVs distributed in the vehicular network. The Ricean model of fading is used in the implementation of the proposed IWDH-HP-RDD scheme. In the initial part of analysis, the proposed IWDH-HP-RDD scheme and the compared PDRLS, CVPLS and RCIC-CS are evaluated using percentage increase in localization accuracy, percentage increase in warning data dissemination, percentage decrease in localization error and percentage decrease in latency for varying number of SVs.

Figures 3.2 and 3.3 exemplar the results of the proposed IWDH-HP-RDD scheme and the compared PDRLS, CVPLS and RCIC-CS evaluated with respect to percentage increase in the localization accuracy and warning data dissemination for varying number of SVs. The localization accuracy and warning data dissemination rate of the proposed IWDH-HP-RDD scheme for varying number of SVs are found to be improved due to the degree of approximation incorporated in the multi-lateration method. The localization accuracy of the proposed IWDH-HP-RDD scheme for varying number of SVs is identified to be improved by 5.21%, 6.76% and 7.62% when compared to the baseline PDRLS, CVPLS and RCIC-CS approaches. The warning data dissemination rate of the proposed IWDH-HP-RDD scheme for varying number of SVs is also determined to be enhanced by 5.94%, 6.85% and 7.94% when compared to the baseline PDRLS, CVPLS and RCIC-CS approaches.

Figures 3.4 and 3.5 demonstrate the results of IWDH-HP-RDD scheme and the compared PDRLS, CVPLS and RCIC-CS evaluated with respect to percentage decrease in localization error and percentage decrease in latency

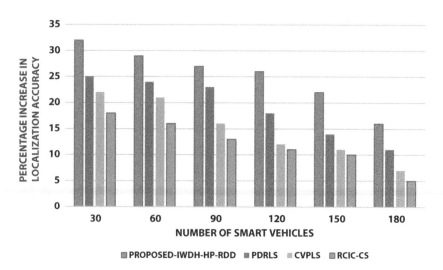

Figure 3.2 Percentage increase in localization accuracy of the IWDH-HP-RDD scheme for varying number of smart vehicles.

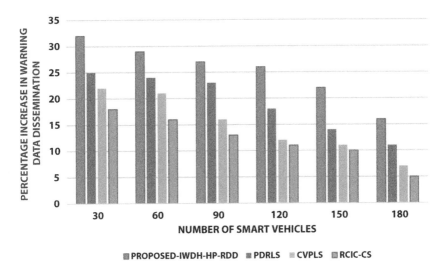

Figure 3.3 Percentage increase in warning data dissemination of the IWDH-HP-RDD scheme for varying number of smart vehicles.

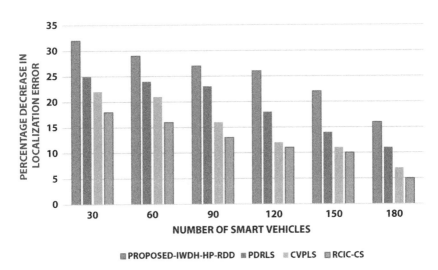

Figure 3.4 Percentage decrease in localization error of the IWDH-HP-RDD scheme for varying number of smart vehicles.

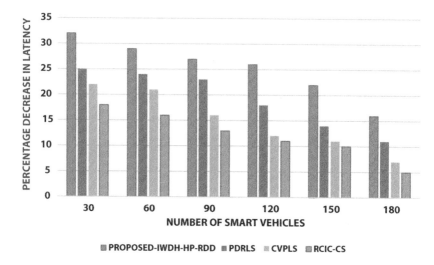

Figure 3.5 Percentage decrease in latency of the IWDH-HP-RDD scheme for varying number of smart vehicles.

for varying number of SVs. The percentage decrease in localization error and percentage decrease in latency of the proposed IWDH-HP-RDD for varying number of the SVs are considered to be phenomenally improved due to the addition of multi-lateration approach in position estimation. The percentage decrease in localization error of the proposed IWDH-HP-RDD scheme for varying number of the SVs is proved to be enhanced by 4.98%, 5.86% and 6.58% when compared to the baseline PDRLS, CVPLS and RCIC-CS approaches. The percentage decrease in latency of the proposed IWDH-HP-RDD scheme for varying number of SVs is also determined to be enhanced by 5.94%, 6.42% and 7.68% when compared to the baseline PDRLS, CVPLS and RCIC-CS approaches.

In the second part of analysis, the proposed IWDH-HP-RDD scheme and the compared PDRLS, CVPLS and RCIC-CS are evaluated using percentage increase in localization accuracy and warning data dissemination, percentage decrease in localization error and latency for varying number of anchor smart vehicles. Figures 3.6 and 3.7 demonstrate the results of the proposed IWDH-HP-RDD scheme and the compared PDRLS, CVPLS, and RCIC-CS evaluated with respect to percentage increase in localization accuracy and warning data dissemination for varying number of NLOS smart vehicles. The localization accuracy and warning data dissemination rate of the proposed IWDH-HP-RDD scheme is determined to be improved due to the multilateration method included in the process of position estimation associated with the unknown NLOS SVs. Thus, the

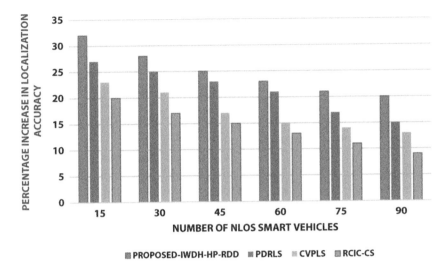

Figure 3.6 Percentage increase in localization accuracy of the IWDH-HP-RDD scheme for varying number of NLOS smart vehicles.

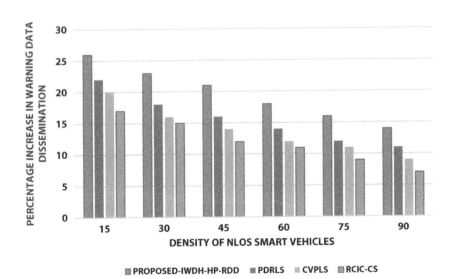

Figure 3.7 Percentage increase in warning data dissemination of the IWDH-HP-RDD scheme for varying number of NLOS smart vehicles.

localization accuracy of the proposed IWDH-HP-RDD scheme for varying number of NLOS smart vehicles is identified to be improved by 4.58%, 6.28% and 7.21% when compared to the baseline PDRLS, CVPLS and RCIC-CS approaches. The warning data dissemination rate of the proposed IWDH-HP-RDD scheme for varying number of smart vehicles is also determined to be enhanced by 5.12%, 6.54% and 7.16% when compared to the baseline PDRLS, CVPLS and RCIC-CS approaches.

Figures 3.8 and 3.9 depict the results of IWDH-HP-RDD scheme and the compared PDRLS, CVPLS and RCIC-CS evaluated with respect to percentage decrease in localization error and percentage decrease in latency for varying number of NLOS smart vehicles. The percentage decrease in localization error and percentage decrease in latency of the proposed IWDH-HP-RDD for varying NLOS smart vehicles are estimated to be increased considerably due to the inclusion of Woodburg formula in the process of localization. The percentage decrease in localization error of the proposed IWDH-HP-RDD scheme for varying NLOS smart vehicles is identified to be improved by 5.64%, 6.89% and 7.64% when compared to the baseline PDRLS, CVPLS and RCIC-CS approaches. The percentage decrease in latency of the proposed IWDH-HP-RDD scheme for varying NLOS smart vehicles is also determined to be enhanced by 6.21%, 7.48% and 8.42% when compared to the baseline PDRLS, CVPLS and RCIC-CS approaches.

In the final part of analysis, the proposed IWDH-HP-RDD scheme and the compared PDRLS, CVPLS and RCIC-CS are evaluated in terms

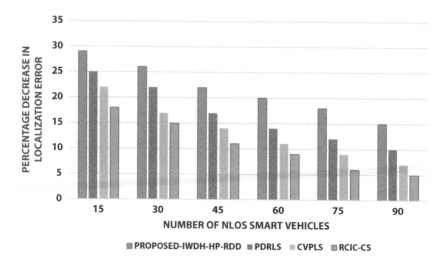

Figure 3.8 Percentage decrease in localization error of the IWDH-HP-RDD scheme for varying number of NLOS smart vehicles.

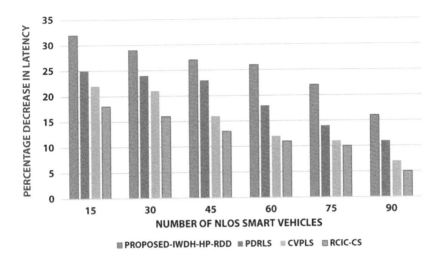

Figure 3.9 Percentage decrease in latency of the IWDH-HP-RDD scheme for varying number of NLOS smart vehicles.

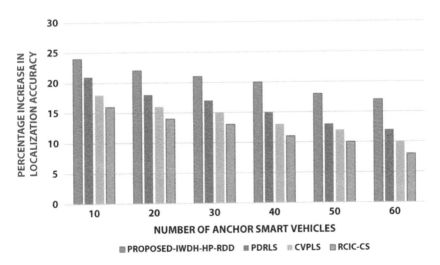

Figure 3.10 Percentage increase in localization accuracy of the IWDH-HP-RDD scheme for varying number of anchor smart vehicles.

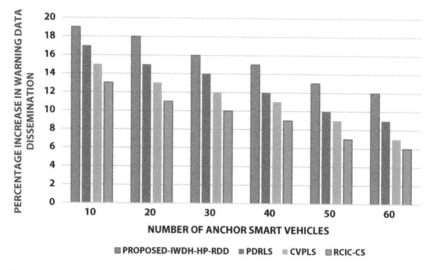

Figure 3.11 Percentage increase in warning data dissemination of the IWDH-HP-RDD scheme for varying number of anchor smart vehicles.

of percentage increase in localization accuracy and warning data dissemination, percentage decrease in localization error and latency for varying number of anchor SVs. Figures 3.10 and 3.11 highlight the results of IWDH-HP-RDD scheme and the compared PDRLS, CVPLS and RCIC-CS evaluated with respect to percentage increase in localization accuracy and warning data dissemination for varying number of anchor SVs. The percentage increase in localization accuracy and warning data dissemination of the proposed IWDH-HP-RDD scheme for varying number of anchor SVs is due to the incorporation of the enhanced weighted hyperbolic estimation process involved in unknown node positioning. The localization accuracy of the proposed IWDH-HP-RDD scheme for varying number of anchor SVs is confirmed to be improved by 5.69%, 6.85% and 7.94% when compared to the baseline PDRLS, CVPLS and RCIC-CS approaches. The warning data dissemination rate of the proposed IWDH-HP-RDD scheme for varying number of anchor SVs is also determined to be enhanced by 5.86%, 6.89% and 7.76% when compared to the baseline PDRLS, CVPLS and RCIC-CS approaches.

In addition, Figures 3.12 and 3.13 depict the results of IWDH-HP-RDD scheme and the compared PDRLS, CVPLS and RCIC-CS evaluated with respect to percentage decrease in localization error and latency for

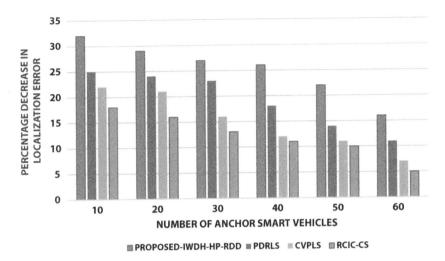

Figure 3.12 Percentage decrease in localization error of the IWDH-HP-RDD scheme for varying number of anchor smart vehicles.

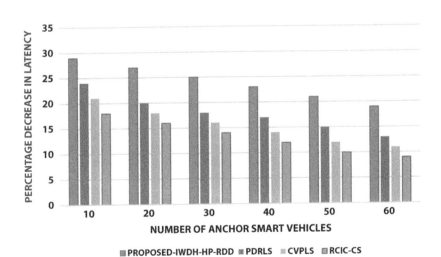

Figure 3.13 Percentage decrease in latency of the IWDH-HP-RDD scheme for varying number of anchor smart vehicles.

varying number of anchor SVs. The percentage decrease in the localization error and latency of the proposed IWDH-HP-RDD for varying number of anchor SVs is improved as it includes the method of least squares for accurate location estimation. The percentage decrease in localization error of the proposed IWDH-HP-RDD scheme for varying number of anchor SVs is identified to be improved by 4.96%, 5.68% and 6.64% when compared to the baseline PDRLS, CVPLS and RCIC-CS approaches. The percentage decrease in latency of the proposed IWDH-HP-RDD scheme for varying number of anchor SVs is also found to be enhanced by 5.74%, 6.86% and 7.92% when compared to the baseline PDRLS, CVPLS and RCIC-CS approaches.

In addition, Tables 3.2 and 3.3 present the performance of the proposed IWDH-HP-RDD scheme and baseline PDRLS, CVPLS and RCIC-CS approaches for parameters including Warning message dissemination rate, Channel utilization rate, Rate of neighborhood awareness and Success rate in localizing NLOS nodes.

Table 3.2 Proposed IWDH-HP-RDD scheme: warning message dissemination rate and channel utilization rate.

Schemes used for comparison	Warning message dissemination for varying number of anchor nodes used for localization (in %)			
	10	20	30	40
Proposed IWDH-HP-RDD	99.34	99.06	98.76	98.54
PDRLS	96.12	96.04	95.62	95.29
CVPLS	95.84	95.39	94.68	94.32
RCIC-CS	95.04	94.69	94.32	93.48
Schemes used for comparison	Channel utilization rate for varying number of anchor nodes used for localization			
	10	20	30	40
Proposed IWDH-HP-RDD	99.14	99.04	98.76	98.38
PDRLS	97.42	96.43	95.21	93.87
CVPLS	95.84	94.29	93.92	91.24
RCIC-CS	92.98	93.64	92.85	90.68

Table 3.3 Proposed IWDH-HP-RDD scheme: rate of neighborhood awareness and success rate in localizing NLOS nodes.

Schemes used for comparison	Rate of neighborhood awareness for varying number of anchor nodes used for localization			
	10	20	30	40
Proposed IWDH-HP-RDD	99.18	99.02	98.76	98.52
PDRLS	96.58	95.42	94.86	93.18
CVPLS	95.73	94.12	93.64	92.76
RCIC-CS	94.64	92.36	90.21	89.74
Schemes used for comparison	Success rate in localizing NLOS nodes for varying number of anchor nodes used for localization			
	10	20	30	40
Proposed IWDH-HP-RDD	99.42	99.31	99.23	99.16
PDRLS	97.29	96.46	95.12	94.48
CVPLS	95.56	93.48	92.94	90.14
RCIC-CS	94.12	92.29	91.29	90.64

The aforementioned results clearly depict that the proposed IWDH-HP-RDD scheme is significant enough in improving the parameters of Warning message dissemination rate, Channel utilization rate, Rate of neighborhood awareness and Success rate in localizing NLOS nodes on par with the baseline PDRLS, CVPLS and RCIC-CS approaches.

3.5 Conclusion

In this chapter, an Improved Weighted Distance Hop Hyperbolic Prediction–based Reliable Data Dissemination (IWDH-HP-RDD) mechanism is presented for enhancing the location estimation degree of unknown NLOS SVs in a vehicular network. It is proposed with the benefits of multi-lateration method and method of least squares in order to reduce the possibility of localization error to the maximum level. The simulation results conducted using EstiNet simulator clearly prove that the proposed IWDH-HP-RDD mechanism is capable of increasing the localization accuracy and warning data dissemination rate by 5.98% and 6.18% when compared to the benchmarked schemes. The results also prove that the percentage decrease in localization error of the proposed IWDH-HP-RDD scheme for varying number of anchor SVs is improved on an average by 5.12% and 6.62% when compared to the baseline PDRLS, CVPLS, and RCIC-CS approaches.

References

1. Gazzah, L., Najjar, L., Besbes, H., Improved hybrid AML algorithm without identification of LOS/NLOS Nodes, in: *Proceedings of 81st IEEE Vehicular Technology Conference*, pp. 1–5, 2015.
2. Yousefi, S., Chang, X.W., Champagne, B., Cooperative localization of mobile nodes in NLOS, in: *Proceedings of 25th IEEE Annual International Symposium on Personal, Indoor, and Mobile Radio Communication*, pp. 275–279, 2014.
3. Li, W., Jia, Y., Du, J., TOA-based cooperative localization for mobile stations with NLOS mitigation. *J. Franklin Inst.*, 353, 6, 1297–1312, 2016.
4. Teng, J., Snoussi, H., Richard, C., Zhou, R., Distributed variational filtering for simultaneous sensor localization and target tracking in wireless sensor networks. *IEEE Trans. Veh. Technol.*, 61, 5, 2305–2318, 2012.
5. Li, W., Jia, Y., Du, J., Zhang, J., Distributed multiple-model estimation for simultaneous localization and tracking with NLOS mitigation. *IEEE Trans. Veh. Technol.*, 62, 6, 2824–2830, 6, 2013.
6. Zhang, Z., Wang, C., Tao, X., Zeng, L., Research on the effect factor of WSN nodes ranging using WTR method in NLOS environment, in: *Proceedings of International Conference on Mechatronics. Electronic, Industrial and Control Engineering*, Atlantis Press, 2014.
7. Fujita, T. and Ohtsuki, T., Low complexity localization algorithm based on NLOS node identification using minimum subset for NLOS environments, in: *Proceedings of IEEE Global Telecommunications Conference*, pp. 1–5, 2008.
8. Sorrentino, A., Nunziata, F., Ferrara, G., Migliaccio, M., An effective indicator for NLOS, nLOS, LOS propagation channels conditions, in: *Proceedings of 6th European conference on antennas and Propagation*, pp. 1422–1426, 2012.
9. Zhang, P., Zhang, Z., Boukerche, A., Cooperative location verification for vehicular ad-hoc networks, in: *IEEE International Conference on Communications*, pp. 37–41, 2012a.
10. Zhang, Z., Mao, G., Anderson, B.D., On the information propagation process in multi-lane vehicular ad-hoc networks, in: *Proceedings of IEEE International Conference on Communications*, pp. 708–712, 2012b.

11. Gentner, C. and Groh, I., Analytical derivation of the false alarm and detection probability for NLOS detection, in: *Proceedings of 73rd IEEE Vehicular Technology Conference*, pp. 1–5, 2011.

12. Xiao, B., Yu, B., Gao, C., Detection and localization of sybil nodes in VANETs, in: *Proceedings of the workshop on Dependability issues in wireless ad hoc networks and sensor networks*, pp. 1–8, 2006.

13. Čapkun, S., Čagalj, M., Srivastava, M., Secure localization with hidden and mobile base stations, in: *Proceedings of IEEE INFOCOM*, 2006.

14. Song, J.H., Wong, V.W., Leung, V.C., Secure location verification for vehicular ad-hoc networks, in: *Proceedings of IEEE Global Telecommunications Conference*, pp. 1–5, 2008.

15. Leinmüller, T., Schoch, E., Kargl, F., Maihöfer, C., Decentralized position verification in geographic ad hoc routing. *Secur. Commun. Netw.*, 3, 4, 289–302, 2010.

16. Ros, F.J., Ruiz, P.M., Stojmenovic, I., Acknowledgment-based broadcast protocol for reliable and efficient data dissemination in vehicular ad hoc networks. *IEEE Trans. Mob. Comput.*, 11, 1, 33–46, 2010.

17. Abumansoor, O. and Boukerche, A., A secure cooperative approach for non-line-of-sight location verification in VANET. *IEEE Trans. Veh. Technol.*, 61, 1, 275–285, 2011.

18. Bai, X., Gong, M., Gao, Z., Li, S., Reliable and efficient data dissemination protocol in VANETs, in: *Proceedings of 8th International Conference on Wireless Communications. Networking and Mobile Computing*, pp. 1–4, 2012.

19. Zemouri, S., Djahel, S., Murphy, J.A., fast, reliable and lightweight distributed dissemination protocol for safety messages in Urban Vehicular Networks. *Ad Hoc Netw.*, 27, 26–43, 2015.

20. Pramuanyat, N., Nakorn, K.N., Kawila, K., Rojviboonchai, K., LARB: Location-aware reliable broadcasting protocol in VANET, in: *Proceedings of 13th International Joint Conference on Computer Science and Software Engineering*, pp. 1–6, 2016.

21. Alodadi, K., Al-Bayatti, A.H., Alalwan, N., Cooperative volunteer protocol to detect non-line of sight nodes in vehicular ad hoc networks. *Veh. Commun.*, 9, 72–82, 2017.

22. Dua, A., Kumar, N., Bawa, S., ReIDD: reliability-aware intelligent data dissemination protocol for broadcast storm problem in vehicular ad hoc networks. *Telecommun. Syst.*, 64, 3, 439–458, 2017.

23. Oliveira, R., Montez, C., Boukerche, A., Wangham, M.S., Reliable data dissemination protocol for VANET traffic safety applications. *Ad Hoc Netw.*, 63, 30–44, 2017.

24. Sattar, S., Qureshi, H.K., Saleem, M., Mumtaz, S., Rodriguez, J., Reliability and energy-efficiency analysis of safety message broadcast in VANETs. *Comput. Commun.*, 119, 118–126, 2018.

25. Ciabattoni, L., Foresi, G., Monterìù, A., Pepa, L., Pagnotta, D.P., Spalazzi, L., Verdini, F., Real time indoor localization integrating a model based

pedestrian dead reckoning on smartphone and BLE beacons. *J. Ambient Intell. Humaniz. Comput.*, 10, 1, 1–12, 1, 2019.

26. Amuthan, A. and Kaviarasan, R., Weighted inertia-based dynamic virtual bat algorithm to detect NLOS nodes for reliable data dissemination in VANETs. *J. Ambient Intell. Humaniz. Comput.*, 10, 11, 4603–4613, 2019a.

27. Amuthan, A. and Kaviarasan, R., Rank Criteria Improved Confidence-based centroid scheme for Non Line of Sight node localizations in vehicular networks. *J. King Saud Univ.-Comput. Inform. Sci.*, 2019b (In Press).

28. Nascimento, P., Kimura, B., Guidoni, D., Villas, L., An integrated dead reckoning with cooperative positioning solution to assist GPS NLOS using vehicular communications. *Sensors*, 18, 9, 2895–2912, 2018.

4

Remaining Useful Life Prediction of Small and Large Signal Analog Circuits Using Filtering Algorithms

Sathiyanathan M.[1]*, Anandhakumar K.[1], Jaganathan S.[2] and Subashkumar C. S.[1]

[1]Department of EEE PSG Institute of Technology and Applied Research, Neelambur, Coimbatore, India
[2]Department of EEE Dr. N.G.P. Institute of Technology and Applied Research, Kalapatti, Coimbatore, India

Abstract

This chapter addresses filter algorithms for the diagnosis and prognosis of failure in analog circuits, using Unscented Kalman Filters (UKFs) and Unscented Particle Filters (UPFs). Most of the industrial process uses sensors and actuators to the increase the production without conceding the quality of the product. The sensors and actuators (normally an electric motor) are connected with a power conditioning circuit which consists of several active and passive devices. The sensor is a highly sensitive element and has primary contact with the industrial process. The sensed signals are considered to decide controllers/processors to operate the motors through the power converters. These elements are in the manufacturing/control process round the clock. The failures in anyone the component may be on sensor networks or power converter leads to process failure. To avoid failures in the industrial process and also to ensure the safe operation of associated components, filtering algorithms are proposed. Particularly, small-signal sensor circuits and large-signal power circuits are monitored through filtering algorithms to forecast the failure of individual components in a circuit and also to forecast the remaining useful life (RUL) of that component. This will help the users to replace the circuit to regulate the manufacturing process.

Keywords: Analog circuits, failure prediction, filtering algorithms, remaining useful life

---

Corresponding author: sathiyangm@gmail.com

C. Venkatesh, N. Rengarajan, P. Ponmurugan and S. Balamurugan (eds.) Smart Systems for Industrial Applications, (93–114) © 2022 Scrivener Publishing LLC

4.1 Introduction

The sensors and power conditioning units play a vital role in the industry for process automation. These elements are important in the industrial process for monitoring or identifying the end product of the process. Moreover, the sensors have primary contact with the product and provide complete information about the product or object in the form of analog signals to the computer or microcontroller unit in the automated system. Based on the information obtained from the sensors, all the actuators and power conditioning devices are operated to speed-up the process. The sensors and associated analog circuits are utilized 24/7 in an operation. The outputs of the sensing element may be voltage or current that depends on the frequency. The sensor network contains a sensor element, a signal conditioning circuit to record the output signal of the sensor element in a range which can be interpreted by the remaining electronic circuit and then filters the device to reduce or suppress electronic noise. Signals from the sensor are influenced by this signal conditioning circuit and most sensors are analog output signals. The proposed fault prognosis process flow diagram is illustrated in Figure 4.1.

A filter is a circuit that enables some frequencies and compensates for others. The filter will also remove large frequencies from signals that contain unwanted or insignificant frequencies as well. The four main types of filters are as follows:

- low-pass filter
- high-pass filter
- band-pass filter, and
- notch filter (or the band-reject or band-stop filter)

The response curves are used to study the behavior of analog filters used in sensor networks. A response curve shows an attenuation ratio versus

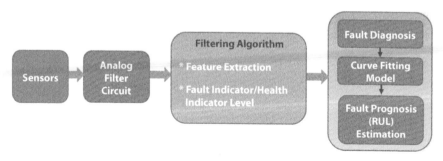

Figure 4.1 Fault prognosis process flow diagram.

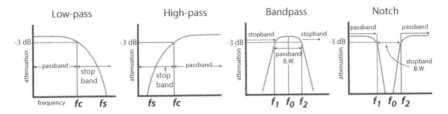

Figure 4.2 Frequency response curves of different analog filter circuits.

frequency as shown in Figure 4.2. Attenuation is denoted in decibel units (dB) and frequency can be expressed in two forms: either the angular frequency in rad/s or frequency, f in Hz, i.e., cycles per second. These two forms are correlated by ω = 2πf.

In this chapter, an anti-aliasing filter also known as a low-pass filter is presented for fault prognosis algorithm implementation and RUL prediction. Many techniques have been used to design an analog low-pass filter; the Sallen-Key Filter is one of the most popular filter configurations used. A Sallen-Key Filter is essentially a cascade of RC filter stages with a non-inverting amplifier configuration at each stage. The Sallen-Key, along with all the techniques which can be used to build analog filters for sensors, employs conventional analog design methods with many manual mathematical computations and hence can be vulnerable to mistakes in design. The failure in any of the components will affect the quality of the signal given to the controller which may lead to a malfunction in the control signal is provided to the actuators. Besides, finding the failure component in a complex sensor network or circuit is a difficult task that will affect the industrial operation. To tackle the above-mentioned problems, fault prognosis algorithms are developed which are used for a multitude of applications for fault diagnosis, forecasting, and the remainder of a component or whole circuit.

The chapter is organized as follows. Section 4.2 presents a literature survey where the problems associated with fault prediction and remaining useful life (RUL) prediction are discussed, various filtering algorithms are studied and presented. Section 4.3 describes the system architecture and its characteristics. Section 4.4 elaborates the filtering algorithms. Finally, Section 4.5 discusses the simulation results of RUL predictions.

4.2   Literature Survey

To ensure the reliability and availability of engineering systems, maintenance programs are now necessary. Accurate forecasts of the RUL of industrial equipment could include advanced maintenance schedules, improve the availability of equipment and reduce running costs as indicated in the article [16, 20]. However, existing deep learning methods for RUL prediction are not completely successful due to the following two reasons. First, relying on a single objective function to estimate the RUL will limit the learned representations and thus affect the prediction accuracy. Second, while longer sequences are more informative for modeling the sensor dynamics of equipment, existing methods are less effective to deal with very long sequences, as they mainly focus on the latest information. The fault prognostic was done for different analog circuits, battery, resistor, capacitor, etc., are presented in this literature [9, 19]. The model-based and data-driven methodologies are the two most important methodologies in the forecasts of analog circuits. In the model-based approach, a complex theoretical model of the system is used to find the degree of failure and the time remaining for failure. Similarly, it is predicted that statistical facts from the method will not affect before failure/rupture happens in the data-driven approach. In addition to evidence-driven methods, integrating facts from model-based approaches can however improve prognostic ability and provide important data. The data-driven methodology is the basis for the failure prognosis in the three main phases of the electronic circuit. At first, fault features of an analog circuit and its components are extracted. Secondly, to reach the component quality level, a fault indicator/health indicator has been developed. Finally, to find the RUL device and its elements, the threshold stage is employed. The advances in filtering algorithms, including UKF and UPF process flow, are described in this section by the mathematical model and the effects of the simulation.

The preventative measure creates a large number of failures in rotating machinery in rotating electric machines. In [1, 15], the condition-based diagnosis and forecast of failures in electric drives are presented, where the extended Kalman Filter (KF) is used to identify the fault in the bearing, in particular the remainder of the lifetime of rolling stock (RUL). The main reasons are the lack of accurate models of physical degradation and limited data on label training. In [5, 13], a new method of RUL prediction for rollers focused on the time-variable KF is proposed, which can work to prevent balance the different deterioration stages of the rollers and carry out the RUL forecast efficiently. In normal and gradual deterioration phases the progression of the tracking data is a linear trend; changes in the rapid degradation process are not linear. The filter models of Kalman are then constructed using linear and quadratic functions. A relative sliding window is constructed to adjust the bearing depreciation process. Dynamically, filter models can be switched to data monitoring at multiple stages. The RUL can be measured correctly. To show the viability and validity of the suggested process, there are two classes of data sets running to failure. Moreover, in [6], for estimating the RUL with Switching Kalman Filter (SKF), non-linear functions with linear functions are proposed that allow us to choose the most probable mode of degradation so that they can make better forecasts.

The life cycle of the electric car depends on the battery's use and costs. In specific, battery aging eventually deteriorates and affects the efficiency of the battery. As part of the knowledge in [2], the identification of the condition of the battery and its health is important. Battery health monitoring allows the user to secure and replace batteries in advance to avoid damages from accidental battery faults and to minimize repair costs. Battery health detection This paper points forth and contrasts two mathematical models to describe the battery's lifetime behavior. Experimental life-cycle research data were used for validating the precision of the empiric model. The most reliable model was subsequently used for predicting battery RUL in the Unscented Kalman Filter (UKF). This work is an early step in the implementation of a battery health monitoring system. In [3, 11], the prediction of the RUL, battery power, and charging status (SOC) of lithium-ion batteries are provided with the novel PF-based filtering process. The KF and particles swarm optimization mechanism is built with this PF tool (PSO). In this work, the fast reduction of lithium-ion batteries will be used to represent the decay of the lithium-ion battery and then to find the RUL of the battery using the proposed PF algorithm. The UKF algorithm is similarly fused with the neural back propagation (BP) net to improve lithium-ion battery prediction precision. The BP neural network automatically predicts the residual of UKF. The UKF uses the projected remaining parameters to change iteratively the degradation model [4]. In [8], the accuracy of predictive approaches to current predictive approaches is based on the ability to model the development of the CM signal reliably. It thus ultimately relies on the amount of the random noise signal from the CM. In [18], some situations, RUL estimation is impracticable even though signals are corrupted by high levels of random noise. To mitigate this problem, a robust RUL method is proposed based on a limited KF. To ensure adequate predictability, regardless of the noise levels of the signal evolution, the suggested system models, CM signaling is subject to a series of inequalities. A numerical study and a case study with real-world data on car platinum acid batteries show the advantages of the proposed RUL forecasting process.

To make that happen, a system requires a degradation model to predict and act before any failure. Ideally, physics-based models are used because they are precise yet difficult to construct, and it is virtually impossible in complicated systems with many interactions. A model degradation composed in [7, 14] of a Multilayer Perceptron (MLP) and a KF for an airplane turbine or turbofan for its RUL prediction. The results show that the model outperforms other more complex models. The fault location is considered to be identified in [10] and the evolution of the pipeline's blocking particles will continue to be studied. Wax will create a solid deposit at the pipe wall to minimize the radius of the pipe and also take advantage of this phenomenon. The movement through pipelines is determined dramatically by the creation of a solid deposit, which depends on the volume of wax in the fluid. The context for estimating the non-observable condition of the system is often used for stochastic filters. The expanded Kalman filter (EKF) algorithm is used to estimate the state vector based on the background of all the measurements obtained, thus allowing accurate results for the state estimate of deterioration given in [11, 12]. Failure of the superb buck converter circuit and estimating the remaining usable life (RUL) is recommended in [17]. To determine the health status of the circuit a Mahalanobis distance (MD) is used. Time sets of various MD form the time series of the circuit. The SVR was improved by an updated grey wolf optimizer (MGWO) algorithm before calculating the RUL in compliance with the working state time series obtained.

4.3   System Architecture

The fault prognostic approach takes into account a Sallen-Key, low-pass filter with a baseline frequency of 25 kHz. The tolerance range is 5% and the default tolerance range is 15% for all circuit components. Characteristics of the actual component status (i.e., without a fault) derived as the component's tolerance range varies within this range. If any of the fundamental components differ beyond their tolerances, then fault responses are achieved. In Figure 4.3, the input signal sensitivity is increased and essential components are treated as components like R_1, C_1, R_2, C_2, R_2, and C_3. Two faults are taken into account for each critical component: firstly, a defect value greater than the upper limit (+5% to 15% of the component's tolerance); secondly, a fault value smaller than the bottom limit (−5% to 15% of the component's tolerance). Eight fault cases occur, and one faultless status is taken into account for the assessment. The execution of circuit failure prognosis stage is defined as follows.

The Sallen-Key filter gives the flexibility of modifying the filter characteristics (cut-off frequency and Q) using R, C values, and amplifier gain. A low-pass filter is used for eliminating high-frequency noise from the system.

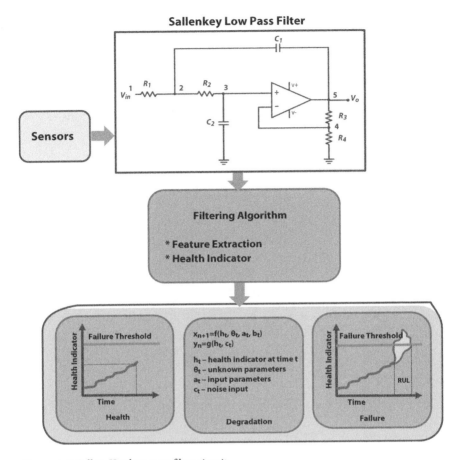

Figure 4.3 Sallen-Key low-pass filter circuit.

4.4 Remaining Useful Life Prediction

The hybrid form of the particle filter (PF) and UKF algorithm is known as the unscented particle filter (UPF). In the standard form of PF, the dynamic state-space form employed in the Bayesian inference framework is shown as follows.

4.4.1 Initialization

The time-domain mathematical model of Sallen-Key LPF describes the dynamic characteristics of systems, including the state transition and measurement equations which can be expressed as follows:

$$H_o^n = f(a_{01}, b_{01}), n = 1, 2, \ldots, N_s \tag{4.1}$$

$$I_o^n = g(a_0, c_0) \tag{4.2}$$

where f and g are the state-transition and measurement functions respectively. The state variables and measurement data of the system are given as a_o and I_o, respectively. Similarly, b_o and c_o are the process noise and measurement noise variables, respectively. The noises are liberated with the system state variables.

$$\overline{H}_o^n = U[a_o^n] \tag{4.3}$$

$$H_{o1}^n = U[(a_o^n - \overline{a}_o^n)(a_o^n - \overline{a}_o^n)] \tag{4.4}$$

From Equations (4.3) and (4.4), when time is zero, $\overline{H}_o^n$ and H_{o1}^n are the mean and covariance of a_o, respectively.

$$\overline{H}_o^{n,x} = [\overline{a}_o^n \, 0 \, 0]^T \tag{4.5}$$

$$H_1^{n,x} = \begin{bmatrix} h_1 & 0 & 0 \\ 0 & h_2 & 0 \\ 0 & 0 & h_3 \end{bmatrix} \tag{4.6}$$

The mean of $\overline{X}_o^{i,a}$ and covariance of $X_1^{i,a}$ from time 1 obtained from Equations (4.7) and (4.9).

4.4.2 Proposal Distribution

The final sigma points of the particle and the weights shall be obtained as follows:

$$\overline{X}_k^i = \sum_{i=1}^{N_s} \omega_k^i x_k^i \tag{4.7}$$

$$X_k^i = \sum_{i=1}^{N_s} \omega_{k1}^i (x_o^i - \overline{x}_o^i)(x_o^i - \overline{x}_o^i)^T \tag{4.8}$$

The weights are normalized from the following equation:

$$\omega_k^i = \omega_k^i / \sum_{i=1}^{N_s} \omega_k^i \tag{4.9}$$

4.4.3   Time Update

To move the particle to further prediction, the next update functions are completed.

$$X_o^{i,x-} = f(X_{o1}^{i,x+}, X_{o1}^{i,u+}) \tag{4.10}$$

$$x_k^{i-} = \sum_{j=0}^{N_s} \omega_j^i X_o^{i,x-} \tag{4.11}$$

$$X_k^{i-} = \sum_{j=0}^{N_s} \omega_j^i (X_o^{i,x-} - x_k^{i-})(X_o^{i,x-} - x_k^{i-})^T \tag{4.12}$$

$$y_k^{i-} = h(X_o^{i,x-}, x_{o1}^{i,v+}) \tag{4.13}$$

$$z_k^{i-} = \sum_{j=0}^{N_s} \omega_j^i y_k^{i-} \tag{4.14}$$

4.4.4   Relative Entropy in Particle Resampling

The size of the sample is below the limit, i.e., the value of N_s, new particles, and covariance weights are provided by Equations (4.15) and (4.16). The relative entropy is inserted into the new random samples to reduce the error between samples and covariance.

$$X_k^{i+} - X_k^{j+} = 0 \tag{4.15}$$

$$\sum_{j=1}^{N_s} \omega_k^j \geq r_k^i \tag{4.16}$$

The divergence of Kullback-Leibler is often called relative entropy (KLD). The distance between the random distribution of two particles or particles is calculated. Relative entropy or KLD is a more formally efficient assessment approach to compare two distributions, x_k^{i+} and x_k^{j+}, as follows:

$$F(X_k^{i+}, X_k^{j+}) = \sum x_k^{i+} \log \frac{x_k^{i+}}{x_k^{j+}} \qquad (4.17)$$

In general, x_k^{i+} is the true value of estimated distribution and x_k^{j+} comes from the analog circuit model to approximate that true distribution.

4.4.5   RUL Prediction

The rest of the useful life transition is calculated from parameters of the degradation model, also called state-space variables of the device.

$$x_k = [a_k; b_k; c_k; d_k] \qquad (4.18)$$

where a_k, b_k, c_k, and d_k are the model variables and k is the cycle number of RUL.

$$a_k = a_{k-1} + \omega_a \qquad \omega_a \sim N(0, \sigma_a)$$

$$b_k = b_{k-1} + \omega_b \qquad \omega_b \sim N(0, \sigma_b)$$

$$c_k = c_{k-1} + \omega_c \qquad \omega_c \sim N(0, \sigma_c) \qquad (4.19)$$

$$d_k = d_{k-1} + \omega_d \qquad \omega_d \sim N(0, \sigma_d)$$

where $0 \rightarrow$ Gaussian noise and $\sigma \rightarrow$ standard deviation.

A frequent adjustment in the component value, i.e., rise and fall in value, from the tolerance range (i.e., $\pm 5\%$ real tolerance to 15% fault tolerance), results in the degradation model. In circuit output, the deterioration model of components like R_1, C_1, R_2, and C_2 plays a major role. The fault level increases here by 0.5% each time the index is indexed.

$$f(y) = a_k * \exp(b_k * k) + c_k * \exp(d_k * k) \qquad (4.20)$$

The proposed circuit curve fitting model is performed using Equation (4.20) from the health index (HI) data obtained using characteristics derived during different simulated failure conditions. This HI is shown in Figure 4.4 with a block line which indicates the boundary at which the

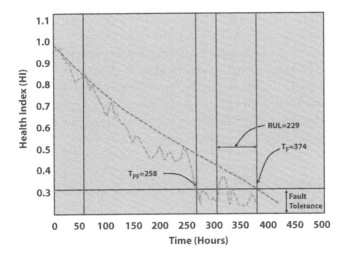

Figure 4.4 RUL prediction model curve of passive component.

circuit works in a normal state. If it crosses this HI, then the circuit may fail. In the following circuit, the red line indicates the actual life of the component, and the green line indicates the estimated life of the component under the change in input condition. The total lifetime of the component is considered as 500 hours

Figure 4.4 shows that the initial fault (i.e., pre-fault) is detected at $T_{PF} = 258$ hour, and circuit failure time is estimated as $T_F = 374$. But the UPF and UKF algorithms have identified the after the pre-fault time and the total RUL of the circuit is estimated as 229 hours. Similarly, for the lower tolerance range of components (i.e., +5%), predictions are made. The estimated hours are used to perform the service or used to replace the faulty component from the system.

4.5   Results and Discussion

The life prediction is made by setting the degree of failure of each portion near the tolerance range in the Sallen-Key low-pass filter. The input is used for a random noise; the run time is 50 s. The number of iteration samples for the Gaussian distribution is set to 200 in the IUPF m-file code. In any defect scenario, a simulation extracts 200 original samples. For the analog circuit RUL calculation, the proposed approach has a good output and the estimated error is less than 5%. Besides, as compared with the UKF algorithm, the UPF algorithm shows greater efficiency in evaluation indices. It is widely agreed that the fault threshold is 80% of the rated value of the item. The variable is subject to failure if the prediction is under this threshold. The exponential model of growth is used for the degradation curves. The MATLAB curve adapting toolbox is used to obtain the exact exponential model, with the necessary model parameters shown in Table 4.1. Figure 4.5 and Figure 4.6 shows the HI of the elements R_1, C_1, R_2, and C_2. HI is greater than 0.95 in correlation.

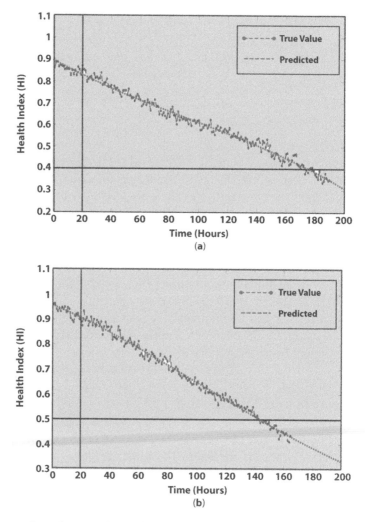

Figure 4.5 Curve fitting model of Sallen-Key low-pass filter without fault: (a) resistor R1, (b) capacitor C_1, (c) resistor R_2, and (d) capacitor C2.   (*Continued*)

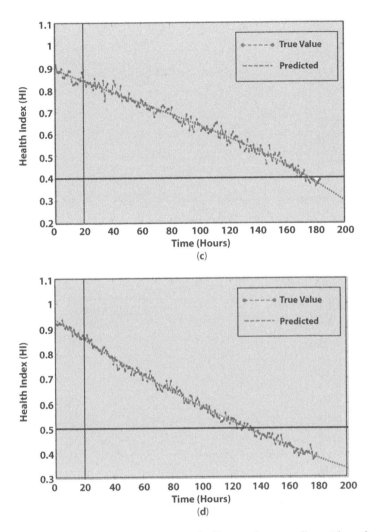

Figure 4.5 (Continued) Curve fitting model of Sallen-Key low-pass filter without fault: (a) resistor R1, (b) capacitor C_1, (c) resistor R_2, and (d) capacitor C2.

Table 4.1 Sallen-Key LPF degradation model parameters.

Component	a_k	b_k	c_k	d_k
R_1	0.9273	0.22649	−0.17230	1.02224
R_2	0.9345	0.11462	−0.14580	2.98590
C_1	0.9789	0.16791	−0.12993	4.25647
C_2	0.9247	0.45978	−0.32348	2.26547

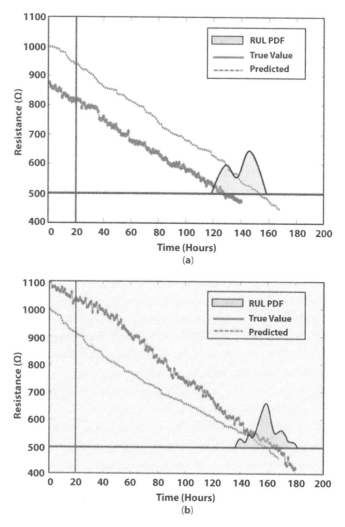

Figure 4.6 RUL prediction results: Sallen-Key low-pass filter: (a) R_1 below the tolerance, (b) R_1 above the tolerance, (c) C_1 below the tolerance, (d) C1 above the tolerance, (e) R_2 below the tolerance, (f) R_2 above the tolerance, (g) C_2 below the tolerance, and (h) C_2 above the tolerance. (*Continued*)

The maximum failure is 0.0436 suggesting that with this represented relation the system model can be defined. The factor of correlation is 0. 9811, the degradation model will characterize the component degradation process. Figure 4.3 shows the RUL prediction curve.

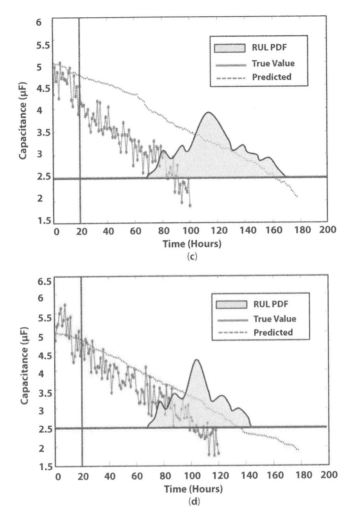

Figure 4.6 (Continued) RUL prediction results: Sallen-Key low-pass filter: (a) R_1 below the tolerance, (b) R_1 above the tolerance, (c) C_1 below the tolerance, (d) C1 above the tolerance, (e) R_2 below the tolerance, (f) R_2 above the tolerance, (g) C_2 below the tolerance, and (h) C_2 above the tolerance.   (*Continued*)

The health deterioration curve begins from the highest value, and at the start, no fault is regarded. Table 4.2 assesses and contrasts the UPF and UKF algorithms and provides a quantitative performance comparison. In contrast with the UKF algorithm, the UPF algorithm has better abilities with an average convergent width interval. Similarly, the proposed approach also

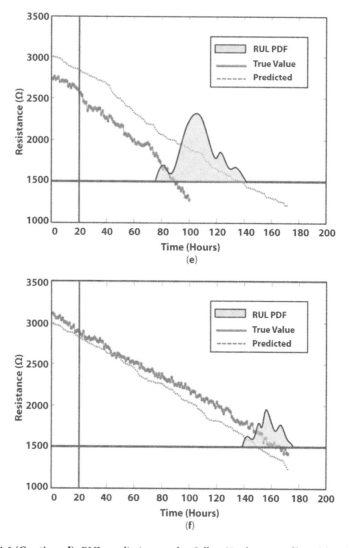

Figure 4.6 (Continued) RUL prediction results: Sallen-Key low-pass filter: (a) R_1 below the tolerance, (b) R_1 above the tolerance, (c) C_1 below the tolerance, (d) C1 above the tolerance, (e) R_2 below the tolerance, (f) R_2 above the tolerance, (g) C_2 below the tolerance, and (h) C_2 above the tolerance. (*Continued*)

has a decent performance in RUL estimation. The UPF methods can be obtained from Tables 4.2 for a good RUL estimate and the maximum RUL relative error is 10%. This shows that the approach is ideal for non-linear systems like analog circuits in sensors or non-Gaussian systems. Moreover,

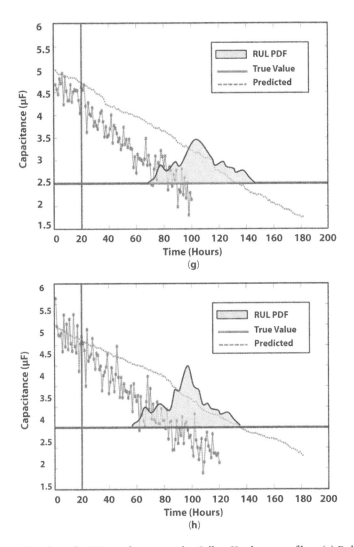

Figure 4.6 (Continued) RUL prediction results: Sallen-Key low-pass filter: (a) R_1 below the tolerance, (b) R_1 above the tolerance, (c) C_1 below the tolerance, (d) C1 above the tolerance, (e) R_2 below the tolerance, (f) R_2 above the tolerance, (g) C_2 below the tolerance, and (h) C_2 above the tolerance.

the proposed UPF algorithm is superior to the simple PF algorithm, and the maximum relative error can be reduced by 5%. The 95% converging interval of the UPF algorithm, particularly with the unsafe RUL number, is much more convergent and contains the actual value. The RUL estimates are very uncertain.

Table 4.2 Performance result of proposed UPF and UKF.

Component	Tolerance (%)	Failure range (%)	UPF			UKF		
			Relative error	RUL (hours)	Convergence time (sec)	Relative error	RUL (hours)	Convergence time (sec)
R_1	+5	15	0.06290	10,024	1,233.15	0.30247	10,028	823.02
	−5	15	0.16613	9,347	1,231.18	0.18931	9,230	820.12
R_2	+5	15	0.24959	12,384	1,123.20	0.38937	12,391	809.27
	−5	15	0.14025	10,283	824.37	0.33424	10,233	881.39
C_1	+5	15	0.19373	32,940	942.14	0.32456	32,939	801.32
	−5	15	0.17941	30,283	923.59	0.23245	30,392	880.39
C_2	+5	15	0.29121	28,493	1,399.82	0.34960	27,983	1,232.80
	−5	15	0.12670	29,449	1,002.13	0.22553	29,321	1,180.19

4.6 Conclusion

The analog circuit in the area of sensors and communication systems is commonly used as a Sallen-Key low-pass filter. The ongoing operation of a highly variable or noise-assisted analog circuit will increase the risk of circuit component failure. The RUL forecast thus becomes a difficult challenge for scientists. In the conventional filter-algorithms, UKF and UPF, several researchers have shown ROL prognostic methods (UPF). However, because of its estimation and defective status of the circuit elements, the forecast results are not reliable. To evaluate the distance between the samples, the UPF algorithm was used in the RUL prognosis with relative entropy for the exact sample of the particles. In this procedure, the UPF of the covariance matrix produces a collection of sigma samples and then compares the sigma samples using relative entropy. The final results are spread to the forecast stage.

References

1. Singleton, R.K., Strangas, E.G., Aviyente, S., Extended Kalman Filtering for Remaining-Useful-Life Estimation of Bearings. *IEEE Trans. Ind. Electron.*, 62, 3, 1781–1790, Mar. 2015.
2. Sangwan, V., Kumar, R., Rathore, A.K., An Empirical Capacity Degradation Modeling and Prognostics of Remaining Useful Life of Li-ion Battery using Unscented Kalman Filter. *2018 8th IEEE India International Conference on Power Electronics (IICPE)*, Dec. 2018.
3. Mo, B., Yu, J., Tang, D., Liu, H., Yu, J., A remaining useful life prediction approach for lithium-ion batteries using Kalman filter and an improved particle filter. *2016 IEEE International Conference on Prognostics and Health Management (ICPHM)*, June 2016.
4. Xiao, Z., Fang, H., Li, Z., Chang, Y., Remaining Useful Life Prediction of Lithium-ion Battery Based on Unscented Kalman Filter and Back propagation Neural Network. *2019 IEEE 8th Data Driven Control and Learning Systems Conference (DDCLS)*, May 2019.
5. Alberto-Olivares, M., Gonzalez-Gutierrez, A., Tovar-Arriaga, S., Gorrostieta-Hurtado, E., Remaining Useful Life Prediction for Turbofan based on a Multilayer Perceptron and Kalman Filter. *2019 16th International Conference on Electrical Engineering, Computing Science and Automatic Control (CCE)*, Sept. 2019.
6. Cui, L., Wang, X., Wang, H., Ma, J., Research on Remaining Useful Life Prediction of Rolling Element Bearings Based on Time-Varying Kalman Filter. *IEEE Trans. Instrum. Meas.*, 69, 6, 2858–2867, June 2020.

7. Lim, P., Goh, C.K., Tan, K.C., Dutta, P., Estimation of Remaining Useful Life Based on Switching Kalman Filter Neural Network Ensemble. *Annual conference of the prognostics and health management society 2014*, pp. 1–8, Jan. 2014.

8. Son, J., Zhou, S., Sankavaram, C., Du, X., Zhang, Y., Remaining useful life prediction based on noisy condition monitoring signals using constrained Kalman filter. *Elsevier J. Reliab. Eng. Syst. Saf.*, 152, 38–50, Aug. 2016, https://doi.org/10.1016/j.ress.2016.02.006.

9. Duan, B., Zhang, Q., Geng, F., Zhang, C., Remaining useful life prediction of lithium-ion battery based on extended Kalman particle filter. *Int. J. Energy Res.*, 44, 1724–1734, Mar. 2020, https://doi.org/10.1002/er.5002.

10. Moulahi, M.H. and Hmida, F.B., Extended Kalman Filtering for Remaining Useful Lifetime Prediction of a Pipeline in a Two-Tank System, in: *Diagnosis, Fault Detection & Tolerant Control*, vol. 269, pp. 211–233, Feb. 2020, https://doi.org/10.1007/978-981-15-1746-4_11.

11. Qi, J., Mauricio, A., Sarrazin, M., Janssens, K., Gryllias, K., Remaining Useful Life Prediction of Rolling Element Bearings Based on Unscented Kalman Filter. *Advances in Condition Monitoring of Machinery in Non-Stationary Operations. CMMNO 2018. Applied Condition Monitoring*, vol. 15, Springer, pp. 111–121, Feb. 2019, https://doi.org/10.1007/978-3-030-11220-2_12.

12. Baptista, M., Henriques, E.M.P., de Medeiros, I.P., Malere, J.P., Nascimento, C.L., Jr., Prendinger, H., Remaining useful life estimation in aeronautics: Combining data-driven and Kalman filtering. *Reliab. Eng. Syst. Saf.*, 184, 228–239, April 2019, https://doi.org/10.1016/j.ress.2018.01.017.

13. Cheng, C., Ma, G., Zhang, Y., Sun, M., Teng, F., Ding, H., Yua, Y., A Deep Learning-Based Remaining Useful Life Prediction Approach for Bearings. *IEEE/ASME Trans. Mechatron.*, 25, 3, 1243–1254, June 2020.

14. Wang, Z.-Q., Hu, C.-H., Si, X.-S., Zhang, J.-X., Wang, H.-Y., A new remaining useful life prediction approach for independent component based on the Wiener process and Bayesian estimating paradigm. *2013 25th Chinese Control and Decision Conference (CCDC)*, July 2013.

15. Qin, A., Zhang, Q., Hu, Q., Sun, G., He, J., Lin, S., Remaining Useful Life Prediction for Rotating Machinery Based on Optimal Degradation Indicator. *Hindawi Shock Vib.*, 2017, 12, Mar. 2017, https://doi.org/10.1155/2017/6754968, 6754968.

16. Okoh, C., Roy, R., Mehnen, J., Redding, L., Overview of Remaining Useful Life Prediction Techniques in Through-life Engineering Services. *Proc. CIRP*, 16, 158–163, 2014.

17. Wang, L., Yue, J., Su, Y., Lu, F., Sun, Q., A Novel Remaining Useful Life Prediction Approach for Superbuck Converter Circuits Based on Modified Grey Wolf Optimizer-Support Vector Regression. *Energies*, 10, 459, 2017, https://doi.org/10.3390/en10040459.

18. Lau, J.W., Cripps, E., Cripps, S., Remaining useful life prediction: A multiple product partition approach. *Commun. Stat. - Simul. C.*, 2020, 1–12, May 2020, https://doi.org/10.1080/03610918.2020.1766499.

19. Fan, B., Hu, L., Hu, N., Remaining useful life prediction of rolling bearings by the particle filter method based on degradation rate tracking. *J. Vibroengineering*, 17, 2, 743–756, Mar. 2015.

20. An, D., Choi, J.-H., Kim, N.H., Prediction of remaining useful life under different conditions using accelerated life testing data. *J. Mech. Sci. Technol.*, 32, 2497–2507, June 2018, https://doi.org/10.1007/s12206-018-0507-z.

5

AI in Healthcare

S. Menaga* and J. Paruvathavardhini†

Jai Shriram Engineering College Coimbatore, India

Abstract

This chapter on "AI in Healthcare" encompasses the emerging new technologies of AI in the field of healthcare, the newly developed and tested algorithms for various medical analysis in different fields. It showcases how Artificial Intelligence is able to harvest the advance medical knowledge through the literature, thereby assisting in the attempt to provide care for the optimal patient by assisting physicians in making superior decisions clinically. It also concentrates on how AI is trained using various technical algorithms and medical tools to streamline the diagnoses of various diseases. It emphasizes the need of AI on the latest clinical trends which has solutions on Radiology, Pathology, Immuno-Oncology, Neuroscience, Neuro-degenerative disorders, and various chronic disorders, in the platform of chemical and pharmaceutical for drug design and development.

It stipulates the need of AI in the vast medical field where rapid progress is required to analyze the human cognitive functions. It sets forth the popular AI techniques of machine learning algorithms, which is focusing for the structural data such as neural network and classical support vector machine, and for the processing of unstructured data, the modern deep learning as well as natural language processing is used.

It also imparts the significance of AI in Tele-Healthcare. Various new techniques are discussed on how a patient can be monitored by his medical advisor through automated text messages and online portals. Different healthcare chatbots are also reviewed here like Forsky (conversational diary-food track, counts calories, nutrition-related), WebMD (health conditions, general symptoms, medicine and various treatment options, recognize pills, and local health schedules), Ada (used to make informed decisions about their health based on the virtual doctor's database of knowledge), SkinVision (a skincare app that analyzes using the image of the skin). Finally, new technical ideas are explored on how to develop

---

Corresponding author: sri.ece09@gmail.com
†*Corresponding author*: vardhini.jpv@gmail.com

C. Venkatesh, N. Rengarajan, P. Ponmurugan and S. Balamurugan (eds.) Smart Systems for Industrial Applications, (115–140) © 2022 Scrivener Publishing LLC

new rapid test kits using AI to handle the pandemic situations of diseases where the culture test results take 4 to 5 days.

Keywords: Machine learning, deep learning, neural networks, natural language processing, pharmaceutical medication, Cobot, wearable sensors, AI in medical imaging

5.1   Introduction

At the point when a significant number of us hear the expression "Artificial Intelligence" (AI), we envision robots carrying out our responsibilities, delivering individuals out of date. The main aim of AI is to impersonate human cognitive function. It was initiated in the year of 1950s by the academicians and it has undergone many failures while testing practically. Then, the optimization of AI was divided into subfields based on technical considerations for further research, and finally, it has been enormous technology in all the fields. In the most recent periods, the use of AI has been an explosive growth in the domain of healthcare which once was thought as a futuristic threat to mankind. Many research studies were initialized on AI in healthcare and it was slowed down due to lack of funding. But in recent days, many global corporations and organizations are very much interested in investing in the creative innovation of AI applications. It is assessed to offer over $15 trillion to the world economy constantly 2030 and the best effect will be in the field of medical care.

Also, since AI-driven PCs are modified to settle on choices with minimal human intercession, some marvel if machines will before long settle on the difficult decisions we currently depend on our primary care physicians. The quickly developing openness of clinical information and the advances of large information indicative procedures have finished the capability of the current effective employments of AI in the healthcare framework [1]. One approach to explore healthcare services requests and exponentially expanding multifaceted nature in care and treatment alternatives to proactively envision future interest, dangers, and well-being needs and utilize this information to better care allocation and patient-focused treatment division. With present day, medicine confronting a noteworthy test of procuring, breaking down, and applying organized and unstructured data information to treat or oversee maladies

With the assistance of significant clinical inquiries, expected AI strategies can separate human services suitable data discharged in the colossal amount of information, which can keep up the medicinal services dynamic. Current healthcare innovation in different clinical zones has spread to the few spearheading new companies on the planet, which helps individuals in more beneficial and longer lives.

5.1.1 What is Artificial Intelligence?

AI is the advanced growth through computer machines that are proficient in carrying out tasks which generally needs human intelligence, such as object identification, decision-making, solving of difficult problems, and so on. The four main benefits of AI is that it is capable of prediction with increased accuracy level, it assists in processes of making decisions, it solves complex problems, and it performs high-level computation which usually takes more number of days when human involves. Therefore, AI has become a part of everybody's day-to-day life.

AI in healthcare is revolutionizing the medical industry. AI is not one innovative technology but it is a bunch of different innovation combined together. Most of these technologies have rapid significance to the medical service field, but still they broadly differ in supporting some particular procedures [1]. Some specific AI developments of large significance to healthcare are characterized and depicted beneath.

AI can be categorized into three gatherings: machine learning (ML) techniques, the deep learning methods, and the NLP techniques.

5.1.2 Machine Learning – Neural Networks and Deep Learning

ML is one of the utmost and broadly recognized types of AI. ML strategies were examined structured data includes imaging, hereditary, and electronic patient (EP) data. The ML algorithm is information driven; thus, it should not be expressly customized. On the off chance that more information (variable) is brought, the results (forecasts) would be more exact. In the healthcare area, there are huge amounts of clinical information, which, whenever handled, can give supportive bits of knowledge in giving the correct treatment and the ML methodology endeavor to collect patients' traits or conclude the probability of the malady outcomes.

In medical care, the most generally perceived utilization of conventional ML is precision drug—what therapy shows are likely going to persuade a patient reliant on various patient attributes and the therapy context [2]. The incredible dominant part of AI and precision prescription applications require a training dataset for which the result variable (e.g., starting stage of malady) is known; this is called supervised learning. The Figure 5.1 shows the different types of technology in AI.

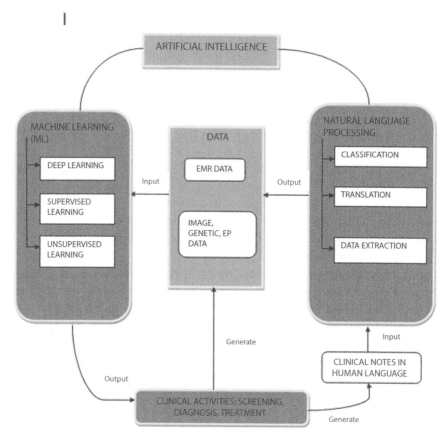

Figure 5.1 Artificial intelligence in healthcare.

A more intricate kind of ML is the neural network—an advancement that has been available since the 1960s has been settled in healthcare research for a couple of many years [3] and has been used for classification applications like choosing if a patient will acquire explicit infections. It checks for issues concerning to data sources, yields and loads of factors or "highlights" that partner contributions with yields. ML have been compared to the way that neurons procedures signals, anyway the relationship to the mind's capacity is moderately powerless.

Deep learning or neural system models with numerous degrees of highlights or factors that anticipate results. There might be a great many types in such models that are revealed by the quicker handling of the present visual preparing elements and cloud architectures. Also, we can use a typical deep learning in medicinal services to acknowledge the tumorous injuries in radiology images [4]. Deep learning is progressively being applied to radiomics, or the identification of clinically important highlights in imaging information beyond what can be seen by the human eye [5]. Both deep learning and radiomics are generally found in oncology-arranged picture investigation. Their mix seems to guarantee more prominent precision in the conclusion than the past age of mechanized instruments for image analysis, known as PC supported detection or CAD.

Deep learning is likewise progressively utilized for speech recognition and, in that capacity, is a type of natural language processing (NLP). In contrast to earlier types of statistical analysis, each element in a deep learning model commonly has small importance to a human eyewitness. Thus, the clarification of the model's results might be exceptionally troublesome or difficult to interpret.

5.1.3 Natural Language Processing

Since 1950s, the main aim of the AI analysts is to understand the human language. The AI, NLP, incorporates in the applications of speech recognition, text examination, understanding, and various goals related to language. There are two fundamental approaches to deal with it: statistical NLP and semantic NLP. Statistical NLP relies upon AI (deep learning neural systems explicitly) and has added to a progressing increment in accuracy of recognition. It requires an enormous "corpus" or collection of language from which to learn [12].

In medicinal services, the predominant uses of NLP include the formation, comprehension, and arrangement of medical documentation and distributed examination. NLP frameworks could analyze unstructured clinical notes on patients, plan reports (e.g., on radiology assessments), translate patient communications, and direct conversational AI.

5.2 Need of AI in Electronic Health Record

EHR is a computerized arrangement of each individual patient data, collected into one dataset. They incorporate clinical history of the patient like information about the medicines, analyze, remedies, vaccination records, hypersensitivities to treatments or allergies to foods, pictures produced through radiology test, and laboratory test outcomes. Clinicians will be able to review the patient's clinical data and play out various investigations. Digital medical records have presented a large group of issues, including upsetting clinician work processes, restricted interoperability, and making information over-burden.

The basic segments of Electronic Health Record (EHR) are as follows: EHR is always updated every time when a particular patient undergoes a diagnosis, so that the data will be available at any time anywhere to the clinicians for analysis or predictive purpose.

- Accessibility: EHR updates and arrange continuously for the utilization of information science functions includes diagnostics and give analysis to expressive and prescient purposes. The information is accessible consistently and gets imparted to the entirety of the gatherings that are engaged with thinking about the patient (research centers, strength doctors, radiologists, drug stores, emergency clinics, and so on.)
- Security: Only approved clients can obtain entrance and change EHR data which is safely put away by expanding access to the board convention, information encryption, anonymization, and schedules for information misfortune protection.
- Advancement of the work process: EHR can robotize routine capacities in suppliers' work processes. EHR robotization can also measure oversee healthcare information handling guidelines (HITECH, HIPAA, and PIPEDA) by starting the convention that is needed while processing the data.

With AI entering the healthcare field, it is removing the EHR burn-out and burden away from doctors, improving interoperability, and it is meaning to use the information for state health and human administration endeavors [6].

ML and NLP can assist in recording the clinical encounters of the patients, sorting out the enormous EHR information banks for discovering significant documents, checking patient fulfillment, and so forth. With the execution of this cutting edge innovation and the development of AI, EHR sellers are attempting to improve their products.

5.2.1   How Does AI/ML Fit Into EHR?

The extent of information that clinical offices produce is expanding and that data's complexity nature is expanding. The EHR can be processed and examined using the ML algorithms and the data mining in EHR is performed using two methodologies:

ML is an incredible alternative for some components of EHR [7], for example,

- **Data mining:** A ton of information is required for gaining experiences in clinical practice. To gather this information, it consumes large amount of time. The extent of information that clinical offices create is expanding and that information's complication is growing. The utilization of ML calculations is a need for handling and investigating data while data mining.
- **Discovery of medical data:** In the case of finding patient information and therapy, ML is utilized to gather relevant data in the history of clinical treatment record, to additionally help in making clinical decision. The EHR data set is further mined to compare the investigations and proceed with the new prescription to the patients.
- **Data extraction:** In this case, a ML application is applied to assemble appropriate information dependent on terms and results over the EHR information base. A model would figure out what prescription attested to accept for explicit sicknesses and the conditions for which they were diagnosed [7]. Similar apparatuses could be utilized for the experimental examination which can redesign accessible information to encounter explicit necessities, for example, analyzing lipid profiles from test result patterns.

5.2.2 Natural Language Processing (NLP)

NLP is utilized eventually in EHR tasks.

Almost all clinical records are in text structure joined with chart diagrams and graphs.

The primary uses for NLP are as follows:

- **Searching a document:** This is used as a feature of widened data mining tasks and also as a simple directing tool utilized inside. The substance acknowledgment is frameworks which have skill on a particular set of terms and assignments identified with different tests and clinical tests. The outcome is an amazing time spare for clinical staff in finding explicit data from huge stores of information.

- **Clinical record:** NLP is utilized in speech recognition and consequently formats it appropriately.
- **Report creation:** NLP can envision information in the printed structure. These models are prepared from prior reports and formats.

5.2.3   Data Analytics and Representation

Information representation is the thing that empowers EHR to be powerful at making information open and reachable. An EHR is basically a graph diagram loaded with crude information with respect to different aspects of a patient's clinical state. The job of ML for this situation is to decipher that information into an open structure.

5.2.4   Predictive Investigation

The most essential advancement which is introduced by EHR is smoothing out the information pipeline for extra change. As all patient information and reference information bases entwine at different focuses into one system particularly, the utilization of available information for predicting the potential results dependent on already existing information is not just conceivable, it is profoundly effective. Predictive investigation can help the doctor in settling on choices by giving different choices while taking potential courses of action into thought. Models for prescient investigation are prepared one case at a time case on EHR information bases. By gathering different information, basic examples are recognized alongside malady improvement aspects as well as a patient's response to fluctuating treatment strategies.

5.2.5   Administrative and Security Consistency

Healthcare clearly works with information that is exceptionally sensitive. EHR can be powerless against information penetrates or misfortune. Yet, EHRs are limited by administrative guidelines on gathering, handling, and capacity of individual information, for example, GDPR or HIPAA guarantees associations on confidentiality of patient information.

EHR and the execution of ML have raised the healthcare industry higher than ever. The chart of more extensive patient information EHR makes accessible outcomes in better results for patients. ML-filled EHR are giving clinician's straightforwardness in the structure for information science that gives exact information and profound experiences. The outcome is composed healthcare that conveys medicines that mend patients in an opportune way with more positive results.

5.3 The Trending Role of AI in Pharmaceutical Development

In the last few years, AI in the pharmaceutical industry has moved from still being fiction to real scientific fact. Pharmaceutical medication revelation requires dealing with and investigating enormous databases of substance mixes and consequently intends to look over a colossal measure of compound data. This can be accomplished by utilizing AI methods (MLTs) that can work and arrive at their objective in a generally brief timeframe. In medicate disclosure, what makes a difference is not just handling a lot of information in a brief timeframe yet additionally a capacity to correspond or relate various information to sub-atomic structure or potential properties [8].

The wide areas of MLT based applications in biotechnology are as follows: Figure 5.2 gives a basic idea about the steps involved in drug development.

1. Screening of more number of libraries based on ligands;
2. Structure of possible ligands and their pharmacophoric values as a medication;

Figure 5.2 Steps in developing a drug.

3. Quantitative structure-activity relationship (QSAR)studies;
4. Biological activeness or functionality of drug receptors and curtailing of drugs to them aided by molecular dynamics (MD)simulations;
5. Virtual drug screening; and
6. Estimated toxic level properties of specified drugs.

In all these areas, chiefly ANN will be a valuable tool together with MD programs.

5.3.1   Drug Discovery and Design

Target distinguishing proof and approval can be accomplished utilizing AI to recognize natural elements to target. For instance, AI and NLP can be utilized to check tremendous books of clinical writing and hereditary datasets to search for hints about quality infection relationship, to recognize new targets. AI is used in the drug discovery process without any human interference [10].

There are many companies in the market which has started using the AI techniques for drug discovery and also medical imaging. This medical imaging is used to identify the diseases and suggest medications to that disease, or it is used to assist the clinical physicians to make decisions on the medical-related images in kind of diseases. The principle point of medication curtailing to a receptor atom is to have the option toward perceiving in what way a given medication particle well fits into a particular receptor. As far as a quantifiable portion is concerned, the point is to have the option to anticipate the coupling partiality of that medication to a given receptor. That is, identifying the binding site on the receptor molecule for the specified class of drugs as shown in Figure 5.3.

Though the specific drug is given, the ultimate aim in the drug curtailing is to predict the binding affinity for that drug on a particular receptor molecule. For such an inquiry, it is understood that the best medication for a given receptor is the one that ties most unequivocally to the receptor. In any case, there will be situations where a medication which ties inadequately to a receptor can have a solid impact as a prescription and the other way around. The molecules will also need an entire support of other properties prediction—such as absorption, distribution, metabolism, elimination, and toxicity (ADMET) as the impact of a medication must be qualified. The impact can be the strength to restrain another organic capacity. Furthermore, from the drug discovery, AI can

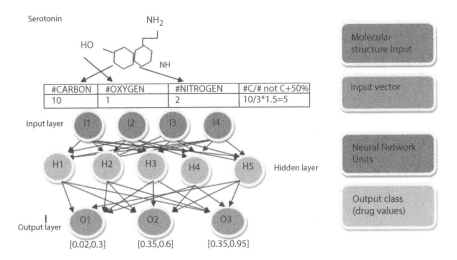

Figure 5.3 Training and operation of an ANN for the drug Serotonin assembled into three parts as input layer, hidden layer, and output layer of a neural network [10].

be used to find the drug's life cycle, optimize production process, and gather clinical data and response data rates from the population using the drugs.

5.3.2   Diagnosis of Biomedical and Clinical Data

It is a known fact that the patient's record is maintained electronically with the help of AI and it is called as EHR. So, the different clinical trials of the patients can be used in the R&D process to test the different medical combinations on the different diseases, and these records will also be maintained, which can be used by the clinicians in case of doubt in understanding the different genetic attribute on the condition of a patient or about combination of all the previous records of the patient [8].

5.3.3   Rare Diseases and Epidemic Prediction

In the last few years, we can see that many new diseases are being emerged based on the various environmental, geological, and biological factors. So, these diseases can be diagnosed with the help of the patient biology, analytics, medical imaging and biopsies, etc. In such cases, immediate action has to be taken to identify new drugs, so here the AI is used to try out many combinations using ML technology to find out the exact combination of drugs to cure the disease.

5.3.4 Applications of AI in Pharma

AI can introduce many opportunities to enhance the production process in the field of the pharmaceutical industry. There are many different manufacturing process steps which are as follows:

- Controlling of quality
- Design time will be reduced
- Analytical maintenance
- Minimizes wastes
- Production reuse will be improved.

Through optimizing the production process in a more faster and efficient manner by using AI, the old process and intervention of humans can also be eliminated [11].

5.3.5 AI in Marketing

The pharmacological sector is a sales-driven segment, as AI is more helpful in refining the elegance of promoting and procedures that organizations use. Organizations realize that investigating and finding the legitimate type of advertising is the most ideal path for them to help their incomes and lead them to a gainful road [9]. Using the EHRs, the company can find out the requirements of a customer and this allows them to persuade a direct marketing technique which ultimately makes the customer buy the product. This decreases the chances of wastage of money or time in the implementations of marketing strategies.

5.3.6 Review of the Companies That Use AI

Many companies like Novaritis [14], Pfizer, Roche, Sanofi, and GlaxoSmithKline (GSK) are using ML techniques in which most of them are created as an in-house project. Pfizer collaborated with CytoReason (leader in ML for drug discovery and development) to develop cell-centered models of the immune system. Novartis along with Tech startup PathAI have created a system using which they are able to diagnose cancer. Sanofi along with Exscientia (AI-driven company) tried to explore and validate combinations of drug targets for metabolic disorders like diabetes.

GSK joined hands with Google to generate biomedical medicines which came out as an implantable device which could modify electromagnetic signals that passes along the nerves in the human body, this also includes abnormal or distorted impulses are the symptoms in many illnesses.

Thus, the implementation of AI in pharmacy is really a challenging and promising task, as it is these medicines which cure the fatal diseases. Many more companies are focusing on accelerating treatments on rare diseases like cancer in different parts. The usage of AI and ML technology is democratized such that even smaller companies can also use it.

5.4   AI in Surgery

The technology in AI is getting improved day by day that too especially in the healthcare industry. Various fields are like maintain the EHR, finding new drug combinations for various diseases, assisting the clinicians in diagnosing various diseases and early detection of diseases with the help of EHRs and medical imaging. Now as advancement, the researchers have tried to perform surgery with the help of robots specialized with AI techniques. They are trained by specialists in such a way that the doctor can perform surgery even when they stay miles apart as shown in Figure 5.4. [13].

One of the greatest progressing banters in a medical procedure is the degree to which complex clinical intercessions ought to be incorporated to improve results. For the NHS, "large" has frequently implied better, and more specific. For patients, where their medical procedure happens can have the effect between feeling generally quiet about an overwhelming possibility, or causing extraordinary concern by including good ways from family members during recuperation. This can be especially significant for more established individuals who might be too delicate to even consider traveling significant distances, just as for individuals on low livelihoods and those with caring obligations. More seasoned individuals are likewise bound to live external metropolitan zones and this pattern is set to increment.

5.4.1   3D Printing

The 3D printing which is also a part of AI technology helps to make the anatomical transplantation surgery more precise and safer. It helps in planning a surgery, its range, and effectiveness of it. It helps the clinicians to analyze and extract data from the patient's medical imaging pictures clearly and create an anatomical model to be replaced in the patient [14].

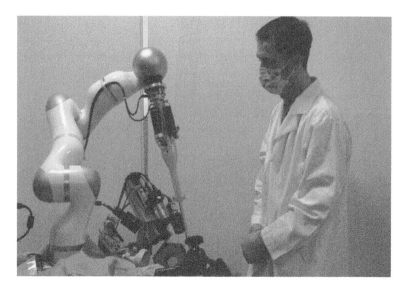

Figure 5.4 A Cobot assisting the surgery.

The models created are robust and has improved the patient choice and expectation. It also helps the doctors to explain the procedure of the surgery to the patient which he is about to undergo. It is widely implemented in all hospitals in all kinds of department.

5.4.2 Stem Cells

It is a rapidly developing research area and a very effective type of treatment in the NHS, bone marrow stem cell transplants, leukemia, and sickle cell anemia. As advancement in ophthalmology, a gene modified bone marrow stem cell transplants can also be done to cure patients with severe disorders. Stem cell transplants can be used to treat macular degeneration, which helped to improve vision in many of the patients. Many researches are further continued to create new regenerative medicine using the stem cells to cure retinal diseases.

5.4.3 Patient Care

AI can support surgeons in post-operative monitoring of the patients regarding their pulse monitoring, post-operative infections such as level of wound healing or detecting any bacteria with the help of the smart gadgets. Also, new patients coming with significant disorders can be regularly monitored on how the medications are effecting or giving any changes in their body conditions.

5.4.4   Training and Future Surgical Team

More new sophisticated technologies are developed in the new era for assisting the doctors in gynecological, colorectal and cardiothoracic surgeries, and reconstructive surgeries in head and neck. AI technology is used in suturing the open or incision wounds to decrease the extent of surgical procedures and reduce the exhaustion of a surgeon. This is done with the help of Raven robot and PR2 robot (as shown in Figure 5.5). These robots are taught with the complete surgical work flow model using the ML techniques, which can also navigate the complex situations and environment.

An automatic surgical phase in laparoscopic technique is achieved using the AI by training the robots through conventional neural networks (semantic segmentation) using a large dataset containing videos and images. One more significance of AI in surgery is that it can predict the risk factors of the post operation, which helps the patients to demand for a surgery or not [16]. Figures 5.6 and 5.7 show image processing analysis of a surgical image used to predict inimical events during the surgery.

For most common diseases like pharyngitis, rhinosinusitis of ear, nose, and throat, otitis media, ML training along with artificial neural networks can also be done with the help of rhinologic data (by using computed tomographic images that is classified with osteomeatal complex by convolutional neural networks). Then, the decision-making performances will be tested with various other diseases to check whether the robot has got completely trained. In neuro-surgery, the spectroscopic images of clinically identified lesions are trained and tested.

Figure 5.5 Picture of a moving robot used in suturing.

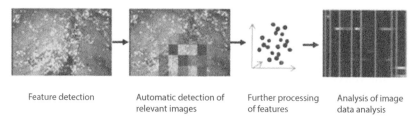

| Feature detection | Automatic detection of relevant images | Further processing of features | Analysis of image data analysis |

Figure 5.6 Image processing analysis of a surgical image used to predict inimical events during the surgery.

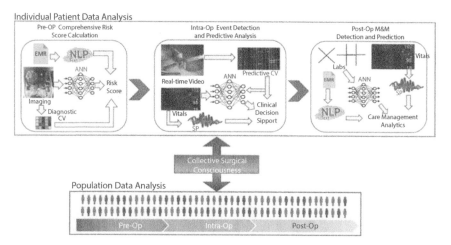

Figure 5.7 Collective process of surgical decision by AI using multimodal data using ML technology [15].

AI is used to recognize the oral cancers with computer archive from the images. The magnetic resonance imaging (MRI) is used in the prediction of sound wire thickness by using one of the soft computing field component called support vector machines. Tonsillectomy surgery which is related to bleeding complications can be trained with the help of fuzzy logic. This kind of surgery is performed on adenoidectomy patients.

Alongside, new and greater innovations are reckoned in the field of surgery. The surgeons are expecting flexibility and adaptability from NHS to promote wider healthcare which could reduce workload and risk factors.

Liquid biopsies with analysis of fragments of tumor deoxyribonucleic acid found in peripheral blood can help the early detection of cancer, and that part can be safely removed with the help of AI assisted surgery without affecting the other parts.

Earlier interventions were limited to only in assistance, but later, it was extended to diagnosis of different diseases and now in the field of surgery. Thus, AI technology combining with synergetic subfields has the ability to support the clinicians and surgeons in critical surgeries. It also helps in the pre-operative and post-operative care of the patients which reduces the burden of the doctors. It is playing a significant role in devising a new research in the field stem cell treatment which is still a challenge for the doctors.

5.5   Artificial Intelligence in Medical Imaging

In all kinds of diseases, the diagnosis and the clinical decisions mainly rely on the medical imaging which consists of X-rays, CT scan, MRI scans, cardiovascular echo, and many other imaging modalities. It is a significant source of patient data which is also considered as the complex one (shown in Figure 5.8) [23]. AI technique gives a major support to the clinicians in the field of radiology and pathology and it is proved that it gives a valuable and accurate solutions.

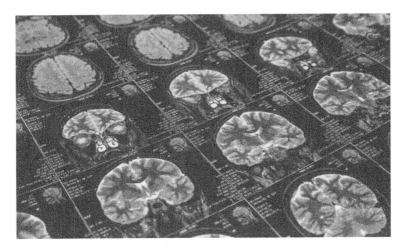

Figure 5.8 Image of a CT scan [17].

5.5.1   In Cardio Vascular Abnormalities

The chest radiograph is one of the imaging test that is preferred for the patients who come with the complaint of shortness of breath (Figure 5.9) [17]. An automated screening tool called Cardiomegaly is used as a marker

Original Image

Findings

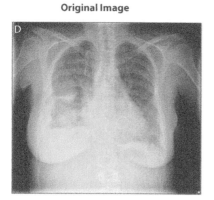
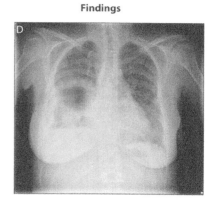

Figure 5.9 Medical imaging using AI in cardiovascular findings [19].

for the heart disease initially. AI is used in the identification of left atrial enlargement, coagulation of muscle structures in the left ventricle wall from chest X-rays, monitors blood flow changes, and rule out the problems regarding pulmonary diseases, which starts to give the preliminary treatment to the patients. So, ML technique has been implemented to train the algorithm regarding this chest radiology.

5.5.2   In Fractures and Musculoskeletal Injuries

The X-rays or MRI scans are preferred for the patients who complaint for an injury or long time chronic pain, especially for elderly patients who come

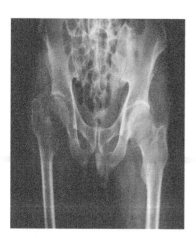
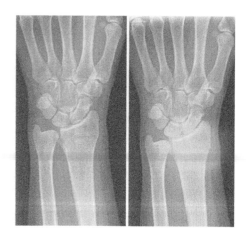

Figure 5.10 Medical imaging using AI identifying hip fracture and wrist fracture [20, 21].

with hip fractures. It helps the doctors to come to a conclusion regarding the surgery (Figure 5.10) [20]. By using AI radiology tool, patient who complains with neck and head trauma can be assessed for odontoid fracture (fracture in cervical spine). Very quick analysis is required in some critical cases that come with deadly injury, and it is very important to diagnose the problem properly in such a way that the risk factor is reduced. So, ML technology will help to reduce the false negative rate to major extent.

5.5.3   In Neurological Diseases and Thoracic Complications

Neuro is a significant system of the human which allows the human to think, act, and react to situation or environment. The disorders should be perfectly diagnosed as in case of any misdiagnose will lead to a complexity in the whole nervous system [17]. So, the AI is perfectly trained using the ML technology in developing a promising image biomarker.

Pneumonia is another life threatening condition when left untreated. Sometimes, it is difficult for the clinicians to differentiate pneumonia from the patient's pre-existing lung conditions like malignancies or cystic fibrosis from the radiology images. In such cases, AI is used which accurately identifies the pneumothorax condition in high-risk patients. It also helps to predict the subtle pneumonias which usually projects under the dome of the diaphragms in the front chest radiographs (Figure 5.11).

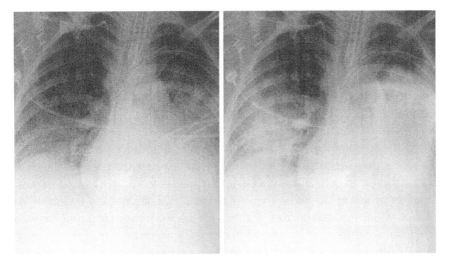

Figure 5.11 Medical imaging technique to spot pneumonia [18].

5.5.4   In Detecting Cancers

AI is often used in screening of breast and colon cancer from the radiology images. It plays a significant role in microcalcification of tissues to identify the stage of cancer (whether benign and malignant) by using measurable imaging features to more accurately classify the stages of doubt for ductal carcinoma in situ (DCIS), so that unnecessary biopsies can be avoided [17]. The patients who are undergoing screening for colorectal cancers may be found with polyps which are precursors of cancers. CT colonography (CTC) helps in examining the colon and rectum for polyps, as less experienced radiologists may miss this polyps presentation so the AI can be used to efficiently detect it which helps to reduce false positives or false negatives. Extra nodal extension (ECE) of cancer is sometimes not predicted earlier and found only during the time of surgery but by using performant algorithms in AI these ECEs can be easily predicted. This helps in prevention of spreading in pre-operative condition and treatment in postoperative condition. So, AI can analyze and diagnose cancer accurately.

Therefore, imaging on the whole is a definitive tool in the field of healthcare, which is further armed with the technology of AI to the betterment of treatment of patients.

5.6   AI in Patient Monitoring and Wearable Health Devices

Conceivably, the digitization of human services gives the chance to upgrading the patients (prescient, exact, preventive, and customized) of medication. Health relevant products are fueled by AI, which are gushing into our lives, from virtual specialist apps to wearable sensors and drugstore chatbots. Creating mobile-based apps to examine patient concerns, missing typical clinical language, to more readily comprehend the patient's condition and at last suggest care choices [22].

Despite the fact that the most energizing and refined advances are in operating theaters, moderately basic smart phone innovation is set to positive influence on patients before and after operation happen. As of now, the NHS application empowers individuals to book straightforward general expert (GP) appointments on the web. Then, the GoodSAM application commissions "smart phone initiated doctors" through a framework which incorporates with ambulance vehicle administration dispatch frameworks to trigger a reaction from close by, prepared, spectators while an emergency vehicle is on route.

5.6.1 Monitoring Health Through Wearable's and Personal Devices

Human healthcare devices are smart ones that can be able to gauge important signals from the human body or unique physiological boundaries of the patient. The sensing devices utilized are particularly appropriate for this somewhat harsh condition and could adapt to temperature, blood pressure, pulse, and so forth. The critical inquiry of connecting human body with the sensor, etc., has been comprehended. Sensing device combination (for example, unsheathing of data from few sources) might create included worth to the healthcare devices [22]. Movement ancient represent a distinctive and significant test for measurement tasks in close to human healthcare conditions. Likewise, many other human healthcare wearable devices shall give remedial estimates in emergency like electric incitement (for example, for an initiated heart contraction, acoustic sensation, or heart defibrillation) or inject drugs.

Personal healthcare devices are wearable one. Most importantly, numerous individual healthcare gadgets can be worn on or inside the body of a patient. Indeed, gadgets like these might be embedded (like for example heart pacemakers or cochlear inserts) or outside gadgets incorporated into garments or things of everyday use (like watches, glasses, and so on.). Besides, individual healthcare gadgets will in general be little and light to dodge inconvenience while wearing them. In this manner, scaling down and reconciliation are significant issues. Personal healthcare gadgets ordinarily have some installed vitality gracefully framework. For some situation, a rechargeable or normal battery might be adequate, whereas different devices may depend on an active recharging procedure or utilize an independent body power age and appropriation innovation. All physical body worn devices and all inserts must be associated together in a system domain. The designer of the wearable device or jacket should highlight a point or a transport association might be built up by methods for optical filaments woven into the article of clothing (material coordination) or by methods for a remote body zone arrange. Nonetheless, in a more extensive and less incorporated sense, the meaning of individual medicinal services devices might be stretched out to incorporate the present work area devices that would already be able to be utilized in one's own residential condition. A business tele-monitoring administration as of now in activity permitting household estimation of weight, electrocardiogram (ECG), beat rate, pulse and glucose focus, and transmission of that data to a clinical expert group by means of the Internet.

5.6.2 Making Smartphone Selfies Into Powerful Diagnostic Tools

Proceeding with the subject of outfitting the intensity of versatile gadgets, specialists accept that pictures shot from smart phones and additional usage of customer side branded sources will be a significant enhancement to clinically based quality imaging—particularly needless populaces or growing countries. The variety of lenses used in the cameras of today's smart phone is changing or upgraded in every single models, and it creates pictures that would be feasible for examination by AI processes that are combined with the Android phone apps. Ophthalmology and dermatology derive beneficiaries of this pattern as a beginning stage.

Some famous research analysts from UK have developed up a device that recognizes formative sicknesses through breaking down picture of a child's face. The developed algorithm was able to recognize discrete highlights, for example, eye, child's jaw line and nose position, and different properties that may demonstrate a craniofacial irregularity. Presently, the developed tool can coordinate the conventional pictures on to an excess of 90 disorders to give a helpful clinical decision.

Using cell phones to gather pictures of skin injuries, eyes, wounds, meds, or different subjects may have the option to help needless regions get used to a lack of experts while decreasing the chances to-determination for particular complaints. Cell phones have demonstrated specific guarantee is HIV management. Specialists from Brigham and Women's Hospital (BWH) have as of late built up a rapid, minimal effort CD4 counter by incorporating headways in consumer gadgets and micro fabrication. Although ongoing WHO rules stress viral burden testing for HIV the executives. Antenatal screening is another region of medicinal services that cell phone based gadgets can possibly improve in creating nations. In 2015, the Sia Lab at Columbia University built up a cell phone dongle equipped for distinguishing HIV and syphilis in pregnant ladies in only 15 minutes, with the objective of decreasing unfriendly impacts of the infections in the both moms and infants.

Almost every significant part in the business has begun to construct AI programming and equipment into their devices. That is not an occurrence. Consistently, in this developed globe, we produce approximately above 2.5 million terabytes of information. The mobile phone makers accept that they can utilize the stored information with AI techniques to give substantially customized, quicker and more intelligent administrations.

5.7   Revolutionizing of AI in Medicinal Decision-Making at the Bedside

When the human healthcare industry moves from charge for administration, so too is it moving advance a lot from responsive care. Stretching out beyond chronic infections, expensive intense occasions, and abrupt deterioration is the objective of each supplier, and repayment structures are at last permitting them to build up the cycles that will empower proactive, prescient interventions. AI would give a major part of the bedrock to that progression by driving prescient investigation and clinical decision uphold devices that illuminate providers to issues some time before they may some way or another perceive the need to act. AI is able to give earlier exhortations to conditions like seizures or sepsis, which as often as possible require concentrated examination of significantly complex datasets.

ML is capable of support clinical choices about whether to keep on with care for basically unwell patients, consider a situation, the persons who have undergone a state of unconsciousness (coma) later than cardiac arrest, say Brandon Westover, MD, PhD, and Director of the MGH Clinical Data Animation Center [24].

Normally, suppliers ought to ostensibly examine EEG data from the patients, the cycle is monotonous and emotional, and the results may shift by way of the ability and knowledge of the individual clinician. Utilizing AI for clinical choice help, hazard scoring, and timely cautioning is one of the challenging part of advancement for this progressive way to deal with information examination. By driving advance medical tools and frameworks that make clinicians more aware of subtleties, more beneficial while conveying care, and bound to stretch out beyond creating issues, AI will introduce another time of clinical quality and energizing discoveries in caring of patients. "In any case, on the off chance that with an AI calculation, parcels and numerous information from several patients, that's simpler to coordinate what you're considering to long haul designs and possibly distinguishes inconspicuous upgrades that would affect your choices around care."

5.8   Future of AI in Healthcare

We should accept that AI can be used to carry out different task in the human healthcare in the mere future. The AI with the support of ML provides an essential capacity behind the improvement of exactness medication that is broadly accepted to be a woefully required development in patient care. Although the conventional method of medical treatment is based on giving diagnosis depending on the demonstrated testing, the latest technology in AI can adopt these procedures with greater excellence. As an advancement in AI for imaging examination, most of the radiology and pathology pictures will be analyzed eventually by a smart machines like computers which is based on artificial neural networks. Discourse and wording acknowledgment are as of now utilized for undertakings like patient communiqué and catch of the clinical comments and the utilization of these comments will increase will increase.

Discussing about advanced innovation of AI in healthcare is not alone sufficiently proficient, but the challenge is using it in daily life of a person or a patient. For far reaching selection to occur, AI frameworks shall be endorsed using controllers, coordinated with the EHR frameworks, normalized to an adequate extent that comparative items function in a similar manner, will be educated to doctors, and this will be provided to an open or private organizations as a paid framework and frequently updated. There are some difficulties that are observed in using AI in day-to-day life; however, it will take some time to get adopted to these new technologies. Therefore, we may see some restricted use of AI in personnel healthcare or clinical practice around 5 years and more broadly in use within 10 years.

In future, post-operative checking will have the option to happen distantly with the patient demonstrating specialists how their injuries are healing utilizing their own cell phone camera. Smart watches can screen heartbeat, and obviously numerous individuals effectively gather information on their pulse, their calorie utilization, and their activity through such gadgets. For more perplexing information assortment, momentary wearable, implantable, or ingestible sensors could help screen indispensable signs and distinguish post-operative diseases maybe by identifying microbes in an injury and checking the body's center temperature.

It furthermore gives off an impression of being logically clear that AI systems would not displace human clinicians for tremendous scope, yet rather will expand their endeavors to consider patients. After some time, human clinicians may push toward endeavors and occupation structures that draw on strangely human capacities like compassion, impact, and tremendous picture coordination. Possibly, the principle restorative administration providers who will lose their situations after some time may be the people who would not work close by computerized reasoning.

5.9 Conclusion

AI technologies have been used for various purposes in the field of healthcare. It is certainly a potential technology used for accurate clinical decisions in identifying a disease from images, biopsies, and chronical conditions. It also plays a major role in the drug discovery based on the diseases; it helps the pharmaceutical industry in developing new combination medicines in the epidemic situations (i.e., when new types of diseases arise). This is done with the help of the EHRs which is also maintained by using the AI technology. The data are segregated using the ML and used in the different fields like drug discovery, reference of the patient conditions by the clinicians all over the world. AI plays a significant role in surgery, where the surgeons are supported to a greater extent in handling critical situations. There are many applications developed for the smart phones today for different healthcare services, in which the patient can upload his/her condition and get the suggestion and treatment over the gadget.

References

1. Davenport, T. and Kalakota, R., The potential for artificial intelligence in healthcare. *Future Healthc. J.*, 6, 2, 94, 2019.
2. Lee, S.I., Celik, S., Logsdon, B.A. *et al.*, A machine learning approach to integrate big data for precision medicine in acute myeloid leukemia. *Nat. Commun.*, 9, 42, 2018.
3. Sordo, M., *Introduction to neural networks in healthcare*, OpenClinical, Published in IEEE international conference on neural networks. 2002, www.openclinical.org/docs/int/neuralnetworks011.pdf.
4. Fakoor, R., Ladhak, F., Nazi, A., Huber, M., Using deep learning to enhance cancer diagnosis and classification. *A conference presentation The 30th International Conference on MachineLearning*, 2013.
5. Vial, A., Stirling, D., Field, M. *et al.*, The role of deep learning and radiomic feature extraction in cancer-specific predictive modeling: a review. *Transl. Cancer Res.*, 7, 803–16, 2018.
6. Jason, C., Xtelligent HEALTHCARE MEDIA Dec 02, 2019. how-can-artificial-intelligence-ai-improve-clinician-ehr-use, https://ehrintelligence.com/news/how-can-artificial-intelligence-ai- improve-clinician-ehr-use.
7. West, H., Healthcare and Data Science: How EHR and AI Can Go Hand-in-Hand, Informatics from TECHNOLOGY NETWORKS, March 30 2020. https://www.technologynetworks.com/informatics/articles/healthcare-and-data-science-how-ehr-and-ai-can-go-hand-in-hand-332840.
8. Tiernay, S., European Pharmaceutical Review publisher, March 2020, https://www.europeanpharmaceuticalreview.com/article/114914/artificial-intelligence-in-pharma-utilising-a-valuable-resource/.

9. Goyal, K., Applications of Artificial Intelligence in the Pharmaceutical Industry, published in upGrad blog, April 2020, https://www.upgrad.com/blog/artificialintelligence-in- pharmaceutical-industry/

10. Bohr, H., *Drug discovery and molecular modeling using artificial intelligence*, pp. 61– 83, Academiapress, 2020.

11. McLeod, T., SARTORIUS, Aug-2020.https://blog.umetrics.com/the-trending-role-of-artificial-intelligence-in-the-pharmaceutical-industry. https://doi.org/10.1016/B978-0-12-818438-7.00003-4

12. Faggella, D., emerRJ, The AI Research and Advisory company, Feb2020, https://emerj.com/ai- sector-overviews/ai-in-pharma-and-biomedicine/.

13. Sennaar, K., The AI Research and Advisorycompany, published in emerj, The AI and research advisory company, https://emerj.com/ai-sector-overviews/machine-learning-in-surgical-robotics-4-applications/.

14. Kerr, R.S., Surgery in the 2020s: implications of advancing technology for patients and the workforce. *Future Healthc. J.*, 7, 1, 46, 2020.

15. Hashimoto, D.A., Rosman, G., Rus, D., Meireles, O.R., Artificial intelligence in surgery: promises and perils. *Ann. Surg.*, 268, 1, 70, 2018. Doi: 10.7861/fhj.2020-0001

16. Iyer, R., Gentry-Maharaj, A. *et al.*, Predictors of complications in gynaecological oncological surgery: a prospective multicentre study (UKGOSOC— UK gynaecological oncology surgical outcomes and complications). *Br. J. Cancer*, 112, 3, 475–484, 2015.

17. Bresnick, J., Health it Analytics, Xtelligent Healthcare Media, https://healthitanalytics.com/news/top-5-use-cases-for-artificial-intelligence-in-medical-imaging.

18. Couzin-Frankel, J., AAAS, https://www.sciencemag.org/news/2019/06/artificial-intelligence-could-revolutionize-medical-care-don-t-trust-it-read-your-x-ray.

19. Rouger, M., ESR (European Society of Radiology), Published in AAAS Science article https://ai.myesr.org/healthcare/medical-imaging-ai-the-bubble-will-break-in-2-3-years/.

20. D'Onofrio, K., docfireNEWS, https://www.docwirenews.com/condition-center/orthopedicscc/can-ai-predict-hip-fracture/.

21. McMillan, R. and Dwoskin, E., docwirenews, The Wall Street Journal, May 03, 2019 https://www.wsj.com/articles/ibm-crafts-a-role-for-artificial-intelligence-in-medicine-1439265840.

22. Leonhardt, S., Personal healthcare devices, in: *AmIware Hardware Technology Drivers of Ambient Intelligence*, pp. 349–370, Springer, Dordrecht, 2006.

23. Hosny, A., Parmar, C., Quackenbush, J., Schwartz, L.H., Aerts, H.J., Artificial intelligence in radiology. *Nat. Rev. Cancer*, 18, 8, 500–510, 2018. https://www.springer.com/gp/book/9781402041976

24. Ranschaert, E.R., Morozov, S., Algra, P.R. (Eds.), *Artificial Intelligence in Medical Imaging: Opportunities, Applications and Risks*, pp. 9–23, Springer, 2019.

6

Introduction of Artificial Intelligence

R. Vishalakshi[1][*] and S. Mangai[2][†]

¹Department of Information Technology Excel, Engineering College, Komarapalayam, India
²Department of Bio Medical Engineering, Velalar College of Engineering and Technology, Erode, India

Abstract

Artificial Intelligence (AI) is influencing the situation where advancement happens. What are the suggestions for our comprehension of the plan? Is AI simply one more advanced innovation that, much the same as numerous others, would not fundamentally question what we think about the plan? Or on the other hand, will it make changes in structure that our present systems cannot catch? To address these inquiries, we have researched two spearheading cases at the boondocks of AI, Netflix and Airbnb (supplemented with investigations in Microsoft and Tesla), which offer a special window on the future advancement of the plan. We found that AI does not subvert the essential standards of Design Thinking (individuals focused, abductive, and iterative). Or maybe, it empowers to defeat past restrictions (in scale, extension, and learning) of human intense configuration measures. With regard to AI production lines, arrangements may even be more client-focused (to an outrageous degree of granularity, for example being intended for everyone), more imaginative, and ceaselessly refreshed through learning emphasizes that length the whole life pattern of an item. However, we found that AI significantly changes the act of plan. Critical thinking errands generally carried on by creators are currently robotized into learning circles that work without restrictions of volume and speed. These circles think in a fundamentally unexpected manner in comparison to a fashioner: they address complex issues through straightforward undertakings, iterated exponentially. The article thusly proposes another system for understanding structure practice in the time of AI. We likewise talk about the suggestions for the plan and development hypothesis. In particular, we see that, as inventive critical thinking is essentially directed by calculations, human structure progressively turns into a

---

*Corresponding author: vishalakshiraj@gmail.com
†Corresponding author: lshamangai@yahoo.com

C. Venkatesh, N. Rengarajan, P. Ponmurugan and S. Balamurugan (eds.) *Smart Systems for Industrial Applications*, (141–172) © 2022 Scrivener Publishing LLC

movement of sense-making, for example, to comprehend which issues bode well to be tended to. This move in the center calls for new speculations and brings the plan nearer to the initiative, which is, inalienably, an action of sense-making.

Keywords: Artificial intelligence, tesla, self awareness, robotics, user interface, expert system

6.1   Introduction

As per the father of Artificial Intelligence (AI), John McCarthy, it is *"The science and technology of creating intelligent machines, particularly intelligent computer applications"*.

AI is a method of creating a software think intelligently, a computer-controlled robot, or a computer in a similar way the smart humans think. AI can be achieved by researching how humans understand and how the human mind thinks, determine, and work while attempting to resolve the problem and then utilizing the effects of this analysis as a foundation of evolving intelligent systems and software.

The term "Artificial Intelligence" is frequently utilized to define computers or systems that replicate "cognitive" responsibilities that humans associate with human consciousness, like "problem-solving" and "learning". **AI (Artificial Intelligence)**, sometimes referred to as **machine intelligence**, is intelligence shown by the machines, in contrast to the **natural intelligence** shown by the animals and humans. Prominent AI textbooks describe the area as the survey of "intelligent agents": every device that recognizes its natural environment and takes measures that increase its opportunity to effectively attaining its targets.

6.1.1   Intelligence

The capability of a machine to determine, motivation, identify connections and similarities, learn lessons from experience, save and retrieve information from memory, problem-solving, to understand complicated ideas, use real language easily, categorize, generalizations, and adjust new circumstances. The intelligence is indefinable. It is comprised of the following:

- Linguistic intelligence
- Perception
- Problem-solving
- Learning
- Reasoning

6.1.2   Types of Intelligence

Intelligence	Description	Example
Linguistic intelligence	The capability to talk, understand, and utilize methods of semantics, syntax, and linguistics	Orators, Narrators
Musical intelligence	The opportunity to create, connect with, and comprehend the meanings that have been created of sound, comprehension of rhythm, pitch	Composers, Singers, Musicians
Logical-mathematical intelligence	The capability of usage and comprehend interactions in the lack of objects or actions. Ability to understand complicated and conceptual ideas	Scientists, Mathematicians
Spatial intelligence	The capacity to understand spatial or visual data, modify it, and re-establish visual pictures with no reference to the objects, build 3D images, and to move around and twist them	Physicists, Astronauts, Map Readers,
Bodily kinesthetic intelligence	The capability to utilize part or complete body for fashion products or problem-solving and the ability to control fine and abrasive motor abilities, and control the objects	Dancers, Players,

(Continued)

(*Continued*)

Intelligence	Description	Example
Intra-personal intelligence	The capability to distinguish between an individual's own emotions, objectives, and motives	Gautam Buddha
Interpersonal intelligence	The capability to identify and make differences among other people's emotions, attitudes, and objectives	Interviewers, Mass Communicators

6.1.3 A Brief History of Artificial Intelligence From 1923 till 2000

Year	Milestone/Innovation
1923	Karel Čapek play called "RUR" (Rossum's Universal Robots) opens in London, the initial usage of the word "robot" in English.
1943	Organizations for neural networks set out.
1945	Isaac Asimov, a Columbia University alumnus, invented the term *Robotics*.
1950	Claude Shannon printed *Detailed Analysis of Chess Playing* as a seek. Alan Turing established a Turing Test to evaluate intelligence and issued *Computing Machinery and Intelligence*.
1956	John McCarthy invented the term *Artificial Intelligence*. Presentation of the main running AI system at Carnegie Mellon University.
1958	John McCarthy creates a LISP programming language for AI.
1964	At MIT Danny Bobrow's study demonstrated that pcs could comprehend natural language sufficiently well to resolve algebra word difficulties properly.
1965	Joseph Weizenbaum, a highly interactive challenge that holds on a dialogue in English at MIT built *ELIZA*.

(*Continued*)

(*Continued*)

Year	Milestone/Innovation
1969	At Stanford Research Institute, *Shakey*, a robot, was established y Researchers which is outfitted with problem solving, perception, and locomotion.
1973	At Edinburgh University, *Freddy* built the Assembly Robotics unit was built who was the Famous Scottish Robot, adept at utilizing foresight to discover and construct models.
1979	The leading computer-controlled independent vehicle, which is referred to as Stanford Cart, was constructed.
1985	In the illustration program, *Aaron* was produced and exhibited by Harold Cohen.
1990	Major innovations in all regions of AI: • Games • Scheduling • Natural language understanding and translation • Web Crawler, Data mining • Virtual Reality, Vision • Multi-agent development • Case-based interpretation • Considerable experiments in machine learning
1997	Then, the Deep Blue Chess Program overcomes the world chess champion, Garry Kasparov.
2000	Interactive robot domestic animals come to be available on the market. MIT shows *Kismet*, a robot with a challenge that articulates feelings. The robot *Nomad* investigates isolated areas of Antarctica and detects meteors Figure 6.1 illustrates the AI usage for the past 7 decades.

6.2   Introduction to the Philosophy Behind Artificial Intelligence

The phenomenon of humans takes the lead to admire, *"Can a machine believe and act like people do?"* though harnessing the power of the computer systems. Consequently, the growth of AI began with the aim of establishing comparable intelligence in systems that we discover and take into consideration high in human beings is shown in the Figure 6.2 as follows.

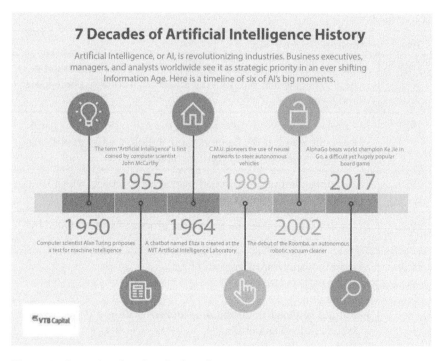

Figure 6.1   Seven decades of artificial intelligence.

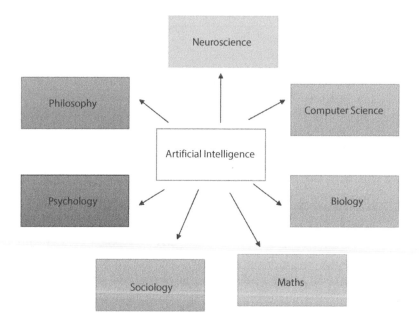

Figure 6.2   Phenomenon of AI.

6.2.1 Programming With and Without AI

The programming with and without AI is completely different in the following methods.

Programming with AI	Programming without AI
A computer program with AI can respond to the generic issues it is supposed to resolve.	A computer program without AI can answer the problems it is intended to solve.
AI programs are able to absorb additional changes that have been made by putting extremely impartial pieces of data altogether. Therefore, one can make changes to as much as a minute element of the program without interfering with its structure.	Variation in the program is leading to a transformation in its structure.
Quick and simple program modification.	Modification is not easy and fast. It could result in influencing the program negatively affected.

6.3 Basic Functions of Artificial Intelligence

The data analysis is a fundamental function of the algorithms of AI. Allow me to place it this manner. How do you believe human beings understand different things? They examine. They monitor and that is the way in which they learn. Machines understand a similar approach. An enormous amount of data is the feeding into the systems, and they recognize and understand, recognize and understand, recognize, and understand. Because they are the systems and do not normally get sick, not like humans, this method of knowledge is certainly not coming to an end. Data that is feeding into the systems could be real-life occurrences. How human beings communicate with each other, exactly how people perform, how human beings react, etc. So, in other words, systems are taught to feel like human beings, by watching and understanding from humans. That is exactly what is known as Machine Learning which is a subdivision of AI.

6.3.1 Categories of Artificial Intelligence

There are four kinds of AI. These are as follows:

1. self-awareness,
2. theory of mind,
3. limited memory, and
4. reactive machines.

6.3.1.1 Reactive Machines

The most fundamental kinds of AI systems are entirely sensitive and have the capability neither to constitute memories nor to utilize previous capabilities to communicate existing determinations. This kind of intelligence includes the computer understanding the world directly and working on anything it sees.

During the late 1990s IBM's chess-playing supercomputer, Deep Blue, beat international chess player Garry Kasparov, which is the perfect illustration of this kind of machine.

Deep Blue will be able to distinguish the parts on a chessboard and understand how each move. It will be able to make projections regarding what moves could be next for it and its challenges, and it will be able to select the most optimum moves from between the opportunities available.

Also, Google's AlphaGo, one that has defeated the highest individual Go specialists, cannot assess all possible future steps either one. This analysis method is much more complex in comparison to Deep Blue's, utilizing a neural network to assess developments in the game.

These techniques do enhance the capability of AI systems to perform certain games safer, but they will not be able to be easily modified or that apply to other circumstances.

6.3.1.2 Limited Memory

This kind includes systems can take a look at the past. Self-driving cars make some of this even now. For instance, they monitor the direction and speed of other cars. That could not be accomplished in a simply one instant, but more accurately entails detecting particular objects and surveillance them over a period. These reflections will be added to the self-driving cars' preprogrammed descriptions of the world, which also consist of traffic lights, lane markings, and other essential components, like bends in the road.

6.3.1.3   Theory of Mind

Systems in the following, most technologically advanced, grade not only form statements regarding the world but also regarding other entities or agents in the world. In psychology, this is known as "theory of mind"—the insight that human beings, objects, and creatures in the world can have emotions and thoughts that influence their own behavior.

This is vitally important to the way in which people formed groups since they allowed us to have social relationships. Without insight into intentions and motives of each other's, and without considering what someone else understands either regarding me or the natural environment, which work together is at greatest difficult, in the worst-case scenario unfeasible.

6.3.1.4   Self-Awareness

The very last step of AI evolution is to construct structures that can create statements about each other. Eventually, AI scientists will need to not only comprehend the awareness but develop machines that are equipped with it. Awareness is sometimes referred to as "self-awareness" for a reason. This is a significant step to comprehend human intelligence by itself, and it is extremely important if we need to evolve or design systems that are higher than extraordinary at categorizing what they look at in front of them.

6.4   Existing Technology and Its Review

There are types of innovations performed in AI. A comprehensive analysis is as in accordance with the following:

6.4.1   Tesla's Autopilot

It is the first in the world to AI-fueled powering experience. Tesla's Flight Control is one of the excellent instances of the computerized revolution Figure 6.3 shows Tesla's Autopilot vision and its specification while driving. It is the semi-independent driving characteristic that comprises the prevention of accidents, collision, automatic braking, lane change, and speed adjusting. Tesla gets the information for autopilot from every car that uses the new computerized lane or steering change system and utilizes it to educate its algorithms. Then, Tesla takes such algorithms, tests them out, and integrates them in to operational software. In this sophisticated technology car utilizing AI, the individual in the driver's seat is there only for the necessary legal reasons. He does not need to do anything since the car is powered by itself.

Figure 6.3 Tesla's autopilot [3].

6.4.2   Boxever

It is an insightful client cloud that relies vigorously upon AI to improve the client's involvement with the moving industry. So, it can be rethinking the client's understanding through AI and utilization of AI. Boxever enacts the states around every client obviously. It gives a single relevant perspective on all the clients. Boxever is a brand dependent on AI utilizing one-to-one personal settings the features of boxever is shown in Figure 6.4 as follows.

6.4.3   Fin Gesture

It is the most recent innovation dependent on AI that is as a brilliant ring, which makes an interpretation of the hand signals into orders Figure 6.5 illustrates the finger gesture equipment with embedded sensors. This gadget is used to wear on the thumb and afterward utilizes it to perceive every section of each finger on all fours takes advantage of orders. It essentially utilizes Bluetooth to communicate the orders to other systems.

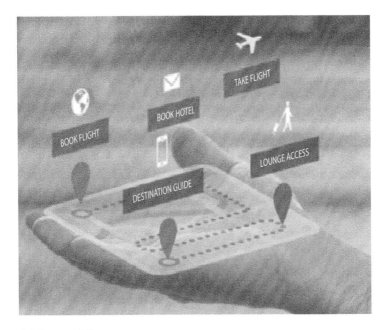

Figure 6.4 Boxever [4].

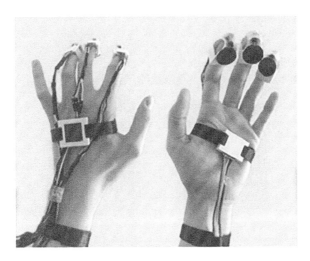

Figure 6.5 The embedding method sensors in a finger and hand gestures process.

6.4.4   AI Robot

The robot created on the world for performing troublesome assignments is not only a robot however it is an AI. It perceives facial highlights as well as understands our disposition. The robot has nicknamed Jia is shown in Figure 6.6 as follows. She can consider to be the world as similar that people do. We can ask for anything. She comprehends what we state and what is its significance. She controls all our associated tools with our voice, provides insights concerning climate, plays music, news, plans gatherings, sets alerts, and so forth.

Figure 6.6 AI robot [6].

Figure 6.7 Vinci [7].

6.4.5   Vinci

Figure 6.7 illustrates about Vinci is the main savvy earphones with AI that can get you. You just need to tell Vinci and it responds appropriately. You can alter paths likewise and give data about your huge inquiries.

6.4.6   AI Glasses

AI glasses have been observed to be an incredible enchantment of AI particularly for the kids experiencing autism [8]. The kids experiencing this ailment cannot perceive the feelings through outward appearances. Chemical imbalance glass is the wearable glass that utilizations AI and constant expressive gestures so individuals experiencing mental imbalance can collaborate. At whatever point a patient needs to utilize it, he wears it on his eyeballs. The glass has a forward-looking camera that utilizes AI and computerized reasoning that perceives the outflows of others. The wearable is associated with the Smartphone application so patient's folks and experts can verify the measure of progress in feelings perceiving capacity of the patient.

6.4.7   Affectiva

One of the highly significant developments in AI can be viewed in enthusiastic knowledge. Think for some time, imagine a scenario in which innovation

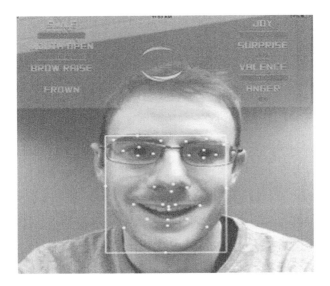

Figure 6.8 Affectiva [9].

could adjust to human feelings. The appropriate response is Affectiva is the feeling of acknowledgment programming that carries enthusiastic insight into the advanced world which is illustrated in Figure 6.8. It does not just change how human interactions collaborate with innovation yet how people essentially cooperate. It is a programmed facial coding framework that prompts enhancement, forecast, and assessment. It realizes exactly how we are feeling from the appearance of our face. In this way, it is creating feelings once again into advanced understanding.

6.4.8   AlphaGo Beats

AlphaGo is a tight artificial knowledge, which is very broadly used to compete the table game Go. It overwhelms a human expert go player in 2015 is shown in Figure 6.9. It utilizes the Monti Carlo tree seeks to discover its movements dependent on AI by the Artificial Neural system by broadly preparing both PC player and human.

6.4.9   Cogito

Cogito is a specialist framework semantic canny stage is shown in Figure 6.10. The innovation accepts any sort of text as a contribution to any design and afterward plays out a profound etymological investigation by experiencing all the various advances required for the semantic examination. It is a genuinely softer AI programming for client support that utilizes conduct investigation to act in-call examination and see the feeling of customers through

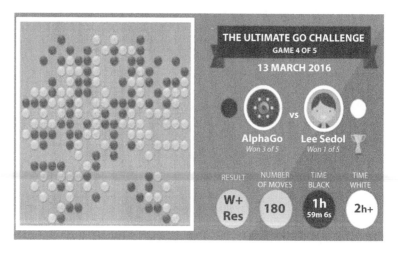

Figure 6.9 AlphaGo beats [10].

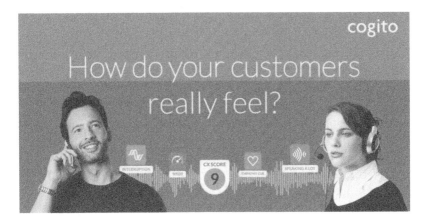

Figure 6.10 Cogito [11].

their working examples, verbal prompts, and other community signs. It depends on a portrayal of information referred to as the Cogito Knowledge Graph. This product measures different capacities, for example, the capacity to peruse, grasp, learn, and understand the significance of words and articulations. It gets shrewd by utilizing human experience and gaining from the composed information.

6.4.10   Siri and Alexa

Siri is fundamentally a PC program that functions as a wise individual collaborator and information guide shown in Figure 6.11. It is some portion of Apple Inc's iOS. At the end of the day, it is the voice collaborator of Apple. With the assistance of AI, Siri gone through an enormous arrangement of cerebrum transfers through moving its silicon-controlled brain to Ai fueled psyche.

After different endeavors and trails, when apple began utilizing AI, there happened a sensational improvement in Siri's voice acknowledgment.

Figure 6.11 Siri [12].

At that point utilizing AI over and over, it gets softer and more started to comprehend our common language. We can converse with Siri as we talk with our companions and it encourages us to complete different things, for example, sending messages and play calls. It can show us the best course in any area as it works sans hand.

It can likewise plan dates, establish our updates, discover bearings, and offer responses to every one of our questions. Same as Siri, another AI-based innovation is Alexa shown in Figure 6.12. It fundamentally feels in the same way as an AI. She is the individual right hand that is living in the cloud and continually tuning in to us through various accessible physical devices that think carefully and similarly, she can hear better than Siri.

Figure 6.12 Alexa [13].

Figure 6.13 Pandora [14].

6.4.11   Pandora's

Pandora's AI is one of the most progressive strategies that have an extraordinary effect today which is demonstrated in Figure 6.13. It is recognized as the melodic DNA. Nearly dependent on 400 melodic qualities, every tune is physically dissected by the master group of performers and it has likewise the history for suggesting tunes that would somehow go undetected, however, individuals characteristically love.

6.5   Objectives

- The goals of AI research are thought, information interpretation, organizing, education, ordinary language preparation, recognition, and the ability to move and manage objects. There are distance targets in the overall insight area.
- Methods integrate factual methods, conventional coding AI, and computational knowledge. In the period of the AI research recognized with the pursuit and mathematical improvement, fake neural systems, and techniques reliant on measurements, probability, and economic matters, we utilize numerous devices. Software engineering is pulling in AI in the area of brain research, arithmetic, science, phonetics, theory, etc.
- **To Create Expert Systems:** The machines which display the smart behavior, understand, determine, describe, and recommendation by its users.
- **To Execute Human Intelligence in devices:** Establishing machines that recognize, feel, comprehend, and perform like humans.

6.5.1   Major Goals

- Robotics
- Computer Vision
- Natural Linguistic Processing
- Machine Learning
- Knowledge reasoning
- Planning

6.5.2   Need for Artificial Intelligence

At present, the measure of information on the planet is humongous to such an extent that people miss the mark concerning engrossing, deciphering, and settling on choices of the whole information, no even piece of the information. This perplexing dynamic requires creatures that have higher psychological aptitudes than people. This is the reason we are attempting to construct machines superior to us, at the end of the day, AI. Another significant trademark that AI machines have yet we do not is tedious learning. People are seen to discover tedious errands exceptionally exhausting. Exactness is another factor wherein we people need. Machines have very high precision in the undertakings that they perform. Machines can likewise face challenges rather than people.

6.5.3   Distinction Between Artificial Intelligence and Business Intelligence

Factors	Business intelligence	Artificial intelligence
Concept	It entails intelligent decision making.	It includes human-like computer intelligence.
Focus	It deals with deep learning and machine learning algorithms.	It deals with the values of numerical analysis.
Application	It is utilized in data warehousing and data mining methods.	It is utilized primarily in fuzzy logic, virtual gaming, image recognition, robotics, etc.
Scope	Its latitude has been linked by what has occurred in the past.	Its scale is linked to events that have taken place in the future.
Contributions	It is contributing to data analysis, enterprise reporting, and OLAP.	It is contributing to topics such as computer science and biology.
Algorithm	It utilizes the linear aggression module for categorizing data.	It utilizes the breadth-first algorithm (BFS) and is followed by the principle of FIFO.

(Continued)

(*Continued*)

Factors	Business intelligence	Artificial intelligence
Drawback	It has disadvantages like inappropriate technologies and misappropriation of data.	It has disadvantages like a danger to safety privacy.
Intention	The main objective of business intelligence is to analyze the data and forecasting the future from the previous information.	The main purpose of Artificial Intelligence is to build the systems which have the capability of acting like the human mind.
Tools	It utilizes data mining tools, query software, spreadsheets for analysis.	It utilizes sophisticated algorithms to produce logic.

6.6   Significance of the Study

AI expert frameworks structure a significant zone of exploration in a half and half field known as man-made consciousness (computerized reasoning). Man-made consciousness unites PC researchers and architects. Clinicians and language specialists with laborers in different zone use the different applications as per the needs and demands based on their work environment. Such an intermingling of numerous foundations and perspectives is important to wrestle with three of the principle unsolved issues of master frameworks research.

1. By what method can the client of such a framework convey the issue to the PC in a characteristic manner? The issues of making PCs manage regular. Language in spoken or even composed structure is huge. An exceptionally enormous measure of certain information is required for discourse understanding. Forthcoming essential advancements in regular language understanding. Current master frameworks accept ideal understanding and an ability on the client's part to "play the PC's down".

2. By what means should the PC manage the expressed issue? This is likewise a principal question: it prompts further inquiries of the interior portrayal of information. The association of

the chose portrayal to encourage the quest for a specific thing and the expansion of new things. Also, the utilization of good judgment general principles for thinking. Conclusion and critical thinking. These are, obviously, the inquiries that analysts have been posing to themselves corresponding to human reasoning, arranging and learning. One part of man-made reasoning exploration is the common advantage that can result from mental examination and work on "educated" PCs.

3. In what manner can individuals control and cheek the activity of a specialist framework? This is additionally a urgent inquiry—if the client is given just a proposal, without knowing the explanation behind that counsel. At that point the framework is not generally working as a guide, however more like a tyrant. Then again, if the PC consequently presents all the choice focuses and auxiliary data used to create the proposal, this might be excessively dull. The program, in this way, needs to adjust itself to the standard needs of its present client.

In any case, have the offices to give a total record of its "thinking" if that is required. Notwithstanding these three fundamental inquiries, research on master frameworks likewise connections to deal with PC vision and discourse info and yield as methods for gaining information and giving a reaction to ask for. These prerequisites strengthen the quest for new PC structures and programming strategies that underlie the ebb and flow chip away at people in the future of data frameworks.

6.6.1   Segments of Master Frameworks

Master frameworks are PC frameworks that utilization information and deduction or thinking methodology to tackle issues regularly managed by a specialist, i.e., somebody who has aptitude and mastery in the zone of concern. Such frameworks are worried about a specific application zone or area—for example, diagnostics, and arranging—which is typically truly restricted. Master frameworks are a subset of man-made reasoning which models the capacity of people to issue. Master frameworks have the capacity to cape with high degrees of unpredictability and fragmented information, just as to give clarifications of finishes of reach. A specialist framework can for the most part choose the following stage to be taken in a critical thinking strategic.

Information-based master frameworks, or on the other hand information frameworks for short, utilize human information to tackle issues, that require human knowledge. Information frameworks speak to and apply of information electronically. These abilities at last will make information frameworks huge and more impressive than the previous advances for putting away and sending information, books, and show programs. Today, books store the biggest volume of information.

Inevitably, the most PCs today perform undertakings as per the dynamic rationale of ordinary projects, and these projects do not promptly oblige huge measures of information. Projects comprise of two unmistakable parts, calculations, and information. Calculations decide how to tackle explicit sorts of issues, and information describe boundaries in the specific issue close by. Human information does not fit this model, notwithstanding. Since much human information comprises of rudimentary sections of ability. Applying a lot of information requires better approaches to compose dynamic parts into able wholes. The information frameworks reenact master human execution, and they present human-like facade to the client.

Generally, PC programming has utilized an algorithmic way to deal with procedural to taking care of issues; as such, it utilized an unbending bit by bit approach. These two methodologies can work accurately, the entirety of the potential blends of information sources and information esteems must be remembered for the program. In master frameworks, the product is non-procedural. It chooses itself how to continue, and it can manage sudden situations in a manner like a human.

The product can work out the subsequent stage for that specific circumstance. The significant distinction between the two kinds of programming lies in the manner that the program is sorted out and how the information is utilized. There are commonly two levels in customary programming—the information and the code or control. This program code contains the control data and the undertaking information, as such, subtleties on the best way to approach tackling the issue.

In master frameworks, there are three key levels and three relating parts. These are as follows:

1. Information, which is regularly provided through the UI.
2. Control, the surmising motor.
3. Undertaking information, the information base.

A regular design for a standard-based framework is appeared in As Can Be Seen, the undertaking information is isolated from the control. This partition infers seclusion and implies that new information can be included without modifying the control segment. This may improve considerably with respect to profitability and viability. The figure shows a more

definite portrayal of a specialist framework utilized in a systems administration condition. Here, the information base, or working memory, speaks
to explicit information about the area being referred to. This will incorporate, for instance, the parts and geography of the system.

6.6.1.1   User Interface

The human-PC interface or UI innovation permits clients to communicate
with the framework. The client presents the issue and has the ends introduced to him. A noteworthy element of some master frameworks is that
they can legitimize the ends came to just as clarify why certain choices
were utilized or disposed of. There are various manners by which the activity can be shared between the framework and the client. The most clear
strategy is that where the framework decides the progression of the intelligent meeting by provoking the client with inquiries and posing for information to be inputted. In this example, the client cannot chip in data.

In the case of an analytic framework, the speculations would be picked
by the framework and the client would be posed inquiries until the theory
was affirmed or invalidated. Such a framework is ideal for students, however, not for those clients with elective recommendations for taking care of
the issue. Man-made brainpower is characterized as a development of the
capacities of PCs to incorporate the capacity to reason.

To learn improvement: What is more, to recreate human tactile capacities.
The present PCs can deliver reams of paper, perform billions of computations,
and control the progression of thousands of messages, however at the day's end,
they know close to they did at its beginning. A significant part of the exploration in the zone of man-made brainpower is planned for enabling PCs to
imitate human thinking and, subsequently, learn. Presently, PC "information"
is gotten from human information. Maybe, later on, PCs will learn and add to
their own insight base. Scientists in computerized reasoning hold out incredible guarantee for the upcoming master frameworks, one of a few regions of
man-made consciousness research. Rough, however, successful master frameworks are presently being marketed for clinical conclusion, oil investigation,
and a few different zones. A specialist framework is an information-based
framework to which preset principles are applied to tackle a specific issue,
for example, deciding a patient's sickness. Present master frameworks depend
principally on real information—a distinct quality of PCs. We people, however, take care of issues by consolidating real information with our quality—
heuristic information—that is, instinct, judgment, and derivations. The truly
extreme choices include both verifiable and heuristic information. Thus,
analysts are attempting to improve the PC's capacity to assemble and utilize

heuristic information. This considerable innovative obstacle disrupts the general flow of human-like master frameworks. Notwithstanding, this obstacle will in the long run be cleared, and master frameworks will proliferate for basically every calling. Lawyers will have mock preliminaries with master frameworks to "pre-attempt" their cases. Specialists will regularly ask a "second feeling". Architects will "talk about" the auxiliary plan of a structure with a specialist framework. Military officials can "talk" with the "master" to design combat zone methodology. City organizers will "ask" a specialist framework to propose ideal areas for recreational offices.

6.6.1.2   Expert Systems

In frameworks where the activity is shared, the entire dynamic cycle is shared among client and framework. In a symptomatic framework, the clients can choose a theory and at each stage remark with regard to whether to proceed with a similar course or change it. Clearly, this sort of framework is considerably more unpredictable to structure. A definitive interface would be one permitting the client to take the entirety of the activity, to have the option to include quite a few proposals in a characteristic language structure. This is exceptionally mind boggling and is under steady turn of events.

6.6.1.3   Inference Engine

The Inference Engine is that aspect of the program which reasons and decides how to apply the information in the information base to the realities and premises introduced at the UI. It plays out this undertaking so as to reason new realities which are then used to reach further determinations. The derivation motor is the dynamic part of a specialist framework since it steers through information and advances the entire collaboration. The point of the surmising motor is to mirror human thinking so the client can comprehend why the framework has picked the means it has. There are, indeed, different deduction procedures which model distinctive thinking techniques; these incorporate in reverse and forward binding, think about a diagnostics master. He would begin with a speculative shortcoming and afterward reason in reverse to show up at potential side effects. In forward changing, the converse move is made; this strategy models the thinking taken by a setup master. He would begin from a rundown of prerequisites to decide a definite 16 agenda of what might be important to fulfill the necessities. Both these strategies can be utilized in a similar framework, as certain parts of the issue might be more qualified to one than the other. As was referenced before, master frameworks can manage information that are muddled or fragmented. Methods for prevailing upon unsure information inputted by the client are basic in the derivation motor. This vulnerability is frequently important for the information base, since that degrees of assurance can be related with the consequents of rules; i.e., the "at that point" part of an "assuming at that point" rule.

6.6.1.4   Voice Recognition

PC-based voice-acknowledgment frameworks have just been made that perceive around 100 verbally expressed words. A voice-acknowledgment framework accessible for PCs, for instance, permits the client to provide orders to the PC vocally instead of composing them at the console. As our comprehension of voice-acknowledgment procedures develops, PCs will turn out to be more adroit an understanding expressed orders. Later on, the mouthpiece may supplant the console as the central methods for human-computer collaboration and information input.

6.6.1.5   Robots

Modern robots—machines that have human-like aptitudes or adroitness—are as of now grinding away welding vehicle parts, working inside atomic reactors, and interesting specialists. The present robots, notwithstanding, are truly minimal beyond what unique reason and man-made brainpower could prompt another age of silicon-based clever creatures. On the off chance that smart robots occur, carbon-based shrewd creatures (people) should modify—and the modification, as sci-fi essayists have been letting us know for a long time, may not be simple.

6.7   Discussion

As AI is diffusing in our general public, plan researchers and professionals wonder how this will affect our comprehension of structure. Will it influence the manner in which we practice structure? Furthermore, assuming this is the case, will it even scrutinize its fundamental standards? How about we start by tending to the primary inquiry?

6.7.1   Artificial Intelligence and Design Practice

Until today, advanced innovations have mostly spread into the activities of associations, lessening the expenses and season of assembling and conveying items and administrations. However, the plan of those items and administrations was a human concentrated cycle. Alluding back to Figure 6.14, regardless of whether the "making" was quick and modest, the "structuring" was substantial in time and assets. It fundamentally was an irregular movement, directed incidentally and for a fragment of clients, through tasks. Man-made brainpower drastically changes this situation, in a way that is key for development researchers: it moves advanced robotization upstream, into the space of the structure. On a less difficult level, these mechanization capacities can be utilized to empower architects to do what they did previously, however quicker. For instance, Airbnb is building up an AI framework that underpins the mechanization of an average plan task: the interpretation of mockups drawn by architects legitimately into part determinations for programming engineers. The framework depends on normalizations and orders of all plan parts. Simulated intelligence can perceive Airbnb's plan segments that may have been hand-drawn on a planning phase and consequently render them into the genuine particular and source code for models. In the event that the utilization of AI would be restricted to the mechanization of existing plan undertakings, as in the model over, the quintessence of configuration practice would stay immaculate. Nonetheless, the instances of Netflix and Airbnb talked about in the past meeting show that the effect of AI on configuration works out positively past mechanization of existing plan practice; it significantly changes it. As such, AI is the marker for a revelation in the manner we take a gander at plan [26–28]. What establishes the framework for reevaluating configuration practice are the critical thinking abilities fused in AI. Through AI, they empower to delegate to calculations the meaning of definite structure decisions normally made by planners: which interface to show to a client, which substance to make, how to situate an item contrasted with contenders. This has significant ramifications both regarding the article and of the cycle of the structure. The main emotional change is in the object of configuration practice (the "what" of plan). Customarily, fashioners made arrangements (items, administrations, encounters) to be conveyed at scale. What a client experienced was recently considered and created by planners; down to the degree of subtleties: for example, a picture to be shown on a screen. On the other hand, with AI, the particular arrangement experienced by an individual client (for example what she sees on the screen of her cell phone), is not just conveyed yet additionally structured "at the time" by a critical thinking circle fueled by AI. As it were, with regard to AI, architects do not structure arrangements (these are created by the AI motor); they plan the critical thinking circles. This difference in the object has problematic ramifications. Particularly because most AI calculations do not reason as a fashioner, for example, they just not computerize the thinking about a fashioner; they work in an alternate way. Though we will in general accept that AI recreates human conduct and thinking (what is normally alluded to as "solid AI"), the majority of the applications we talked about in the instances of Netflix and Airbnb are occurrences of "powerless" AI: they depend on amazingly straightforward undertakings (for example, perceiving a shape in a picture or if two pictures have various shapes). To lay it out plainly, power-less AI is naturally "stupid". However, by reproducing these undertakings a great many occasions (and by supporting them with masses of information), feeble AI can give complex expectations, which even outperforms human abilities. The ramifications for researchers and teachers of configuration are amazing. How would you structure critical thinking circles? How would you imagine configuration decides that depend on incredibly basic undertak-ings, however, that once reproduced occasions and times once more, can independently give amazingly complex answers for clients? Fashioners are not taught along these lines. Their psychological edges are prepared to foun-dationally grasp complex undertakings. To use the intensity of AI, they need a remarkable ability: to envision what an imbecilic framework can do while working at scale. As the object of configuration changes (from planning answers for structuring critical thinking circles) additionally, the cycle of the plan (the "how" of configuration) changes also. This is apparent in the event that we contrast Figure 6.14 and Figure 6.15 recently outlined: with regard to AI Factories, the structure cycle is part of two lumps. Initial, a human-serious plan stage where the arrangement space is considered and the crit-ical thinking circles are planned; and afterward, an AI-fueled stage, where the particular arrangement is created for a particular client by the calcula-tion. As this second lump of the cycle requires for all intents and purposes zero expense and time, the advancement of the arrangement can be initiated for every individual client, in the exact second wherein she requests it. This thusly empowers to use the most recent accessible information and learning, and in this manner to make, inevitably, a superior novel arrangement. There is no more item or administration outline that goes about as a cradle among plan and use. Structure, conveyance, and use, they all occur, to some degree, at the same time.

Figure 6.14 Design practice in the context of traditional human-intense operating models.

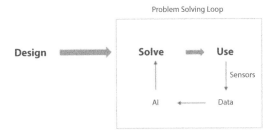

Figure 6.15 Design practice in the context of AI Factories.

6.8 Applications of AI

Research areas	Real-life application
Expert Systems Instances: Clinical systems, flight-surveillance systems	
Natural Linguistic Processing Illustrations: Automatic voice output, speech recognition, Google Now feature	
Neural Networks Illustrations: Pattern recognition devices like character recognition, integrity recognition, face recognition	

(Continued)

(*Continued*)

Research areas	Real-life application
Robotics Instances: Manufacturing robots for carving, coating, cleaning, drilling, precision checking, painting, spraying, moving	
Fuzzy Logic Systems Instances: Automobiles, consumer electronics, etc.	

6.8.1 AI Has Been Developing a Huge Number of Tools Necessary to Find a Solution to the Most Challenging Problems in Computer Science

These are as follows:

- Languages
- Control theory
- Neural networks
- Classifiers and statistical approaches to learning
- Probabilistic techniques for ambiguous reasoning
- Logic
- Search and optimization

6.8.2 Future of AI

The future of AI is as follows:

- Healthcare
- Business
- Music
- The perfect lawyer
- Military Bots

6.9   Conclusion

AI is not cared for some other computerized innovation. It does not simply mechanize activities. It mechanizes realizing, which is the center of development. It accordingly offers remarkable chances to significantly lessen the expense and season of building up another arrangement. In this article, we have opened a window on the suggestions for configuration, by investigating the techniques of spearheading organizations in AI: Netflix, Airbnb, Tesla, and Microsoft. The cases propose that AI does not sabotage the suppositions and standards of Design Thinking. Or maybe, by eliminating past constraints in scale, extension, and learning, it empowers to additionally authorize plan in its center: it understands a definitive type of individuals centeredness, with encounters that can be intended for every distinctive individual and consistently improved dependent on singular client information; AI may upgrade inventiveness, by growing the extent of the structure space past item classifications and businesses; at long last, it brings cycles and analyses at the center of the working models of firms. We have acquainted a system to examine this change and catch the idea of structure in the new setting of AI Factories. With the coming of man-made reasoning, a huge piece of critical thinking (fundamentally, what we used to call "advancement") is moved to calculations. They continue improving and looking for better arrangements because of their learning circles. These calculations think in a fundamentally unexpected manner in comparison to a fashioner: they think regarding little imbecilic tasks, which, notwithstanding, when scaled up and iterated thousands or even a huge number of times, can address complex issues. For chiefs, understanding the new idea of the plan practice in the period of AI is subsequently major to abstain from applying the correct structure rules (that stay immaculate) to an inappropriate cycle (which rather is altogether unique about the past). For researchers, the suggestions regarding plan speculations are likewise significant. We need two new sorts of systems. Initially, we have to give planners new models that help them in their new undertaking: not of structuring arrangements, however of planning the critical thinking circles that will build up the arrangements. Second, and more important for the administration of plan and advancement, we have to fortify our comprehension of the vital component of structure: the meaning of a significant heading. In AI Factories, the human side of configuration progressively turns into an act of sense-making (characterizing which issues bode well to address). As it were, the disciplinary separation among structure and the board has begun to contract effectively 20 years prior (see likewise [1]). Nonetheless, in the past, it was the board hypothesis that drew nearer to structure, in look for new systems that could uphold critical thinking. Presently rather, we anticipate that plan should draw nearer to the executives. Furthermore, the separation will contract on another measurement: the components of sense-making. The space for pollution between the two controls, and specifically between a plan (with its hypotheses of confining and evaluate) and initiative (with its speculations of sense-making and dialogic), is applicable; it is fundamentally undiscovered, and it vows to be one of the most interesting excursions for development researchers in the years to come.

References

1. Trainor M, Bieber J, Timberlake J. John Black-Engaged Learning With Digital Media: The Points of Viewing Theory (Chapter 14) lyrics.
2. Brown T, Katz B. Change by design: How design thinking transforms organizations and inspires innovation. New York, NY: HarperBusiness; 2019.
3. Carr D. Giving viewers what they want. The New York Times. 2013 Feb 24;24(02): 2013.
4. Chandrashekar A, Amat F, Basilico J, Jebara T. Artwork personalization at netflix. Netflix Technology Blog. 2017 Dec 7;6:67-72.
5. Chang R. Using machine learning to predict value of homes on Airbnb. Airbnb, available at: https://Medium. Com/Airbnb-Engineering/Using-Machine-Learning-to-Predict-Valueof-Homeson-Airbnb 9272d3d4739d. 2017.
6. Csikszentmihalyi, M., Motivation and creativity: Toward a synthesis of structural and energistic approaches to cognition. *New Ideas Psychol.*, 6, 2, 159–176, 1988a.
7. Csikszentmihalyi, M., Solving a problem is not finding a new one: A reply to Simon. *New Ideas Psychol.*, 6, 2, 183–186, 1988b.
8. Dai P. Helping guests make informed decisions with market insights.
9. Domingos, P., A few useful things to know about machine learning. *Commun. ACM*, 55, 10, 78–87, 2012.
10. Dorst, K., *Frame Innovation. Creating New Thinking by Design*, MIT Press, Cambridge, 2015.
11. Elsbach, K. and Stigliani, I., Design Thinking and Organizational Culture: A Review and Framework for Future Research. *J. Manag.*, 44, 6, 2274–306, 2018.
12. Galle, P., Philosophy of design: an editorial introduction. *Des. Stud.*, 23, 3, 211–218, 2002.
13. Gibson, J.J., The theory of affordances, in: *Perceiving, Acting, and Knowing: Toward an Ecological Psychology*, R. Shaw and J. Bransford (Eds.), 1977.

14. Kelley, D. and Kelley, T., *Creative Confidence: Unleashing the Creative Potential within Us All*, Crown Publishing, New York, 2013.

15. Krippendorff K. On the essential contexts of artifacts or on the proposition that "design is making sense (of things)". Design issues. 1989 Apr 1;5(2):9-39.

16. Liedtka J. Perspective: Linking design thinking with innovation outcomes through cognitive bias reduction. *Journal of product innovation management.* 2015 Nov;32(6):925-38.

17. Love T. Philosophy of design: a meta-theoretical structure for design theory. Design studies. 2000 May 1;21(3):293-313.

18. Margolin V, editor. Design discourse: history, theory, criticism. University of Chicago Press; 1989 Sep 15.

19. Marglolin V, Buchanan R, editors. The idea of design: a design issues reader. MIT Press; 1996.

20. Norman DA, Verganti R. Incremental and radical innovation: Design research vs. technology and meaning change. Design issues. 2014 Jan 1;30(1):78-96.

21. Simon, H.A., *The Sciences of the Artificial,* The MIT Press, Cambridge, 1982, Simon, H.A., Creativity and motivation: A response to Csikszentmihalyi. *New Ideas Psychol.,* 6, 2, 177 -181, 1988.

22. Spangler T. Netflix Eyeing total of about 700 original series

23. Ghoddusi H, Creamer GG, Rafizadeh N. Machine learning in energy economics and finance: A review. *Energy Economics.,* 2019 Jun 1;81:709-27.

24. Stigliani, I. and Ravasi, D., Organizing thoughts and connecting brains: Material practices and the transition from individual to group-level prospective sensemaking. *Acad. Manag. J.,* 55, 5, 1232–1259, 2012.

25. Verganti, R., Design, meanings, and radical innovation: A meta-model and a research agenda. *J. Prod. Innov. Manag.,* 25, 5, 436–456, 2008.

26. Verganti, R., *Design-driven innovation – Changing the rules of competition by radically innovating what things mean,* Harvard Business Press, Boston, 2009.

27. Verganti, R., Designing Breakthrough Products. *Harv. Bus. Rev.,* 89, 10, 114–120, 2011a.

28. Verganti R. Radical design and technology epiphanies: A new focus for research on design management. *Journal of Product Innovation Management.* 2011 May;28(3):384-8.

29. Verganti R, Öberg Å. Interpreting and envisioning—A hermeneutic framework to look at radical innovation of meanings. Industrial Marketing Management. 2013 Jan 1;42(1):86-95.

30. Wilson M. Inside The Hip Redesign Of Holiday Inn Express: Ideo helps the budget hotel chain rethink everything from beds to mood lighting.

7

Artificial Intelligence in Healthcare: Algorithms and Decision Support Systems

S. Palanivel Rajan* and M.Paranthaman

Department of Electronics and Communication Engineering M. Kumarasamy College of Engineering, Karur, Tamilnadu, India

Abstract

The purpose of this chapter is to discuss the role of Artificial Intelligence (AI) in medical platform, especially to create a device that performs the same as a human organ does. We are going to discuss AI-driven healthcare devices that use machine learning, deep learning, and natural language processing, analyzing methods of clinical data in the form of text and images. Different platforms such as BioXcel Therapeutics, BERG, XtalPi's ID4, Deep Genomics, IBM's Watson, and Google's DeepMind Health, and techniques reduce the mortality rate in complicated medical diagnosis and surgeries. Finally, the challenges and risks of an automated clinical system will be explained.

Keywords: Artificial Intelligence, healthcare, machine learning, deep learning, natural language processing, IBM Watson, Google DeepMind

7.1 Introduction

The system which has the capability of acquiring knowledge and applying it for a particular application is called intelligent systems. Applying the acquired knowledge to a particular application needs experience. This experience can be acquired by training the past information. Intelligent systems resemble human thinking abilities by training with past experiences. We are already living in the Artificial Intelligence (AI) world employing automatic process which we experience in our daily activities

Corresponding author: drspalanivelrajan@gmail.com

C. Venkatesh, N. Rengarajan, P. Ponmurugan and S. Balamurugan (eds.) Smart Systems for Industrial Applications, (173–198) © 2022 Scrivener Publishing LLC

from face recognition to the virtual assistant. In healthcare also, AI has assisted the physician to some extent. Deep research and clinical trials are going on for a fully automated clinical system that replacing humans and to decide prognosis and treatment for the patients. New kinds of diseases spread that affect the aging population around the world [1]. The clinical data is getting increased day by day. The curated data becomes complex and insufficient to predict the required data for the patients. Suggestions may be developed from the dataset which will help the physician to decide the prognosis. The art of AI has become part of the new frontier in medicine [2]. A few years back, it helped the doctor predict cardiovascular risk factors from retinal fundus photographs. AI could do this because it was able to dive into that deep blue sea and analyze all the pitfalls and risks for diseases in a way far better and faster than human doctors. If we give an optimistic sight to it, then we can find that AI is for help and not destruction. Humans are lazy but consider themselves as superheroes. But AI is the real cheetahs that could analyze every pattern rapidly and produce proper diagnosis. AI can be of help before a doctor come into action. It is a great breakthrough if the AI system could scan the X-ray report and diagnose a patient of pneumonia. This secures double bacon, one of the patients as he gets faster cure and the other for the doctor as he can provide swift treatment [3].

Even though AI was introduced in the late 1950s it is gaining importance only after introducing its subsets machine learning and deep learning. Using statistical analysis and developing algorithms enable the cognitive thinking of the system. The system learns information from experience and updates its knowledge frequently. We are moving toward an automatic clinical system in which a system decides for treatment with or without assisted by humans. Machine learning is a subset of AI that connects a computer with a statistical model to develop new algorithms for automation. The algorithm is set free to explore related data to learn things and applied to particular applications. So, there need for explicit rules to the system not required. Supervised and unsupervised learning are the two approaches to learning. Patients affected by neurological diseases are at risk of losing their physical movements and speaking ability with the other people [4]. AI along with brain-computer interface can assist them to almost restore their physical activities. A non-invasive method of diagnosing diseases can be automated using novel AI methods. For example, the diagnosis and prognosis of radiological results can be automated. An intelligent system can have the capability to analyze the CT scan reports, x-rays, and MRI images. As we aware COVID-19 pandemic changes our lifestyle completely. If we could develop an intelligent system that will diagnose through virtual biopsies, then it reduces the spreading of the diseases from one human to another. There are many systems in a clinical trial based on AI methodologies.

Natural language processing and deep learning methods have the potential to change the hospital environment. A fully automated hospital system can be developed by using novel deep learning systems with support from NLP. There were vast handwritten clinical data available all over the world. Those data have to be converted into the digitized format and curated into meaningful data. Numerous clinical trials on natural language processing are going on and hopefully, that will come into the market soon to assist the patients.

Self-learning and self-correcting abilities of AI devices will help assist the physician. To assist clinical practice at hospitals or in biotelemetry, AI-driven software or devices are much needed as the population of patients increasing. Therapeutic and diagnostic errors can be reduced by AI devices as they learned a large medical database. Moreover, real-time analysis medical inferences from a large patient group are possible in AI-driven software. If any risk factor is identified, then it can be immediately notified to corresponding authority in the medical field. With less time and in reduced cost, the tasks done only by humans such as continuous patient monitoring, hospital administrations, and early detection of diseases will be simplified by implementing AI. Next, the focus is on the diseases that cause more deaths, such as diseases related to neurology, cardiology, and cancer. Implementing AI to the repeated activities at the hospital and the most critical functions that are difficult by a human needs the AI device to be learned by itself. Biomarker discovery relies on identifying previously unrecognized correlations between thousands of measurements and phenotypes. Omics technologies have enabled the high-throughput measurement of thousands of genes and proteins, and of millions of genomic and epigenomic aberrations. Several high-performing machine-learning models generate results that are difficult to interpret by unassisted humans. Although these models can achieve better-than-human performance, it is not straightforward to convey intuitive notions explaining the conclusions of the models [5].

This chapter is organized into two sections: methodologies followed by machine learning algorithms and intelligent tools on clinical trials as well as in the market. Methodologies in the sense, the workflow of machine learning and deep learning and the collection of researches happened and reported. Recent researches on machine learning for disease diagnosis and prognosis and also assisting physicians in some cases were identified and explained, followed by deep learning and natural language processing methods that were listed. Last is a brief collection of the pharma industry contribution in adapting AI to their products.

7.2   Machine Learning Work Flow and Applications in Healthcare

Machine learning focuses on developing a mathematical model to learn and apply the learned things on which it is employed. We can call it a statistical learning theory. Without explicit programs, ML can work by learning itself. Teaching how to do is the only thing humans can give as input to machines. Data preparation (data sources), basic or advanced algorithms, automation, and iterative process and ensemble modeling are the steps involved to create a good machine learning system.

The difference between machine learning algorithms and the traditional program is the logic to solve the problem. Machine learning writes its logic with the input and expected output. To develop a model, a machine learning system needs to be trained. It collects the past data and also periodically updating the database. Then, the collected data in raw format may require pre-processing. Based on the data collected, it builds model algorithms.

The workflow of the machine learning system is shown in the Figure 7.1. There are four steps to build a machine learning system. First, the data needs to be collected from the data providers based on the application of the ML

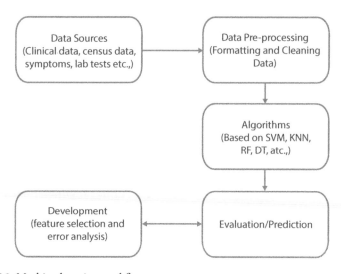

Figure 7.1 Machine learning workflow.

system. The data in machine learning can be a text, sound, or image, that is not being perceived. Those unprocessed data have to be interpreted and stored in the database. To build a model, gaining knowledge from interpreted information is needed. The properties of data are represented in 5 V's: as we are living in a faster-growing world, the huge amount of data is generating every second (Volume); the generated data may be in different forms as discussed earlier (Variety); the rate of data generation per second (Velocity); information interpreted from the data must be meaningful (Value) and it should be helpful to researchers; finally, the correctness and certainty of data (Veracity).

This chapter deals with machine learning in a healthcare application. So, the medical database needs to set up for training and implementation of the machine learning system. Several categories may be there in medical data. We can collect data from clinical trials, genome data, census data, family history of the patients and their symptoms, laboratory test reports, disease history, and clinician notes. Using wearable devices also data can be generated. These data may be in raw format and requires pre-processing to organize it or to categorize it clearly with a label or unlabeled. This interpretation must be done so that model can be build and trained easily.

7.2.1   Formatting and Cleaning Data

One of the significant processes in building a model for machine learning is formatting cleaning data. Formatting and cleaning the raw data is like someone walking on a knife-edge. The result may boost our machine learning algorithm efficiency or it drops the efficiency. So, better data gives better results. Most of the data scientists spend a huge time on working in cleaning the data. A very simple algorithm may provide excellent results of complex problems only if the data is well-cleaned. As discussed earlier, the data may be in different types, so we need different cleaning strategies for each type of data that we have in the database.

Removing unwanted things, structural error or difference, and missed data management are the three steps involved in the data formatting and cleaning process. Removing unwanted things includes the direct removal of redundant information, irrelevant observations, and false/suspicious data. Next, the structural errors can be identified when the data is transferred to a different location while categorizing it. During the classification or clustering of data, this kind of error will occur. To avoid this error data should be categorized as labeled or unlabeled.

Third, missed data management is a somewhat tricky job in the machine learning process. Any format of missing data in the observation should be handled carefully. We cannot remove directly as we did in previous steps. It might be important information about the particular problem. After interpreting and analyzing, only the removal or prediction decision should be taken. There are two ways to manage missing information: either dropping the entire observation which has missing data or predicting the missing information based on past observation saved in the database.

7.2.2   Supervised and Unsupervised Learning

If labeled data is used to train the model with a supervisor, then it is called supervised learning. Labeled means it is already tagged with the correct result. If the model is required to solve a similar problem, then it refers and gives the result. Unsupervised learning does not need a supervisor to train the data. The model itself discovers solutions by learning. Simply unsupervised learning deals with only unlabeled data, whereas supervised learning deals with only labeled data. Real-world complex problems can be solved easily by unsupervised learning. Classification and regression, clustering, and association are the widely used methods to train a model in supervised and unsupervised learning, respectively.

Classification is the process to differentiate and categorize the data using a model called classifiers. Regression is a statistical method of estimating the relation between two variables or more than two variables. The types of classifiers and regression models will be discussed in the upcoming section.

Clustering is the process of dividing the dataset into subsets such that subset data are similar. Clustering is the categorization of similar and dissimilar data in the database. It is an unsupervised learning method deals only with unlabeled data or data in raw format. Clustering algorithms used to build a machine learning model will be discussed later.

Predictive modeling can help solve undesired problems arise during classification or clustering. If the classifier output has more similar features, then the model cannot give good output. So, a predictive probabilistic model is needed to reduce the dimensions of the data such that the classifier gives less redundant results.

7.2.3   Linear Discriminant Analysis

LDA was used for the prediction of knee injury among athletic participants. The classification is based on biomechanical and demographic factors. The simulator was used to find the damaged structure of the knee. Anterior cruciate ligament, medial collateral ligament, and menisci are the most commonly damaged structures. There were 32 variables given as input for predicting knee injury. In this work, the authors used a 5-factor model, a 10-factor model, and 15-factor model for prediction. Bootstrap forest partitioning determines the input variables for the simulator. It reduces the number of input variables as 5, 10, and 15 forms the 32 variables collected. The confusion matrix of each model was analyzed. LDA is a data dimensionality reduction method that is useful for developing advanced machine learning algorithms. Using this analysis, a biomechanical prediction model can be built for the automatic prediction of a knee injury [6].

LDA combined with a genetic algorithm to optimize the parameters of the neural network which is used as a prediction model for Parkinson's disease. In this research, a potential automatic diagnostic system was proposed to classify PD patients. PD is a neurogenic disorder target older people of age more than 60. A hybrid intelligent method was developed and experimented with PD patients. It also provides generalization capabilities. For pattern classification at the initial level, LDA was used. The reason for employing LDA on PD analysis is to improve the predictive model and to reduce the time complexity. After this dimensionality reduction, the data is ready for classification. The neural network is used for classification and it depends on hyperparameters. The inappropriate parameter may lead to an unfit network. So, fitness function is used for generalization [7].

Implementation of LDA and Principal Component Analysis (PCA) to classify patients either affected by Coronary Artery Disease or a normal person was discussed. PCA is used as a linear dimensionality reduction method to reduce the population into subsets with important information. It removes the maximum variance and searches for the second linear combination. The classification accuracy of 84.5% and 86% were achieved by using LDA and LDA along with PCA, respectively [8].

LDA is used to build a linear framework to analyze blood base gene expression and also RNA sequences data [9]. To develop biomarkers for prognosis, adaptive immune response–based pattern recognition is needed. The repertoire fingerprinting method was proposed by the author, which uses PCA to reduce the dimension and to classify patterns of an immune response [10].

7.2.4   K-Nearest Neighbor

Classification using K-nearest neighbor and random forest classifier for Rheumatoid Arthritis was discussed. RA is a progressive disease causing joint destruction. Wearable sensors or thermal sensors are widely used to collect data for RA [11]. K-nearest neighbor algorithm is used to identify lung cancer was reported. Before classification, there were dimensionality reduction techniques employed to reduce the complexity. KNN can be used for nonlinear classification to predict the unlabeled samples [12].

In cancer treatment, active small molecules that inhibit protein kinases play a major role. In this aspect, the classification of active inhibitors from a large set of the population is demonstrated. KNN is used as a classifier and a genetic algorithm is used for complexity reduction. KNN is a non-parametric algorithm that has no explicit phase of training; hence, it is also called a lazy learning method. There will not be assumptions on missing data because KNN is considered as non-parametric [13].

Molecular-level disease prediction is a great challenge in cancer identification and bioinformatics. The identification of specific genes is a goal that is difficult to achieve in cancer research. The genes causing cancer disease can be identified only with excellent classifiers which work on a microarray basis because the success of the research mainly depends on the classifier [14]. KNN is used to evaluate the texture analysis of MRI images. Texture analysis is used to differentiate phyllodes tumors and fibroadenoma. A case-based clinical study was carried out and explained [15].

7.2.5 K-Means Clustering

K-means clustering is an unsupervised machine learning method used to optimize hospital staff management. The proposed method was useful in categorizing patients and hospital staff securely [16]. Clustering obese and overweight population work was carried out. K-means clustering is involved in predicting the distance measures and creating a new cluster or subset [17].

The data handling process may be the weakest area to leak the data to unknown persons. No patient or the clinician wants to disclose the treatment details explicitly to others. To avoid privacy issues in healthcare IoT, a privacy-preserving classification method is proposed. The layers of healthcare IoT are shown in Figure 7.2. K-means clustering along with homomorphic encryption was employed to preserve the data. After implementing this method, there is no way to recognize either patient or the hospital by the data analyst. The cluster can be identified by K-means clustering for each iteration [18].

Earlier detection is crucial to increase the survival of non-small lung cancer patients. DNA copy numbers are used to point out the normal cell as well as cancer cells. A nonlinear clustering approach is employed to separate cancer cells from normal cells. Sixty-three blood samples of cancer patients were used for training and testing of the classifier [19]. To classify skin and breast cancer, the K-means clustering approach is used. Usually,

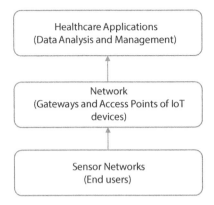

Figure 7.2 Healthcare IoT layers.

cancer datasets are larger when compared to any other medical datasets. So, the simple and efficient classifier has to be used to distinguish the cells [20].

7.2.6   Random Forest

Prediction of severe sepsis and organ space infections using a random forest classifier was reported. Molecular and clinical data were collected for laparotomy for trauma at level 1. The machine learning model was trained by 117,113 records of patients for SS and OSI prediction, respectively [21]. During data pre-processing, missing data prediction is one of the significant processes. Missing data imputation can be done by random forest was reported [22].

The random forest model was proposed to predict the Type A Aortic Dissection. The input variables given to the classification are demographics, symptoms, medical history of the patient, laboratory test, and imaging to predict TAAD [23]. miRNA disease prediction using a random forest model was proposed. Here, the proposed RF model is applied for regression not for classification. To predict the category of the disease, many decision trees were trained and integrated [24].

7.2.7   Decision Tree

The decision tree prediction model for Cerebal Palsy was proposed. The model was built by collecting data from hospitals as a case study and interview with CP patients and non-CP patients. The individual risk of CP can be predicted by the model reported [25]. Intrauterine Adhesions recurrence prediction using the decision tree model was developed. Patients' hysteroscopy data, clinical data, and demographics were collected from the hospital. The portion of data was used to training and testing of decision tree prediction model. This model assists the clinician to decide with an accurate prediction of IUA [26].

In hospital, heart attack can be preventable using a simple prediction model based on the decision tree. A case-control study of 21,337 patient's data was collected and analyzed. The decision tree takes seven variables from the collected data to predict acute coronary syndrome [27].

7.2.8   Support Vector Machine

A Gastric Cancer prediction based on a support vector machine (SVM) was proposed. Using SVM, a long noncoding RNA model was built. The lncRNA model consists of 16 features. This model can classify Microsatellite Instability status. The relation between MSI and lncRNA has displayed the potential of lncRNA role in immunotherapy of GC patients. Assessment of prognosis values, disease-free survival, and overall survival prediction was carried out by the lncRNA model [28].

Early prediction of Type 2 diabetes is important to avoid huge risks in saving a patient's life. Based on the SVM, a prediction model was built by using the Oral Glucose Tolerance Test. Training and testing of the model using OGTT and demographic data collection were carried out. This automatic tool that predicts the diabetes mellitus (type 2) uses SVM. The patient's plasma glucose level plays an important role in the early prediction of diabetes rather than insulin and demographics [29]. SVM is used as a classifier for optical coherence tomography in the diagnosis of multiple sclerosis [30].

The implementation of SVM for the prediction of lumbosacral joint compression was explained. Since Electromyography-based SVM implementation was attempted, the complexity of the data collection becomes difficult. Because this method uses kinetic, kinematic, anthropometric, and electromyography data. The objective of the SVM-based model is to identify the deviated function when compared to the original input [31].

SecProMTB is an advanced model was constructed to identify the Mycobacterium Tuberculosis. Because MTB can dominate immunogenicity in pathogenesis. Identification of secreted proteins in before biological experiment and imbalanced classification addressing are the two main objectives of constructing this SecProMTB model [32].

The role of SVM in earlier detection of gastric cancer was reported. SVM was trained and tested by using 100 samples to classify cancer and normal area of the image. Color-based image classification approach is used in the analysis of affected areas on huge endoscopic image population [33].

7.2.9   Artificial Neural Network

Early diagnosis of Alzheimer's disease is by identifying a set of lipid peroxidation. Cell damage due to the stealing of electrons by free radicals is called lipid peroxidation. In this research, plasma and urine samples were collected from healthy people and Alzheimer's disease diagnosed patients. The artificial neural network model was constructed to classify the patients at risk of having Alzheimer's disease. The ANN model was developed using demographic factors as independent variables and one dependent variable. Initially, the dataset was divided into training, testing, and validating datasets randomly. More number of training iterations gives better ANN model. The network may be in multiple layers and one or two-layer were hidden among them. This multilayer network reduces prediction errors. The number of layers depends on the complexity of the system. The developed ANN model explains the correlation between lipid peroxidation and the diagnosis of complex diseases like Alzheimer's [34].

For successful treatment of orthognathic surgery, diagnosis and treatment planning is very important. The patient's facial aesthetics depends on the proper planning of handling orthognathic surgery decisions. In general, orthognathic surgery decisions should be made by skilled clinicians who have learned on trial and error methods in his experience. The training of unskilled clinicians is a complex, costly, and time-consuming process. Instead of unskilled laborers, if we train a machine learning model either supervised or unsupervised, then it reduces the burden of management. Using the ANN model, the unskilled orthodontist can provide good decisions. For extraction determination and surgery decisions, a new signature model based on ANN was proposed. A total of 316 patients' sample clinical data were used for training the network. The network consists of one hidden layer in the feed-forward architecture. Out of 316 samples, 160 were decided to surgery and 156 were decided non-surgical treatment. After the training of the ANN model, the success rate was analyzed. After testing and validation, this model can provide decisions on surgery or non-surgery, type of surgery, and extraction status [35].

ANN was constructed to perform the classification of patients with type 2 diabetes, patients with prediabetes, and healthy patients. Two-layer feed-forward network with one hidden layer was constructed. Sigmoid transfer function and 15 neurons hidden layer was trained with 190 samples. The clinical information and the test results of HbA1c and fasting plasma glucose were curated. Out of 320 samples collected, 120 samples were used for testing the ANN model. It shows the accuracy level of 94.1% and 93.3% in the classification of patients with prediabetes and patients with type 2 diabetes, respectively [36].

7.2.10 Natural Language Processing

Natural Language Processing is a part of AI that uses machine learning and deep learning. NLP tries to make computers understand human languages. It is a computational task to detect human languages like speech or text. In clinical research, an electronic health record is protected information of the patients in digitized format curated from clinical records, lab tests, and the patients. NLP follows two methods, using prescribed rules and using machine learning algorithms to convert clinical notes into digitized format [37].

THE rule-based NLP approach was dominant in the late 1980s. It requires human interactions to define grammar and vocabularies and an algorithm based on the defined rules. In machine learning–based NLP, the computer creates its algorithm based on learning the records. Human interactions may or may not be needed for the ML-based NLP method. Implementing a rule-based method is very complex in the aspect of defining rules and creating algorithms. Because human language is highly flexible and writing all rules and patterns will be much difficult. The other reason is ruled-based method is not equipped to understand the context of the sentence. Interpreting a single sentence may give good results but interpreting a paragraph or a whole document may not give a fruitful result [38].

Machine learning–based NLP avoids the problems faced in the rule-based method. The machine itself writes the algorithm by learning and predicting approach by parsing old verified clinical records. There is a large set of databases available to train the NLP model. Automatic data extraction from a large volume of clinical notes using NLP for lung cancer is proposed. In lung cancer research, the accuracy of the automatic extraction of predefined information from clinician notes was demonstrated [39].

A comparative study of rule-based interpretation and ML interpretation was conducted in the field of breast cancer research. A collection of comprehensive vocabulary was made by interviewing pathology, radiology reports, and skilled clinicians. The objective of this study is to identify the timing and presence of metastatic recurrence. The neural network model was developed to find the recurrence by parsing clinical notes from EHRs [40].

From radiology reports, the identification of Incidental Lung Nodules was done by NLP. From vast EHRs, the authors have collected 950 random CT reports and manually reviewed it for ILN. To automate the detection process of ILN, an NLP model was developed, trained, and tested against the manually reviewed datasets. The specificity and sensitivity of 82.2%

and 91.1%, respectively, were obtained by the NLP tool for the identification of ILN [41].

In orthopedics, Surgical Site Infection identification depends only on manual interpretation of medical records. The automatic interpreting process may help the researcher to identify SSI easily by using the NLP tool. A combination of estimated logistic regression models and NLP derived variables outcome was demonstrated for the infection surveillance system. In addition, 97% of SSI was identified by the proposed NLP tool when compared to manual abstraction. This automated tool can aid the early detection and prevention of surgical complications and reduces economic cost [42].

7.2.11   Deep Learning

Deep learning is unsupervised learning using novel neural networks. Convolutional neural networks and the datasets are important components in the development of a deep learning system. CNN consists of processing layers in cascade form. The input, feature extraction, and output are the three processing layers of CNN.

Deep learning in ophthalmology research gives significant outcomes in detecting retinopathy and age-related macular degeneration. There are many guidelines suggested for the classification of diabetic retinopathy. Researchers need to know the difference between the classification methods before training and testing deep learning algorithms. DL algorithms can be used as an aiding tool for diagnosis, prognosis, and treatment [43].

A deep learning approach for brain tumor classification was demonstrated. It uses a residual network for classifying MRI images. A total of 3,064 MRI images dataset were used for testing the enhanced residual network which gives 99% accuracy. The dataset contains three types of brain tumor MRI images [44].

Classification of normal and sclerotic kidney for transplant operation was demonstrated. The suitable kidney selection heavily depends on the pathologist. From the frozen section, the percentage of glomeruli was determined. A deep learning method was implemented to automate this process. The objective of CNN is to identify a suitable kidney from the donor. The algorithm analyzes the whole images and classifies them as sclerosis and non-sclerosis glomeruli. The CNN was trained and tested with large datasets. The success of this method opens the gate for fully digitized pathology [45].

The diagnosis of breast cancer using deep learning was proposed. Radiologists generated multiparametric MRI images for the classification of normal and cancer affected images. CNN was used for feature extraction to differentiate malignant tissues. Single parameter classification was done by SVM classifier and multiparametric classification was done by CNN. Classifier fusion, feature fusion, and image fusion are the three different levels of feature extraction carried out using MRI images [46].

Automatic image analysis in pathology department uses deep learning method. The fully convolutional neural network is used here to segment the images. It aids the pathologist to decide on identifying metastatic, tumor region, and prognosis solution. Whole side imaging is the growing method in the diagnosis of cancer. Deep learning algorithms for pathology image segmentation are gaining importance in WSI [47].

A deep learning model for automatic tissue segmentation is age-related molecular degeneration was demonstrated. Disease progression can be identified by analyzing 3D optical coherence tomography images. The proposed model consists of two components: interpretable tissue segmentation by predicting conversion of OCT and predication based on OCT itself. Prediction conversion is not followed by all clinician and it is not a routine task to be carried out [48].

7.2.12   Ensembles

Instead of using single machine learning algorithms, some researchers used hybrid machine learning methods to increase performance. One of such researches carried out for diabetic retinopathy classification was reported. Hybrid machine learning methods are also called ensemble machine learning. The proposed model consists comprise random forest, decision tree, KNN, logistic regression has experimented on the diabetic retinopathy datasets. After normalization, this dataset was used to train the ensemble model. The performance ensemble model outperformed the performance of individual machine learning algorithms [49].

Another ensemble machine learning approach for breast cancer identification was demonstrated. This model comprises KNN, naïve Bayes, SVM, and logistic regression to classify malignant types among the database selected [50].

The ensemble model for type 2 diabetes diagnosis was reported. After considering 15 machine learning algorithms, this model uses five main classifiers namely random forest, KNN, ANN, naïve Bayes, and SVM [51]. Ensemble learning approach for brain cancer classification reported. The ensemble learning method focused on distinguishing cancer grades using random features. First-order, Grey level co-occurrence matrix, Size zone, run-length matrix, and size are the randomized features considered [52].

7.3 Commercial Decision Support Systems Based on AI

IBM's Watson

IBM' Watson is helping in hospitals to optimize clinical data and treatment. It is currently employed to customize health plans after analyzing patient records. An automated second opinion can be suggested by Watson AI to the patients by sit alongside doctors as advanced supportive technology. A database must be created to train this product. Watson was tested by 55 hospital doctors around the world since it is displayed significant performance in the detection of tumors at the earliest. The use of natural language processing and outstanding knowledge by reading clinical data make such suggestions by Watson AI.

Memorial Sloan Kettering Cancer Centre helped IBM to trail Watson AI in the identification of tumors at an early stage. It assisted to diagnose the lung and breast cancer in the year 2013. Now, the product grown up to 13 different earlier stages of tumors can be identified. It is designed as a decision-making device for the physician to determine better treatment. The decision made by interpreting large databases that are dumped with rich clinical data in structured or unordered formats.

Watson AI is for

- Oncology
- Genomics
- Trial of Clinical Matching
- Diabetes Management
- Drug Discovery

In 2016, IBM made a partnership with Under Armour to provide the cognitive system for personalized coaching. It provides personal care to a particular user in terms of their fitness, daily activities, nutrition management, and sleep on evidence-based. Watson AI offers multiple functionalities and it will directly compete with the doctors, no other AI products do this.

One research study provides the following data. The recommendations made by Watson AI matched with the physician that 81% for colon cancer, 93% for rectal cancer, and 96% for lung cancer.

The major pitfall of Watson AI is the design and development are based on US patients and their clinical records. The other part of the world cannot use such advanced technology. So, this product may be redesigned and reformed based on geographical location [53].

7.3.1   Personal Genome Diagnostics

Cancer cells tend to evolve and grow rapidly. The DNA is also altered because of the unwanted growth of the cells. These mutations must be identified as early as possible to save the life of a human. For AI products or platforms, the information needed is the type of mutations and how it is changing. Even though there are some tools available to carry out this issue, no tools performed as expected levels. Personal Genome Diagnostics proposed a new machine learning approach that improves mutation identification accuracy. For oncology, PGDx Elio developed to empower the medical diagnosis and to suggest the best approach for treatment.

Clinical Workflow:

Step 1: DNA Extraction—Get the patient DNA samples
Step 2: Preparing Library—Stores the DNA samples
Step 3: Target area for capture
Step 4: Sequencing—NGS
Step 5: Machine Learning algorithm
Step 6: Report

The goal of PGDx is to develop a tool, that can be used anywhere in the world. PGDx developing a new tool called dubbed Cerebro. To automate the mutation detection by using the classifier called random forest. It is trained with millions of clinical data around the world. The previous tools developed by PGDx are PGDx Elio tissue and PGDx Elio pharma resolve [54].

7.3.2   Tempus

A new way to generate the genomic sequence proposed by Tempus genomic profiling to make the data-driven decisions. In oncology, Tempus introduced a new method of sequencing to identify mutations in DNA. Tumor/normal match, RNA sequencing, and automatic conversion from solid to liquid biopsy are three ways to provide data for molecular profiling. Pharmacogenomics is an advanced tool introduced by Tempus to aid the physician working in the neurology and psychiatry field. It aids the doctors by providing complex molecular findings of the patients. For example, it provides PGDx information by analyzing the saliva sample of the patient. Tempus iD an NGS for Covid-19 and other respiratory diseases. It is broader the range of sequence the genomes of virus and safe all clinical data for further discovery or advance in research [55].

7.3.3 iCarbonX—Manage Your Digital Life

iCarbonX is the biggest company for genomic sequencing aims to create an AI platform. It launches the digital health platform called Meum. It offers personalized solutions to the individual in an infinite number of ways. The database contains genetics and molecular data and also behavior data. The advanced feature of this platform is it improves automatically by reading the new clinical data and case studies.

As a personal care guide, Meum helps people by continuous monitoring of present and predicting the future. For example, people can store photos of what food they have eaten, Meum automatically suggests when the nutrition factor becomes low by analyzing intake and nutrition in the food [56].

7.3.4 $H_2O.ai$

Driverless AI is a platform created by $H_2O.ai$. The advanced features of this platform are as follows: it recognizes the images automatically, custom visualization, zero inflation model, multinode support for training the datasets and for regression; it quantifies the uncertainty; and also it improves GUI for interpretability machine learning.

To combat the Covid-19 pandemic, $H_2O.ai$ introduces Q AI application. Q AI can easily augment your data and visualize the datasets and predictions. This app is solving problems like predicting hospital staffing, risk segmentation based on population analysis, and Covid-19 spread prediction [57].

7.3.5 Google DeepMind

Google DeepMind was stepped into healthcare in London at the Royal Free London NHS Trust in the year 2015. To develop software for maintaining patient data. One of the largest providers of healthcare in the U.K. brought the new company to use AI as it has a huge amount of clinical data to maintain. DeepMind Health (DMH) Clinical application, Streams was developed to process patient data for clinician only. It provides secure data transmission between end-users [58].

7.3.6 Buoy Health

Buoy health develops a personalized healthcare assistant. Buoy using AI to chat like humans and when a person needs health-related advice, it provides correct solutions by analyzing symptoms. The working of Buoy AI is simple and easy access. The first step is entering symptoms an input to Buoy. Then, it analyzes and gains detailed knowledge about the corresponding person's case and offers the best solutions. The solutions may be a piece of personalized advice that what he/she has to do next or if they require immediate healthcare it can connect them with the nearest healthcare providers [59].

7.3.7   PathAI

Advanced technology is exclusively developed to concentrate only on pathology for most accurate diagnosis and treatment, with well-renowned partners like LabCorp for clinical precision, Bristol-Myers Squibb for drug development, and Bill & Melinda Gates Foundation for ease access of advanced healthcare around the world at a reasonable cost.

Recently, PathAI tests the third phase of clinical trials to analyze the performances of Opdino, a cancer treatment software developed by its partner Bristol-Myers Squibb. PathAI aims to provide the best solutions for cancer treatments by assisting the pathologist in terms of accurate diagnosis [60].

7.3.8   Beth Israel Deaconess Medical Center

BIDMC is one of the largest healthcare providers in New England associated with the Harvard Cancer Center. BILH (Beth Israel Lahey Health) is currently developing an algorithm called SSA (Sepsis Surveillance Algorithm) for continuous monitoring of patients who are at the risk of Sepsis. The development of SSA is based on advanced machine learning to integrate all kinds of clinical data.

BIDMC is also associated with the Bill & Melinda Gates Foundation to help poor people around the world. As a part of this, doctors from BILH visited a northern state of India to set a medical camp. A real-life experience shared by one of the doctors is detailed in ref. It explains how telemedicine and machine learning saved a women's life [61].

7.3.9   Bioxcel Therapeutics

To identify the next generation of medicines for oncology and neuroscience by utilizing AI, Bioxcel therapeutics developed two clinical programs recently. BXCL701 is for the treatment of prostatic cancer and BXCL501 is for the acute treatment of neuropsychiatric disorders [62].

7.3.10   BERG

Interrogative Biology is an AI-powered platform at the clinical stage developed by BERG. The development of this platform aims to create a revolution in the treatment of neurology, oncology, and other rare diseases. It was built using patient biology as frontend and mathematics AI as backend. bAIcs is an analytical platform used to feed the data into Interrogative biology. bAIcs has a huge amount of patient data and also the entire history of that disease.

By combining both Interrogative Biology and bAIcs, BERG introduced a new way to discover and treatment process. Two simple steps have to follow to generate the data in bAIcs. First, the platform identifies the target and analyze the treatment carried out. It collects all the clinical data including samples collected, quality of treatment, and the cost in the next step.

The heart of Interrogative Biology is bAIcs, Bayesian AI-based software. The functions of bAIcs are to gain knowledge using a data-driven method, capable of managing large datasets, the scalable cloud, and parallel operation. In a digital world, bAIcs is used for diagnosis, prognosis, and treatment for patients. Interrogative Biology is a novel automatic platform for different biomedical applications [63].

7.3.11   Enlitic

To advance the medical diagnosis, the enclitic tries to connect AI with humans. It uses deep learning methods to collect worldwide clinical data aims to help doctors diagnose the diseases sooner with better accuracy. For that, it connects world-class data scientists to get the data from radiologists [64].

7.3.12   Deep Genomics

Deep Genomics aims to create a new world for automatic drug development using AI. Project Saturn is the first drug delivery system built for molecular biology. Over 69 billion molecules evaluated against one million targets *in silico*. This AI workbench aims to discover novel therapies for diseases with high risk. Some of the researches in the pipeline are Wilson disease, undisclosed metabolic, and undisclosed retinopathy. This workbench uses deep learning algorithms at the backend to analyze over 10^{50} compounds in molecular biology [65].

7.3.13   Freenome

Multiomics is a platform developed by Freenome to detect cancer using machine learning and molecular biology. Precision therapies will be possible by using this platform that will reduce the burden of clinicians.

Multiomics platform is trained around thousands of positive case blood samples and also trained with healthy blood samples to analyze the variance between positive and negative cases of cancer. This will be very useful in determining cancer at an early stage. To fight more effectively than humans against cancer, it follows a novel way consists of cell-free cancer biology and machine learning.

The cell-free cancer biology process analyzes the RNA, proteins, and DNA in blood plasma. Machine learning decodes the billions of extremely complex patterns related to results obtained in earlier steps to diagnose the early stage of the tumor [66].

7.3.14   CloudMedX

An extreme collection of clinical data to increase access for everyone. It adapts AI for gathering and organizing data from the data providers. Aligned Intelligence is a deep learning platform developed by CloudMedX for predictive analysis. It works in three steps. First, it gathers data from healthcare providers, and the data may be unstructured. Second, it curates and converts the data to identify key patterns. Third, actionable insights for suggesting better solutions. Through the Aligned Intelligence platform, CloudMedX transforms the transplant process to find high-risk patients and prioritize them. This platform is used to match the donor and recipients to provide accurate analysis [67].

7.3.15   Proscia

Proscia provides AI-powered digital pathology solutions. The process of research and diagnosis of cancer is redefined by its digital platform called Concentriq. To advance the practice, Proscia releases its application called DermAI for pathology. DermAI uses a deep learning method to provide automatic solutions and the classification of thousands of various diseases related to skin. DermAI is trained with millions of clinical data from pathologists. It offers an intelligence prioritizing system to optimize the distribution of cases to the doctors so that the high-risk patients to be examined first. Usage of DermAI in clinical labs provides the best solutions to the clinicians and also it updates the library periodically [68].

7.4   Conclusion

A brief note is given about the AI algorithms and intelligent mechanisms that are developed by AI experts. For personal use, AI is going to reside with us. The future healthcare is going to depend on AI systems for diagnosis, prognosis, and treatment. Telemedicine is going to rule the world without a doctor. Instead of doctors, an intelligent system will be employed for the treatment of patients. Narrow-down researches are going on and some approaches are in clinical trials for customized service for the patients.

References

1. Libbrecht, M.W. and Noble, W.S., Machine learning applications in genetics and genomics. *Nat. Rev. Genet.*, 16, 321–32, 2015.
2. Hamet, P. and Tremblay, J., Artificial intelligence in medicine. *Metabolism.*, 69S, S36–S40, 2017.
3. Beam, L. and Kohane, I.S., Big data and machine learning in healthcare. *JAMA - J. Am. Med. Assoc.*, 319, 13, 1317–1318, 2018.
4. Handelman, G.S., Kok, H.K., Chandra, R.V., Razavi, A.H., Lee, M.J., Asadi, H., eDoctor: machine learning and the future of medicine. *J. Intern. Med.*, 284, 6, 603–619, 2018.
5. Ramkumar, P.N. *et al.*, Artificial Intelligence and Arthroplasty at a Single Institution: Real-World Applications of Machine Learning to Big Data, Value-Based Care, Mobile Health, and Remote Patient Monitoring. *J. Arthroplasty*, 34, 2204–2209, 2019.
6. Schilaty, N.D., Bates, N.A., Kruisselbrink, S., Krych, A.J., Hewett, T.E., Linear Discriminant Analysis Successfully Predicts Knee Injury Outcome From Biomechanical Variables. *Am. J. Sports Med.*, 48, 10, 2447–2455, 2020.
7. Ali, L., Zhu, C., Zhang, Z., Liu, Y., Automated Detection of Parkinson's Disease Based on Multiple Types of Sustained Phonations Using Linear Discriminant Analysis and Genetically Optimized Neural Network. *IEEE J. Transl. Eng. Heal. Med.*, 7, 1, 2019.
8. Ricciardi, C. *et al.*, Linear discriminant analysis and principal component analysis to predict coronary artery disease. *Health Inf. J.*, 26, 3, 2181–2192, 2020.
9. Moradi, E., Marttinen, M., Häkkinen, T., Hiltunen, M., Nykter, M., Supervised pathway analysis of blood gene expression profiles in Alzheimer's disease. *Neurobiol. Aging*, 84, 98–108, 2019.
10. Sevy, A.M., Soto, C., Bombardi, R.G., Meiler, J., Crowe, J.E., Immune repertoire fingerprinting by principal component analysis reveals shared features in subject groups with common exposures. *BMC Bioinf.*, 20, 1, 1–10, 2019.

11. Sharon, H., Elamvazuthi, I., Lu, C., Parasuraman, S., Development of Rheumatoid Arthritis Classification from Electronic Image Sensor Using Ensemble Method. *Sensors 2020*, 20, 1671–26, 2019.
12. Wang, C. *et al.*, Exploratory study on classification of lung cancer subtypes through a combined K-nearest neighbor classifier in breathomics. *Sci. Rep.*, 10, 1, 1–12, 2020.
13. Arian, R., Hariri, A., Mehridehnavi, A., Fassihi, A., Ghasemi, F., Protein kinase inhibitors' classification using K-Nearest neighbor algorithm. *Comput. Biol. Chem.*, 86, March, 107269, 2020.
14. Zakaria, L., Ebeid, H.M., Dahshan, S., Tolba, M.F., Analysis of Classification Methods for Gene Expression Data, in: *The International Conference on Advanced Machine Learning Technologies and Applications (AMLTA2019)*, A. Hassanien, A. Azar, T. Gaber, R. Bhatnagar, M.F. Tolba (Eds), 2020, AMLTA, *Advances in Intelligent Systems and Computing*, vol. 921, Springer, Cham, 2019.
15. Schlkopf, B., Tsuda, K., Vert, J.P., *Kernel methods in computational biology*, MIT Press series on Computational Molecular Biology, Berlin.
16. Spini, G., van Heesch, M., Veugen, T., Chatterjea, S., Private Hospital Workflow Optimization via Secure k-Means Clustering. *J. Med. Syst.*, 44, 1, 2020.
17. Li, L., Song, Q., Yang, X., K-means clustering of overweight and obese population using quantile-transformed metabolic data, *Diabetes Metab. Syndr. Obes. Targets Ther.*, 12, 1573–1582, 2019.
18. Guo, X., Lin, H., Wu, Y., Peng, M., A new data clustering strategy for enhancing mutual privacy in healthcare IoT systems. *Futur. Gener. Comput. Syst.*, 113, 407–417, 2020.
19. Kachouie, N.N., Shutaywi, M., Christiani, D.C., Discriminant Analysis of Lung Cancer Using Nonlinear Clustering of Copy Numbers. *Cancer Invest.*, 38, 2, 102–112, 2020.
20. Sithambranathan, M., Kasim, S., Hassan, M.Z., Rodzuan, N.A.S., Identification of Gene of Melanoma Skin Cancer Using Clustering Algorithms. *Int. J. Data Sci.*, 1, 1, 51–56, 2020.
21. Gelbard, R.B. *et al.*, Random forest modeling can predict infectious complications following trauma laparotomy. *J. Trauma Acute Care Surg.*, 87, 5, 1125–1132, 2019.
22. Kokla, J., Virtanen, M., Kolehmainen, J., Paananen, K., Hanhineva, Random forest-based imputation outperforms other methods for imputing LC-MS metabolomics data: A comparative study. *BMC Bioinf.*, 20, 1, 1–11, 2019.
23. Wu, J. *et al.*, Predicting in-hospital rupture of type A aortic dissection using Random Forest. *J. Thorac. Dis.*, 11, 11, 4634–4646, 2019.
24. Yao, D., Zhan, X., Kwoh, C.K., An improved random forest-based computational model for predicting novel miRNA-disease associations. *BMC Bioinf.*, 20, 1, 1–14, 2019.

25. Xiang, S., Li, L., Wang, L., Liu, J., Tan, Y., Hu, J., A decision tree model of cerebral palsy based on risk factors. *J. Matern. Neonatal Med.*, 0, 0, 1–6, 2019.

26. Zhu, R., Duan, H., Wang, S., Gan, L., Xu, Q., Li, J., Decision Tree Analysis: A Retrospective Analysis of Postoperative Recurrence of Adhesions in Patients with Moderate-to-Severe Intrauterine. *BioMed. Res. Int.*, 2019, 2019.

27. Li, H. *et al.*, Decision tree model for predicting in-hospital cardiac arrest among patients admitted with acute coronary syndrome. *Clin. Cardiol.*, 42, 11, 1087–1093, 2019.

28. Chen, T., *et al.*, A gastric cancer LncRNAs model for MSI and survival prediction based on support vector machine. *BMC Genomics*, 20, 1, 1–7, 2019.

29. Abbas, H.T. *et al.*, Predicting long-term type 2 diabetes with support vector machine using oral glucose tolerance test. *PloS One*, 14, 12, 1–11, 2019.

30. Cavaliere, C. *et al.*, Computer-aided diagnosis of multiple sclerosis using a support vector machine and optical coherence tomography features. *Sensors (Switzerland)*, 19, 23, 2019.

31. Li, S.S.W., Chu, C.C.F., Chow, D.H.K., EMG-based lumbosacral joint compression force prediction using a support vector machine. *Med. Eng. Phys.*, 74, 115–120, 2019.

32. Meng, C., Wei, L., Zou, Q., SecProMTB: Support Vector Machine-Based Classifier for Secretory Proteins Using Imbalanced Data Sets Applied to Mycobacterium tuberculosis. *Proteomics*, 19, 17, 1–8, 2019.

33. Ogawa, R. *et al.*, Objective Assessment of the Utility of Chromoendoscopy with a Support Vector Machine. *J. Gastrointest. Cancer*, 50, 3, 386–391, 2019.

34. Peña-Bautista, C., Durand, T., Oger, C., Baquero, M., Vento, M., Cháfer-Pericás, C., Assessment of lipid peroxidation and artificial neural network models in early Alzheimer Disease diagnosis. *Clin. Biochem.*, 72, December 2018, 64–70, 2019.

35. Choi, H.I. *et al.*, Artificial Intelligent Model with Neural Network Machine Learning for the Diagnosis of Orthognathic Surgery. *J. Craniofac. Surg.*, 30, 72019, 1986–1989, 2019.

36. Buza, N. and Dizdar, M., Classification of Prediabetes and Type 2 Diabetes Using Artificial Neural Network. *IFMBE Proceedings 62*, vol. 62, 2017.

37. Juhn, Y., and Liu, H., Artificial intelligence approaches using natural language processing to advance EHR-based clinical research. *J. Allergy Clin. Immunol.*, 145, 2, 463–469, 2020.

38. Hughes, K.S., Zhou, J., Bao, Y., Singh, P., Wang, J., Yin, K., Natural language processing to facilitate breast cancer research and management. *Breast J.*, 26, 1, 92–99, 2020.

39. Wang, L., Luo, L., Wang, Y., Wampfler, J., Yang, P., Liu, H., Natural language processing for populating lung cancer clinical research data. *BMC Med. Inform. Decis. Mak.*, 19, Suppl 5, 1–10, 2019.

40. Banerjee, I. *et al.*, Natural Language Processing Approaches to Detect the Timeline of Metastatic Recurrence of Breast Cancer. *JCO Clin. Cancer Inform.*, 1–12, 2020.

41. Kang, S.K. *et al.*, Natural Language Processing for Identification of Incidental Pulmonary Nodules in Radiology Reports. *J. Am. Coll. Radiol.*, 16, 11, 1587–1594, 2019.

42. Thirukumaran, C.P. *et al.*, Natural Language Processing for the Identification of Surgical Site Infections in Orthopaedics. *J. Bone Joint Surg. Am.*, 101, 24, 1–8, 2019.

43. Ting, D.S.W. *et al.*, Deep learning in ophthalmology: The technical and clinical considerations. *Prog. Retin. Eye Res.*, 72, 100759, 2019.

44. Ismael, S.A.A., Mohammed, A., Hefny, H., An enhanced deep learning approach for brain cancer MRI images classification using residual networks. *Artif. Intell. Med.*, 102, 101779, 2020.

45. Marsh, J.N. *et al.*, Deep learning global glomerulosclerosis in transplant kidney frozen sections. *IEEE Trans. Med. Imaging*, 37, 12, 2718–2728, 2018.

46. Hu, Q., Whitney, H.M., Giger, M.L., A deep learning methodology for improved breast cancer diagnosis using multiparametric MRI. *Sci. Rep.*, 10, 1, 1–11, 2020.

47. Wang, S., Yang, D.M., Rong, R., Zhan, X., Xiao, G., Pathology Image Analysis Using Segmentation Deep Learning Algorithms. *Am. J. Pathol.*, 189, 9, 1686–1698, 2019.

48. Yim, J. *et al.*, Predicting conversion to wet age-related macular degeneration using deep learning. *Nat. Med.*, 26, 6, 892–899, 2020.

49. Reddy, G.T. *et al.*, An Ensemble based Machine Learning model for Diabetic Retinopathy Classification. *Int. Conf. Emerg. Trends Inf. Technol. Eng. ic-ETITE 2020*, 1–6, 2020.

50. Dhanya, R., Paul, I.R., Akula, S.S., Sivakumar, M., Nair, J.J., F-test feature selection in Stacking ensemble model for breast cancer prediction. *Proc. Comput. Sci.*, 171, 2019, 1561–1570, 2020.

51. Sarwar, A., Ali, M., Manhas, J., Sharma, V., Diagnosis of diabetes type-II using hybrid machine learning based ensemble model. *Int. J. Inf. Technol.*, 12, 2, 419–428, 2020.

52. Brunese, L., Mercaldo, F., Reginelli, A., Santone, A., An ensemble learning approach for brain cancer detection exploiting radiomic features. *Comput. Methods Programs Biomed.*, 185, 105134, 2020.

53. IBM Watson products and solutions, https://www.ibm.com/in-en/watson/products-services.

54. Personal Genome Diagnostics (PGDx), https://www.personalgenome.com/company.

55. Tempus, https://www.tempus.com/applications/.

56. iCarbonX – Manage your digital life, https://www.icarbonx.com/en/about.html.

57. H2O.ai, https://www.h2o.ai/products/.

58. Google Deepmind, https://deepmind.com/research.

59. Buoy health, https://www.buoyhealth.com/learn.

60. PathAI, https://www.pathai.com/news/.

61. Beth Israel Deaconess Medical Center, https://www.bidmc.org/centers-and-departments.
62. Bioxcel Therapeutics, https://www.bioxceltherapeutics.com/product-pipeline.
63. BERG, https://www.berghealth.com/research/.
64. Enlitic, https://www.enlitic.com/.
65. Deep Genomics, https://www.deepgenomics.com/platform/.
66. Freenome, https://www.freenome.com/preempt-crc-study.
67. CloudMedX, https://cloudmedxhealth.com/solutions/.
68. Proscia, https://proscia.com/news-resources/.

8

Smart Homes and Smart Cities

C. N. Marimuthu* and G. Arthy

Nandha Engineering College, Perundurai, India

Abstract

We are living in an era of technological revolution. Humans are trying to invade technology at various phases of life. As a result of this, new technological inventions are made at a rapid phase. People also like to have a sophisticated life which also enthused for various inventions. "Smart homes and smart cities" are also a part of human intelligence. Artificial intelligence and Internet of things are deployed by human intelligence for a smart living. In this chapter, the first section will be discussing briefly about the evolution of smart homes, basic architecture, and the various technologies involved in designing a smart home. Further, few specific applications of smart homes are discussed along with the advantages and disadvantages. The second section briefly discuss about the smart cities. It includes smart city framework, architecture of smart cities, and components of smart cities. Added to this, characteristics and challenges of smart cities are discussed.

Keywords: Smart homes, smart cities, Internet of Things (IoT), architecture, technologies

8.1 Smart Homes

8.1.1 Introduction

"Smart Homes" sounds really smart and delightful. Everyone like an altruistic smart act in our day-to-day life. Obviously, we all would like to have a system which turns ON the coffee maker and the heater immediately as we woke up from the bed. Similarly we all love to control the lighting, to control electronic appliances like TV and washing machines, to adjust the

---

Corresponding author: muthu_me2005@yahoo.co.in

C. Venkatesh, N. Rengarajan, P. Ponmurugan and S. Balamurugan (eds.) Smart Systems for Industrial Applications, (199–224) © 2022 Scrivener Publishing LLC

window blinds, temperature control using thermostat, etc., from our couch. Moreover, when we are away from home, smart home can help us to monitor our kids at home, exchange voice messages, control the TV channels which they watch and also can have limitations on the screen time. Motion sensors can be used to find any intruders at our home which enhances our safety and security. These sensors are smart enough to differentiate between pets and burglars. Smart home doors can be locked remotely which dismays most of us midst our busy schedule. The advantages of smart homes cannot be limited to this. The door locks can be opened automatically when we approach them; during night times, the lights can be turned ON in the pathways which helps elderly people, automatic alarms from security systems, refrigerators which gives food recipe ideas based on the available ingredients, lights can be turned OFF automatically if no one is present inside rooms, notify elderly persons about their regular medications, and medical checkups and many more. The applications and advantages of smart homes are not limited to this. It extends its graceful hands in every aspect of our life.

As like two sides of a coin, every technology has its own pros and cons. In this digital era, a smart home becomes an inevitable part of our life. On the other hand, it is expensive. When the numbers of connected devices increase, the cost also increases. Moreover, this technology may not be user friendly for the elderly people. Also, it makes our life style sedentary. Above all, since all the data are shared in the common pool it is important to focus more on the privacy and security policies.

In this chapter, we will be discussing about the evolution, architecture, technologies, and different applications of smart homes in Section 8.1 and about smart cities in Section 8.2.

8.1.2 Evolution of Smart Home

A smart home is the one where the electronic gadgets of that home are interconnected to each other so that they can communicate with each other. Commands can be given to them through remote control or voice or smart phones. Figure 8.1 shows a sample smart home.

The idea of smart home emerged since 1898 when the first remote control was invented by Nikola Tesla. In the beginning of 1900s, the industrial revolution led to the introduction of various household appliances like vacuum cleaner followed by the washing machine, refrigerator, dish washers, etc. These equipment are not smart or automatic, but they paved the way for smart machines. Later in 1930s, many efforts were taken to introduce automatic machines. But the inventers could not materialize them. In 1966, the

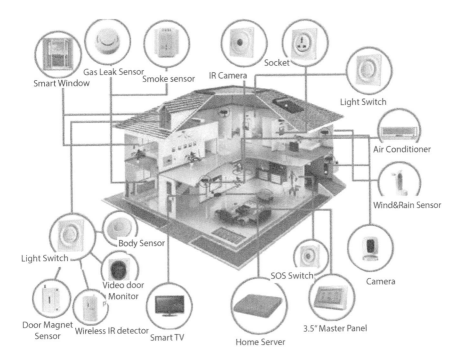

Figure 8.1 A sample smart home.

first smart automation system, called the Echo IV was developed which create shopping lists, turn ON and OFF the electrical appliances, and helps to control the temperature inside the home. In 1966, a kitchen computer was developed which helps in creating recipes with the available raw materials. It was very costly due to which could not succeed commercially.

The development of microcontroller in 1971 was a boon to the electronic industry. The cost of various electronic appliances was reduced due to their design using of microcontrollers. After this, during 1980s, various systems like the programmable thermostat, systems for home security, and automatic door opening systems were introduced.

The phrase smart home was coined by the American Association of House builders in 1984 which was just a dream! Later in 1996, the invention of clapper paved the way for smart homes. When the internet technology blooms, the dream of smart home also started to flourish. In 1999, the phrase Internet of Things (IoT) was defined by Kevin Ashton of MIT. In 1998 and early 2000, smart home products like portable MP3 players and smart phones were introduced in the market. High-speed broadband home networking technologies to connect multiple devices emerged in

2003. Numerous consumer gadgets occupied the market. Globally, smart home automation became the marketing trend after 2000. The life was made easier for the consumers by controlling the heaters, televisions, lights, doors, MP3 players, security alarms, etc., via remote controllers and smartphones. A survey by Statistic says that the Indian smart home market is expected to be around $6 billion by 2022.

8.1.3   Smart Home Architecture

Smart home is where the devices of a home interact with each other as well as with the human beings based on the given instructions. Connecting the worldwide internet and the smart objects at our home is a great idea which we call it as the smart home. Before discussing the technology behind this awesome idea, let us have a look at the major components involved in a smart home [1].

Figure 8.2 shows the architecture of smart homes.

The main components of the smart home are as follows:

1. Smart electrical devices or smart plugs
2. Home intelligent terminals or home area networks
3. Master network

8.1.3.1   Smart Electrical Devices or Smart Plugs

The smart home architecture comprises of the smart household devices such as the television, washing machine, air conditioners, refrigerators, smart watches, CCTVs installed for security, home theatres, even the

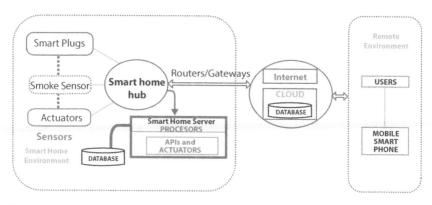

Figure 8.2 Architecture of smart homes.

lights and fans. Moreover, various sensors like the smoke sensors, temperature sensors, motion sensors, and gas leakage sensors constitute the end device [2]. These end devices should be either smart devices or it should be plugged in to smart sockets. Smart plug is an affordable smart home integration option. The smart plug connects our appliances to the internet without any hub. The smart plug has to be inserted in any wall socket and then the selected appliance should be connected to the smart plug. So, any household electrical appliances can be upgraded by connecting it to a smart plug which can be controlled through any smart plug app.

8.1.3.2   Home Intelligent Terminals or Home Area Networks

The smart appliances or the smart plugs are generally app-based devices which are connected through a network, commonly Home Area Networks (HAN) through Wi-Fi, Bluetooth, Zigbee, or Z waves [3]. These devices are connected to a gateway somewhere, which could be accessed through apps on your smart device. To this HAN, wired devices as well as wireless devices could be connected.

8.1.3.3   Master Network

Smart home hub is an important feature of smart home network. A smart home hub is normally a device (hardware) or a mobile app (software) which acts as the master home automation controller. It connects different devices to a common platform and controls all the appliances or the systems in a home. This helps to collect the data from the devices and forward it to the required devices. A smart home hub typically has an integrated switch, which holds the required information regarding the transfer of data. It has some computing capabilities which perform some basic tasks like scheduling and controlling of tasks before transfer of data.

Many smart home devices have their own branded hubs. They may not be compatible with other smart devices. For example, if a gas leakage sensor detects the gas leakage, then it may not be able to command the smart windows to open for the gas to exit or disconnect the power supply for safety. For such circumstances, dedicated smart home hubs will co-ordinate these entire functions. This dedicated hub combines the functionalities of all individual hubs and acts as a centralized control. If all the connected devices in a home run on Wi-Fi, there is no need for a smart home hub. Smart speakers can also be used as smart home hub. But they may not be compatible with all the protocols and devices.

Through the hub, the devices are connected to the smart gateway or the router. Routers are used if all the devices are connected using same protocol and gateway is used if devices with different protocols are connected. Here, let us use the term gateway assuming that different devices using different protocols are connected. The smart gateway is connected to the cloud network. The cloud structure helps in storing the data and giving commands to the hub based on the information received from the user. After performing the task, the hub will update the details in the cloud network. Now, the devices are connected to the internet and the term Internet of Things (IoT) comes to the picture. The total framework is connected to the smart phones through internet which helps to track and control the activities taking place in the smart home from a remote location. For example, if you have scheduled an event like turning ON the washing machine or the food warmer, based on the input information stored on the cloud, then the desired task will take place and the notification is send to the user. Suppose if any intruder enters inside the house, then the motion sensor will send the information to the cloud network through the hub and gateway and immediate notification is send to the user at any part of the world. This smart home architecture enhances our life style and makes it more comfortable with the pervasiveness of internet. To this framework, other applications like any factories or other members of the family, police, doctors, or parents also could be connected.

8.1.4   Smart Home Technologies

The smart home architecture consists of different components as discussed earlier. For the effective communication of all these components, obviously communication protocols are required. The communication protocols can be either wired or wireless. Few of them are X10, Z-waves, Zigbee, Wi-Fi, Bluetooth, etc. Initially, the idea of smart home was possible with any devices connected to electricity in a home. The X10 wired protocol allows appliances to communicate with the help of existing electrical wires. But this mode of communication is not reliable due to the disturbances in the power line. X10 and its protocol are not compatible with other devices and protocols, which is another major drawback.

Then, radio waves were used for communication. All the smart devices relayed on Wi-Fi network. But Wi-Fi networks are battery draining. So, two familiar radio networks especially for smart homes emerged in the market. They are the Z-waves and ZigBee technologies. Both these technologies use the mesh network topology. Z-waves apply source routing algorithm while the ZigBee searches for the best path to reach the receiver. The operating frequency of ZigBee is 2.4 GHz which is very high. The operating frequency of Z-waves is 908 MHz which is very low. The Zigbee can transmit more data due to the high operating frequency but the range attained by the signal is very low. When there are any obstacles between two devices, the range even gets reduced. When the range is low, the reliability will be less. More number of devices can be connected using Zigbee protocol while only 232 devices could be connected using Z-waves [4]. The use of Z-waves or Zigbee purely depends upon the user applications. Unlike communication through electrical wires, the wireless technologies provide more flexibility while connecting devices. For fast data transmission, Zigbee could be used, and for a reliable transmission, Z-waves could be used.

In order to operate and control the smart home from a remote location using smart phones, we require internet. Smart devices with Wi-Fi are easy to install. But devices with Wi-Fi consume more power when compared to Z-Wave and Zigbee devices. More number of Wi-Fi devices in a smart home may hinder the performance of the network. But without Wi-Fi, smart homes cannot be connected with the cloud through which other smart phones or applications are connected. In order to overcome this, Zigbee and Z-wave devices which are independent of Wi-Fi are used in a HAN. If the smart device is compatible with Wi-Fi, then it can directly connect with the existing home Wi-Fi network. Instead, if the smart device uses Zigbee or Z wave, then it requires a gateway. Gateway is used to connect two dissimilar networks.

Another common yet simple wireless technology is the Bluetooth technology. It is easy to install and controlled by mobile app. For instance, fan and light control systems can use Bluetooth technology. It consumes very less energy compare to Wi-Fi. Due to its limited range it cannot be used remotely.

Now, the systems are interconnected globally using the Internet Protocol Suite (TCP/IP). Now, we can connect any device to internet; from a simple sensor to smart phone as well as any appliances at our house and they can communicate with each other which is known as the IoT. The key feature of IoT is the RFID (Radio Frequency Identification number) and sensor technology. IoT-based smart home collects the data, does basic processing, and transmits it to the cloud structure for further processing. Cloud is where a large pool of data is stored and shared for further processing.

8.1.5 Smart Grid Technology

While discussing about homes, smart grid technologies also should be discussed. Smart grid is a two-way digital communication system with distributed generation. Smart grid uses smart meters which helps people to conserve energy. Smart meter acts as an interfacing device between us and our energy supplier. It helps utilities to gather information about the energy consumption of a particular area. Energy consumption limits can also be set if smart energy meters are installed in user premises. Now, the Government of India is under the mission of installing smart energy meters which is an added advantage for smart homes. The energy consumption limit for every smart home appliance is fixed and alert messages are sent when it exceeds the limit. The high energy consuming smart home devices like dish washers, water heaters, and air conditioners are equipped with facilities such that they are turned OFF during peak load demand hours. The end user can also control those devices. For example, if a customer does not care about using a high load appliance during peak load demand hours, then they can use it by paying more.

Nowadays, more awareness is created among people for the installation of home solar system systems and small wind turbines for generating their own energy. The smart grids with the smart energy meters help in collecting and co-ordinating these small power generators. With the help of smart grid, the local power generated is used by the customer. Any excess power requirement is met by the utility.

8.1.6 Smart Home Applications

Let us discuss few smart home applications in this section.

8.1.6.1 Smart Home in the Healthcare of Elderly People

The United Nations Population Fund and Help Age India have released a report regarding the growth rate of elderly people in India. It has predicted that the count of elderly people will grow to 173 million by 2026 [5]. So, it is necessary and important to design and develop systems which support the elderly people. What kind of applications could be equipped in a smart home for these elderly people? Many elder people live alone preferring to manage themselves with all the household chores. Some may require personal assistance. Design of smart home systems with remote monitoring and some facilities for healthcare will be a great support to them. Wearable electronics is also a great leap in the smart healthcare systems. Sensors or actuators can be fixed in any part of the body or can be attached with the worn items like dress, watch, and wrist bands. This is generally used to monitor a person continuously. This is used greatly for elderly people. Moreover, it is used in athletes and military people.

8.1.6.2   Smart Home in Education

The Covid-19 pandemic has led to a great reform in teaching-learning process. Education has now become digital. Smart class rooms were setup at homes. With the help of technology, exams, workshops, and seminars were also conducted online which has changed the scenario totally.

8.1.6.3   Smart Lighting

The ambience of a home is completely decided by the lightings. In a smart home, the sensors can sense our mood swing and the lighting can be changed accordingly, either relaxing or exciting. Moreover, existing applications like the Alexa from Amazon, Siri a virtual assistant from Apple Inc., plays a major role in smart home. If we ask "Alexa, what is the date?" or "Alexa, control the intensity of lights to 20%" or "Alexa, turn off the garage lights" those tasks can be done simply by sitting on a couch.

8.1.6.4   Smart Surveillance

Considering safety and security, surveillance is a must in many places. But in certain places like the bank lockers or homes continuous monitoring is not required because it leads to a lot of data storage and power consumption. So, we go for smart surveillance where the human presence is not available frequently. Smart surveillance systems use sensors which detects and produce alarms only if there is a human intervention. They can also differentiate between a human movement and animal movement like cats.

8.1.7   Advantages and Disadvantages of Smart Homes

There are many advantages of smart homes which include the following: (i) All the devices of a home can be controlled by simply sitting on a couch; (ii) the smart home can be monitored and controlled from any remote location; (iii) very flexible for adding new smart devices with the existing infrastructure; (iv) smart homes are highly secure; (v) efficient use of energy is possible; (vi) design can be customized as per our convenience. Every advancement in technology has its own disadvantages. Few are as follows: (i) initial capital investment of more; (ii) it makes a sedentary life style; (iii) privacy and security issues are a major threat; (iv) for remote villages/places, high-speed internet is yet a dream.

8.2   Smart Cities

8.2.1   Introduction

What defines a smart city and why we are interested on it? Due to the abrupt growth of Information and Communication technology (ICT), we all turn our focus toward smart cities. The concept of smart city differs from one country to another and from one state to another. The Government is encouraging the communities to submit various proposals for smart city projects depending on the current scenario of development and the existing resources. In simple terms, a smart city can be defined as where the existing facilities are made more comfortable, flexible, highly efficient, and feasible with the help of ICT, to improve the quality of life, to provide sustainable ecosystem, and to find smart solutions to very problem [6]. The UK Department of Business considers smart cities as a process rather than an outcome in which more citizens are involved, and hard infrastructure and digital technologies make it a better space for living. The British Standards Institute defines it as "the effective integration of physical, digital and human systems in the built environment to deliver sustainable, prosperous, and inclusive future of its citizens".

The important feature of smart cities is that the digital technologies are used to serve every single citizen. The problems of common man are analyzed, and an application or system is developed with the help of technology. If it is sustainable, then it forms a solution. This forms the bionetwork of smart cities [7] which is shown in Figure 8.3.

Smart cities possess different components, characteristics, necessities, and infrastructure at different countries and states [8]. As per the standardization by the ISO, no specific standards were mentioned. But it is understood that the characteristics of smart cities should provide a quality and safe bionetwork.

In a smart home, all the devices are connected through Wi-Fi or some home networks and can be controlled by remotes or any android mobiles from any part of the world. When it comes to a smart city, the ICT plays a major role. For example, if a smart dustbin is installed in a particular place, then it intimates the respective corporation officials once if it is filled. Similarly, it helps to improve waste management, water management, transportation, e-governance, health, energy management, etc.,

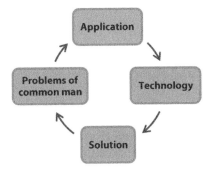

Figure 8.3 Bionetwork of smart cities.

8.2.2 Smart City Framework

ICT is the basic framework of smart cities. It includes the IoT technology, sensors, secure wireless connectivity, and the centralized shared data pool, that is, the cloud control system. The smart city framework involves three basic functions:

(i) **Creation:** At this stage, the data is collected using different sensors, distributed throughout the city. For example, temperature sensor, light intensity, pollution, vehicles, books in library, medical data, etc.

(ii) **Integration:** The data that is collected using sensors is send to the control or management center. Here comes the IoT, where the devices can communicate with each other. Intelligent controllers can play its own role here. Artificial intelligent controllers can also be used at the management center where decisions can also be taken automatically at appropriate places, which ease the burden of the government officials as well as help the citizens smartly at every instance. For example, a smart water meter installed at homes collect data about the water usage and can supply water based on our requirement. It can help drivers to find out the available parking spaces nearer. Also, it can give intimation about the road conditions and the traffic congestion on the route of our travel, thereby can suggest alternate routes too. Therefore, smart cities are a boon for every citizen.

(iii) **Adoption:** The data collected by the sensors can be used by the government for further analysis. Also, they can collect feedback from the citizens which help them to make improvements accordingly.

Smart city helps us to improve the quality of life by making better decisions and helps the government to have smooth relationship with every citizen.

8.2.3 Architecture of Smart Cities

The smart city architecture is a four-layer architecture. The concept of IoT is the key technical background of smart cities. Figure 8.4 shows the architecture of smart city. Much theoretical architectures are available for smart cities. The general layers available in almost any kind of smart city frame work are discussed here. The sensing layer includes any kind of sensors, actuators, devices etc., which can be wired or wireless.

Data capturing is the main task in smart cities because the processing accuracy depends on the clarity and volume of data. The input data is transmitted inside the building or to a short distance using the access networks like Bluetooth, Z-wave, Zigbee, M2M, and RFID. The transmission network is used for transmitting the data over long distances using 3G, 4G, LTE, low-power wide area networks, 6LoWPAN, etc. Then, the

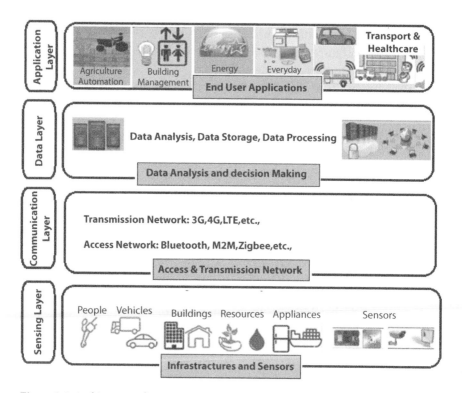

Figure 8.4 Architecture of smart cities.

data is given to the data processing layer where data fusion, data organization, data manipulation, data analysis, data storage, and decision-making takes place. It is the core layer that lies in between the input (sensing) layer and the application layer. Data fusion is where heterogeneous types of data are processed together to make decisions. For example, we may require an input from the camera as well as the sensor to make certain decision, wherein both the data are of different types. Intelligent operations take place in the data layer. Finally, the application layer is through which the citizens enjoy the smartness of the cities.

8.2.4   Components of Smart Cities

The important components of a smart city are shown in Figure 8.5. It includes smart energy, smart infrastructure, smart buildings, smart transportation, smart healthcare, smart technology, smart data center or smart e-governance, and smart citizens and education.

Sensors are installed in near vicinity of every smart city component areas which gather the basic information. This collected information is collected in the database using any existing networks like GSM, 3G, and 4G for smart phones. The collected information is then processed and analyzed using semantic techniques [9]. Let us discuss about the components in detail.

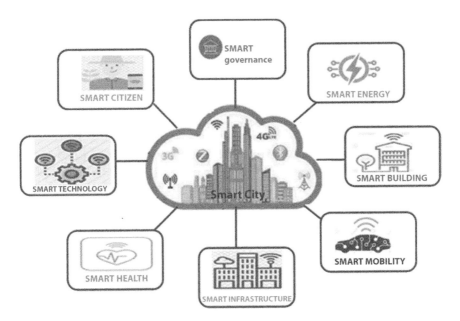

Figure 8.5 Components of smart cities.

8.2.4.1   Smart Technology

Smart technology plays the key role for smart cities. The term "SMART" is an acronym for "Self-Monitoring Analysis and Reporting Technology". The design, implementation, and working of smart cities are all built around the smart technologies. Smart technology begins from the sensors and IoT and now leaps in the revolution of artificial intelligence, machine learning, deep learning, and big data. The smart technologies can never replace a human; instead, they are trained by the human to perform the tasks which we want them to do. Due to the innovation in science and technology and advancement in ICT implementation of smart technologies in smart home and cities, it is becoming cost effective. Smart communication technologies like fiber optics communication to home, Wi-Fi anywhere anytime, Bluetooth technology, and near field communication (NFC) are of great boon. NFC is the base for contact less payments like how the credit cards are being used. Moreover, it forms the groundwork for cashless transaction. The short message service (SMS) also plays a major role in smart technology. The advantages of smart technologies include convenience, it ensures sustainability, it is secure, it saves money and time, and it is highly efficient. Smart technology plays its role from smart grid, smart homes, smart education, smart healthcare, smart industries, and many more. This revolution in technology has broken down all the hindrance in the field of education during the pandemic lockdown. Regular classes, exams, online courses, workshops, admissions, placements, and every sort of activities in education is successfully carried out globally during the Covid-19 lockdown using smart technologies.

8.2.4.2   Smart Infrastructure

Smart infrastructure can be imagined as a case where the different infrastructures of a city like the buildings, hospitals, transport, roads, and bridges communicate with each other as shown in Figure 8.6. Also, the people living in the cities should be able to operate and utilize the infrastructures efficiently. The backbones of the smart cities include a well-established physical network, electrical network, and the digital network or the internet. The ICT coordinates all the networks to make the infrastructure much smarter and to provide a sophisticated life. The smart home infrastructures can be categorised under three major umbrellas: (i) public infra-structure which includes finance, energy, transportation, and hospitals; (ii) home infrastructure; (iii) business infrastructure which includes offices, industries, and data centers. Let us discuss few examples of smart infrastructure for a better understanding.

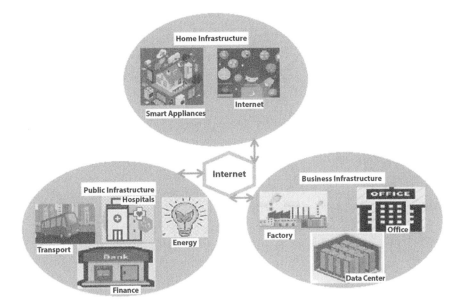

Figure 8.6 Smart infrastructure.

We all like to have a clean and green environment. Air pollution is a major a major concern today. We would have heard that during the Covid-19 lockdown period the atmospheric pollution has reduced to a great extent all over the globe. Now, we have to find a solution to reduce air pollution by managing the traffic efficiently. In [10], a smart sensor was designed for monitoring the air pollution in the city of Thailand. The smart sensor was designed for low power wide area network which consist of a dust sensor, carbon monoxide sensor, carbon dioxide sensor, a noise level sensor, and ozone sensor. With the data observed by the sensors, the air quality index is measured. This can help the people to have knowledge about the quality of air or the air pollution in a particular area which could be transmitted to the users through IoT services.

In India, another major issue is the hygiene. Hence, the Government of India focus on the "Swachh Bharat Mission" program which tries to find various solutions to remove the garbage. Under the component of smart city infrastructure, it is very important to design smart garbage. The smart garbage normally intimates the waste management department for clearing the bins one when it is filled instead of scheduled pick-ups. For the separation of different kinds of wastes, robots could be involved with different sensors.

The problem of traffic congestion is growing day by day. Parking four wheelers is a major problem for people living in cities. It is a daily routine for many people. They waste a lot of time and fuel in searching for a parking space. Moreover, it increases the pollution. Various solutions using the GPS and different sensors are proposed nowadays for this issue. Smart parking systems gather details about the available parking spaces in a selected area and inform it to the drivers. Moreover, predictions can be made where they can likely find a space.

Smart traffic signals not only helps people to overcome waste of time rather saves money as well as reduce the pollution. Using IoT-enabled traffic signals the stop time (red signal) and the go time (green signal) could be adjusted depending on the number of vehicles at the junction. Moreover, the current traffic status could be intimated well in prior to the persons using that particular roadway. This reduces road congestion.

Industries should be upgraded to smart structures. Now, we are at the fourth phase of industrial revolution, i.e., Industry 4.0. A smart factory is where the manual production process is combined with digital technology. Here, the industries relay mainly on real time data and sensors. Tasks are automated with the help of machine learning and artificial intelligence. For instance, if the real time production data is integrated with the predictive record, then the purchase department can be optimized so that the supply of materials can be aligned with the production schedule efficiently. Another example is improving the efficiency gains using machine learning techniques. The data collected from the sensors can be used for the analysis and learning. After machine learning is done, parameters in the software of the machineries can be updated automatically based on the real time scenario which makes the manufacturing process automated. In another case, robots or drones could also be used to handle repeated jobs without any human intervention. Above are few areas where the infrastructures were made smart.

8.2.4.3   Smart Mobility

Smart mobility is the sustainable smart transportation system rather mentioned as intelligent transportation system. Transportation is a major infrastructure which develops the growth of a nation which connects cities and countries. Figure 8.7 shows a pictorial view of Intelligent Transport System (ITS). Economic growth of a country majorly depends on the transportation system.

The ITS updates the users with prior knowledge about the seat availability in a public transport and real-time running information of the bus, and SMS can be delivered to the passenger about the next locations, details about the about traffic, etc. This makes the journey easier and comfortable.

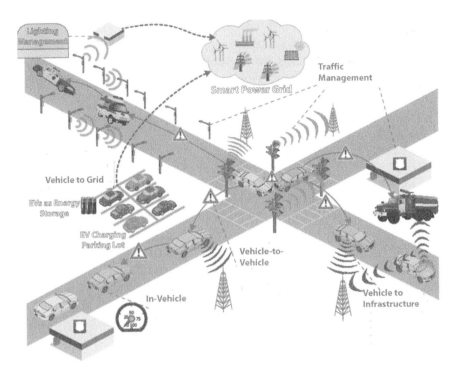

Figure 8.7 Intelligent transportation system [11].

The smart transportation system includes sensors where in the speed of every vehicle could be monitored. RFID-based toll gates also enhance the system which reduces the traffic. Even in airports, electronic passports or RFID-based passports are also implemented which avoids manual checking as well as saves times. Using smart apps for booking taxi, tracking the location of the vehicles, making emergency calls while traveling, and pre-payments through online are few other instances where smart transportation could be realized. In smart transportation, vehicle-to-vehicle as well as vehicle-to-infrastructure communication also takes place which greatly helps to avoid collision and anti-skidding, thereby safety is assured.

8.2.4.4   Smart Buildings

Smart buildings are which we have discussed in Section 8.1. Smart home is an example of smart building. Offices, industries, and apartments are also made smart with the emergence of IoT. Here, let us consider a smart apartment. In an apartment, there are many places where smartness could be practiced. Starting from the door locks, air conditioners, lights, fans, robot vacuum cleaners, smart baby monitors, smart garages, smart cookers, ovens, alarm systems, gas leakage systems, and smart mattress which monitor our sleep patterns, which alarm intimates about our engagements and what not? Few are mentioned here and remaining left to your imagination.

8.2.4.5   Smart Energy

We all prefer a clean energy, green energy, sustainable energy, renewable energy, and smart energy. Generally, if it is a green energy, then we normally refer to it as renewable energy sources like solar and wind. Clean energy is defined as energy without any harmonics or disturbances in the supply. When considered sustainable energy it is not created by human beings, whereas renewable energy is created by human beings. Then, what is smart energy? Smart energy in other terms can be called as "Internet of Energy (IoE)". IoE includes the smart power generation, smart power grids, smart storage, and smart consumption. The smart energy system is shown in Figure 8.8. In essence, any traditional energy, clean energy, green energy, sustainable energy, and renewable energy along with the ICT make smart energy [7].

The smart energy system includes power generation using green energy sources, distribution of the generated power efficiently, and optimized power consumption. Efficient power distribution helps the smart infrastructure, smart grid, smart meters, and the ICT to co-ordinate effectively. Smart meters are also installed at consumer premises to optimize

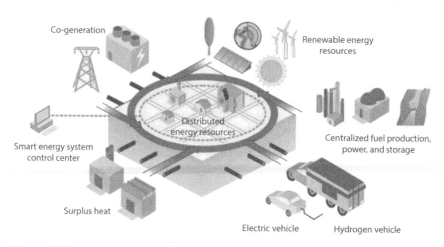

Figure 8.8 Smart energy system [12].

the power utilization. The power consumption details are intimated to the users as well as alert messages were also given if they use heavy load such as dish washers or heaters during high load consuming hours. This helps the uses to save money. It also communicates the reading details for billing without human intervention at the consumer premises. Also, the maximum energy consumption limit alerts can also be given. The core of smart energy system is the smart grid. The smart grid integrates the activities of all connected users like the utility and the consumers. In smart grid, bidirectional communication takes place. Using smart grids, the safety of the system is assured, and it is highly efficient, and quality of supply is good, economical, and with less losses. Nowadays, consumers have starter to generate their own power using solar and wind generators. A smart grid has to synchronize the energy generated from different sources and should provide power without any fluctuation. Electric vehicles are also powered by smart grids.

8.2.4.6   Smart Governance

Smart government or the e-government is an important aspect of smart city. Simple, moral, accountable, responsive, and transparent, i.e., SMART, is the vision behind the Government of India. Smart governance uses the ICT effectively to make decisions by consulting their ideas with the different stakeholders. Social media nowadays plays a key role in analyzing a decision-making because people are much interested in opening up their views through them. During the pandemic period, the e-governance plays a vital role in helping its citizens. Due to the emergence of smart governance, the activities done by the government is transparent, and so the citizens can have detailed information about the funds and developmental works of a city or country. Through web portals, online forums and mobile apps public were able to share their difficulties to the government. Also, public was encouraged to give suggestions to the government. In India, RTI (Right to Information) Act was enacted in 2005 through which an ordinary citizen have the right to ask the government about their decisions, policies, etc., as well as the details of government documents, fund allocations, tenders, etc. This creates a transparency in the government. Moreover, there are websites and apps to report bribery, corruption, civic issues, etc. The features of e-governance mainly include a strong ICT system. During the Covid-19 pandemic lockdown, e-governance gave solution to electricity complaints, travel passes between districts or states, education, and even healthcare consultation all takes place through online.

8.2.4.7   Smart Healthcare

Smart healthcare is a kind of healthcare technology where ICT plays a major role. Diagnosing, monitoring, and preventing the diseases are the good practices that need to be followed concerning our health. Nowadays, people do not find time to take care of their health. The busy schedule makes people to give less priority to health unless it troubles them physically. People are reluctant to notice small signs produced in their body which may later lead to chronic health issues. Smart healthcare systems connect the patients with the doctors or healthcare professionals using intelligent devices. Figure 8.9 shows an example of smart healthcare. The intelligent devices can be biosensors, mobile phones, wearable devices, etc., that help us to monitor our health regularly. They remind us for regular health checkups. Also, they alarm when there is a necessity for a visit to doctor. Early detection of any disease helps to treat easily. The intelligent devices could be connected to smart healthcare services includes remote monitoring of patients, helping patients with chronic diseases like diabetics, blood pressure for monitoring themselves, performance monitoring in the case of physiotherapy patients or patients in rehabilitation centers, etc. The collected real-time data could be monitored by the medical personal in the nearby public health centers or by the hospitals were the patients are associated with. The real-time data will be stored in the cloud which

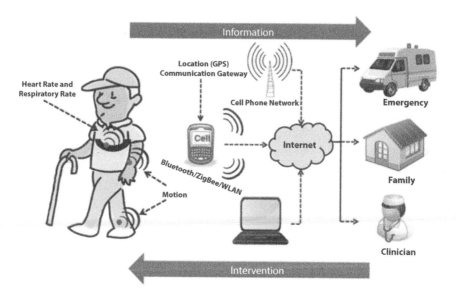

Figure 8.9 Illustration of smart healthcare [13].

facilitates it to be analyzed by doctors from different cities or globally so that easy and clear diagnosis can be made.

Let us consider the Covid-19 situation. Many asymptotic patients were home quarantined due to lack of beds in the hospitals and they were monitored personally or conditions were observed through phone. If we would have developed a good smart healthcare service, then monitoring would have been very easy. By incorporating temperature, respiratory rate sensor, heart rate sensor, and blood pressure sensor in the Covid-positive patients home, they can be closely observed and if they have any drastic symptoms, then, immediately, the data could be alerted to the nearby smart ambulance and hospital.

Another great reformation is the telemedicine. There are many rural areas where hospitals are not easily accessible. Telemedicine services help the people of rural communities by providing immediate medical support in case of medical emergency. Moreover, this service helps the elderly people who cannot visit hospitals with a good nursing care. Many apps were developed to monitor our health. Telemedicine was promoted by the National e-health authority (NeHA) of India with an aim of providing cost-effective and high quality treatment to every citizen. Electronic Health Records (EHR) standards developed in 2013 ensure a secure data transmission [14]. The National Rural AYUSH Telemedicine Network promotes traditional treatments through smart telemedicine. Village Resource Center (VRC) was developed by ISRO for various smart tele-services including telemedicine. During the Corona Virus pandemic, many people who suffer from other medical issues were treated through telemedicine services. The concept of telemedicine is shown in Figure 8.10.

8.2.5   Characteristics of Smart Cities

Deployment of smart cities should focus on the different characteristics or attributes with respect to each and every component. The different characteristics are sustainability, quality of life, urbanization, and smartness [7] as shown in Figure 8.11.

The four pillars of sustainability are environmental, social, economic, and government. A sustainable smart city refers to the one which uses the ICT to maintain the quality in development, operation, and service in all the areas such as infrastructure and governance, energy and climate change, pollution and waste management, social issues, economics, and health. Good physical infrastructure refers to the buildings, railways, road, water facilities, Wi-Fi, uninterrupted quality power supply, etc. Smart infrastructure refers to the ICT. ICT is the backbone which converts good physical infrastructure

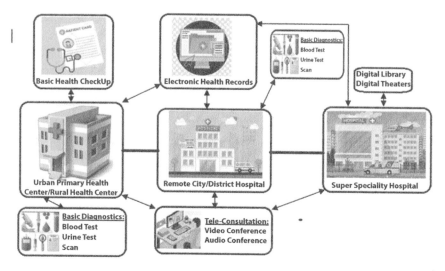

Figure 8.10 Architecture of telemedicine.

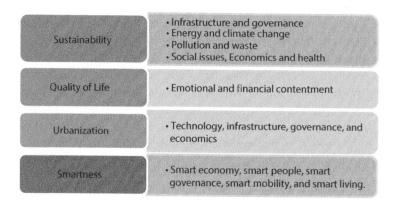

Figure 8.11 Characteristics of smart cities.

to a smart infrastructure. The second character is the Quality of life which includes both the emotional as well as financial contentment. A sustainable smart city provides a quality life both financially and emotionally.

Urbanization refers to movement of people from rural to urban areas due to various reasons. Smart cities are in a developing pace and so people are more curious to move toward urban areas due to the good infrastructure, governance, improved technology, smart healthcare, job availably and steep economic growth. Smart mobility, smart living, smart people, and smart governance lead to smartness in the cities.

8.2.6   Challenges in Smart Cities

Though smart cities improve the quality of life of every individual, it has its own challenges as shown in Figure 8.12. The challenges of smart cities can be at various levels. It can be categorized either at the design or implementation level or the operational level. The implementation level challenges are faced by the government, administration, and citizens. The problem with the government is that it implements a project in collaboration with various sectors including public and private. Effective planning, good leadership, and co-operation of the citizens are all the basic challenges.

Huge funds are required to build a smart city. The cost can also be the initial design cost as well as the maintenance cost. The initial design cost will be very heavy if everything is designed from the scratch. In order to overcome this, we upgrade the existing infrastructure with the help of ICT. Moreover, the funds allocated should be utilized optimally. The operation

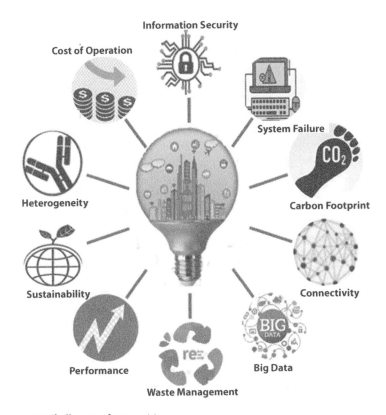

Figure 8.12 Challenges of smart cities.

cost is the maintenance cost which could be reduced by utilizing the components effectively and safely.

Urbanization is another challenge. Due to the advantages of smart cities, the people in rural areas are shifting toward cities. This increases the pollution and the congestion in cities. Heterogeneity is another major problem in transformation of smart cities because it involves different types of sensors or different types of data. These have to be analyzed and stored which again becomes another challenge.

When it comes to smart machines and cities, it involves a lot of data during data collection and data processing. These data has to be transmitted and secured safely. New threats that affect data confidentiality, integrity, accessibility, protection, and privacy [15] have to be rectified. Similarly, it is the responsibility of the government to provide a good connectivity environment. Reducing carbon emissions and waste is mandatory to reduce the operational cost thereby maintaining sustainability.

8.2.7 Conclusion

We have discussed about the various components, architecture, and applications of smart homes and smart cities. Various examples were discussed for the purpose of understanding. But the applications are not limited to the discussion in this chapter. As the technology develops, we will overcome the challenges. Now, we are in the pace of development and it is time for us to contribute ourselves and adapt to the day-to-day changes in the field of ICT.

References

1. Singh, D., Tripathi, G., Jara, A.J., A survey of Internet-of-Things: Future vision, architecture, challenges and services. *IEEE World Forum on Internet of Things (WF-IoT)*, pp. 287–292, Seoul, 2014, 2014.
2. Li, M., Gu, W., Chen, W., He, Y., Wu, Y., Zhang, Y., Smart Home: Architecture, Technologies and Systems. *Proc. Comput. Sci.*, 131, 393–400, 2018.
3. Govindraj, V., Sathiyanarayanan, M., Abubakar, B., Customary homes to smart homes using Internet of Things (IoT) and mobile application. *International Conference On Smart Technologies For Smart Nation (SmartTechCon)*, pp. 1059–1063, 2017.
4. Gislason, D., *Zigbee Wireless Networking*, 1st Edition, Newnes, Oxford, UK, pp. 351–387, 2008.
5. www.mospi.nic.in/sites/default/files/publication_reports/Elderlyin India_2016.pdf

6. www.smartcities.gov.in
7. Mohanty, S.P., Choppali, U., Kougianos, E., Everything you wanted to know about smart cities: The Internet of things is the backbone. *IEEE Consum. Electron. Mag.*, 5, 3, 60–70, 2016.
8. Silva, B.N., Khan, M., Han, K., Towards sustainable smart cities: A review of trends, architectures, components, and open challenges in smart cities. *Sustainable Cities and Society*, Vol. 38, 697–713, 2018.
9. Gaur, A., Scotney, B., Parr, G., McClean, S., Smart City Architecture and its Applications Based on IoT. *Proc. Comput. Sci.*, 52, 1089–1094, 2015.
10. Duangsuwan, S., Takarn, A., Nujankaew, R., Jamjareegulgarn, P., A Study of Air Pollution Smart Sensors LPWAN via NB-IoT for Thailand Smart Cities 4.0. *10th International Conference on Knowledge and Smart Technology (KST)*, 2018.
11. Yılmaz, Y., Uludag, S., Dilek, E., Ayozen, Y.E., A Preliminary Work on Predicting Travel Times and Optimal Routes Using Istanbul's Real Traffic Data. *9th Transist Istanbul Transport Congress and Exhibition*, 2016.
12. Mohseni, S., Brent, A., Kell, S., How 'smart integrated renewable energy systems' can drive sustainable economic development in remote communities, *Renewable Energy World, POWERGEN International*, Dallas, 2020
13. Patel, S., Park, H., Bonato, P., Chan, L., Rodgers, M., A review of wearable sensors and systems with application in rehabilitation. *J. Neuro Eng. Rehabil.*, 9, 1, 21, 2012.
14. Vinoth, G., Chellaiyan, A., Nirupama, Y., Taneja, N., Telemedicine in India: Where do we stand? *J. Family Med. Prim. Care*, 8, 6, 1872–1876, June 2019.
15. Popescul, D. and Radu, L.D., Data Security in Smart Cities: Challenges and Solutions. *Inform. Econ.*, 20, 1/2016, 29–38, 2016.

9

Application of AI in Healthcare

V. Priya[1]* and S. Prabu[2]

[1]Department of CSE, Paavai Engineering College, Namakkal, Tamilnadu, India
[2]Department of ECE, Mahendra Institute of Technology, Namakkal,
Tamilnadu, India

Abstract

Artificial Intelligence (AI) communicates to human intelligence imitation of computers; they are automated to think like humans and replicate their behavior. The word will also denote to any computer which shows human mind-related features such as problem-solving and thinking. The perfect purpose of AI is the measurements to rationalize and take achievement that have the utmost possibility of attaining a specific goal.

An Artificial Neural Network (ANN) is based on the brain, where neurons are linked to the senses in complicated patterns to interpret data, construct memories, and regulate the body. ANN is a programed computational model that aims at replicating the human brain's neural molecular mechanisms.

AI implementations are immeasurable. The technique can be prolonged to various trades and sectors. Throughout the biomedical sector, AI is studied and utilized in clinics for treating medications and multiple therapies, including in the operation room for clinical procedures.

In this chapter, we are going discuss about the basic applications of AI in healthcare and their relationship between the humans. Accordingly, AI aims to mimic certain skills that are perhaps exclusively unique to people, taking advantage of computer technologies in healthcare for better make the disease identification tasks to work faster and even more reliably than a person might ever have accomplished. Neural networks are a simple replication in medication field along with human system for firing electrical signals controlled through knowledge back and forth through the brain. AI playing major role in computer vision, deep learning, and machine learning processes supports in detection of disease and also for surgical supports to the doctors, etc.

Corresponding author: priya.saravanaraja@gmail.com

C. Venkatesh, N. Rengarajan, P. Ponmurugan and S. Balamurugan (eds.) Smart Systems for Industrial Applications, (225–248) © 2022 Scrivener Publishing LLC

In healthcare AI, it is for detecting tumors and diseases, cancer cell identification, and image detection like X-ray and CT scans that help to further medication. Thus, AI is going to be the future of world and this going to become a humans' everlasting link with AI in healthcare.

Keywords: Artificial Intelligence, machine learning, deep learning, healthcare, biomedical application

9.1 Introduction

The word diagnosis is used to describe illness signs or to assess patients for the purpose of assessing health conditions. The history of the patient is also preserved in a form of prescription along with medications needed, streamlining the process and keeping track of the success of the patient. The prescription had been originally saved in form of a paper chart that contains the type of illness, the recommended drugs, the dates of vaccination, the treatment plans, and the test result of particular hospitals for X-rays. The prescription is, however, saved through digital format in the modern era of the internet, that is specified in electronic medical record (EMR) or electronic health record (EHR) [1]. Such digital data can assist different processes in relation to different processes, such as patient health decision-making.

The area of healthcare research that gives computers the ability to learn without being specifically programed is Artificial Intelligence (AI). In the field of medical sciences, AI is one of the most exciting innovations that one has ever come across. As it is obvious from the name, it gives the machine the ability to predict, which makes it more analogous to physicians [2], where machine learning (ML) and deep learning (DL) are the primary process of using AI to automate systems. Although looking forward to the forms of algorithms for ML are supervised learning, unsupervised learning, semi-supervised learning, and reinforcement learning.

9.1.1 Supervised Learning Process

The computer learns from medical data by supervised learning [3]. In other words, we have variables for input and output, and we just have to map a function between the two. The term "supervised learning" derives from the impression that a dataset (training) learns from an algorithm. So, this part is known as "training" in supervised learning, where the computer learns all the features of the input data along with its labels. It is again possible to break supervised learning into two categories: they are regression and classification.

There would be an input variable as well as an output variable, since regression is a supervised learning algorithm, and the thing to bear in mind is that the expected output is a continuous numerical, i.e., the dependent variable is a continuous numerical, e.g., EMR or HER in healthcare monitoring, where both input data as well as the output data also require classification algorithms. Here, in nature, the output variable or dependent variable should be categorical. There are now a range of algorithms available for classification, such as Naïve Bayes (NB), Decision Tree (DT), Support Vector Machine (SVM), and Random Forest (RF).

9.1.2   Unsupervised Learning Process

The computer learns from unlabeled data in unsupervised learning, i.e., the performance for the input data is not previously established. The algorithm here attempts to establish the data's underlying structure. There are several algorithms of unsupervised learning: clustering of K-means, hierarchical clustering, and key component analysis.

9.1.3   Semi-Supervised Learning Process

The computer learns from a mixture of labeled and unlabeled data in semi-supervised learning. In other words, as a combination of supervised learning and unsupervised learning, you might consider as semi-supervised learning.

9.1.4   Reinforcement Learning Process

The algorithm learns through a scheme of rewards and punishment in reinforcement learning, and the aim here is to maximize the total reward. So, to understand reinforcement learning, let us go through this example. The sub-domain of AI is ML and DL, where a machine is equipped with knowledge to learn and make intelligent decisions. AI is a tool that makes it possible for computers to imitate human actions. The theory and growth of computer systems is capable of doing some tasks that involves with human intelligence, like visual perception, decision-making, speech recognition, and language translation, which is AI. AI devices have the capacity to make decisions and they strive to learn and develop themselves when exposed to vast volumes of real-world data. To explain this, Self-Driving Vehicles,

Google Translator, Amazon's Alexa, and Google Maps are some realistic implementations of AI.

DL [4] is subdivision of AI that is used for accomplishing ML. This strongly supports the medical data sets in the diagnosis (image dataset). The future of precision medicine and health management is being advanced by DL and its advances. Just very few samples of the DL in field of healthcare are brain tumors, cancer diagnostics, lung disease, skin disease, etc. Computer-assisted diagnosis will play a significant role in healthcare in the coming years.

9.1.5 Healthcare System Using ML

In the 21st century, just two decades before, it is much clears that AI will be one of the greatest disruptive technologies and also enablers of this century for the human society. This produces deep-rooted concept of AI [5] and it have related services and networks are built to convert and generate tremendous wealth in global efficiency, working habits, and lifestyles. It is no secret that the strong ML methods and tools like Deep Generative Adversarial Networks (GAN), Convolutional Neural Networks (Deep CNN), Deep Reinforcement Learning (DRL), and Gradient-Boosted Tree Model (GBM) are largely driving this transformation.

Traditional sectors of industry and tool are not only fields that affected by AI. The healthcare is an area that is considered as highly appropriate for use of the AI methods and technologies. Healthcare networks have also been primed by mandatory activities such as EMR to implement big data techniques for next-generation data analytics. To add more value to this, AI/ML instruments are intended. In primary/tertiary stage of patient healthcare and the public healthcare systems are estimated to increase efficiency of modelsalong with smart decision-making. This may be the greatest influence of AI tools, as billions of folks all over the world will theoretically change quality of life.

9.1.6 Primary Examples of ML's Implementation in the Healthcare

9.1.6.1 AI-Assisted Radiology and Pathology

Electronically stored medical imaging information has been abundant in recent days (Figure 9.1), and DL models will be supplied with the sort of dataset for detecting and to discover the anomalies and patterns. The imaging data may be interpreted by computers and algorithms in the same

Figure 9.1 Image of AI-assisted radiology and pathology.

way that a highly qualified radiologist can detect irregular spots over the skin, wounds, brain bleeds, and tumors. Therefore, use of AI platforms is to assist radiologists is ready to get growing exponentially. The identification of diseases that is difficult for diagnosing, and also it depends on detection of called edge-cases. Since this types of ML machine is based on the large databases that contain raw images of these diseases (with different transformations) and more accurate for these kinds of detection than humans.

In comparison to traditional business data of the transactional type, patient data is not especially suitable for easy statistical modeling and analysis. The need for the hour is powerful and agile AI-enabled systems capable of linking to multitude of the patient databases also to process diverse mix of the data types (like genomics, blood pathology, medical history, and images). In addition, the systems would be able to process thoroughly by analyses and figure out the secret trends. It should also be able to modify and to visualize the results to human-intelligible ways so the physicians (Figure 9.2) and also other healthcare professionals may work along with high trust also with full clarity on their performance. Interpretable AI and the distributed ML systems suit these kinds of bills very well and they are ready in near future to meet the demands for such systems.

9.1.6.2   Physical Robots for Surgery Assistance

Surgical robots (Figure 9.3) can provide human surgeons with unique assistance [6], increasing the ability to see and manoeuvre in an operation and

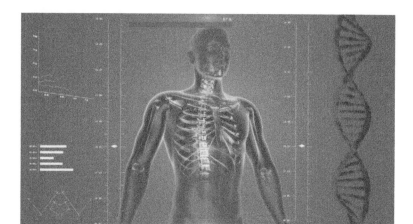

Figure 9.2 Biomedical image of human body.

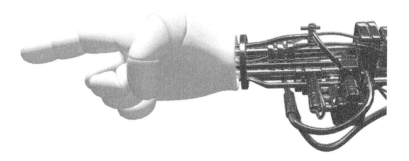

Figure 9.3 Surgical robots.

delivering effectiveness, and minimally, it is invasive incisions and causes less discomfort along with wound stitching and optimum geometry. For such automated surgery robots, they are truly exciting prospects for applications of AI. A software-centric robotic partnership with help of enormous distributed computing. The data-driven observations with advice focused toward on records of surgery (conducted mutually with machines and people) and findings (favorable or not). The virtual reality space is created by AI for the real-time guidance and direction. Thus, possible to do telemedicine and remote surgery are relatively through simple process, where AI with related data-driven approaches are exclusively equipped to resolve some issues, known as root cause fear of excessive bills, long wait, unnecessarily complicated appointment process, and the long-drawn inability to meet exact healthcare provider.

For several decades, the same sets of problems have troubled conventional companies and AI methodologies are now part of solution because, with such pattern matching or optimization problems, intelligent search algorithms and large databases are a big part of AI systems. Advanced AI/ML technologies and strategies must also be leveraged in their regular operating aspects by hospitals and public health organizations. The great thing is that questions data protection, which is for healthcare systems is difficult problem and more complicated, does not posture the major challenges to this type form of AI application. Very frequently, an organizational challenge does not contain sensitive patient data relating to illness, diagnosis, or medication, but it consists of data relating for funding, marketing, capital, or human resources problems, like any other modern business enterprise.

AI-assisted platforms aimed at enhancing experiences of healthcare services for largest segment of ordinary citizens should be the core purpose of such programs. The overriding purpose of systems already implemented in conventional companies is to maximize benefit. By combining empathy with the aim of profit generation, effective AI methods for healthcare operations management must differentiate themselves from traditional systems.

9.1.6.3   With the Assistance of AI/ML Techniques, Drug Discovery

To overcome the hellishly challenging problem of successful [6] drug development, AI and ML strategies are gradually being selected by major names in pharmaceutical industry. These case-studies span all sorts of clinical fields, such as metabolic disorders, cancer therapies, immuno-oncology medications. Going away from conventional long-haul process, the AI technologies are progressively increased by applying to speed up fundamental processes of the early-stage for mechanism discovery and candidate selection. For example, the biotechnology company Berg utilizes its AI platform for analyzing enormous quantities of patient's biological data and outcome data (enzyme, lipid, protein profiles, and metabolite) to illustrate crucial dissimilarities among diseased and the healthy cells to identify new tools for cancer detection.

DeepMind's journal of potential protein structures is accompanying with COVID-19 virus (SARS-CoV-2) utilizing the AlphaFold method was another prominent example in this respect. By using latest techniques in the Markov chain models, reinforcement learning, natural language processing (NLP), and Bayesian inference, several other start-up companies are focused on AI systems to evaluate multi-channel data (patents, research papers, patient records, and clinical trials). The main objectives are to identify patterns and create high-dimensional demonstrations to be stored in cloud, and it is used in drug-discovery process.

9.1.6.4   Precision Medicine and Preventive Healthcare in the Future

Precision medicine, according to U.S. National Library of Medicine [7], has "an new method to the prevention and treatment of diseases which takes into account individual heterogeneity for each individual in genes, climate, and lifestyle". Looking forward [8], this may be one of most impactful advantages of healthcare application of AI. The purpose is incredibly demanding and complex: to find specific treatment choices for a person based on the personal medical background, genetic data, lifestyle decisions, and pathological tests that are constantly evolving. Of course, to address the challenge, we need to put the most effective AI techniques to address the challenge: deep neural networks, advanced reinforcement learning, AI-driven search algorithms/probabilistic graphic models, and semi-supervised learning.

AI-system will also theoretically predict the likelihood of future of patients developing in specific diseases specified early screening or regular annual physical examination data, beyond this prediction and modeling of disease and also treatment. In addition, AI tools may be able to model why diseases are more likely to occur and in what situations and can thus help direct and train doctors for intervene (in a customized manner) before the individuals begin to display symptoms.

9.2   Related Works

9.2.1   In Healthcare, Data Driven AI Models

Currently, AI is disrupting many sectors and the healthcare sector appears to be next. The use of ML and DL in medicine has recently been growing. A type of ML, which is subset of AI, is DL itself and uses layered architecture to analyse data algorithmically. ML is a particular form of computer programming that uses an algorithm to apply statistical operations against inputs without much human intervention to turn them into outputs. While

ML models are improving and improving in their operation, they still need to be regulated and directed to some degree, whereas a DL model can determine whether or not a prediction via neural networks is true or not. In other words, an algorithm in ML requires a person with engineering and domain knowledge to turn data into understandable representations for the learning algorithm to detect patterns. On the other hand, a DL algorithm requires less data pre-processing and is capable of generating its own representations from raw data for pattern detection. In terms of DL methods and favored "modern" ML, the healthcare industry has so far been doubtful because it is explainable. We can, however, see an increase in the use of DL in recent years, especially in visual-based tasks [9].

9.2.2   Support Vector Machine

The most traditional ML process used by healthcare industry [10] is Help Vector Machines. It utilizes a supervised model of learning for outline classification, regression, and detection. The algorithm is used in recent years for predicting heart patients' drug adherence, which helped millions to escape from serious effects, like hospital readmission and at even death. This is used for the classifying proteins, categorization of texts, and image segregation [7]. SVM will be used for regression and classification, but this algorithm is mainly used in classifying problems that require a hyperplane to divide a dataset into two groups. The goal is to select a hyperplane with the greatest possible margin or distance within the training set between the hyperplane and any point, so that new data can be properly classified. Help vectors are information points that are nearest to the hyperplane and that will change its location if removed. In SVM, deciding the parameters in model is the problem of convex optimization, and thus, solution is continuously optimal globally.

In clinical research, SVMs are used widely, for example, to define imaging biomarkers, to diagnose cancer or neurological disorders, and generally to distinguish data from imbalanced datasets or missing-value datasets in Figure 9.4 [11].

9.2.3   Artificial Neural Networks

DL is a group algorithm which obtains signals through previous layer and transfers them to next layer, inspired by the neuron organization in animal brains. A network [12] learns without any human intervention or by analyzing the examples. An ANN also has range of many applications, from pathologists that use it for diagnosis in biochemical research. It is again

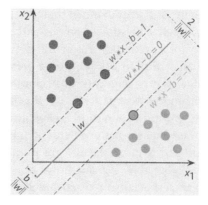

Figure 9.4 Feature extraction using SVM model. (https://www.kindpng.com/imgv/ howJbTx_svm-margin-svm-simple-example-hd-png-download/).

split into two components: the recurrent neural network (RNN) and the convolutional neural network (CNN).

The imaging is the key part of the medical science because, long before the symptoms appear, it may allow a doctor to know about the disease. As a result, many screening procedures are available, like mammograms, colonoscopy, and Pap smears. In this section, CNN has been proven that it to be more critical, as the algorithm is well adapted to the problem of binary classification and multi-class classification. RNN, on other hand, it proves that it is important when it is used in the medical time-series of data analysis for pattern recognition. Figure 9.5 represents the structure of neural network.

With textbook example of breast cancer prediction through mammographic photographs, neural networks have been successfully applied

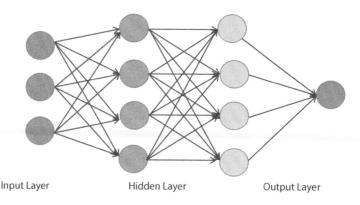

Figure 9.5 Structure of neural network.

to different area of medicines, like diagnostic systems, picture analysis, biochemical analysis, and drug production [12]. A collection of algorithms are inspired through nervous system for DL. More importantly, they inspired by organization of neurons in the animal brains. It consists of unit like artificial neurons that process, receive, and transmit signals from previous layer to the next layer. By "looking" at some examples by without having direct programming through humans, these networks will learn. The CNN and the RNN are two different types of neural networks widely used in field of medicine.

9.2.4   Logistic Regression

This ML model is used with the use of predictor variables for prediction in current scenario of categorical dependent data. It is also used to identify and forecast [13] an event's likelihood, such as the management of disease risk, which helps doctors make important medical decisions. In order to change their daily wellness habits, it also supports medical institutions to target patients at more risk and to curate behavioral health programs. Logistic regression is commonly needed in healthcare to solve the classification problems and estimate likelihood of given case, making it a valuable method for determining the probability of a disease and improving medical decisions.

9.2.5   Random Forest

This algorithm is to build multiple training trees to perform regression and classification at training time, and also it helps to solve issues of over fitting DT that represented in Figure 9.6 [14]. RF is required for the estimation of

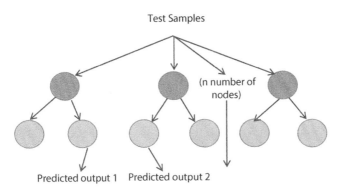

Figure 9.6 Structure of Decision Tree.

the disease at risk and also for ECG and the MRI analysis on the basis of a patient's medical history.

9.2.6   Discriminant Analysis

The discriminant analysis is a ML model used to evaluate adequacy of the classification of objects and it also used to assign single or multiple classes to one object. In the healthcare sector, discriminant analysis is applied from early detection of the diabetic peripheral neuropathy to refinement of the diagnostic features of the blood vessel image. It is also used to identify signs of mental health disorientation and for EHR management systems [7].

9.2.7   Naïve Bayes

This is one of the most powerful ML models that ever recognized to humanity, based on the Bayes theorem, and is highly used for medical data clarification and disease prediction by the healthcare industry. Classification may be referred to as data analysis when it comes to data mining that is also used for deriving models to represent the data groups. Hence, distribution of likelihood is too high, an optimal result will be obtained by the Bayes classifier [7, 8, 15].

9.2.8   Natural Language Processing

In healthcare, large proportion of the clinical material, like clinical laboratory reports, physical examination, operational notes, and the discharge summaries, is in the form of narrative text, which is incomprehensible and unstructured for computer software without any special text processing methods. These problems are solved by NLP and it recognizes set of disease with relevant keywords in clinical data notes depends on historical databases to join and to enrich structured data after validation for helping clinical decision making [8].

9.2.9   TF-IDF

TF-IDF, the simple keyword extraction algorithm, is represented for frequency-inverse text frequency, where the weight of the TF-IDF is statistical indicator of the word value of text in corpus or collection. The value increases in relation to number of times that a word appears in text, but it is balanced by word frequency in corpus. The TF-IDF is used in area of healthcare to assess the similarity of patients in observational trials, as well as for identifying disease associations through the medical records and also to find temporal trends in the databases [9].

9.2.10 Word Vectors

A group of similar models are needed to generate word embedding are considered to breakthrough in word vectors, NLP, or word2vec. Word2vec models are, in their core, two-layer neural networks, shallow that recreates linguistic word contexts. With unique word having a corresponding vector, Word2vec generates a multidimensional vector space from a document. In the vector space, word vectors are arranged in such a way that terms that shares context in near proximity to each other [16, 17]. Word vectors are used for the processing of biomedical terminology, including identifying parallels, standardizing medical words, and it discovers new features of diseases [8].

9.2.11 Deep Learning

DL is the extension of methodology of the traditional neural network to put it simpler like multilayer neural network. The DL may explore much complex non-linear patterns in data by providing more strength compared to classical ML algorithms. As each of them can be trained as a pipeline of modules, DL signifies a scalable method to perform automated feature extraction through raw data, among others. DL models magnificently solve both ML and the NLP tasks in medical applications. CNN, deep belief network, RNN, and multilayer perceptron are widely used DL algorithms, with CNNs foremost the race through 2016 on [18].

9.2.12 Convolutional Neural Network

CNN has been established to manage high-dimensional data or the data with a wide variety of features, like image datasets. Initially, the inputs to CNN [19] are normalized into pixel values on the images as suggested by LeCun. Biological processes that influenced convolutional networks in which pattern of communication among neurons resemble arrangement of animal visual cortex, along with individual cortical neurons that respond to stimuli in small region of receptive area, where receptive fields of various neurons partly overlap so that it occupy entire visual field. By weighting in convolutional layers and the sampling in subsampling layers are alternatively to CNN, then it transfers the pixel values into image. A recursive feature of weighted input values is the final product.

CNN represented in Figure 9.7 has recently been successfully introduced in the medical sector to help the diagnosis of illnesses, such as skin cancer or cataracts [20]. This is a feed-forward neural network where DL model receives an input image to assign weights and the biases to different input image features and is able to differentiate images from each other after doing so. With ample preparation, it is able to "read" features and philtres that in primitive AI methods would have to be programed manually [21]. The RNNs, the second most common in healthcare, are neural networks that uses sequential data. The RNNs are referred to as repeating because for each element of a sequence, they perform the same operation, and the performance depends upon previous computations. The RNNs also have "memory" that captures knowledge several steps back on what has been determined. RNNs are also an effective method of forecasting clinical incidents, which is extremely common in NLP [8].

The fundamental difference between the CNN and RNN is that only a fixed size input can be consumed by the CNN, producing fixed-size output, where the RNN is more multifaceted and it can consume more arbitrary inputs, producing more arbitrary output data sizes, even though it have much more input datasets than CNN is required. In this field of computer vision (medical image analysis, image recognition, and feature detection), NLP (semantic parsing, sentence modeling, speech recognition, retrieval of search queries, and text generation using snippet), and in the earlier stages of medication development (filtering it potentially

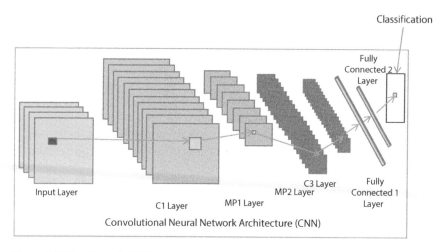

Figure 9.7 Structure of CNN.

beneficial substances and the prediction of medical benefits), ANNs are used [9].

They used the most common algorithms in medical literature for ML. The knowledge is provided by searching on PubMed for ML algorithms in healthcare [8, 17]. Detection of heart disease is playing a primary role in field of medical diagnosis [20]. They developed a model for selecting the features by using feature selection algorithm (FCMIM) to classify the heart disease like minimal redundancy, shrinkage of heart absolute, relief, etc., by using various classifiers like K-nearest neighbor, DT, and NB, where the experimental results show that SVM model produces high levels of accuracy than the other model (FCMIM-SVM) in the identification of heart disease. Modified Artificial Plant Optimization (MAPO) algorithm [21] had been proposed that will be used as optimal feature selector along with other ML methodologies to predict the heart rate. MAPO were compared with some other optimizers to outperform it with best accuracy with correlation and the standard error rate of 09541 and 2.418 that compared with other optimizers.

This [22] aims at finding primary features of prediction of the cardiovascular diseases by using ML models. The prediction model is made by adding different combinations of the features along with various existing methods of classification. A comparison of significant variables displayed with Internet of Medical Things (IoMT) boards, for the data analysis with the effect of high blood pressure that affects the coronary artery disease with the accuracy of 96.6% of accuracy along with F-measure of 96.7%. To predict heart disease risk, the Weighted Associative Classifier (WAC) [23] is used. WAC uses the technique of data mining to create a rule base. The Java Platform framework has been implemented and trained using UCI benchmark data. An integrated view of implementation of automated diagnostic systems for the diagnosis of breast cancer is the focus of the author [24]. The main aim of the paper is to be a reference for readers who want to build a framework of automated decision support like MLPNN, CNN, RNN, and SVM for breast cancer detection. The goal was to establish an ideal classification scheme for this problem with high diagnostic accuracy using SVM model with higher accuracy.

In many applications, feature selection has demonstrated its efficacy by constructing simpler and more detailed models. Big data features [25] such as data velocity and data variety have raised challenges to the problem of feature selection. For big data analytics, authors visualize these obstacles by using scikit-learn. In three patient test groups, a new discriminant feature model [26] to estimate probabilities of the angiographic coronary disease has been tested for the clinical utility and reliability. By applying a Bayesian algorithm, the probabilities which are resulted from application of Cleveland algorithm compared with extracts. The likelihood of illness at the Hungarian and American centres was over-predicted by both algorithms. It has been concluded that when supplied to the patients with intermediate disease incidence and chest pain syndromes, coronary disease probabilities that are derived from the discriminant functions are accurate, and it is clinically useful. The proposed approach is based on the three major cardiac disorders that can be described by the ANN system [27]: aortic stenosis, mitral stenosis, and ventricular septal defects. This method has precision of 92% for the classification of heart diseases.

9.3 DL Frameworks for Identifying Disease

9.3.1 TensorFlow

TensorFlow is a multifunctional open source software library by using data flow graphs for the numerical computation. It has been established to take DL into account, but it is applicable to a much wider range of issues. This will cover the very basics of TensorFlow, not getting far into DL at all. It is possible to use TensorFlow in many programming languages. We are going to provide basic examples, such as linear regression, showing both the python API and the new interface to R.

9.3.2 High Level APIs

It uses high level API like Keras and Eager Execution (API is for writing TensorFlow code and to use Numpy) and by importing data (bring the data into TensorFlow program). Estimators produce high-level API to provide fully-packaged model to get ready for large-scale training the data and production.

9.3.3 Estimators

Premade estimators are basic estimators, to save the train process and checkpoints, to resume it from where it left off (Feature Columns), to handle the wide variety of input data type without changing model with dataset, by using tf.data as the input data, and to create custom estimators for writing own estimator.

9.3.4   Accelerators

By using GPUs, it clarifies how the TensorFlow as sign processes for the device and it shows how to change the arrangements manually. By using these TPUs, it describes how to change estimator program to run over TPU.

9.3.5   Low Level APIs

This introduces basis of TensorFlow outside high-level APIs. Tensors illuminate how to generate, process, and access fundamental objects of TensorFlow. The variables show the information to denote the shared and persistent state of program. The embeddings introduce concepts of embeddings that provide an example to train an embeddings in TensorFlow, which describes how to overlook embeddings along with the TensorBoard Embedding Projector.

9.4   Proposed Work

9.4.1   Application of AI in Finding Heart Disease

It is difficult to diagnose heart disease in patients and needs different data, laboratory tests, and the equipments. This study is not intended to replace traditional methodology used to diagnose and predict the chances of heart failure, but to use emerging technology such as ML to support this method. The ML is not new method and it is used for various applications many times. In order to aid heart consultants through the diagnostic process, cloud-based decision support system was suggested. ML algorithms have been used to predict heart disease in this method. An approach is to apply various clustering algorithms on the dataset of heart disease to realize the best solution that optimizes ratio of accuracy of prediction. In a study carried out by using DT, SVM, NB, and also other ML models, it has proved to be successful in predicting the heart disease through historical data.

9.4.2   Data Pre-Processing and Classification of Heart Disease

After processing of different documents, heart disease data is pre-processed. A total of 303 patient records are included in datasets; they consist 6 records along with some missing values. Thus, 6 records have been deleted from dataset, and pre-processing uses remaining 297 patient records. For the attributes in specified dataset, the multiclass parameter and the binary classification are implemented. The multi-class component is used to screen for heart disease presence or absence. In this case of a patient with heart disease, with the value will be to 1, otherwise value will be set to 0, showing patient's lack of the heart disease. Data pre-processing is supported by translating medical records into binary values for diagnosis, where pre-processing data findings for the 297 medical records suggest that have 137 records which shows value of 1 for presence of heart disease in human, while remaining 160 shows value 0 for absence of the heart disease [15].

Two attributes relating to age and sex are used to classify the patient's personal details from among the 13 features of the data collection. As they contain essential clinical documents, the remaining 11 attributes are considered essential. In order to detect and recognize the nature of heart disease, clinical reports are important. Several (ML) techniques used they are NB, DL, GLM, DT, LR, GBT, RF, and SVM, as previously stated in this experiment. With all the ML methods, the experiment was replicated using all 13 attributes in the Linear Regression with RF prediction process. The clustering of dataset is carried out on basis of DT function variables and the criteria. Then, in order to estimate the consistency, classifiers are subjected to each clustered dataset. Based upon their low rate of error, best performing methods are classified from the data. The efficiency is further optimized by selecting the high error rate of DT cluster and extracting its corresponding classifier characteristics. The classifier's output is evaluated on this data set for error optimization.

The next model selected and executed in the research process is the RF. Since this comes from the classification family, it often referred to supervised learning algorithm. This model first produces more random trees are called as forest at learning process. For example, a dataset contains a "x" number of attributes, choosing a random feature known as "y" first. Use all features; using the best rift form, it generates nodes. Moreover, by repeating these previous steps, algorithm will work to construct a complete LR with RF. Then, the algorithm attempts to merge the trees during the prediction process using the predicted result and voting procedure. By voting in a forest, the aim of merging the random trees is to opt out of highest tree predicted, that boost accuracy level of prediction for future data. The design of the proposed model is represented in Figure 9.8 and the model description is represented in Figure 9.9.

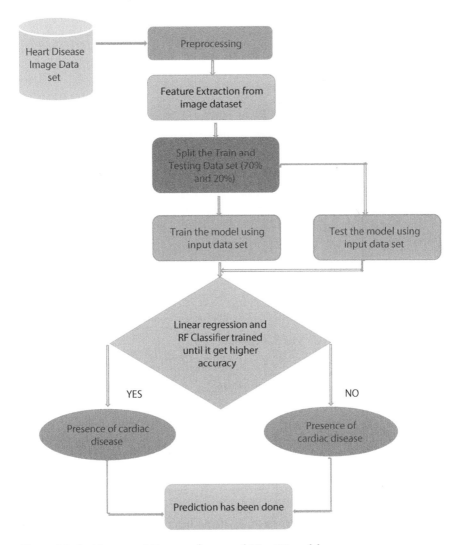

Figure 9.8 Architecture of diagram of proposed LR + RF model.

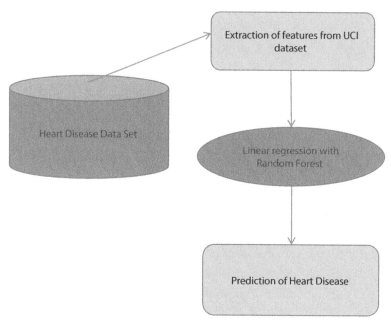

Figure 9.9 Proposed system model overview.

9.5 Results and Discussions

As the performance analysis of AI and ML is various metrics. Here, we considered the values like True Positive (TP), True Negative (TN), False Positive (FP), and False Negative (FN) values using confusion matrix function in scikit-learn. This supports to estimate the accuracy in classification, score of Precisions, F1 score, Recall or Sensitivity, Specificity, and in Area Under ROC Curve (AUC), and it uses True Positive Rate and False Positive Rate to draw the curve to identify the loss function. Accuracy [Equation (9.1)] produces the prediction level of our proposed model.

$$Accuracy = \frac{TP + TN}{TP + FP + FN + TN} \tag{9.1}$$

$$Precision = \frac{TP}{TP + FP} \tag{9.2}$$

This produces [Equation (9.2)] number of right documents returned by the proposed model.

$$Recall = \frac{TP}{TP + FN} \tag{9.3}$$

It [Equation (9.3)] calculates the number of positive values that are returned by our model.

$$Specificity = \frac{TN}{FP + TN} \tag{9.4}$$

Specificity [Equation (9.4)] produces the number of negative values that are created by the model by using confusion matrix in contrast with the Recall function.

$$F1\ score = \frac{2 * (precision * recall)}{(Precision + recall)} \tag{9.5}$$

where [Equation (9.5)] F1 score gives the weighted average of precision and recall. The best value is chosen from F1 and it produces if worst case occurs during classification in proposed model.

Performance is evaluated based upon the above equations to estimate the proposed model, and analysis reports are made by comparing the performance of classifiers through Figure 9.10.

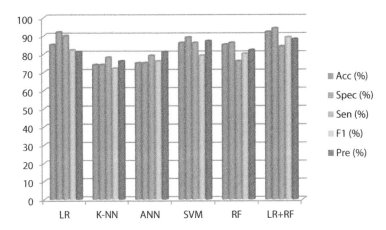

Figure 9.10 Performance analysis of classifiers based on the classifiers.

Table 9.1 Results of classifiers for prediction of heart disease.

Prediction models	Acc (%)	Spec (%)	Sen (%)	F1 (%)	Pre (%)
LR	85	92	90	82	81
K-NN	74	74	78	72	76
ANN	75	75	79	76	81
SVM	86	89	86	79	87
RF	85	86	76	80	82
LR + RF	92	94	84	89	88

9.6 Conclusion

In this proposed model, an efficient ML-based analysis is developed for diagnosing the heart disease which produces 92.23% of accuracy while compared with the other existing classifiers. For comparison, we used LR, K-NN, ANN, SVM, and RF with the proposed model LR along with the RF classifier. While compared with the existing models, LR produces high sensitivity about 90.78% than the proposed model. All algorithms produce less F1 score than the proposed model is shown in Table 9.1. In this research, we compared five parameters for feature selection algorithms through ML models. Thus, the proposed model improves computational cost and computation time by predictive systems with their performance metrics. Thus, the future of biomedical analysis process is moving toward the prediction and recovery of disease through AI with ML, DL, transfer learning, and reinforcement learning algorithms.

References

1. https://www.geeksforgeeks.org/machine-learning/
2. https://intellipaat.com/blog/tutorial/machine-learning-tutorial/introduction/.
3. https://www.edureka.co/blog/artificial-intelligence-tutorial/
4. https://intellipaat.com/blog/tutorial/machine-learning-tutorial/introduction-deep-learning/
5. https://intellipaat.com
6. https://towardsdatascience.com/ai-and-machine-learning-for-healthcare-7a70fb3acb67
7. https://analyticsindiamag.com/top-6-ai-algorithms-in-healthcare/

8. https://medium.com/sciforce/top-ai-algorithms-for-healthcare-aa5007ffa330
9. https://rubikscode.net/2020/03/16/top-ai-algorithms-in-healthcare/
10. Rajkomar, A., Dean, J., Kohane, I., Machine learning in medicine. *N. Eng. J. Med.*, 380, 1347–1358, 2019.
11. Pronovost, P.J. *et al.*, Paying the Piper: investing in infrastructure for patient safety. *Jt. Commun. J. Qual. Patient Saf.*, 34, 342–348, 2008.
12. Shaban-Nejad, A., Michalowski, M., Buckeridge, D., Health intelligence: how artificial intelligence transforms population and personalized health. *NPJ Digit. Med.*, 1, 53, 2018.
13. Gijsberts, C.M. *et al.*, Race/ethnic differences in the associations of the framingham risk factors with carotid IMT and cardiovascular events. *PloS One*, 10, e0132321, 2015.
14. Panch, T, *et al.*, Artificial intelligence: opportunities and risks for public health. *Lancet Digit. Health*, 1, e13–e14, 2019.
15. Revell, T., Google DeepMind's NHS data deal 'failed to comply' with law, 2017, https://www.newscientist.com/article/2139395-google-deepminds-nhs-data-deal-failedto-comply-with-law/.
16. Yan, S. *et al.*, A systematic review of the clinical application of data-driven population segmentation analysis. *BMC Med. Res. Methodol.*, 18, 121, 2018.
17. Fogel, A.L. and Kvedar, J.C., Artificial intelligence powers digital medicine. *NPJ Digit. Med.*, 1, 5, 2018.
18. Sultana, A., Ciuc, M., Strungaru, R., Florea, L., A new approach in breast image registration. *Proceedings of the 2010 IEEE 6th International Conference on Intelligent Computer Communication and Processing*.
19. Anakal S., and Sandhya, P., Clinical decision support system for chronic obstructive pulmonary disease using machine learning techniques. *2017 International Conference on Electrical, Electronics, Communication, Computer, and Optimization Techniques (ICEECCOT)*, IEEE, Mysuru, India, 2017.
20. Li, J.P., Haq, A.U., Din, S.U., Khan, J., khan, A., Saboor, A., Heart Disease Identification Method Using Machine Learning Classification in E-Healthcare. *IEEE Access*, 8, 107562–107582, 2020.
21. Sharma, P., Choudhary, K., Gupta, K., Chawla, R., Gupta D., Sharma, A., Artificial plant optimization algorithm to detect heart rate & presence of heart disease using machine learning. *Artif. Intell. Med.*, 102, 1–14, January 2020.
22. Guo, C., Zhang, J., Liu, Y., Xie, Y., Han, Z., Yu, J., Recursion Enhanced Random Forest With an Improved Linear Model (RERF-ILM) for Heart Disease Detection on the Internet of Medical Things Platform. IEEE Access. Special Section on Deep Learning Algorithms for Internet of Medical Things, 8, 59247–59256, 2020.
23. Soni, J., Ansari, U., Sharma, D., Soni, S., Intelligent and Effective Heart Disease Prediction System using Weighted Associative Classifiers. *Int. J. Adv. Trends Comput. Sci. Eng.*, 3, 6, 2385–2392, June 2011.

24. Übeyli, E.D., Implementing automated diagnostic systems for breast cancer detection. *Expert Syst. Appl.*, 33, 4, 1054–1062, November 2007.

25. Li, J. and Liu, H., Challenges of feature selection for big data analytics. *IEEE Intell. Syst.*, 32, 2, 9–15, Mar. 2017.

26. Detrano, R., Janosi, A., Steinbrunn, W., Pfisterer, M., Schmid, J.-J., Sandhu, S., Guppy, K.H., Lee, S., Froelicher, V., International application of a new probability algorithm for the diagnosis of coronary artery disease. *Am. J. Cardiol.*, volume No. 64, 5, 304–310, Aug. 1989.

27. Ghwanmeh, S., Mohammad, A., Al-Ibrahim, A., Innovative artificial neural networks-based decision support system for heart diseases diagnosis. *J. Intell. Learn. Syst. Appl.*, 5, 3, pp. 176–183, 2013, Art. no. 35396.

10

Battery Life and Electric Vehicle Range Prediction

Ravikrishna S.[1*], Subash Kumar C. S.[1] and Sundaram M.[2]

[1]*Department of Electrical and Electronics Engineering PSG Institute of Technology and Applied Research, Neelambur, Coimbatore, India*
[2]*Department of Electrical and Electronics Engineering PSG College of Technology, Coimbatore, India*

Abstract

To ensure reliable and safe operation of electric vehicles it is important to estimate the State of Charge (SoC) and State of Health (SoH) of the battery accurately and should be able to implement practically in embedded Battery Management System (BMS). The BMS algorithms must calculate the parameters of the electro-chemical battery system which are difficult to be measured directly. The amount of energy is estimated to calculate the distance the vehicle can travel and the amount of energy required for the next recharge. In this chapter, the method for estimating the SoC and SoH are analyzed in dynamic load conditions. The Sigma point Kalman filter is used for estimating the SoC of a battery which is operated at non-linear conditions and varying temperatures. The Approximate Weighted Total Least Square Algorithm which is computationally less intensive and also has fading memory which gives more emphasis on recent measurements is used for estimating the SoH of battery to reduce the errors in computation. Equivalent circuit-based battery model is implemented using MATLAB/Simulink to estimate the SoC and SoH that are estimated using above-mentioned methods, and the results are validated.

Keywords: Battery management system, estimating SoC, SoH, Sigma point Kalman filter

Corresponding author: ravikrishna@psgitech.ac.in

C. Venkatesh, N. Rengarajan, P. Ponmurugan and S. Balamurugan (eds.) Smart Systems for Industrial Applications, (249–268) © 2022 Scrivener Publishing LLC

10.1   Introduction

Energy and problems related to the environment are major challenges in the automobile sector. The increase in price of energy produced due to the shortfall in the available energy resources and pollution caused by combustion engines used in vehicles have transformed the transportation systems to move to energy efficient sustainable technologies for the development of vehicles. The challenge of replacing conventional fossil fuel driven vehicles with electric vehicles (EV) is a necessity to reduce carbon emissions and develop a sustainable world [1]. The crisis owing to shortage of conventional fuels and need for cleaner environment necessitates the usage of EVs. The increase in use of EV leads to increase in charging infrastructure and optimum usage of electrical power. The technology used for storing electrical power is a major hindrance for the growth of the EV market. The batteries used for EV should have sufficient life span and the energy density should be high.

The electrified transportation system involved different types of battery storage devices for the EV. Batteries are electrochemical-based storage devices which consist of two electrodes and an electrolyte. Electricity is produced by the movement of ions in the electrolyte between the electrodes. The rechargeable lead acid battery was used during the initial days, and then, nickel cadmium-based battery was used but had drawbacks of drop in voltage due to ageing of batteries. Then, Nickel-Metal Hydride (NiMH) batteries and Lithium ion batteries were developed. The NiMH batteries are available at reduced cost, even then the high specific energy, high efficiency, lower rate of discharge of battery, and larger lifecycle have caused Lithium ion batteries to be used predominantly in EV compared to other types of batteries [3]. Even though Lithium ion batteries are being widely used for EV, they have drawbacks regarding the safety aspects, determining the charging parameters for a nonlinear, time-variant electrochemical system is challenging [4]. Lithium-ion batteries are widely used by electrical vehicle manufacturers throughout the world for different applications for different types of EVs. Even though widely used by different manufacturers, there are no strict guidelines regarding the charging infrastructure and the safety of the batteries

EVs or hybrid EVs rely on battery banks and fuel cells as their source of electrical power input ranging from few kW to hundreds of kW. EVs rely on battery banks and fuel cells to deliver electrical power. The range of vehicle driven will be based on these energy storage systems. The efficiency, the distance travelled, and the safety can be improved by better management of the energy storage systems.

The electrochemical composition of lithium batteries are very sensitive to thermal, electrical, and mechanical changes that occur. The battery packs used should have dedicated temperature control systems to enhance the safety and improve the performance of the battery.

Even with the invention of modern technologies the energy storage system technology provides hindrance for the EV to compete with conventional vehicles. The status of the battery used has to be measured in real time to enhance the efficiency and safety of the energy storage system, making the Battery Management System (BMS) to play a critical role in control of electrical power from the battery. The BMS has to check for the safe thermal operation of the Li-ion battery and also estimate the State of Charge (SoC) [2].

The powertrain of an electrical vehicle should exhibit features such as high specific energy density to provide long runtime and reduce the volume of the battery, higher power density to provide more ampere of current, excellent thermal efficiency since temperature varies the electrical parameters, should have good charging and discharging cycles, available at affordable cost, and reliable. They should also possess low self-discharge, features of recycling the e-waste generated and with less hazard to the environment.

The range of distance that the EV can travel is based on the factors as shown in Figure 10.1. The design of the EV and the BMS, the way in which the EV is driven by the driver, and the environmental factors play a major role in predicting the range for the vehicle to travel with the current charge available in the battery. This information will be helpful even in finding the nearest charging station.

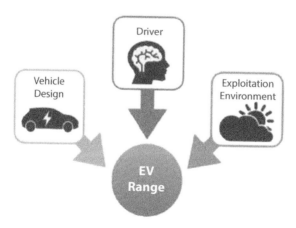

Figure 10.1 Factors influencing EV range prediction.

The SoC and State of Health (SoH) provide information on the working of batteries and the BMS should be able to measure these non-linearities in real time [6]. SoC is defined as the ratio of the depleted instantaneous energy from the battery to the maximum energy to be stored in the battery. Estimating SoC correctly helps to disable the charging of the battery when it is fully charged and charging when the charge goes below the minimum value. There are different algorithms used to estimate the SoC by direct or indirect methods [7].

The various parameters influencing the EV some are constant and some are variable as shown in Figure 10.2. The type of EV, the type of power train used for transfer of power, the number of passengers travelling in the vehicle, the weight of the vehicle, the road terrain in which EV is to travel, and the recharge type and recharge infrastructure act as constant parameters for the design.

The SoC of the battery, the current health of the battery, the behavior of the driver, the traffic in which the vehicle is driven, the dynamic changes that occur in the EV, the type of BMS used, and the environmental factors which are external due to the ambient environment and internal environment inside the EV are taken as variable parameters.

First, the model of the real battery is created by doing open circuit voltage (OCV) test and discharge test at different temperatures and the equivalent circuit parameters of the battery are determined. Then, for estimating the SoC,

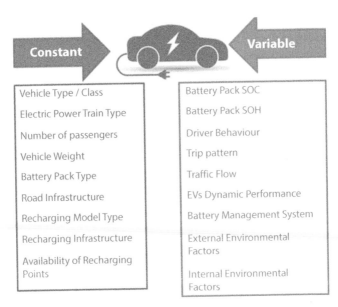

Figure 10.2 Factors influencing EVs battery management system.

the real battery parameters such as terminal voltage, discharge current, and operating temperature are taken online from the real battery and are fed to the Sigma point Kalman filter (SPKF) block which estimates the SoC. The result of the SoC is given to the total least square method block for estimating SoH.

After estimating these two parameters, the battery range and life is predicted using the same and the driver is indicated about that and thereby the performance and overall life of the battery is enhanced.

10.2 Different Stages of Electrification of Electric Vehicles

10.2.1 Starting and Stopping

The function of the control unit at starting or stopping intermittently at traffic signals is to switch off the electrical power to the motor and control the coolers, heaters, and other illumination systems available in the EV.

10.2.2 Regenerative Braking

To harness the power wasted during braking of EVs, a regenerative braking mechanism is used. In conventional braking using mechanical systems the kinetic energy is being dissipated as frictional losses and are dissipated as heat. In a regenerative braking mechanism the kinetic energy is converted into electrical energy and saved in the batteries. These braking systems should be controlled to regulate the flow of power to the battery and high electrical impulses at instant of braking is to be avoided and mechanical braking systems should work in concurrent with electrical braking systems to have an effective braking mechanism.

10.2.3 Motor Control

The motor used should be controlled to deliver the maximum power at maximum efficiency. The driving of the vehicle is influenced by various factors such as road conditions, climatic conditions, the manner in which the vehicle is driven, and the slope and terrain in which the vehicle is driven. The torque demand of the motor varies for these different conditions and batteries have to deliver electrical power to operate the motor at the maximum speed torque point and also to operate at maximum efficiency. Hybrid EVs have electrical power ratings of 30 to 40 kW and an energy demand of 300 to 400 Wh to perform various functions of electrical driven systems. The motor control circuit must use optimum power at reduced losses to enhance the lifetime of the battery [5].

10.2.4   EV Drive

The battery must supply electrical power to the motor drive and the other auxiliary systems. The weight of the system, the aerodynamics, and the different loadings influence the drive system. The drive system transfers electrical energy from one system to another according to its requirement and should have minimum losses in the transfer of power and should not inject unwanted harmonics into the system. The response time of the drive should be fast to respond to different dynamic loading conditions.

10.3   Estimating SoC

The SoC can be estimated by computing the internal resistance and specific gravity for lead acid batteries which has drawbacks in calculating the SoC during the charging conditions, when there is time difference in the conditions of electrolyte at lower voltages. The internal resistance is considered to be important in impedance spectroscopy for SoH estimation. There are implementation difficulties in using these techniques. The direct method of estimating SoC using coulomb counting method does capacity scaled integration of battery current. There are errors induced in the calculation of battery capacity and errors from the sensors used for measuring current. Errors in computation of SoC will lead to error in the determining the range prediction and the battery life. The OCV of the battery is determined from the battery stack and compared with SoC to reduce the errors in measurement. The measurement of these real-time data accurately can be done by means of using Kalman filter and mean square estimator under dynamically varying conditions.

The estimation is done by developing a model of the battery with the present data and comparing with the real-time dynamic data and state estimates are determined and weights are adjusted to determine the error.

10.3.1   Cell Capacity

Based on the operating conditions such as temperature at which the battery is operated, each cell has a safe operating voltage based on the materials used and the chemical composition. The cell capacity can be defined by the way in which current is exchanged between the maximum and minimum potentials of the individual cell. To determine the capacity, a slow discharge is done to accommodate the different conditions of the cell to find the nominal capacity.

10.3.2   Calendar Life

The SoH gives an idea of the remaining life of the battery and the life of the battery has been specified in months or years, which varies based on different operating conditions.

10.3.3   Cycling Life

The life of the battery is determined by the number of charging cycles it can withstand. The number of cycles in EVs cannot be calculated correctly because of the variation in the driving cycle. Each cell used in the battery provides varying data.

10.3.4   SoH Based on Capacity Fade

The degradation of the battery begins immediately after the manufacturing itself owing to the electrochemical reactions taking place. Due to these reactions, the active material properties get changed varying the internal resistance of the battery. This increase in resistance causes more losses internally causing reduction in the capacity [8].

10.3.5   SoH Based on Power Fade

The ageing of the battery leads to higher internal Ohmic resistance leading to more drop in voltage and the power delivered becomes less. The battery end of life is estimated to be twice the internal resistance from the manufactured date or the maximum power delivered is reduced by 70% [9].

10.3.6   Open Circuit Voltage

The OCV is measured during the rest condition of the battery and an interpolation is done with OCV and SoC. This method cannot be applied for dynamically varying current.

10.3.7   Impedance Spectroscopy

The advantage of going for this technique is that the SoC changes can be computed for dynamic varying current in real time. The calculation is done for different values of temperature but varying temperature conditions causes errors in the computation.

The SoH of the battery can also be computed by measuring the charging and discharging cycles, the temperature at which it is operated. During discharge condition, the voltage drop is measured and has an impact on the cycle of operation from which SoH is calculated.

10.3.8   Model-Based Approach

The mathematical model of the cell is constructed from the data available previously in the cell. The model runs in parallel with the real-time system and predicts the output voltage for a certain value of current. The changes occurring in the cell during the time of discharge, the OCV, and the internal resistance are used for estimating the SoC. The errors produced between the model developed and the real-time system is used for correcting the parameters of the model accordingly.

Different models of battery are used for estimating the SoC. The model of battery can be electrochemical in type or it can be of equivalent circuit type as shown in Figure 10.3. The equivalent circuit can be modeled using internal resistance of the battery and capacitors for the electrode surfaces. The equivalent circuit is tested by using a pulse discharge test.

The voltage measured before the application of pulse to the circuit is measured as OCV. The voltage drop is taken as the internal resistance drop. The voltage change between the electrodes is taken as a capacitive circuit. The addition of RC circuits improves the accuracy of the system but increases the computation complexity. This method gives more accurate results. The parameters of the battery can be computed by appropriate optimization techniques to get better results [10].

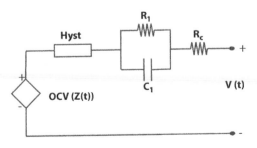

Figure 10.3 Equivalent circuit of battery.

10.4   Kalman Filter

The parameters of the battery change dynamically due to ageing and for the various operating conditions. To calculate the SoC precisely, the parameters of the model should be computed correctly.

Kalman filter–based estimation of state variables and parameters simultaneously improves the accuracy of the results obtained. In Kalman filtering technique, the SoC is taken as the dynamically changing frame and the parameters of the equivalent circuit such as the hysteresis, the internal resistances comprise a slowly moving frame. To limit the state transition, matrix algorithm was limited to two separate frames.

The Kalman filter takes the equivalent circuit model of the battery to be tested as one of the inputs and the terminal voltage, the current discharged, and the temperature of operation of the real battery as the other input. It calculates the error between the model and the battery as shown in Figure 10.4, and the SoC of battery is estimated. Using the total least square method, the SoH of the battery is estimated, and using the data obtained the battery range, life of the battery is calculated.

10.4.1   Sigma Point Kalman Filter

The SPKF is used for accurate prediction for nonlinear systems. In Kalman filtering, the current state is predicted based on the information provided, and then, the filter changes the predicted values for the measurement being done. It also provides information about the uncertainties.

The filter is initialized, and in the measurement interval, six steps are executed. The prior data is given as the first step to predict the present value, and then, in the second step, the covariance of the state estimation

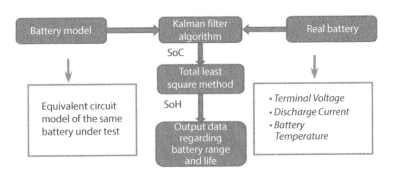

Figure 10.4 Block diagram of the system.

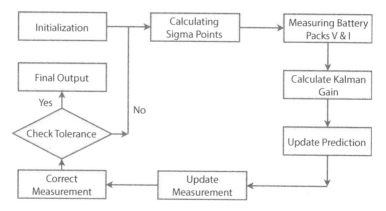

Figure 10.5 Flowchart for SoC prediction.

error is updated. In the next step, the output of the present cell is predicted, and then, in the fifth step, the actual value is compared with the estimated values and state estimate gain values are updated by the Kalman gain and output estimate error. In the final step, the state estimate error covariance is updated [11, 12]. The estimation process of SoC is shown in Figure 10.5.

10.4.2   Six Step Process

The sigma point is chosen in such a way that the mean and covariance of the points matches the mean and covariance of the input random variable to the nonlinear function. The output of the non-linear function is a set of transformed output sigma points. The following are the constants for sigma point computation. The constants are calculated using Central-Difference Kalman filter (CDKF) method.

Constants for sigma point

Method	γ	$\alpha_0^{(m)}$	$\alpha_k^{(m)}$	$\alpha_0^{(c)}$	$\alpha_k^{(c)}$
CDKF		$\dfrac{h^2 - L}{h^2}$	$\dfrac{1}{2h^2}$	$\dfrac{h^2 - L}{h^2}$	$\dfrac{1}{2h^2}$

h = √3
L is the length of input vector.

Step 1: State-prediction time update

The augmented random state vector is formed by combining the state, process noise, and sensor noise at time index k. The augmented posterior state estimate and augmented posterior state-estimation-error covariance matrix for previous time interval is used to generate the augmented sigma points. Then, the sigma-points are propagated through the state function to predict the present value of the state. Finally, the weighted average of these sigma points is calculated for the state prediction as shown in Equation (10.1).

$$\hat{x}_k^- = E\{f(x_{k-1}, u_{k-1}, w_{k-1}) | y_{k-1}\} \approx \sum_{i=0}^{p} \alpha_i^{(m)} f(X_{k-1}^{x,+}, u_{k-1}, X_{k-1,i}^{w,+}) \qquad (10.1)$$

$$= \sum_{i=0}^{p} \alpha_i^{(m)} X_{k,i}^{x,-}$$

Step 2: Error-covariance time update

The covariance for every sigma point "I" is calculated from the previous step.

$$\tilde{X}_{k,i}^{x,-} = X_{k,i}^{x,-} - \hat{x}_k^- \qquad (10.2)$$

Then, the covariance matrix is computed as the weighted sum using the following equation.

$$\sum_{\tilde{x},k} = \left(\tilde{X}_k^{x,-}\right) diag(\alpha^c) \left(\tilde{X}_k^{x,-}\right)^T \qquad (10.3)$$

Step 3: Predict system output

The sigma point with randomness is propagated through the output equation to calculate the system output. Then, weighted sum of the output sigma point is calculated which contains the output prediction.

$$\hat{y}_k = E\{h(x_k, u_k, v_k) | y_{k-1}\} \approx \sum_{i=0}^{P} \alpha_i^{(m)} h(X_{k,i}^{x,-}, u_k, X_{k,i}^{v,+}) \qquad (10.4)$$

$$= \sum_{i=0}^{p} \alpha_i^{(m)} y_{k,i}.$$

Step 4: Estimator gain matrix Lx
The estimator gain matrix is calculated using the following formula.

$$L_k = \sum_{\tilde{x},\tilde{y},k}^{-} \sum_{\tilde{y},k}^{-1} \tag{10.5}$$

$$\sum_{\tilde{y},k} = \sum_{i=0}^{p} \alpha_i^{(c)}(y_{k,i} - \hat{y}_k)(y_{k,i} - \hat{y}_k)^T$$

$$\sum_{\tilde{x},\tilde{y},k}^{-} = \sum_{i=0}^{p} \alpha_i^{(c)}\left(X_{k,i}^{x,-} - \hat{x}_k^-\right)(y_{k,i} - \hat{y}_k)^T \tag{10.6}$$

Equations (10.5) and (10.6) are the covariance matrices calculated from the values computed in steps 1b and 1c.

Step 5: State-estimate measurement update
The state estimator is estimated as follows.

$$\hat{x}_k^+ = \hat{x}_k^- + L_k(y_k - \hat{y}_k) \tag{10.7}$$

Step 6: Error covariance measurement update
Error covariance measurement is updated using Equation (10.8).

$$\sum_{\tilde{x},k}^{+} = \sum_{\tilde{x},k}^{-} - L_K \sum_{\tilde{y},k} L_k^T \tag{10.8}$$

10.5   Estimating SoH

Total least squares (TLS) is applied to battery cell total-capacity estimation. The ith data pair, comprising x_i in x and y_i in y, correspond to data collected from a cell over the ith interval of time, where x_i is the estimated change in SoC over that interval and y_i is the accumulated ampere-hours passing through the cell during that period. The TLS approach assumes that there are errors on both the x_i and y_i measurements and models the data as shown in Equation (10.9). The flowchart for estimating SoH is shown in Figure 10.6 [13].

$$(Y - \Delta y) = Q (x - \Delta x) \tag{10.9}$$

$$X^2_{AWTLS} = \frac{1}{(\hat{Q}_n^2 + 1)^2}\left(\tilde{c}_4\hat{Q}_n^4 - 2\tilde{c}_5\hat{Q}_n^3 + (\tilde{c}_1 + \tilde{c}_6)\hat{Q}_n^2 - 2\tilde{c}_2\hat{Q}_n + \tilde{c}_3\right) \tag{10.10}$$

The Approximate Weighted Total Least Square Algorithm (AWTLS) is computed as given in Equation (10.10). This gives the estimated cell total capacity which is an indication of the battery SoH.

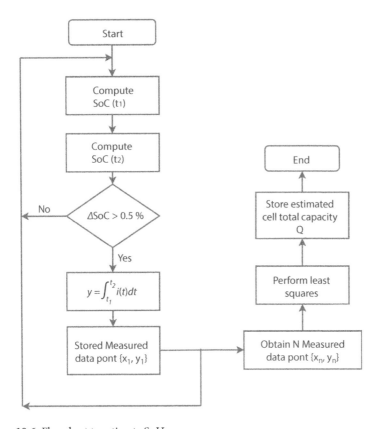

Figure 10.6 Flowchart to estimate SoH.

10.6   Results and Discussion

Here, equivalent circuit parameters of enhanced self-correcting cell model are determined by experimental tests. The characteristics of battery charging and discharging are measured under different operating temperatures and hysteresis conditions. Then, algorithms for estimating SoC and SoH of the battery are developed.

The enhanced self-correcting cell model predicts the terminal voltage which converges to OCV plus hysteresis when the cell rests and converges to OCV plus hysteresis minus all the current time resistance terms on a constant-current event.

The estimation of SoC and SoH (capacity) is simulated using MATLAB. The Urban Dynamometer Drive Schedule (UDDS) profile is used for prediction of the SoC and SoH for an automotive application. The voltage and current for UDDS profile at different temperatures are collected using an ARBIN battery tester.

The plot shown in Figure 10.7 displays the measured voltage versus time for 19 repetitions of the UDDS profile (with rests in between) and also shows a subplot for one profile. The UDDS profile is multiplied by

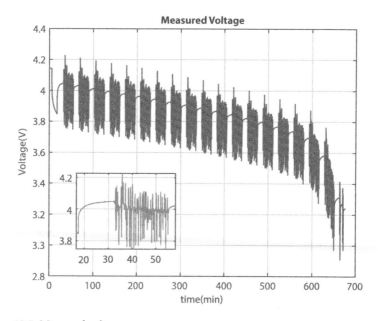

Figure 10.7 Measured voltage.

the C-rate of the cell to convert to current in amperes and the normalized current for 19 repetitions of UDDS with one zoomed profile is shown in Figure 10.8. The plot shown in Figure 10.9 displays the reference SoC which is computed using coulomb counting method.

The SoC estimation errors for different temperatures are shown in Figures 10.10 and 10.11, and the RMS SoC estimation error was 0.84% for 5°C and 0.53% for 25°C, respectively. The error bounds are shown in Figures 10.12 and 10.13, and the true SoC values were outside the estimation-error bounds of the filter for 10.5% of the time for 5°C of battery temperature and 3.67% of the time of battery temperature. The nonlinear hysteresis is much more significant at 5°C temperature than at more typical (warmer) operating temperatures. The biggest contributing factor to this error is most likely that the cell model describes open-circuit voltage poorly in that range at this temperature.

In Figure 10.14, the red color line shows the estimated capacity of a 10-Ah battery with measurement interval of 300 seconds and is within the error bounds. The AWTLS converges to the true total capacity.

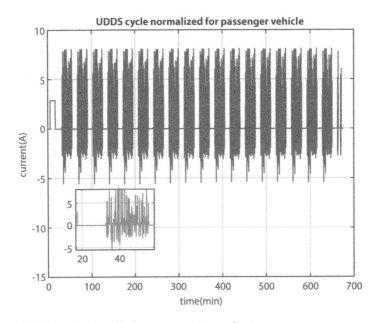

Figure 10.8 Normalized profile for an automotive application.

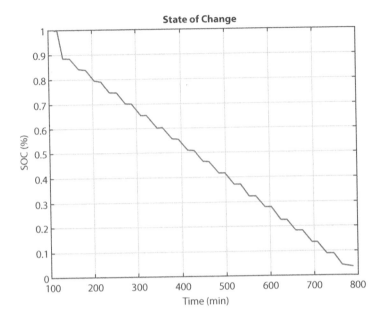

Figure 10.9 Reference SoC.

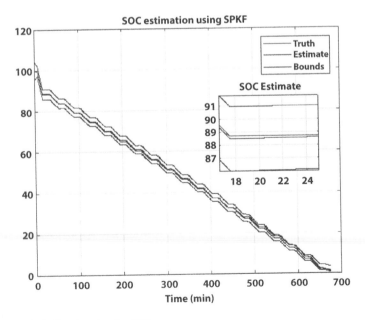

Figure 10.10 SoC estimation for 5°C.

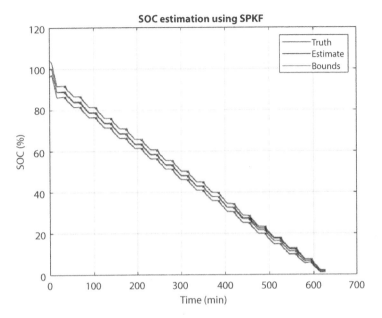

Figure 10.11 SoC estimation for 25°C.

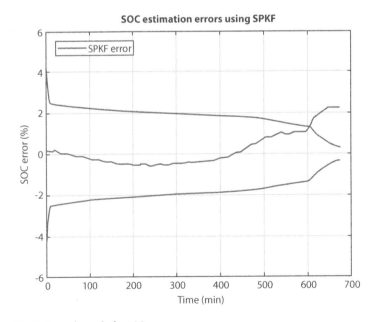

Figure 10.12 Error bounds for 5°C.

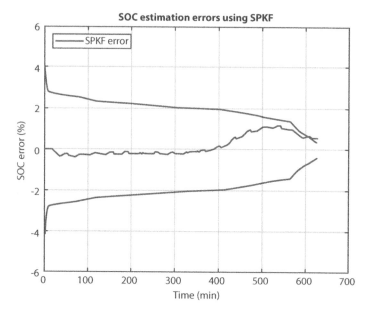

Figure 10.13 Error bounds for 25°C.

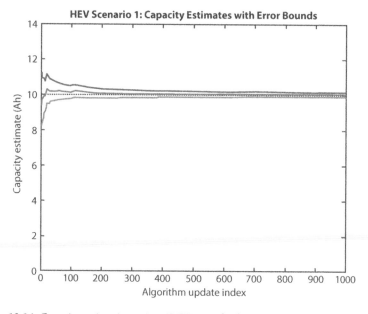

Figure 10.14 Capacity estimation using AWTLS method.

10.7 Conclusion

For prediction of battery range and life in battery EV, it is important to have accurate, computationally less intensive, and memory-efficient algorithms to estimate SoC and SoH. SPKF method estimates the SoC of battery with high accuracy even if the system is highly non-linear and AWTLS method estimates the SoH. AWTLS uses recursive method which is computationally less intensive and also has the ability to implement fading memory, and hence, this method can be practically implemented in BMS.

References

1. Li, Z., Khajepour, A., Song, J., A comprehensive review of the key technologies for pure electric vehicles. *Energy*, 182, 824–839, 2019.
2. Ali, M.U., Zafar, A., Nengroo, S.H., Hussain, S., Junaid A.M., Kim, H.J., Towards a smarter battery management system for electric vehicle applications: A critical review of lithium-ion battery state of charge estimation. *Energies*, 12, 3, 446, 2019.
3. Miao, Y., Hynan, P., von Jouanne, A., Yokochi, A., Current Li-ion battery technologies in electric vehicles and opportunities for advancements. *Energies*, 12, 6, 1074, 2019.
4. Eldeeb, H.H., Elsayed, A.T., Lashway, C.R., Mohammed, O., Hybrid energy storage sizing and power splitting optimization for plug-in electric vehicles. *IEEE Trans. Ind. Appl.*, 55, 3, 2252–2262, 2019.
5. Masias, A., Lithium-Ion Battery Design for Transportation, in: *Behaviour of Lithium-Ion Batteries in Electric Vehicles*, pp. 1–33, Springer, Cham, 2018.
6. Vazquez, S., Lukic, S.M., Galvan, E., Franquelo, L.G., Carrasco, J.M., Energy storage systems for transport and grid applications. *IEEE Trans. Ind. Electron.*, 57, 12, 3881–3895, 2010.
7. Piller, S., Perrin, M., Jossen, A., Methods for state-of-charge determination and their applications. *J. Power Sources*, 96, 1, 113–120, 2001.
8. Vetter, J., Novák, P., Wagner, M. R., Veit, C., Möller, K. C., Besenhard, J. O., Hammouche, A., Ageing mechanisms in lithium-ion batteries. *J. Power Sources*, 147, 1–2, 269–281, 2005.
9. Zenati, A., Desprez, P., Razik, H., Rael, S., A methodology to assess the State of Health of lithium-ion batteries based on the battery's parameters and a Fuzzy Logic System, in: *2012 IEEE International Electric Vehicle Conference*, IEEE, pp. 1–6, 2012, March.
10. Jossen, A., Fundamentals of battery dynamics. *J. Power Sources*, 154, 2, 530–538, 2006.

11. Plett, G.L., Sigma-point Kalman filtering for battery management systems of LiPB-based HEV battery packs: Part 2: Simultaneous state and parameter estimation. *J. Power Sources*, 161, 2, 1369–1384, 2006.

12. Plett, G.L., U.S. Patent No. 7,321,220. Washington, DC: U.S. Patent and Trademark Office, 2008.

13. Plett, G.L., *Battery management systems, Volume II: Equivalent-circuit methods*, Artech House, Norwood, USA, 2015.

11

AI-Driven Healthcare Analysis

N. Kasthuri* and T. Meeradevi

Department of ECE Kongu Engineering College, Perundurai, India

Abstract

AI plays a major role in almost all fields. Healthcare is one of the fields where AI can outperforms the existing techniques used in healthcare technologies. Breast cancer identification at the earliest stage is a challenging task where AI can be applied to determine whether the cancer cells are present or not with highest accuracy. As per 2013, World Health Organization survey statistics reported that approximately 508,000 women died due to breast cancer across the world during the year 2011. It is possible to identify the breast cancer in its primary stage, and hence, it can be healed. But, the cancers are identified at last stage for most of the women.

Early recognition of breast cancer is very important to increase the survival rate. Machine learning technique and technologies are used for the identification and classification of cancer in an accurate level. Classifier such as stochastic gradient decent (SGD), support vector machine (SVM), nearest neighbors (KNN), naïve Bayes, random forest, and convolutional neural network (CNN) are the various machine learning techniques that can be used for the classification of various tumors.

The dataset has been taken from Mammography MIAS database. There are totally 322 images. The Gray Level Co-Occurrence Matrix (GLCM) are used to extract the features from the images, thereby converting the useful information from image space to feature space. These features are used to classify the presence or absence of cancer cells using Machine learning classifiers.

Two different classes of breast cancer tumors are categorized as benign and malignant. Invasive ductal carcinoma and invasive lobular carcinoma are considered as the main category of breast cancer. The breast cancer which is curable is ductal carcinoma when it is found at earliest stage. The other type that can

Corresponding author: kasthuri.ece@kongu.edu

C. Venkatesh, N. Rengarajan, P. Ponmurugan and S. Balamurugan (eds.) Smart Systems for Industrial Applications, (269–286) © 2022 Scrivener Publishing LLC

rapidly spread to lymph nodes and other parts of the body and starts in a lobule of the breast is called as invasive lobular carcinoma.

In addition to mammogram images, the histopathology images are taken for analysis and the deep learning models are used to provide better classification. The images are fed as an input to these models and the features are extracted using the principles of convolution and these features are used to classify the images. The Kaggle dataset is used to train the deep learning model. Breast histopathology images around 200,000 images are available; hence, it is possible to train the CNN classifier with higher accuracy to classify Benign (non-cancerous) and malignant (cancerous).

Keywords: Breast cancer, stochastic gradient decent, support vector machine, K-NN, naïve bayes, random forest, CNN, GLCM

11.1 Introduction

Around 25% to 32% of female in India are affected by Breast cancer. The statistics says that one women in every 4 minutes is spotted with this type of cancer and also one women dies for every 13 minutes due to this cancer type in India. In 2012, the number of women died due to this type of cancer was approximately 70,218. This was happened mainly due to the lack of awareness among the women. In addition to that, due to detaining in screening and diagnosis process, the mortality rate is high. More than 50% of patients in India are suffering from breast cancer, where the possibility of survival is significantly low. In India, breast cancer causes sudden increase for the age group of 30 to 50.

The benign and malignant are the two types of tumors categorized in breast cancer. Benign tumors are not harmful to health, while malignant tumors are harmful to health. Invasive ductal carcinoma, ductal carcinoma *in situ*, and invasive lobular carcinoma are different categories of breast cancer. The breast cancer like ductal carcinoma is curable if it is found at early stage. The other type like invasive lobular carcinoma can rapidly spread to lymph nodes. It starts in a lobule of the breast and spread to all parts of the body. Worldwide every year, one million women are diagnosed with breast cancer. The rate of survival at the early stage is high and 81% is found to be the 5-year survival rate.

The abnormality classes of breast cancer are calcification (CALC), circumscribed masses (CIRC), speculated masses (SPIC), ill-defined masses (MISC), architectural distortion (ARCH), and asymmetry (ASYM). This paper presents a novel five classifier method using machine learning algorithms and deep learning algorithm. The performance of the following machine learning algorithms such as stochastic gradient descent (SGF), support vector machine (SVM), nearest neighbors, naïve Bayes, and random forest classifiers is analyzed, and deep learning model is also developed to classify the presence or absence of cancers using the Kaggle dataset.

11.2   Literature Review

Veta *et al.* [1] presented that the most common cancer occurring in women is breast cancer, and image processing techniques are used in detecting the breast cancer with advanced technologies. The high-throughput histopathology slide digitization is obtained by using whole slide imaging (WSI) scanners. Tissue preparation, staining, and slide digitization processes are used in detecting breast cancer. To produce high quality ground truths, annotation by multiple observers is needed in addition to the large observer variability. But, it is time-consuming and expensive, particularly for large datasets.

Spanhol *et al.* [2] analyzed that almost all conventional classification systems depend on the data representation, and it uses expert domain knowledge of data to produce beneficial features. In deep learning, it can extract and arrange the discriminative details from the data and does not require domain expert for feature extraction. The advanced deep learning method for the classification of breast cancer cells uses histopathological images from BreakHis database. The convolutional neural network (CNN) model is used to extract the features of high-resolution histopathological images taken from BreakHis database. Compared to machine learning techniques, CNN model produces better results.

Aswathy *et al.* [3] proposed that the most common disease that occurs in women worldwide is breast cancer especially in India. Most of the cancer cases occur in urban areas, and it also affects men. There are at least 25–32 patients affected with breast cancer out of 100 cancer patients. Nowadays, there are several advanced methods and technologies that exist for the identification of breast cancer. For detecting breast cancer at early stage, digital image processing techniques such as ANN and CNN are used. The CNN takes histopathological image as input, extracts the feature, classifies the image using fully connected layer, and provides advanced results compared to ANN.

Yaghoobi *et al.* [4] mentioned that number of new breast cancer cases and death rate is 124.8 and 21.9 per 100,000 women per year, respectively. These rates are age-adjusted and are based on 2008–2012 new cases and deaths rates. The breast cancer includes conventional detection methods such as biopsy, thermograph, mammography, and ultrasound imaging. Among these techniques, mammography is the best method for early detection of breast cancer. In order to classify mammography more efficiently, features are extracted using Gray-Level Co-Occurrence Matrix (GLCM), and cumulative histogram features were used. Decision tree classifier system is used for classification of cancer. Discrete version of imperialist competitive algorithm, a new algorithm, was introduced as a global optimization algorithm in discrete space for finding best features among the features extracted. The accuracy obtained using this method was 96.58%. Accuracy can be modified by selecting appropriate features.

Arauajo *et al.* [5] explored breast cancer leads to death occurs in women worldwide. Previously, this breast cancer that causes death is diagnosed using biopsy, and the end results of biopsy may be wrong and it is also time consuming. To improve the accuracy, computer-aided diagnosis system is used as it reduces the cost. Feature extraction is done by using conventional method, and to overcome the difficulty of feature-based approach, deep learning model is used as an alternative. The four classes such as normal tissue, benign lesion, *in situ* carcinoma, and invasive carcinoma are the different classification of an image and are in two classes—carcinoma and non-carcinoma. The features extracted using CNN are applied to SVM. Precision of 77.8% and 83.3% occurred for four classes and for carcinoma or non-carcinoma, respectively, are attained.

Zhou *et al.* [6] mentioned that breast cancer is one of the familiar and fatal cancers among most of the women worldwide. As histopathological images, database is consists adequate phenotypic particulars and plays an indispensable part in identification and treatment of breast cancers. In order to enhance the precision and objectivity of breast histopathological image analysis (BHIA), artificial neural network (ANN) approaches like

MLP and PNN are the most widely used ANNs. These techniques are most widely used for the segmentation and classification of breast histopathological images. In each of these techniques, texture feature and morphological features are used for feature extraction. For early recognition and treatment of breast cancer, the deep learning model such as CNN has achieved better results in classification and segmentation of these images.

Khuriwal *et al.* [7] proposed deep learning method CNN for detecting breast cancer using MIAS mammogram database. The database contains 200 images and 12 features. The 12 features have obtained after applying preprocessing and the preprocessing involves watershed segmentation, color-based segmentation, and adaptive mean filter. After obtaining the features, they dataset has been splitted into training and testing data which are used in prediction of the breast cancer. Before training, the data preprocessing is done to attain high accuracy. Compared to machine learning models, deep learning algorithm has gained more accurate result. The proposed model has attained 98% accuracy in diagnosing breast cancer. In future, additional features and also real-time image database can be used to acquire better results for predicting the breast cancer.

Shwetha *et al.* [8] explored early detection and diagnosis is the most useful methodology to oversight the tumor progression. For such early detection of cancer, mammogram images are nowadays recommended for diagnosing of breast cancer malignancy. To detect the breast cancer at the early stage, they proposed CNN classification approach which is one of the deep learning approaches. Mobile net and Inception V3 architectural models have been used for analysis of mammogram images into two categories: normal and abnormal. On diagnosing breast cancer using Inception V3 architecture model, 83% accuracy has been attained.

Kumar *et al.* [9] proposed CNN for prediction of breast cancer. CNN is a deep learning technique which has been used in feature extraction of an image and classifies an image using these extracted features. The dataset has taken from breast cancer histopathological images and consists of 7,909 breast images. These sets of images contain two different classes: benign and malignant. CNN is class of deep feed forward ANN that has been used in recognition of images. It is viewed that accuracy of the classification depends on how CNN extracts and learns the features of the images at different layers with variation in the parameter. Here, CNN is used with variation in parameter for classifying the images. Predicting breast cancer using this model has attained better efficiency of about 90%

which is to be improved using various techniques and increasing the features of the images.

Bardou et al. [10] analyzed in the field of healthcare informatics that, using biopsy, the breast cancer can be recognized, in which the tissues are separated and studied below microscope. The detection of breast cancer is based on the qualification of the histopathologist and there may be a chance for wrong prediction if the histopathologist is not well-trained. However, due to the recent technologies in computer vision, the quality of the diagnosis can be improved. CNN is used for classification and obtained an accuracy of 98.33% for the binary classification and 88.23% for the multi-class classification.

Ganggayah et al. [11] used machine learning models for diagnosing and visualizing important factors of breast cancer. The dataset has been taken from the University Malaya Medical Centre, Kuala Lumpur, Malaysia. The dataset is consists of 23 predictor variables and dependent variables that indicate the survival of patients. Random forest model and decision trees were built and validation was executed. Both algorithms yield similar results. Decision tree obtained lowest accuracy rate of (79.8%) and random forest acquired highest accuracy of (82.7%).

Sivapriya et al. [12] explored that effective way to classify data and the dataset from Wisconsin breast cancer is used for classification of breast cancer using SVM, logistic regression, naïve Bayes, and random forest methods. Among these methods based on the performance of the classifiers, random forest attains the high accuracy of 99.76% with the least error rate.

Dabeer et al. [13] mentioned that one out of eight females is affected due to breast cancer worldwide. The diagnosis of breast cancer is done by detecting the malignancy in the cells of breast tissues. In modern medical image, processing techniques are used in detecting the cancer cells by capturing the histopathology images using microscope. Various algorithms and methods are used for detecting breast cancer because manual detection of cancer cell is a wearisome and may lead to human error. So, computer-aided mechanisms are performed to obtain better results. Nowadays, deep learning mechanism is used where features are extracted through CNN and classification of cells using fully connected network. The histopathological image datasets are trained using CNN and attained 99.86% of accuracy with better results.

Mohapatra et al. [14] supervised experimental analysis using text datasets and histopathology image datasets to forecast the benign and malignant tumors. The conventional machine learning algorithms like logistic regression, SVM, KNN, and decision tree are used for detection in text datasets, and deep learning model is used for detecting cancer cells in histopathology images. PCA and LDA methods are used to extract the features to provide good accuracy in both the models. While dealing with large datasets with high-resolution images, deep learning perform well compared to machine learning. Various architectures of CNN were applied to the high-resolution images. The histopathological images are given as input to CNN network. For final classification, the model produces an 81% accuracy after varying number of hidden layers between input and output layers and the hyperparameters. Using GPU for processing, the model produces an accuracy of 89% with high-resolution images.

Benhammou *et al.* [15] explored about a public dataset called BreakHis, and the datasets are categorized into four magnification levels and classified as either benign or malignant and its subcategory as (A/F/PT/TA/PC/DC/LC/MC). To overcome the magnification problem, it is categorized into four different reformulations. These reformulations are used in classification breast cancer cells. Among the models, developed Magnification Independent Multicategory reformulation using deep learning is the best approach.

11.3   Feature Extraction

The spatial relationship among the pixels is used to describe the textures. The statistical methods are used to obtain features. One such statistical method which can characterize the texture of an image is the GLCM. It shows how often pairs of pixel occur with specific values and in a specified spatial relationship occur in an image and help to extract statistical features. The GLCM indicates the number of times that the pixel with value i occurred in the specified spatial relationship to a pixel with value j in the input image. In GLCM, the number of gray levels is represented by G, mean as μ and μx, μy,σ x, σ y are the means and standard deviations of Px and Py. The matrix element P(i, j| Δ x, Δ y) is the relative frequency separated by a pixel distance(Δ x, Δ y).

11.3.1   GLCM Feature Descriptors

The 22 features are extracted to classify the breast image into cancerous and non-cancerous. These 22 features of GLCM for mammographic images were taken and written in Excel format which is converted into Microsoft Excel Comma Separated Values File (.csv). This .csv format is given as input for various classifiers for different test size and the accuracy is calculated as shown in Figure 11.1.

diagnosis	F1	F2	F3	F4	F5	F6	F7	F8	F9	F10	F11	F12	F13	F14	F15	F16	F17	F18	F19	F20	F21	F22
M	13.16066	0.046067	0.995771	0.985771	771.9126	68.9535	0.0402	0.407597	1.384132	0.980661	0.980462	0.593402	13.09701	5.563316	39.49196	1.349799	0.046067	0.169219	-0.87368	0.939788	0.995593	0.999307
M	9.004301	0.043739	0.993248	0.993248	473.6003	45.59659	0.041693	0.334482	1.599168	0.978161	0.978158	0.541402	8.951236	4.811424	23.42642	1.568697	0.043739	0.179632	-0.87816	0.958233	0.995146	0.999327
M	11.04837	0.079454	0.991459	0.991459	729.5068	70.12472	0.049583	0.425288	1.410572	0.977896	0.977552	0.627344	11.00906	5.074138	32.27749	1.365845	0.079454	0.190809	-0.85892	0.938293	0.994751	0.998928
M	6.530847	0.028845	0.995373	0.995373	742.5238	80.51053	0.02883	0.61407	1.014342	0.985588	0.985587	0.778913	6.48775	3.703294	19.77695	0.994291	0.028845	0.130894	-0.88198	0.893408	0.996797	0.999556
M	8.941019	0.059969	0.992587	0.992587	798.6154	82.26218	0.03261	0.507143	1.224055	0.986223	0.985866	0.697875	8.901888	4.449051	26.66152	1.193091	0.059969	0.133877	-0.89302	0.928026	0.996616	0.999214
M	9.554308	0.039396	0.995598	0.995598	887.9022	93.85728	0.03925	0.517212	1.21294	0.980399	0.980389	0.708188	9.503681	4.516448	28.95536	1.185227	0.039396	0.165851	-0.86534	0.918027	0.99564	0.999394
M	6.226781	0.036083	0.993207	0.993207	407.9726	51.51942	0.035018	0.554789	1.11335	0.982597	0.98258	0.736049	6.185867	3.788794	17.88069	1.088342	0.036083	0.151839	-0.87026	0.905584	0.996119	0.999449
M	10.39268	0.076712	0.991402	0.991402	767.1589	76.04616	0.060352	0.427601	1.467948	0.971711	0.971321	0.637243	10.35493	4.886654	29.82188	1.414792	0.076712	0.228001	-0.83466	0.936095	0.993452	0.998875
M	7.780235	0.031192	0.995661	0.995661	1008.059	102.1826	0.028328	0.580589	1.097138	0.986294	0.986239	0.758204	7.734791	3.686171	23.73628	1.075551	0.033192	0.12745	-0.88537	0.90965	0.996896	0.999511
M	15.21312	0.055733	0.995751	0.995751	1399.867	109.9752	0.053037	0.350284	1.679592	0.973851	0.973751	0.571278	15.14934	5.893585	44.27388	1.639266	0.055733	0.208635	-0.86537	0.960652	0.904135	0.999148
M	10.14173	0.062975	0.992589	0.992589	707.7504	72.05561	0.047358	0.394773	1.527917	0.97787	0.977626	0.608728	10.09739	4.86813	28.36659	1.486505	0.062975	0.188557	-0.86693	0.950518	0.99488	0.9991

Figure 11.1 Feature extraction in excel format.

11.4 Classifiers

The various optimization methods are used to classify the images of cancerous and non-cancerous.

11.4.1 Stochastic Gradient Descent Classifier

The normally used optimization method in machine learning and deep learning algorithms is gradient descent in which the slope of a function is called as gradient, and it represents the degree of change of a parameter with the amount of change in another parameter. In iterative method, gradient descent is adapted to identify the parameters that minimize the cost function as much as possible.

The word "stochastic" is a process used to represent a random probability. In SGD, for each iteration, certain instances are randomly chosen instead of the entire dataset. In each iteration, the total number of samples from a dataset which is used for calculating the gradient is treated as batch. The whole dataset can be used to achieve minimal error but the problem arises when the size of the dataset is too high. For example, if the dataset consists of million samples data, it takes huge time to reach to the optimal value to complete one iteration if gradient descent optimization technique is used. Hence, the computational complexity is high in this method.

In order to solve this problem, SGD uses a batch size of one to perform each iteration, and the samples are shuffled randomly and selected to perform the iterations. The classification is based on the evaluation and updating the coefficients for every iteration in order to decrease the error for next training instance while training the data. This procedure is repeated for fixed number of iterations to improve the accuracy of the classifier.

11.4.2 Naïve Bayes Classifier

This is a classification algorithm for binary and multiclass classification. The classification is based on Bayes theorem. naïve Bayes classifier presumes that the appearance of a particular feature in a class is unrelated to the appearance of any feature.

Naïve Bayes classifier is one of the probabilistic classifiers, which helps in building the fast ML models to perform quick predictions. The predictions are based on the probability of an object and Bayes theorem is used for classification. Naïve Bayes is basically used in text classification that includes a high-dimensional training dataset. Three types of naïve Bayes model such as Gaussian, Mutinomial, and Bernoulli are used based on the feature distribution.

The naïve Bayes classifier algorithm predicts the occurrence of a certain feature but it is independent of the occurrence of other features. It depends on the principle of Bayes theorem. It uses prior knowledge to determine the probability of a hypothesis and it depends on conditional probability.

11.4.3   K-Nearest Neighbor Classifier

KNN is a simple algorithm that uses the entire data for its training. Whenever a new data given as an input to classifier for prediction, it searches through the entire training data for k-most similar instances and the data with similar instance is returned as output. This algorithm is based on supervised learning technique, and it finds the similarity between the new data and available data. Finally, it assigns the category to the new data to which category it belongs. This algorithm can be used for regression as well as for classification. If the prediction is based on the mean or the median of the K-most similar instances, then it is regression problem. But, for classification problem, the output can be calculated as the class with the highest frequency from the K-most similar instances

11.4.4   Support Vector Machine Classifier

SVM is the robust method of classification algorithm which follows supervised learning model that analyze the data for classification and regression analysis. The data is plotted in n-dimensional space with the value for each feature extracted that is to be separated by a hyperplane and it differentiates the two different classes. SVM algorithm uses a hyperplane to segregate n-dimensional space into classes. Also, SVM chooses the extreme points that help in creating the hyperplane which is called as support vectors. For linearly separable data, linear SVM can be used, and for non-linearly separable data, non-linear SVM can be used for classification. In order to classify the data points, the best decision boundary are to be found and it is straight line for two features. The support vectors are closest to the hyperplane, and as it supports the hyperplane, it is called as Support vector.

11.4.5   Random Forest Classifier

Random forest is a supervised learning algorithm. Random forest classifier can be used for classification and regression. In this algorithm, decision trees are created by the classifier on randomly selected data samples. Based on the prediction from each tree, the best solution is selected for classification problems. The robustness of the forest is decided by the number of trees. In a decision tree, each branch of the tree represents a possible decision. This classifier provides a better solution than a single decision tree as it reduces the overfitting by averaging the result. This classifier results into a good model as it searches for the best feature among a random subset of features. So this considers a random subset of the features during splitting of a node.

11.4.6   Working of Random Forest Algorithm

- **Step 1:** From a given dataset, the random samples are selected.
- **Step 2:** For every sample, this algorithm constructs a decision tree and from every decision tree the results are predicted.
- **Step 3:** For every predicted result, votings are calculated.
- **Step 4:** Higher voting is selected as prediction result.

The accuracy level of different classifiers for various test size were calculated and tabulated in Table 11.1 for analysis.

The algorithm is tested for various test size and shows that the accuracy for lesser test size is high when compared to other test sizes.

11.4.7   Convolutional Neural Network

CNN is a kind of neural network architecture that contains the first layer called convolutional layer as an input layer. It extracts features from each input image using the principle of convolution directly, and hence, it is called as self-learning feature extractor. Therefore, it can extract the features and perform the classification using same CNN layout. The convolutional layer acts as a basic building block of CNN architecture. This layer contains a set of learnable kernels that contains small receptive field but it amplifies through the full depth of the input. The Rectified Linear Unit

Table 11.1 Accuracy for different classifiers.

Classifiers	Test size = 10%	Test size = 20%	Test size = 30%
Stochastic Gradient Descent	87.88%	84.62%	83.51%
Support Vector Machine	SVC Accuracy: 87.88% Linear SVC Accuracy: 87.88%	SVC Accuracy: 84.62% Linear SVC Accuracy: 84.62%	SVC Accuracy: 83.51% Linear SVC Accuracy: 81.44%
Nearest Neighbors	87.88%	84.62%	82.47%
Naïve Bayes	72.73%	78.46%	73.20%
Forest and tree methods	Random Forest Accuracy: 87.88% Extra Trees Accuracy: 87.88% Decision Tree Accuracy: 75.76%	Random Forest Accuracy: 84.62% Extra Trees Accuracy: 80.00% Decision Tree Accuracy: 73.85%	Random Forest Accuracy: 82.47% Extra Trees Accuracy: 80.41% Decision Tree Accuracy: 72.16%

(ReLU) is used as an activation function to provide nonlinearity in each layer. This architecture uses this activation function to learn the parameters in each layer to provide better classification accuracy.

Pooling layer is used as the next layer in CNN architecture to provide non-linear down-sampling. This layer is used to reduce the dimensionality using Min or Max pooling and it works independently on every depth slice of the input. The next layer that can be used is dropout layer that can avoid the overfitting. Few neurons that learnt already does not allow the other neuron to learn making a less chance for every neuron to learn. So, based on the result performance, this layer may be added to the architecture.

In CNN architecture, the features extracted from the input image act as input to the first layer and several hidden layers are used to perform the classification. In every hidden layer, every neuron is connected to every other neuron so it is called as fully connected layer. In CNN model, the fully connected layer is used at the last stage to perform classification. The type of activation which is used to perform the classification is softmax activation and it classifies the patterns based on the probability.

In CNN architecture in every layer, the convolution operation is followed by pooling operation in order to extract the feature pattern. The model can use several layer to extract the feature pattern that can act as an input to the final fully connected layer. In fully connected layer, several hidden layers are used to increase the classification accuracy. The final layer uses the softmax activation to provide classification based on the probability measure.

Figure 11.2 shows the CNN with its layers. It can perform both feature extraction and classification under the same architecture. The input

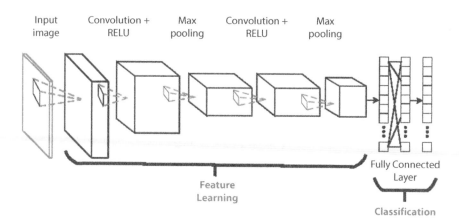

Figure 11.2 Convolutional neural network with its layers.

image is given to the architecture and series of convolution and pooling operations are performed, to extract the features followed by a number of fully connected layers. The softmax activation is used for classification in multiclass classification. The ReLU activation function used to perform the training several times faster and also it avoids the problem of vanishing gradient problem

The first layer which is used in this architecture is the convolution layer to extract features from an input image followed by pooling layer to reduce the dimension. This set of convolution with pooling is performed in several layers. These layers use several filters to create feature vector. These filters or kernels can perform operations such as edge detection, blurring, and sharpening by applying suitable filter stack on to the image. Zero padding is used to perform the convolution operation to all pixels in the image. This adds a value 0 to all sides of an image in such a way to perform convolution of the whole image.

11.4.7.1   Activation Function

The type of activation function that can perform nonlinear function in this architecture is ReLU. This function chooses a maximum value so as to introduce non-linearity in the ConvNet denoted as $f(x) = max(0,x)$. The other nonlinear activation functions are tanh and sigmoidal functions that can also be used but the performance of ReLU is better than the other types.

11.4.7.2   Pooling Layer

The pooling operation is used to reduce the dimension of an image in the feature space and the different types of pooling operations are as follows:

- Max Pooling: It considers the largest value over the scanned region of the feature map.
- Average Pooling: It considers the average value over the scanned region of the feature map.
- Sum Pooling: It considers the sum value over the scanned region of the feature map.

11.4.7.3   Fully Connected Layer (FC)

The last layer in this architecture is FC layer, and the matrix from the convolutional layer is flattened to get the matrix in single dimension, and this single dimensional vector acts as an input to the FC layer. This FC layer acts as a conventional neural network architecture. The feature map matrix will be converted as vector (x1, x2, x3, ...) and fed as an input to FC layer. Several hidden layers are used in FC layer and the final activation function such as softmax or sigmoid is used to classify the outputs in the output layer which is the last layer in this architecture.

11.5   Results and Conclusion

For this model, the Kaggle histopathology images which contain 5,000 and 10,000 images were stored in Google Drive, which are given as input to the model. The validation loss, validation accuracy, test loss, and test accuracy are calculated for all the two set of images. Analysis of this parameters by having the epochs = 100 and batch size = 50 was done. The outputs from all the images are taken and shown in Figures 11.3–11.6.

11.5.1   5,000 Images

Validation Parameters

Test Parameters

```
Epoch 00097: val_accuracy did not improve from 0.83800
Epoch 98/100
4000/4000 [==============================] - 12s 3ms/step - loss: 0.0133 - accuracy: 0.9965 - val_loss: 1.2996 - val_accuracy: 0.8140

Epoch 00098: val_accuracy did not improve from 0.83800
Epoch 99/100
4000/4000 [==============================] - 12s 3ms/step - loss: 2.6881e-04 - accuracy: 1.0000 - val_loss: 1.3391 - val_accuracy: 0.8160

Epoch 00099: val_accuracy did not improve from 0.83800
Epoch 100/100
4000/4000 [==============================] - 12s 3ms/step - loss: 0.0052 - accuracy: 0.9992 - val_loss: 1.8950 - val_accuracy: 0.7630

Epoch 00100: val_accuracy did not improve from 0.83800
<keras.callbacks.callbacks.History at 0x7f7b095d6588>
```

Figure 11.3 Validation parameters.

```
score = model.evaluate(testX, testY, verbose=0)
print('Test loss:', score[0])
print('Test accuracy:', score[1])
```

```
Test loss: 1.8949585704803467
Test accuracy: 0.7630000114440918
```

Figure 11.4 Test parameters.

```
Epoch 00097: val_accuracy did not improve from 0.84650
Epoch 98/100
8000/8000 [==============================] - 25s 3ms/step - loss: 8.0303e-06 - accuracy: 1.0000 - val_loss: 1.9864 - val_accuracy: 0.8170

Epoch 00098: val_accuracy did not improve from 0.84650
Epoch 99/100
8000/8000 [==============================] - 25s 3ms/step - loss: 7.9079e-06 - accuracy: 1.0000 - val_loss: 1.9897 - val_accuracy: 0.8180

Epoch 00099: val_accuracy did not improve from 0.84650
Epoch 100/100
8000/8000 [==============================] - 25s 3ms/step - loss: 7.6578e-06 - accuracy: 1.0000 - val_loss: 1.9866 - val_accuracy: 0.8190

Epoch 00100: val_accuracy did not improve from 0.84650
<keras.callbacks.callbacks.History at 0x7f4bec4ee7b8>
```

Figure 11.5 Validation parameters.

```
score = model.evaluate(testX, testY, verbose=0)
print('Test loss:', score[0])
print('Test accuracy:', score[1])
```

```
Test loss: 1.986630111694336
Test accuracy: 0.8190000057220459
```

Figure 11.6 Test parameters.

11.5.2   10,000 Images

Validation Parameters

Test Parameters

The test accuracy gets improved if the number of images for training and testing increased. This shows that the networks get trained using the given input images and these trained networks get tested with the test data. The various analyses have been performed for various batch sizes and the number of hidden layers.

For CNN model, the validation and testing parameters for 5,000 and 10,000 images are calculated. It is observed that the validation and testing parameters are increases as the number of images increases for same batch size and epoch. On comparing ANN and CNN, it is observed that the accuracy level of CNN is higher than the accuracy level of ANN.

Table 11.2 shows the confusion matrix obtained to evaluate the performance of the system for the classification of breast cancer. Total number of images is 10,000 with 8,000 as malignant and 2,000 as benign, out of which 80% is used for training and 20% used for testing. Also, the network was tested with various combinations of training and testing values.

The overall accuracy of 95% is achieved using this architecture. The performance of the model is improved if the network is supplied with the new

Table 11.2 Performance metrics.

Parameters	Benign	Malignant
TP	1520	6080
TN	6080	1520
FP	80	320
FN	320	80
Error rate	0.01	0.01
F1 score	0.8836	0.968151
Sensitivity	0.95	0.95
Specificity	0.98701	0.8260
Accuracy	0.94915254	0.961111
Precision	0.95	0.95
Recall	0.8260	0.98701
Overall accuracy	95%	

images in such a way that it should learn additional information from the images.

References

1. Veta, M., Pluim, J.P.W., van Diest, P.J., Viergever, M.A., Breast Cancer Histopathology Image Analysis: A Review. *IEEE Trans. Bio-Med. Eng.*, 61, 5, 1400–1411, May 2014.
2. Spanhol, F.A., Oliveira, L.S., Petitjean, C., Heutte, L., Breast Cancer Histopathological Image Classification using Convolutional Neural Networks, in: *2016 International Joint Conference on Neural Networks (IJCNN)*, pp. 2560–2567, 2016.
3. Aswathy, M.A. and Jagannath, M., Detection of breast cancer on digital histopathology images: Present status and future possibilities. *Inform. Med. Unlocked*, Elsevier, 8, 74–79, Nov 2016.
4. Yaghoobi, H., Barandagh, A.G., Mohammadi, Z., Breast Cancer Diagnosis Using, Grey-level Co-occurrence Matrices, Decision Tree Classification and Evolutionary Feature Selection. *J. Knowl.-Based Eng. Innov.*, 3, 8, 511–521, Jan. 2017.

5. Araujo, T., Aresta, G., Castro, E., Rouco, J., Aguiar, P., Eloy, C., Polonia, A., Campilho, A., Classification of breast cancer histology images using Convolutional Neural Networks. *PloS One*, 12, 6, e0177544, Jun 2017.

6. Zhou, X., Li, C., Rahaman, M.M., Yao, Y., Ai, S., Sun, C., Li, X., Wang, Q., Jiang, T., A Comprehensive Review for Breast Histopathology Image Analysis Using Classical and Deep Neural Networks. *IEEE Access*, 4, 1–25, 2016.

7. Khuriwal, N. and Mishra, N., Breast Cancer Detection From Histopathological Images Using Deep Learning. *IEEE Conference*, Nov-2018.

8. Shwetha, K., Spoorthi, M., Sindhu, S.S., Chaithra, D., Breast Cancer Detection Using Deep Learning Technique. *Int. J. Eng. Res. Technol.*, 6, 13, 1–4, 2018.

9. Kumar, K. and Rao, A.C.S., Breast Cancer Classification of Image using Convolutional Neural Network. *Recent Advances in Information Technology RAIT-2018*.

10. Bardou, D., Zhang, K., Mohammad, A.S., Classification of Breast Cancer Based on Histology Images Using Convolutional Neural Networks. *IEEE Access*, 6, 24680–24693, May 2018.

11. Ganggayah, M.D., Taib, N.A., Har, Y.C., Lio, P., Dhillon, S.K., Predicting factors for survival of breast cancer patients using machine learning techniques. *BMC Med. Inform. Decis. Mak.*, 19, 1–17, 2019.

12. Sivapriya, J., Kumar, A.V., Siddarth, S.S., Sriram, S., Breast Cancer Prediction using Machine Learning. *Int. J. Recent Technol. Eng. (IJRTE)*, 8, 4, 4879–4881, November 2019.

13. Dabeer, S., Khan, M.M., Islam, S., Cancer diagnosis in histopathological image: CNN based approach. *Inform. Med. Unlocked*, 16, 1–9, Aug 2019.

14. Mohapatra, P., Panda, B., Swain, S., Enhancing Histopathological Breast Cancer Image Classification using Deep Learning. *Int. J. Innov. Technol. Explor. Eng. (IJITEE)*, 8, 7, 2024–2032, May, 2019.

15. Benhammou, Y., Achchab, B., Herrera, F., Tabik, S., BreakHis based Breast Cancer Automatic Diagnosisvusing Deep Learning: Taxonomy, Survey and Insights. *Neurocomputing*, 375, 9–24, Sept 2019.

12

A Novel Technique for Continuous Monitoring of Fuel Adulteration

Rajalakshmy P.[1*], Varun R.[2], Subha Hency Jose P.[3] and Rajasekaran K.[4]

*[1]Department of Robotics Engineering, Karunya Institute of Technology
and Sciences, Coimbatore, India*
[2]Qualcomm, Hyderabad, India
*[3]Department of Biomedical Engineering, Karunya Institute of Technology
and Sciences, Coimbatore, India*
[4]Staan Biomed Engineering Pvt. Limited, Coimbatore, India

Abstract

A proper discrimination between detecting adulteration in fuel and identifying non-compliance of fuel quality standards is of utmost importance in the automotive sector. In other words, it implies that adulteration of fuel can be done by confining to the standards of fuel quality. Therefore, the compliance with fuel quality standards does not essentially indicate that the fuel is not adulterated. Density is one of the most important quality characteristics of crude oil. By knowing the density of fuel, say, petrol, it is possible to detect whether it is pure petrol or petrol mixed with other solution. Therefore, density measurement in petrol is critical to determine the quantity of petrol present in underground sump. Pure petrol has a density of which is set as a standard range by leading oil companies. Density is indicative of the presence of adulterated additive such as pentane, mineral turpentine oil, kerosene, and water. But the current problem faced by leading retailers of crude oil is that the technology currently in use is extremely prone to failure and sometimes gives incorrect measurement due to the wear and tear of the mechanical moving parts involved. Hence, there is a need to develop an indigenous and failsafe technique to detect fuel adulteration which actually rolls down to identifying a suitable measurement technique to measure the fuel density. A novel technique for continuous measurement of fuel density has been discussed in this chapter.

Keywords: Density, online, fuel, adulteration, continuous, measurement

*Corresponding author: rajalakshmy@karunya.edu

C. Venkatesh, N. Rengarajan, P. Ponmurugan and S. Balamurugan (eds.) *Smart Systems for Industrial Applications*, (287–306) © 2022 Scrivener Publishing LLC

12.1   Introduction

Fluid density is a predominant physical property that is used widely to characterize fluids and classify them to be put into use in various fields of application like cosmetics, environmental, pharmaceuticals, food, beverage, and the hydrocarbon industry. Petroleum and petroleum-based products underpin various sections of the modern world, primarily supplying energy to power industries, home automation systems, operate vehicles, and aircrafts to transport goods to various parts of the world. This great demand for petrol has also resulted in the adulteration of petrol with cheaper alternatives. The difference in price between different fuels is the primary factor that leads to petrol adulteration. Whenever products with similar and comparable qualities have a large variation in the price and the consumers lack efficient tools to distinguish between them, then the unscrupulous dealers and operators are inclined to exploit these conditions for unlawful means of making profit. Such unlawful practices are prevalent worldwide. It is lucrative to add industrial solvents and other cheaper fuels like kerosene in petrol. Such practices of adulteration lead to several losses that include irreparable damage to the vehicle engine as well as ill impacts on the air quality. Doping petrol with kerosene may leave harmful deposits on the engine.

Petrol is a major fuel used for transport, and adulteration of petrol at the point of sale in the dispensing stations and during transportation has turned out to be a serious issue in our country. Transport fuels like petrol and diesel are major transport fuels in India, and hence, these are mixed with cheaper products like waste hydrocarbon. Adulteration of transport fuel can lead to economic disaster, increased emission of harmful gases, and deterioration of engine performance. Statistics reveal that the country is facing a financial loss of approximately 50,000 Crores per year just due to the losses incurred by adulteration. Some of the consequences of adulteration are as follows:

1. Malfunctioning of the vehicle engine and failure of vehicle parts;
2. Increased emission of hydrocarbons that result in air pollution;
3. Ill effects on human health due to the emission of harmful and carcinogenic; pollutants
4. Significant financial loss in the country due to the loss of tax revenue.

There exist well-defined codes, standards, and specifications that are clearly spelt in different countries. These standards indicate the minimum quality that must be ensured when the fuel is supplied to the end user.

This implicitly poses a constraint on the standards to be followed by the engine designers in order to conform that the automobiles operate on the specified fuel quality. In India, it is the BIS (Bureau of Indian Standards) that sets the standards for the required specifications of petrol and diesel.

12.1.1   Literature Review

There has been different methods proposed for measuring density of the diesel and petrol which do not require advanced lab equipment as discussed in the literature [1–3]. The application of statistical techniques to determine the fuel adulteration is discussed [4]. Fiber optic techniques have also been adopted for fuel density measurement [5]. The density measurement techniques for ethanol blended fuels using approximation techniques has proven to be an acceptable one [6]. The resistive measurement techniques used for density and viscosity measurement of diesel fuels at different working conditions is discussed in [7]. The advanced methods in use are digital measurement techniques and online monitoring using intelligent controllers [8, 9]. Methods used to predict the values of density and viscosity of diesel fuels is discussed [10]. In [11], density is measured by subjecting the fuel to pressure of up to 500 MPa using a micro-PVT and maintaining the fuel between a temperature of 298, 323, 348, and 373 K. This device is based on piston-in-bottle design and is operated by a translational-rotary displacement of a metal rod, which is used to compress the liquid at constant rate. In [12], fuel adulteration is detected by heating petrol or kerosene to their respective boiling point temperatures, thereby evaporating any constituent and leaving the residue which can be used the amount of various adulteration substitutes. The level of kerosene left in adulterated petrol is measured using infrared or a camera. In [13], polarimetry is used to determine the density. Polarimetry is the measurement and interpretation of the polarization of transverse waves; by measuring the polarimetry of the fuel, a relation can be derived such that change in density of the fuel can have an impact on the polarimetry. Therefore, by calibrating polarimetry against density a portable device can be designed. In [14], a multimode optical fiber which has diameter of 980- and 20-μm-thick cladding which is removed this now exposed optical fiber cable is now submerged in a bath the fuel which is to test for adulteration one end of the cable is connected to a LED transmitter and the other is connected to an optical detector whose output is measure by a PIC microcontroller. Now, by measuring the change in refractive index with a refractometer, a co-relation between adulation and refractive index can be established.

12.1.2   Overview

The quality of petrol is determined as a measure of the fuel density. The existing methodology adopted in retail outlets is prone to failure due to mechanical effects. Moreover, the corrosion of the metal leads to inaccurate indication of density value of the petrol. The proposed system aims to measure the density of petrol using an accurate and reliable technique that is also a stable system. As the system is mounted in a static position, it does not get damaged easily and it also does not get affected by the environmental factors. The sensor used is a differential pressure sensor that works based on the pressure drop that occurs across a filter.

12.1.3   Objective

The primary objective of the proposed work is summarized as given below.

- Develop a sensor system that can measure density in real time and can be interfaced and integrated with the existing system.
- The new sensor must be able to determine density with high accuracy and must be able to operate in all types of conditions.
- The sensor must not be prone to failure and must be able to distinguish between petrol and water.

12.2   Existing Method

In order to check and calibrate the instrument being developed for petrol density measurement, the accurate density of the petrol sample must be determined. To achieve this, a hydrometer is used. A typical hydrometer is shown in Figure 12.1. The hydrometer has already been calibrated to indicate the

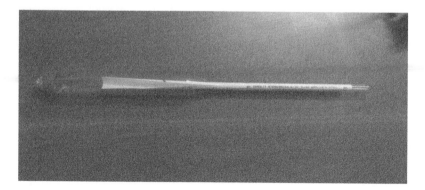

Figure 12.1 Petrol hydrometer.

specific gravity reading for petrol. Hydrometer scales can vary depending on the liquid that is required to be measured. In this case, a petrol hydrometer is designed to show the specific gravity range from 0.700 to 0.750 g/ml at 15°C. The hydrometer works based on Archimedes Principle and is used to measure the relative density of liquids.

12.2.1   Module-1 Water

The concept of measurement of density using the force applied by the liquid is a novel experiment. Therefore, in order to prove the concept and validate the developed system, initially, water is used as standard liquid as its density is known, around 0.9982 g/ml at 20°C and 0.9970 g/ml at 25°C as certified by UKAS ISO/IEC17025 and ISO Guide 34 for pure water, which is around 999 kg/m³ at 20°C and 997 kg/m³ at 25°C.

Water is considered as a standard liquid for comparing because its density variations are very small at different temperature with respect to atmosphere temperature at 1 atmospheric pressure, knowing that the density of water is around 995.7 to 998.2 kg/m³ at 20°C and 30°C, respectively. The table of temperature vs water density as approved by ITS-90 is shown in Table 12.1.

The graph representing the density of water at different temperatures is shown in Figure 12.2 and the density of water in different conditions is shown in Table 12.2. Hence, the pressure that is applied by water on a particular surface area can be calculated by using the formula $P = \rho \times g \times h$ where ρ is the density of the liquid, g is acceleration due to gravity, and h is height.

Thereby substituting the values which are known in the above equation, the pressure that can be applied by any liquid can be calculated; in this case, in order to prove the concept, we must theoretically calculate the pressure that can be applied by the liquid and compare it with the output of the sensor being used for this particular water test in order to prove that

Table 12.1   Water density table approved by ITS-90.

Temp (°C)	Density (g/cm³)
30	0.9957
20	0.9982
10	0.9997
4	1.0000
0	0.9998
−10	0.9982
−20	0.9935

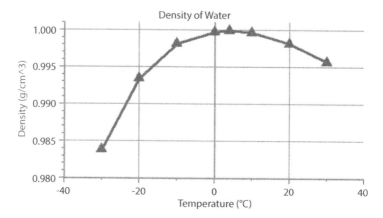

Figure 12.2 Water density at different temperatures.

Table 12.2 Water density table.

Temp (°C)	Density pure water (g/cm³)	Density pure water (kg/m³)	Density tap water (g/cm³)
4	1.0000	1000	0.99999
20	0.9982	998.2	0.99823
40	0.9922	992.2	0.99225
60	0.9832	983.2	0.98389
80	0.9718	971.8	0.97487

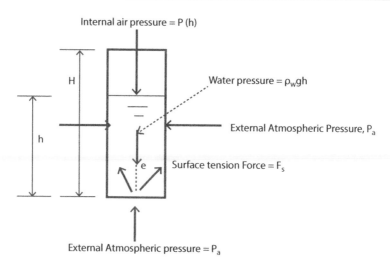

Figure 12.3 Effect of water pressure on air column inside a cylindrical pipe.

density of a liquid can be measure using pressure. The effect of water pressure on air column inside a cylindrical pipe is shown in Figure 12.3.

12.2.2 Module-2 Petrol

In the case of measuring the density of petrol, the same above-mentioned equation can be used but density of petrol is much lower compare to water. The density of petrol ranges from 0.71 to 0.77 kg/L which is around 719.7 kg/m^3 as stated by Bell Fuels "Lead-Free gasoline Material Safety Data Sheet" NOAA. The density of petrol is much lower when compared to water, and hence, in the case of petrol, a sensor with the ability to measure minute pressure changes is required. The above-equation can used to measure density by substituting the known value of height h, gravity g, and pressure, p measured by the sensor to give the corresponding density value. The density of petrol varies depending on the quality of crude oil used in production of petrol. Petrol is deemed fit for sale based on its density value which must be in range of 0.65 to 0.75 kg/L. Hence, different outlets can have different density values depending on the batch and the quality of crude oil used in the process of the producing petrol and diesel.

12.2.3 Petrol Density Measurement

After proving the concept that density of a liquid can be measurement using pressure by using water as a standard test liquid, now, the same concept is applied to petrol to determine its density and confirm the resulting reading with the results of manual testing using hydrometer to show that the instrument is showing the providing the correct density reading of the petrol sample being measured.

12.2.4 Block Diagram

Figure 12.4 shows the methodology adopted for petrol density measurement. The Pressure Instrument is the same type as used in water density measurement but has a different design to help control the air bubble that is formed at the end of the two pipes which continuously expands due vaporization of petrol to petrol vapor which leads to unstable pressure formation

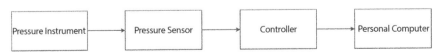

Figure 12.4 Block diagram for petrol density measurement.

at the ends of the pipe. The pressure is given as input to a pressure sensor, and the data is then acquired from the register of the sensor and is transmitted to controller which then sends the relevant data to the computer which can be viewed on the monitor.

12.2.5   Components of the System

The building blocks of the measurement system is listed below.

- Pressure Instrument
- Sensor
- Controller
- Personal Computer

12.2.5.1   Pressure Instrument

The pressure instrument consists of two copper pipes with the same inner diameter of 5 mm. These copper pipes are attached to the sensor and give the pressure which is developed by the water. The two copper pipes have a constant height difference between which is maintain throughout testing.

12.2.5.2   Sensor

The density of petrol is very low compared to the density of water. Due this fact, the same sensor can be used but the sensitivity and degree of accuracy of the output will be affected as a result. For this reason, Honeywell's range of Standard Accuracy Silicon Ceramic (SSC) Series is used. It is a piezoresistive silicon pressure sensor. The sensor used for testing is the SSCSDRN010MD2A3, as shown in Figure 12.5. It has digital interface, where the data is read from the register (0X28) and is sent to the controller using the I2C protocol. The data received at the controller have been processed by algorithm programmed into the controller.

The sensor has pressure rating ranging from −10 mbar to +10 mbar and has an operating voltage of 3.3-V DC and has an output resolution of 12 bits. It is calibrated to operate over the temperature range of −20°C to 85°C.

Extremely tight accuracy of ±0.25% FSS BFSL (Full Scale Span Best Fit Straight Line) reduces software needs to correct system inaccuracies, minimizing system design time. It avoids additional calibration and helps to improve system efficiency. It often simplifies software development. It promotes system reliability and reduces potential system downtime. It can simplify the design process. The sensor has an in-build temperatures sensor as well which can be using to monitor its operational temperature to ensure that it does not over

Figure 12.5 Honeywell SSCSDRN010MD2A3 pressure sensor.

Table 12.3 Output at significant percentage for the sensor.

%Output	Digital counts (decimal)	Digital counts (hex)
0	0	0x0000
10	1,638	0x0666
50	8,192	0x2000
90	14,746	0x399A
100	16,383	0x3FFF

heat that may be caused due to petrol vapor expansion. The percentage output of the sensor for various conditions is tabulated in Table 12.3.

12.2.6 Personal Computer

The personal computer is used to display the immediate data that is transmitted from the sensor and display it with other relevant information such as temperature, pressure reading, and the corresponding density for that pressure reading.

12.2.7 Petrol Density Measurement Instrument Setup

In this section, the design approach for the apparatus used to measure petrol density has been discussed along with the problems faced during testing for each of the setups, and list of updates that have been brought to each setup after the problem was analyzed. The step by step modification of the experimental set up is shown in Figures 12.6 to 12.8.

12.2.7.1 Setup 1

The initial setup just consisted of just two metal pipes which were of different heights, and this acted as the pressure instrument and was connected directly to the sensor via plastic piping to reduce pressure loss and maximize pressure transfer to the sensor.

But this setup was unstable and not accurate enough to display the right density value. This was mostly caused due to the unevenness of the pipes and lack of proper support to hold the sensor and pipes in a fixed position.

Figure 12.6 Initial setup.

Figure 12.7 Improved instrument.

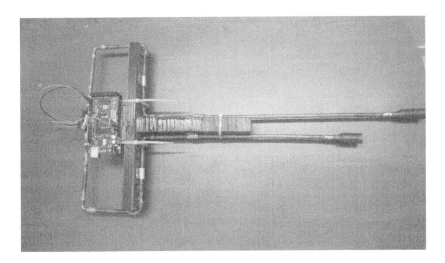

Figure 12.8 Final apparatus setup.

12.2.7.2 Setup 2

In this setup, the piping and sensor are transferred a fitted on a T-shaped designed holder. Holes are made for piping to be passed through the horizontal part of the T-holder and after which is followed by copper metal pipes. It is in this setup that the seals connecting each section of the plastic flexible tube and copper pipes were made air tight and as result of this led to the formation of an air bubble at the end of the metal pipe which was submerged in petrol. This air bubble would often escape very easily resulting in a drop-in pressure which was observed at the sensor output. This air bubble is formed due to the constant vaporization of petrol to vapor leading to unstable air pressure escaping in the form of air bubbles.

12.2.7.3 Setup 3

In the previous setup, it was observed that due to flexible plastic tubing there is a huge lose in air pressure due to possible inner imperfection in the material. For this reason, the entire setup was replaced with completely metal piping which was welded in to place to ensure that there was no possibility of leakage of pressure. Only a small section required flexible tubing to connect the sensor to the metal piping.

12.2.7.4 Setup 4

In the previous setup, it was still observed that air bubbles that were being formed at the end of the pipe which was placed in contact with the petrol medium were escaping and were causing pressure drop which lead to false reading from the sensor. For this reason, an additional wider section of copper pipe with a diameter of 1.5 cm is welded at the end of the 0.6 cm pipe leading from the sensor to the petrol medium.

12.2.7.5 Final Setup

In the final setup, the sensor and the controller are attached to the apparatus and a set of zip ties is used to prevent a flexing in the flexible plastic tubing. Additional rubber adhesive is used at all welded points to ensure that seals are air tight.

After several tests, it has been noted that the air bubble problem that plagued the pervious setups was reduced. The air bubble is more spread-out across a larger surface area, but the problem still exists but is much more control. For much better control over the air bubble, a ½ inch diameter pipe should be welded in any future update.

12.3 Interfacing MPX2010DP with INA114

The MPX2010DP sensor is interfaced with instrumentation amplifier directly on the PCB board by connecting the first pin of the MPX2010DP to ground. The layout diagram of the connection is shown in Figure 12.9. Then, the second pin (+vout) is connected to the instrumentation amplifiers third pin (+vin). The fourth pin (−vout) is connected to the amplifiers second pin (−vin). By directly interfacing the sensor with the amplifier on the PCB, any noise that may be caused due to faulty wiring is eliminated.

A connector is to deliver power to both the sensor and amplifier but must first pass through a de-coupling circuit to remove any noise. Finally, a single connecting pin used to connect the output pin (6) of the amplifier to a CRO or multi-meter.

12.3.1 I2C Bus Configuration for Honeywell Sensor

The Honeywell sensor used is an Open collector type that allows for features like concurrent operation of more than one master.

The pull-up resistor Rp that we have in used in the designer of the PCB is 4.7 kΩ resistance. There are two 4.7 kΩ which connect the Vcc supply of pin 2 with the SDA pin 3 and SCL pin 4 of the sensor. A four-pin connector is used at the other end of the sensor to supply the sensor with 3.3 V and Ground form the controller as well to connect the SDA and SCL pins of the

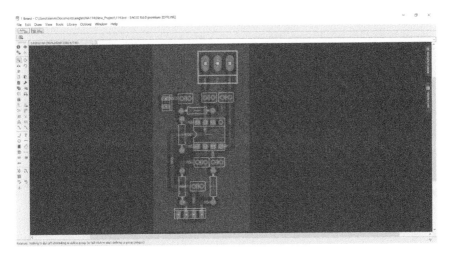

Figure 12.9 MPX2010DP interfaced with INA114 in Eagle.

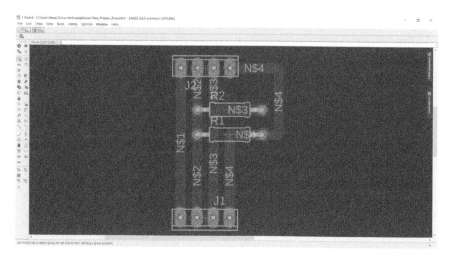

Figure 12.10 Pull-up resistor PCB board for SSCSDRN010MD2A3 in Eagle.

controller with the SDA and SCL pins of the sensor. The PCB layout of the pull up resistor is shown in Figure 12.10.

12.3.2   Pressure and Temperature Output Through I2C

Honeywell's SSCSDRN010MD2A3 pressure sensor is designed to transmit the output over the I2C protocol. The sensor transmits the data bit by bit and must be processed by the controller in order for the data to be converted into meaningful information that everyone can understand. The data transmitted by the sensor is shown in Figure 12.11. The test results of petrol density measurement for various trials is tabulated in Table 12.4. The output obtained from the sensor is plotted against the ASTM values and the graph is shown in Figure 12.12.

Two Byte Data Readout

	Data Byte 1	Data Byte 2
A6 A5 A4 A3 A2 A1 A0 1	S1 S0 B13 B12 B11 B10 B9 B8	B7 B6 B5 B4 B3 B2 B1 B0
Slave Address [6:0] Read	Status Bridge Data [13:8]	Bridge Data [7:0]

Three Byte Data Readout

	Data Byte 1	Data Byte 2	Data Byte 3
A6 A5 A4 A3 A2 A1 A0 1	S1 S0 B13 B12 B11 B10 B9 B8	B7 B6 B5 B4 B3 B2 B1 B0	T10 T9 T8 T7 T6 T5 T4 T3
Slave Address [6:0] Read	Status Bridge Data [13:8]	Bridge Data [7:0]	Temperature Data [10:3]

Four Byte Data Readout

	Data Byte 1	Data Byte 2	Data Byte 3	Data Byte 4
A6 A5 A4 A3 A2 A1 A0 1	S1 S0 B13 B12 B11 B10 B9 B8	B7 B6 B5 B4 B3 B2 B1 B0	T10 T9 T8 T7 T6 T5 T4 T3	T2 T1 T0 X X X X X
Slave Address [6:0] Read	Status Bridge Data [13:8]	Bridge Data [7:0]	Temperature Data [10:3]	Temperature Data [2:0]

☐ Bits generated by master
▨ Bits generated by slave (sensor)

Figure 12.11 I2C bits readout.

Table 12.4 Testing results of petrol density measurement.

Sample	Hydrometer reading(g/ ml@15°C)	Thermometer reading	Corresponding density of ASTM table	Density output of the sensor trial-1	Density output of the sensor trial-2	Density output of the sensor trial-3
IOCL	0.720	29.5°C	733 kg/m^3	730.6 kg/m^3	731.5 kg/m^3	730.2 kg/m^3
BPCL	0.719	27.5°C	730.3 kg/m^3	730.6 kg/m^3	730 kg/m^3	730.3 kg/m^3
HPCL	0.721	29°C	733.3 kg/m3	732.6 kg/m^3	733.3 kg/m^3	732.3 kg/m^3

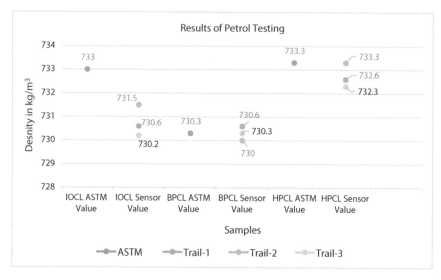

Figure 12.12 The sensor output value and ASTM value obtained are plotted.

12.4 Results and Discussion

Similar to water setup, the height difference is fixed permanently at 10 cm due to the additional piping which as to be welded together in order to pass the air pressure as input to the sensor. Since it has been proven that density of a liquid can be measure using pressure. The density of petrol is first

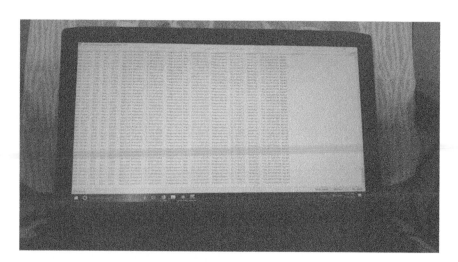

Figure 12.13 Sensor output observed on laptop.

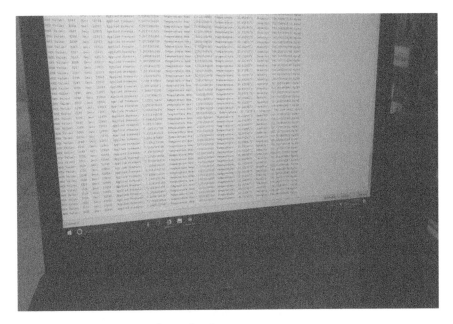

Figure 12.14 Sensor output observed on laptop.

measured using a hydrometer which gives the specific gravity of the petrol, and then, the temperature of the petrol is also measurement. After this, the density of the petrol is determined using an ASTM 53B table which gives the corresponding density value of the petrol sample with respect to the specific gravity and temperature.

For testing, three samples of petrol are used form different outlets; the samples are form IOCL (Indian Oil Corporation Limited), BPCL (Bharat Petroleum Corporation Limited), and HPCL (Hindustan Petroleum Corporation Limited).

The density of the samples is determined using the hydrometer and is compared with the density reading given as output by the sensor. The output of the sensor obtained as html output is shown in Figures 12.13 and 12.14.

12.5 Conclusion

The experimental setup for proving the concept that the density of a liquid can be measured using the force that the liquid exerts on air has been designed and tested for water due to its almost constant density at different temperature, thereby proving the concept. The same concept is used for developing another apparatus for measuring the density of petrol. The apparatus has been tested and the reading taken as output is compared with a hydrometer reading for the same petrol and the reading have been verified and plotted on a graph.

References

1. Roychowdhury, A., Ghose, G., Banerjee, L., Chattopadhyaya, V., A report on the independent inspection of fuel quality at fuel dispensing stations, oil depots and tank lorries, Centre for Science and Environment, 2002.

2. Caruana, C., Azzopardi, J.P., Farrugia, M., Farrugia, M., Common rail diesel engine, fuel pressure control scheme and the use of speed — Density control, *25th Mediterranean Conference on Control and Automation (MED)*, 2017. 10.1109/MED.2017.7984120.

3. Belov, E.N., Lutsenko, V.I., Kabanov, V.A., Khomenko, S.I., Methods for evaluation of petrol quality, *Microwave Conference, Microwave & Telecommunication Technology*. 1999.

4. Pranjali, P. and Wadhekar, A.R., Estimation of petrol adulteration using statistical feature analysis approach. *Circuit, Power and Computing Technologies (ICCPCT), 2016 International Conference on*, 2016.

5. Sadat, A., Fiber optic method to determine adulteration in petrol. *Emerging Research Areas and 2013 International Conference on Microelectronics, Communications and Renewable Energy (AICERA/ICMiCR), 2013 Annual International Conference on*, 2013.

6. Man, J., Density Measurement Of Ethanol Blended Fuels. *Int. J. Mod. Phys.: Conf. Ser.*, 24, 1360009, 2013.

7. Schaschke, C., Fletcher, I., Glen, N., Density and Viscosity Measurement of Diesel Fuels at Combined High Pressure and Elevated Temperature. *Processes*, 1, 30–48, 2013.

8. Roshan, Ahmed, A.A., Krishnan, M.R., Srinivasan, S., Digitalized Flow Quantity and Adulteration Measurement in Petrol. *Int. J. Eng. Res. Technol. (IJERT)*, 8, 6, 2019.

9. Joshi, P. and Thakur, R., Online Monitoring Of Petroleum Fuel Parameters In Storage Tank Using Microcontroller. *Global J. Eng. Sci. Res. Manag.*, 3, 4, 127–132, 2016.

10. Hoang, A.T., Prediction of the density and viscosity of biodiesel and the influence of biodiesel properties on a diesel engine fuel supply system. *J. Mar. Eng. Technol.*, 2018.

11. Schaschke, C., Isobel Fletcher and Norman Glen, "Density and Viscosity Measurement of Diesel Fuels at Combined High Pressure and Elevated Temperature". *Processes*, 1, 30–48, 2013.

12. Felix, V.J., Udaykiran, P.A., Ganesan, K., Fuel Adulteration Detection System. *Indian J. Sci. Technol.*, 8, S2, 90–95, January 2015.

13. Patil, M., Madankar, A., Chakole, V., Portable Fuel Adulteration Detection System. *J. Embed. Syst. Process.*, 4, 1, 1–7, 2019.
14. Kudea, V.P. and Patil, A., Detection of Fuel Adulteration in Real Time Using Optical Fiber Sensor and Peripheral Interface Controller. *Int. J. Optics Photonics (IJOP)*, 11, 2, 95–102, 2017.

13

Improved Merkle Hash and Trapdoor Function–Based Secure Mutual Authentication (IMH-TF-SMA) Mechanism for Securing Smart Home Environment

M. Deva Priya[1], Sengathir Janakiraman[2] and A. Christy Jeba Malar[3]*

[1]*Department of Computer Science & Engineering, Sri Krishna College of Technology, Kovaipudur, Coimbatore, Tamil Nadu, India*
[2]*Department of Information Technology, CVR College of Engineering, Mangalpally, Vastunagar, Hyderabad, Telangana, India*
[3]*Department of Information Technology, Sri Krishna College of Technology, Kovaipudur, Coimbatore, Tamil Nadu, India*

Abstract

The rapid advent in the demand of Internet of Things (IoT) services necessitates the protection of information content disseminated among different entities included in the IoT architecture. The problem of ensuring security in IoT is emerging as a major challenge in day-to-day life. In smart home systems, it is still more challenging as the implementation and requirements of IoT systems are diversified in nature. In smart home environment, the entire system consists of diverse smart devices cooperating among themselves through the Internet. Thus, the wireless network and low capacity devices demand sufficient degree of security when they collaborate. Further, IoT platforms face major challenges in the deployment of reliable authentication mechanisms, since the resource-restricted IoT devices and edge devices may not have sufficient storage and strong computational ability for the purpose of implementing and executing authentication algorithms. In this chapter, an Improved Merkle Hash and Trapdoor Function–based Secure Mutual Authentication (IMH-TF-SMA) mechanism is proposed with lightweight properties for enhancing the degree of security in smart home scenario. In the

Corresponding author: a.christyjebamalar@skct.edu.in

C. Venkatesh, N. Rengarajan, P. Ponmurugan and S. Balamurugan (eds.) Smart Systems for Industrial Applications, (307–332) © 2022 Scrivener Publishing LLC

proposed IMH-TF-SMA mechanism, nodes establish sessions and authenticate anonymously based on the controller nodes by using symmetric keys and dynamic identities in an unrelated way. It sets up a virtual domain for enforcing strict security policy among the nodes under interaction and also enforces restricting potentialities in sending and receiving commands and instructions during the process of cooperation. It is also implemented as a challenge response scheme for verifying the sender identity. The experiment evaluation confirms its strength in resisting the known attacks that are possible in a smart home environment.

Keywords: Improved Merkle hash function, Trapdoor Function, mutual authentication, AVISPA toolkit, Burrows-Abadi-Needham (BAN) logic

13.1   Introduction

Internet of Things (IoT) is envisioned to be applied over a huge variety of applications. There is tremendous increase in the amount of information shared across the internet due to IoT services. Moreover, the financial and human resource demands of application domains vary. In case of domestic environments, human issues are significant as the technical issues. Reliable transfer of information among diverse entities in the IoT architecture is challenging. IoT systems have their own demands and forms of implementation. The drastic growth of internet users and wireless devices has led to an increase in smart homes. Remote services with control to home devices offered by various service providers are appealing. Smart home is a significant application of IoT which enables users to take control of the smart home appliances through the internet. Smart home technologies involve remote use of resources and context-aware services using transportable devices and wireless communication. A smart home includes low ability devices like sensors and wireless networks which demand acceptable degree of security when working together. The wide variety of services includes surveillance cameras, door locks and smart lighting that can be distantly retrieved and managed. Increase in wireless communications and enhanced use of information technologies have enabled humans to adjust their lifestyle. Nevertheless, remote monitoring of home appliances opens up the room for numerous threats against ensuring privacy and security.

Security plays a vital role in smart home environment with an extensive range of wired and wireless devices. The IoT devices accessed within an environment or distantly through the internet necessitates appropriate security schemes so as to circumvent revealing of any secure data or access rights. As the smart homes are technology dependent, there comes the demand for a security scheme with reduced human intervention. Authentication plays a significant role in ensuring security in IoT networks. Without guaranteeing that the legal party is the one who claims to be, additional security aspects are hopeless. Moreover, with the improved movement of IoT devices, old forms of authentication including username and password are less efficient. Various security issues have led to the suggestion of numerous methods of authentication. These schemes demand an authentication token like a smartcard or limiting access to a specific physical location. IoT devices include an extensive collection of sensors from which a huge quantity of data can be collected. Real-time security schemes can support secure user access using the relative information to confirm requests. This information can be recovered to support authentication at the beginning and throughout the session without the need for user communication which evades the danger of being exposed.

In smart home networks, a protected remote user authentication scheme becomes essential to enable only legitimate users to access these devices. Nevertheless, the accessible cryptographic schemes satisfy the security goals. As the smart devices connect over insecure channels, the sensitive data from these devices may be interrupted and modified effortlessly by a malevolent opponent. Hence, an anonymous authentication scheme that assures secure communication is the need of the hour. An illegitimate user can access the data sent by smart devices. As these appliances are connected to the internet enabling the efficient use of technology, there are chances for illegitimate access to some constrained data and devices. Automated energy consumption control trusts on context-dependent incessant authentications of users for the execution of time-critical tasks. The user movement and importance of tasks play a major role. Unceasing authentication is a healthy method to guarantee validity of user authenticity. There are high chances of attacks like device seizure, user, gateway, device impersonation and privileged-insider attacks. The main goal is to reduce the implementation complexity and attain computation efficacy. The control of devices should be limited to legitimate users alone, thus abstaining from malevolent activities. There are many cryptographic mechanisms for safeguarding communication between IoT devices and the capacity of such mechanisms depends particularly on devices with limited computing resources. There is a necessity for a reliable and effective mechanism that safeguards communication between devices with restricted interference. To overcome such limitations, supervised method of authentication that incorporates Merkle hash tree and Trapdoor Function–based signature is required as a lightweight process.

The main contributions of the proposed chapter are presented as follows:

i)   An Improved Merkle Hash and Trapdoor Function–based Secure Mutual Authentication (IMH-TF-SMA) mechanism is proposed with reduced computational complexity attaining maximized security against possible attacks in smart home scenario.

ii) This IMH-TF-SMA mechanism is proposed with the merits of ephemeral trapdoor keys to add strength to the authentication process.

iii) The simulation experiments of the proposed IMH-TF-SMA mechanism are also conducted using Automated Validation of Internet Security Protocol and Applications (AVISPA) tool for evaluating its predominance in terms of computation overhead, communication overhead, storage bits and degree in preservation for varying number of users.

13.2   Related Work

Various authors have dealt with providing solutions for ensuring security in smart homes. In Japan, different forms of smart home appliances are available and efforts are taken for interactive home appliances as well. As these appliances are exposed to several security challenges in terms of technical, social and practical aspects, Pishva and Takeda [1] have come out with some solutions. They have inspected a number of security challenges and have shown that the security demands are based on the functions of the devices. The demands for security of the appliances based on different functions are identified. Public Key Infrastructure (PKI) is identified as the recommended authentication scheme. It considers the agreement with the existing standards and links with suitable settings. It demands cooperation among the producers, network and service providers. They have designed a framework, wherein common home gateways are used to handle security issues based on products. This will enable the users, manufactures and service providers to overcome resource restrictions of every smart appliance. Authentication using passwords helps in authorizing users as it is easy. Joseph et al. [2] have trained a Neural Network (NN) rather than verification table to preserve passwords. Traditionally, networks trained using Back Propagation Networks (BPNs) consume more training time.

The authors have propounded Resilient Backpropagation (RPROP) which is implanted into the Multi-Layer Perceptron (MLP) NN to speed up the training. The performance in terms of Mean Square Error (MSE), training time and number of epochs are found for varying number of hidden neurons and grouping of transfer functions. Tansig and Purelin are used in hidden and output layers respectively with 250 hidden neurons.

Vaidya *et al.* [3] have proposed a strong and effective authentication method using strong passwords to offer secure distant access in smart homes. The propounded technique uses lightweight modules comprising of hashed password that can be used once, and also hash-chaining scheme along with cost effective smart card technology. This scheme focuses on stolen smart card attack and forward confidentiality with missing card including functional demands without verification table and time synchronization. This mechanism seems to offer strong authentication.

The design challenges for effective and secure password-based authentication are widely examined. In the work proposed by Vaidya *et al.* [3], the password-based authentication scheme uses One-Time Passwords (OTPs) using smart card. Kim and Kim [4] claim that there are two flaws in the scheme and have propounded a technique to eradicate them. They have assessed the system for password guessing and forwarding secrecy attacks and have proposed HMAC-based OTP (HOTP) method for user authentication in smart homes. User authentication forms the base of any cryptographic method. In the literature, protocols are available for user authentication including Transport Triggered Architecture's (TTA's) standard Encrypted Extensible Authentication Protocol-PW (EEAP-PW). However, they face some security issues. Kim and Jung [5] have proposed a smartcard-based authentication protocol for home network which offers authentication and key agreement to deal with the password guessing, impersonation and replay attacks.

Kumar *et al.* [6] have propounded a lightweight and secure session key establishment scheme for smart home scenario. To ensure trust in the network, every device uses a small authentication token and forms a secure session key. The technique involves security features to circumvent Denial-of-Service (DoS) and eavesdropping attacks. The propounded scheme offers better computation and communication efficiency. Verification confirms security as expected or not. To deal with the design flaws, an official verification is demanded before implementation. Formal verification is carried out using AVISPA security analyser tool. Premarathne [7] has considered the circumstantial information and user behavioral features. The author has proposed context-based continuous authentication model that uses multiple attributes to effectively utilize energy. Position and nature of tasks are taken as the contextual features for authentication. This relative significance–based feature selection scheme is based on N-model. The trustworthiness of the propounded model is examined as a restriction model using linear temporal logic. Incessant authentication of a user using the circumstantial information is based on user mobility and the environment. The time taken for task executions by genuine users is taken into consideration. It involves multiple features to accomplish time-efficient energy management in smart homes.

Santoso and Vun [8] have propounded an authentication scheme using Elliptic Curve Cryptography (ECC), wherein the method deals with offering robust security in positioning IoT devices for smart home in addition to handiness in using the system. The system uses a Wi-Fi network applied on the AllJoyn framework by means of an asymmetric ECC to complete authentication during the operation of the system. The Wi-Fi gateway acts as the controller to enable preliminary configuration of the system. It is accountable for validating the connection between IoT devices enabling users to establish, use and regulate the system using Android-based mobile with the suitable application.

Peter and Gopal [9] have presented a multi-level authentication system that offers diverse security properties which comprise of integrity, authentication, security and privacy conservation, besides acting as a countermeasure against IoT attacks. It is both computation and communication efficient. This Single-Level Authentication (SLA) technique is proposed to authenticate the smart device and the home gateway. Lin and Bergmann [10] have designed gateway architecture for resource-restricted devices to ensure system availability. To support auto management of the system, system auto-configuration is needed to improve system security. Programmed update of software/firmware is required to sustain the secure system process. Rapid user mobility complicates the use of usernames and passwords in static security schemes. Ashibani *et al.* [11] have introduced a context-based authentication framework based on contextual information including user's profile, calendar, request time, location and access behaviors for efficient access of home devices. Informed decisions of whether to admit or repudiate access requests can be taken easily using this incessant authentication model. Wireless networks that connect users and IoT devices support access control between networks. The firewall is involved in blocking the access to the network by permitting access only to the devices that host the Secure Gateway Application (SGA).

Information and Communication Technology (ICT) is applied to huge number of applications like smart living, health and transportation.

In smart home applications, the occupants monitor numerous smart devices using ICT. To ensure secured communication between smart devices and users, Wazid *et al.* [12] have propounded a remote user authentication scheme for resource-restricted smart devices with restricted resources using one-way hash functions, bitwise XOR operations and symmetric encryptions/decryptions. The efficiency of the scheme is demonstrated using Real-Or-Random (ROR) model. Security analysis and verification is done using AVISPA. The proposed user authenticated key establishment scheme includes a registration authority, numerous smart sensing devices, gateway and users. The Registration Authority (RA) takes control of the offline registration of the devices and the gateway. The user also registers at the RA using his smart phone to enter his details including identity, password and biometric.

Recently, it is seen that the attacks show how the internet-based smart homes become unsafe spots for numerous ill purposes, taking away the privacy of the inhabitants. An observer can take the identity of a specific appliance through public channels, from which the inhabitant's life pattern can be known. Kumar *et al.* [13] have propounded an Anonymous Secure Framework (ASF) for effective authentication and key agreement enabling device privacy. One-time session key enables renewing of the session key for smart devices and reduces the hazard of using a retrieved session key. The computation complexity involved in the framework is found to be low. Pirbhulal *et al.* [14] have designed a secure IoT-based smart home automation system called Triangle-Based Security Algorithm (TBSA) to enable energy-effective data encryption using proficient key generation mechanism. WSNs connect to the internet through Wi-Fi to provide reliable data transmission among numerous nodes in the network. The propounded TBSA algorithm involves less energy. Signcryption is used for authentication, integrity and confidentiality rather than linking encryption and signature schemes. Ashibani and Mahmoud [15] have presented an identity-based signcryption mechanism for smart home communication. It supports integrity and confidentiality in addition to the capability of defending communication between devices against probable attacks.

The IoT devices demand an existing infrastructure that cannot be managed by the owner as it requires a security stack appropriate for assorted devices built in the available operating systems or IoT frameworks. Chifor *et al.* [16] have propounded a lightweight authorization stack, wherein a Cloud-connected device transmits commands to the user's smart phone for authorization. This framework is user device–based and deals with the security issues in an unreliable Cloud platform. The solution chosen is IoT

Kaa which has a web interface for organization and a code generator module for supporting multi-programming languages. Internet services like If This Then That (IFTTT) incorporates assorted devices and enable the user to adapt configurations through IFTTT recipes. Former researches have dealt with a scenario based on Feature-Distributed Malware (FDM), where the victim's IFTTT account can be compromised to operate on the recipes through his device. Baruah and Dhal [17] have propounded a secure IFTTT-based Smart Home framework by including appropriate captcha-based OTP authentication and Physical Unclonable Function (PUF). The performance of the system is analyzed using AVISPA and the framework is presented using High-Level Protocol Specification Language (HLPSL) which shows the roles of each agent. Alshahrani and Traore [18] have propounded a lightweight protocol involving mutual authentication and key exchange for IoT-based system using the identity and collective keyed hash chain. Nodes can authenticate incognito and form a session with the controller using active identities and symmetric keys. Virtual domain separation is used in the implementation of security policy and capabilities of nodes are restricted for transmitting instructions or commands. Cumulative keyed hash chain mechanism is designed to identity the sender. Fog computing concept is exploited to improve identity guarantee. Security is ensured using the Burrows-Abadi-Needham (BAN) logic and AVISPA toolkit.

Dey and Hossain [19] have propounded a lightweight and secure session-key establishment scheme using Diffie-Hellman (DH) key exchange. A reliable service provider offers algorithm parameters to devices enabling the establishment of public key between the home gateway and a smart device. The security of the proposed scheme is examined using AVISPA. Altering critical information taken from a wearable can lead to severe consequences. This information should be encrypted, thus increasing the complexity in querying. Poh et al. [20] have proposed a scheme to ensure privacy called the PrivHome. It provides user and data authentication, safe data storage, confidentiality of data and entity to prevent an illegitimate user from altering the data transmitted between the user and devices, service provider and gateway. The gateway has no access to data. The protocols are established exclusively on symmetric cryptographic techniques.

Shuai et al. [21] have propounded an authentication scheme using ECC which does not involve verification table for authentication. A random number scheme is used to fight against the replay attack and it can circumvent the clock synchronization problem. The severe official proof and empirical examination reveal that the propounded mechanism yields the anticipated security features and fights against attacks. In contrast to the existing schemes, this scheme offers a subtle balance between security and efficacy and is appropriate for real world environments.

The existing schemes emphasize on secure authentication and communication through a reliable third party without considering the privacy issues. Some protocols allow users to inefficiently validate themselves to a huge quantity of devices. To deal with the above-mentioned issues, Lyu *et al.* [22] have propounded a model for smart homes using IFTTT with an anti-tracking mutual authentication technique including key agreement. Precisely, this technique offers IFTTT gateway as control command initiator and protector to permit a user to confidentially access the system. The scheme is based on ECC, nonces, XOR operation and hash functions to attain mutual authentication taking into account the anonymity and forward security. Ashibani *et al.* [23] have proposed an incessant authentication framework that takes the contextual data for user authentication. This mechanism offers security against illegitimate access and does not necessitate supplementary user interference.

Khalid *et al.* [24] have propounded a decentralized authentication and access control scheme for lightweight IoT devices. This fog computing-based scheme involves public blockchain. This authentication scheme based on blockchain supports distributed authentication and authorization among devices belonging to the same or different system. Elliptic Curve Digital Signature Algorithm (ECDSA) algorithm is employed for generating public and private keys for devices and fog nodes. Panda and Chattopadhyay [25] have designed ECC-based mutual authentication protocol for IoT and cloud servers. The security features are strictly confirmed by using AVISPA tools. The capacity of the system to resist attacks related to device privacy, impersonation attack, replay attack, password guessing attack and mutual authentication is also examined. The performance is examined in terms of computational, communication and storage overheads and computational time. Fakroon *et al.* [26] have proposed a scheme for user authentication that considers both physical context and transaction history. It does not maintain a verification table and evades clock synchronization issues. The main aim is to ensure message and agent secrecy. The system is found to involve reduced communication overhead and computational cost. The performance of the system is analyzed through formal analysis using BAN, informal analysis and model check using AVISPA tool. The protocol specifications in HLPSL are broken into roles that define the actions of an agent.

13.3 Proposed Improved Merkle Hash and Trapdoor Function–Based Secure Mutual Authentication (IMH-TF-SMA) Mechanism for Securing Smart Home Environment

In this section, a system model used for the implementation of the proposed IMH-TF-SMA mechanism is initially detailed and presented in Figure 13.1. In the implementation model, the smart home equipments are interconnected to the wireless standard IEEE 802.11 based on the internet. The addressing strategy of IPv6 protocol is utilized for facilitating address to the users, equipments and smart appliances by offering a dynamic method for allocating the address through auto-configuration. The system model comprises of four core entities such as i) Smart Home Network (SHN), ii) Smart Home Server (SHS), iii) Central Unit (CU) and iv) End User (EU). The smart home network comprises of monitoring equipments and smart devices such as smart mobiles, mobile laptops, smart fans, smart lights, smart oven, smart TV, smart kitchen devices, smart webcam and smart locks. On the other hand, monitoring devices are utilized for significant monitoring of home environment through the inclusion of smart sensor and detectors. The SHS receives data continuously from the smart sensors and devices. In this context, the attacker can capture, aggregate and communicate the monitored secret information to the feasible number of other malicious attacks in the environment. This possibility of attacker in compromising the data motivates the option of designing the IMH-TF-SMA mechanism for enhancing the degree of security in a smart home scenario.

The SHS facilitates the option of unique addressing of the complete set of smart home appliances in order to distinctly identify them. Moreover,

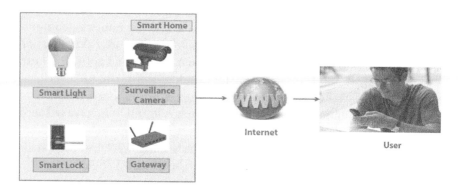

Figure 13.1 Smart home environment.

SHS enables encryption and decryption of the packet, since new user registration cannot be achieved without his verification. The central or trusted authority termed as Smart Home Edge Server (SHES) is potent in monitoring and controlling the aggregation of monitored data. In addition, the end users are the smart home owners who have the authority of accessing the services of smart home through laptops and smartphones.

13.3.1 Threat Model

In the proposed IMH-TF-SMA, a popular DY (Dolev-Yao) threat model is included for enabling the attackers to launch possible kinds of attacks. The attackers are made to launch either a passive attack or an active attack which impacts the performance and functionality of the system. The attackers have the capability of deleting, modifying and forging the received messages. In this threat model, the smart home appliances and devices are considered to be trusted and are assumed to be non-compromised by any type of security treats, since the compromise of smart home appliances and devices results in dramatic degradation in the performance of the network. It is considered that the user devices or the smart cards can be stolen or lost, through which the data and secret identities can be utilized and forged by the attackers. In this context, it becomes essential to safeguard smart home environment from diversified attacks and secure the data exchanged in the scenario. This proposed IMH-TF-SMA approach is developed as a secure authenticable protocol with the capability to resist multiple attacks such as password guessing, DoS attack, device compromisation, masquerade attack, message replay and message forgery. It is also utilized for sustaining forward secrecy, confidentiality, integrity and mutual authentication. In addition, Table 13.1 is presented for highlighting the possible vulnerable threats especially being faced in IoT platforms.

13.3.2   IMH-TF-SMA Mechanism

In this section, the proposed IMH-TF-SMA mechanism is presented with the merits of assigning distinct addressing for smart home devices. This proposed scheme utilizes a modified distinct 64-bit ID which is stored in the home server, edge server and user smart card for the purpose of unique identification and authentication. When a smart home device needs to be accessed by a user, the user's request is forwarded to the edge server by encapsulating the ID bits. They are embedded into each IPv6 packets. The edge server after receiving the request packets extracts the bits of the identified packets and checks the distinct identity pre-stored in the edge server

Table 13.1 Threats and their influences in the IoT environment.

Attack name	Layer of attack	Influences introduced by the attack	Threat imposed
BrickerBot	Application layer	It can adversely impact the complete system.	An attack has the probability of escalating the privileges to access unauthorized data/functionality.
Mirai	Network and perception layer	It eliminates the legitimate data transmission and introduces DoS attacks.	An adversary can jam the communication links.
Smart baby monitors	Network layer	It derives username and passwords (useful information) in an illegal manner.	It can intercept the network traffic, and this performs the process of eavesdropping.
Persirai	Attack layer	It has the possibility of stealing private data and even smartphone could be hacked.	An attacker has the capability to access the web interface and run a random JavaScript code in the victims' browser.
Stuxnet attack	Perception layer	It introduces lesser service lifetime of the node and node outage.	The power consumption of the sensor nodes are intentionally increased in order to prevent from sleep or operation.

(Continued)

Table 13.1 Threats and their influences in the IoT environment. (*Continued*)

Attack name	Layer of attack	Influences Introduced by the attack	Threat imposed
Nest Thermostat	Perception layer	It takes complete control over the systems and has the possibility of accessing the change in hard disk and OS.	It can physically access the smart device hardware and software.
PsycoBoT	Perception layer	It attains complete control over the device that has the possibility of being monitored.	It has the capability of updating the firmware with the malicious code.
DDoS attack	Network layer	It launches different routing attacks and has the capability of visualizing the encrypted communications.	It exploits packet routing process by dropping, spoofing, redirecting and misdirecting the packets.
Replay attack	Perception and network layer	It can mislead the complete IoT systems set for operation.	The fraudulent packets can be injected into the communication links.

database. Further, this identity is stored in the home server for forwarding it to the end user during the registration phase through the smart card. This proposed IMH-TF-SMA mechanism comprises of five main steps such as i) phase of initialization, ii) phase of addressing, iii) phase of registration, iv) phase of login authentication and v) phase of session agreement.

13.3.2.1   Phase of Initialization

In this phase, the home gateway is connected with the home network through the Internet. The home user identity presents the smart card information through $(U_{ID}\|ID_{UG}\|ID_{NES}\|ID_T)$, which is forwarded to the Neighborhood Edge Servers (NES). Once the request is received by the NES, it verifies the received timestamp based on $\Delta T \geq (T_2 - T_1)$ (where "ΔT" is the timestamp which is mutually accepted by the trusted entities). If the verified timestamp is valid, then the process of authentication is continued. Or else, the packets are discarded from the smart home environment. Further, the NES calculates $(U_{ID}\|ID_{UG}\|ID_{NES}\|ID_T\|R_N)$ and extracts identities from the user and validates them. The NES utilizes the user variable identity stored in them for facilitating encryption based on Trapdoor Function and Merkle Hash Tree algorithm. The encrypted data is again stored in the NES database. This NES allocates an 8-bit identifier to the home equipments existing in the smart home environment. The NES furthermore forwards the encrypted data and 8-bit identifier to the SHS to be stored in the database. In addition, the 8-bit identifiers are broadcast by smart devices which are to be stored in their memory. This 8-bit identifier and 56-bit encrypted data are integrated for constructing the 64-bit distinct identity. Finally, NES calculates $(U_{ID}\|ID_{UG}\|ID_{NES}\|ID_T\|R_N)$ based on the secret key and forwards it to the user. Finally, the user validates the identities and derives distinct identity and stores them in the memory of the user devices.

13.3.2.2   Phase of Addressing

In this phase of addressing, initially, the NES broadcasts the 64-bit network prefix to the SHS once the assignment of 64-identifier of the host component is attained. Then, the 64-bit identifier and the 64-bit network address are integrated together with any one secret key generated by the smart devices in order to determine the entire 128-bit header address to be stored in the key table of SHS.

13.3.2.3   Phase of Registration

Similar to NES, the user verifies the received timestamp based on $\Delta T \geq (T_2 - T_1)$ (where ΔT is the timestamp which is mutually accepted by the trusted entities). If the verified timestamp is valid, then the process of authentication is continued. NES after the process of verification grants or generates a short token identity and session key for the associated SHS. This process of registration is mainly achieved based on the identities unique to the entities participating in the smart home environment.

13.3.2.4 Phase of Login Authentication

In this phase, the session key and the smart card are provisioned to the user with which it is possible to extract the password identity and biometric information. The verification of identities is performed based on trapdoor and Merkle hash tree construction. Then, the hash value of the trapdoor is calculated using "$H_{V(OP)}$" based on Equation (13.1), when the condition is $V_r^g \neq V_r^o$ is satisfied. In this context, the SHS verifies the received Timestamp based on $\Delta T \geq (T_2 - T_1)$. If the verified timestamp is valid, then the process of authentication proceeds. Then, the SHS extracts the identity from the communicated message based on a random number and a virtual identity. Further, the SHS computes,

$$TP_{HV}(H_{V(OP)}, V_r) = \left(\beta^{(H_{V(OP)}, MK_{HT})} * MK_{HT}^{-V_r}\right) \bmod q \qquad (13.1)$$

for extracting associated identities to check the keys and tokens shared between the entities of the smart home environment. In addition, the SHS stores the identity after verification in the key table and also forwards it to the user using the private key. Once it is received on the user end, the user verifies the received timestamp based on $\Delta T \geq (T_2 - T_1)$. If the verified timestamp is valid, then session agreement can be achieved.

13.3.2.5 Phase of Session Agreement

The core objective of this phase is to concentrate on the exchange of session keys and session key agreement establishment for securing the network during the process of communication. This session key agreement phase is applied only when the addressing and login authentication is achieved using virtual identities. In this phase, the user can extract the previously shared session from the message in order to check the identities through the use of authorizing keys. Finally, the user calculates the hash key value based on Equation (13.1) using secret key and it is shared to the SHS through the open channel. In this section, the complete process involved in the implementation of the proposed IMH-TF-SMA mechanism based on trapdoor and Merkle hash function is detailed (Figure 13.2–Figure 13.4).

Generation of Private and Public Keys with Initiated Trapdoor and Merkle Hash Function

Step 1: Initiate the generation of long term private and public key pair (PK_{LT}, PU_{LT}) as specified in Equation (13.2)

$$PK_{LT} \in Z_q^* \text{ and } PU_{LT} = \beta^{PK_{LT}} \in Z_q^* \qquad (13.2)$$

Step 2: Also initiate the generation of long term Merkle Hash and Trapdoor Function pair (MK_{HT}, TD_{FN}) based on Equation (13.3)

$$TD_{FN} \in Z_q^* \text{ and } MK_{HT} = \beta^{TD_{FN}} \in Z_q^* \qquad (13.3)$$

Step 3: Select the value of "n_{bs}" in order to estimate the blocks number in the segment

Step 4: Compute the Merkle Hash Tree such that the value of "m" is determined based on the Power of 2 as presented in Equation (13.4)

$$n_{bs} = mS_l \qquad (13.4)$$

Step 5: Generate the private and public ephemeral key pair (PK_{EK}, PU_{EK}) as specified in Equation (13.5)

$$PK_{EK} \in Z_q^* \text{ and } PU_{EK} = \beta^{PV_{EK}} \in Z_q^* \text{ under the}$$
$$\text{condition } 0 \le 1 \le s - 1 \qquad (13.5)$$

Step 6: Generate the Merkle hash and Trapdoor Function–based ephemeral pair (MK_{EK}, TD_{EK}) based on Equation (13.6)

$$TD_{EK} \in Z_q^* \text{ and } MK_{HT} = \beta^{TD_{EK}} \in Z_q^* \qquad (13.6)$$

Signature Generation Process Based on Trapdoor Function and Merkle Hash Tree Function

Step 7: For "S_p" from "0" to "$s - 1$" do

Step 8: Obtain "$t_p(S_p)$" and "$H_{V(OP)}$" generated during registration and store them in the pool of system signature

Step 9: For "S_p" from 0 to "$S_k - 1$" do

Step 10: Build "MH_{TR}" with "n" data blocks and store the root hash value "$MH_{TR(HV)}$" and hash value of "$MH_{TR(V)}$"

Step 11: Calculate the value of collision "HC_{VALUE}" based on the condition

$$MH_{TR(V)} = TD_{EK}(MH_{TR(HV)}) \tag{13.7}$$

Step 12: Construct the information of authentication "$ATH_{(j)}$"
Step 13: Send ($m_{(i)}$, $ATH_{(j)}$) to the authenticating receivers
Step 14: End For
Step 15: End For

Process of Authentication Verification
Step 16: Calculate $H_{V(OP)} = H_{TFN-MHT}$ ($DB_{Sign} \| MK_{HT}$)
Step 17: Calculate the hash value of trapdoor using "$H_{V(OP)}$" based on Equation (13.1)
Step 18: If $V_r^g \neq V_r^o$, then
Step 19: Authentication fails
Step 20: Save TP_{HV} ($H_{V(OP)}, V_r$) in the system buffer in order to utilize it as the "j" trapdoor hash value
Step 21: Authentication is successful
Step 22: End If

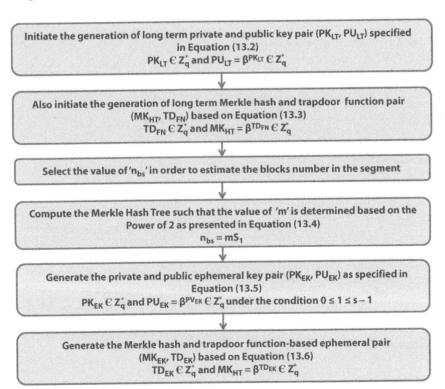

Figure 13.2 Generation of private and public keys with initiated Trapdoor and Merkle Hash Function.

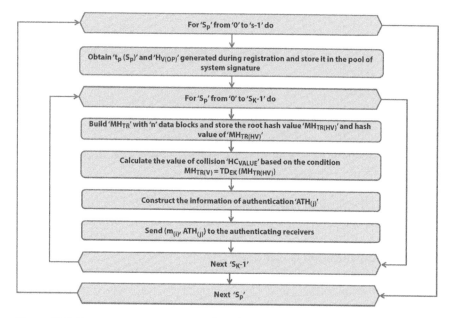

Figure 13.3 Signature generation process based on Trapdoor Function and Merkle Hash Tree Function.

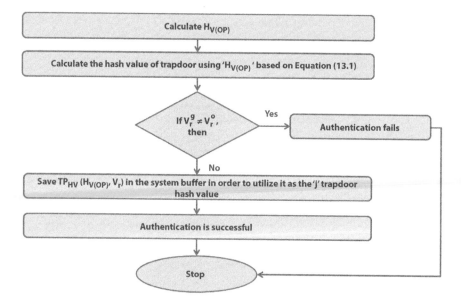

Figure 13.4 Process of authentication verification.

13.4   Results and Discussion

The predominance of the proposed IMH-TF-SMA mechanism and the benchmarked approaches are evaluated based on computation overhead and communication overhead, storage costs and degree in preservation with respect to the number of users. The simulation experiments of the proposed IMH-TF-SMA mechanism are conducted using AVIPSA tool, since it is considered as widely utilized platform for validating the predominance of the security protocol. It is a role-based language in which the agents are responsible for executing the proposed smart home authentication protocol. The security protocol is specified and defined in the AVIPSA tool based on HLPSL. The main goal of using HLPSL in the AVIPSA tool is to facilitate the properties that play a vital role in verifying security concentrating on message authentication and data secrecy during message exchanges between agents. In addition, Figures 13.5 and 13.6 are presented for highlighting the performance of the proposed IMH-TF-SMA scheme and the benchmarked Contextual-Based Continuous Authentication Framework (CBCAF) [23], Provable Security-Based Anonymous Authentication Scheme (PS-AAS) [21] and PRIV-HOME [20] schemes evaluated based on computation and communication overheads for varying number of users. The proposed IMH-TF-SMA scheme is identified to significantly decrease the computation and communication overheads, since the lightweight potentialities of Trapdoor Function and supervised characteristics of Merkle Hash tree play a vital role in reducing the time incurred as well as unnecessary generation of control packets. Thus, the computation overhead of the proposed IMH-TF-SMA scheme for varying number of users is significantly reduced by 6.74%, 7.98% and 8.63% when compared to the benchmarked CBCAF, PS-AAS and PRIV-HOME schemes. The communication overhead of the proposed IMH-TF-SMA scheme for varying number of users is also potentially minimized by 7.82%, 8.26% and 9.26% in contrast to the benchmarked CBCAF, PS-AAS and PRIV-HOME schemes.

Figures 13.7 and 13.8 show the performance of the proposed IMH-TF-SMA mechanism and the benchmarked evaluated based on storage cost and degree of preservation for varying number of users in the smart home environment. The storage cost incurred by the proposed IMH-TF-SMA scheme is considerably reduced due to the inclusion of capable cache strategy. It is also considered to provide maximized privacy preservation, since the utilization of ephemeral trapdoor hash function is capable of resisting known attacks in smart home environment. The storage cost of

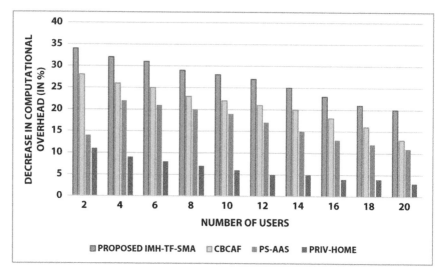

Figure 13.5 Decrease in computational overhead of the proposed IMH-TF-SMA mechanism for varying number of users.

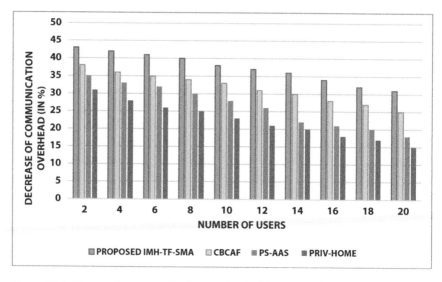

Figure 13.6 Decrease in communication overhead of the proposed IMH-TF-SMA mechanism for varying number of users.

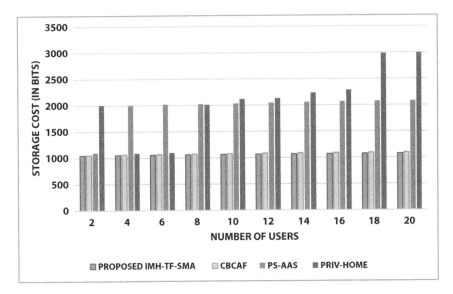

Figure 13.7 Storage cost of the proposed IMH-TF-SMA mechanism for varying number of users.

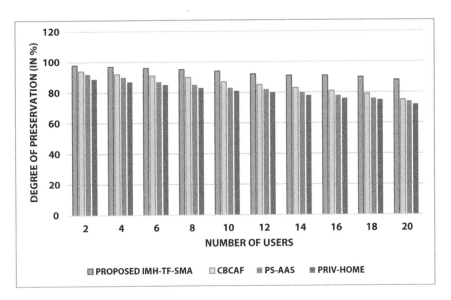

Figure 13.8 Degree of preservation of the proposed IMH-TF-SMA mechanism for varying number of users.

the proposed IMH-TF-SMA scheme is significantly reduced by 4.84%, 5.46% and 6.24% when compared to the benchmarked CBCAF, PS-AAS and PRIV-HOME schemes. The degree of preservation of the proposed IMH-TF-SMA scheme is also potentially minimized by 5.69%, 6.72% and 7.54% in contrast to the benchmarked CBCAF, PS-AAS and PRIV-HOME schemes. In addition, Finally, Figure 13.9 depicts the predominance of the proposed IMH-TF-SMA scheme and the benchmarked schemes evaluated based on time incurred in executing the Trapdoor Function. The time incurred in executing the Trapdoor Function utilized by the proposed IMH-TF-SMA scheme is significantly reduced by 6.89%, 7.92% and 8.18% when compared to the benchmarked CBCAF, PS-AAS and PRIV-HOME schemes.

Tables 13.2 and 13.3 present the computational times required for attaining crypto-operations in the proposed IMH-TF-SMA mechanism and the security-based functionality features of the proposed IMH-TF-SMA mechanism and compared authentication schemes.

From the results presented in Tables 13.2 and 13.3, it is clear that the proposed IMH-TF-SMA mechanism incurs comparatively least amount of computation in carrying out the cryptographic functions of private and public ephemeral keys generation, Merkle Hash tree generation, implementation of Trapdoor Function and encryption and decryption using

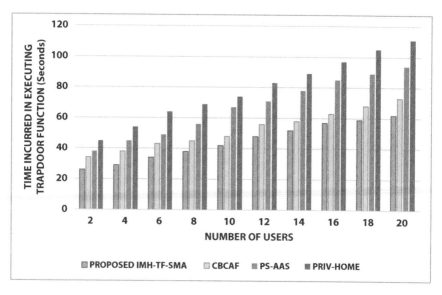

Figure 13.9 Time incurred in executing Trapdoor Function of the proposed IMH-TF SMA mechanism for varying number of users.

Table 13.2 IMH-TF-SMA: Computational times required for crypto-operations.

Crypto-operations	Computation time
Private and Public Ephemeral Keys Generation	14.92 milliseconds
Merkle Hash tree generation	0.2682 milliseconds
Implementation of Trapdoor Function	0.3569 milliseconds
Encryption and Decryption using symmetric keys	4.9251 milliseconds

Table 13.3 Security-based functionality features of the proposed and compared authentication schemes.

Functionality features	PRIV-HOME [20]	PS-AAS [21]	CBCAF [23]	Proposed scheme
Impersonation attacks	Yes	Yes	Yes	Yes
Replay attacks	Yes	No	Yes	Yes
Privileged insider attack	Yes	Yes	Yes	Yes
Password guessing attack	Yes	No	Yes	Yes
Mobile device loss attack	Yes	Yes	Yes	Yes
Phase of password update	Yes	Yes	Yes	Yes
User anonymity	Yes	Yes	Yes	Yes
Forward security	Yes	Yes	Yes	Yes
Untraceability	Yes	Yes	Yes	Yes

symmetric keys. It is also identified that the proposed scheme is capable of handling all the security-based functionality features and resisting the attacks which include impersonation attacks, replay attacks, privileged insider attack, password guessing attack, mobile device loss attack, phase of password update, user anonymity, forward security and untraceability with maximized efficiency.

13.5 Conclusion

In this chapter, Improved Merkle Hash and Trapdoor Function–based Secure Mutua Authentication (IMH-TF-SMA) mechanism is proposed as an attempt to develop a smart home authentication framework with lightweight properties by utilizing Trapdoor Functions and Merkle Hash Tree. This IMH-TF-SMA mechanism utilizes the trapdoor function dynamically to handle the attacks in the smart home scenario. The results prove that the storage overhead of the proposed IMH-TF-SMA scheme is significantly reduced by 4.84%, 5.46% and 6.24% when compared to the benchmarked CBCAF, PS-AAS and PRIV-HOME schemes. The results confirm that the degree in preservation of the proposed IMH-TF-SMA scheme is also potentially minimized by 5.69%, 6.72% and 7.54% in contrast to the benchmarked CBCAF, PS-AAS and PRIV-HOME schemes. The computational overhead of the proposed IMH-TF-SMA scheme is significantly reduced by 3.12%, 4.98% and 5.84% in contrast to the benchmarked CBCAF, PS-AAS and PRIV-HOME schemes. In the near future, it is also planned to utilize a decision tree-based supervised hashing technique to resist attacks that are possible during user authentication in a smart home environment.

References

1. Pishva, D. and Takeda, K., Product-based security model for smart home appliances. *IEEE Aerosp. Electron. Syst. Mag.*, 23, 10, 32–41, 2008.
2. Joseph, A., Bong, D.B.L., Mat, D.A.A., Application of neural network in user authentication for smart home system. *World Acad. Sci. Eng. Technol.*, 53, 1293–1300, 2009.
3. Vaidya, B., Park, J.H., Yeo, S.S., Rodrigues, J.J., Robust one-time password authentication scheme using smart card for home network environment. *Comput. Commun.*, 34, 3, 326–336, 2011.
4. Kim, H.J. and Kim, H.S., AUTH HOTP-HOTP based authentication scheme over home network environment, in: *International Conference on Computational Science and Its Applications*, Springer, Berlin, Heidelberg, pp. 622–637, 2011, June.
5. Kim, H. and Jung, H., Smartcard-Based User Authentication Protocol over Home Network, in: *Future Information Technology, Application and Service*, pp. 181–189, Springer, Dordrecht, 2012.
6. Kumar, P., Gurtov, A., Iinatti, J., Ylianttila, M., Sain, M., Lightweight and secure session-key establishment scheme in smart home environments. *IEEE Sensors J.*, 16, 1, 254–264, 2015.

7. Premarathne, U.S., Reliable context-aware multi-attribute continuous authentication framework for secure energy utilization management in smart homes. *Energy*, 93, 1210–1221, 2015.

8. Santoso, F.K. and Vun, N.C., Securing IoT for smart home system. *2015 International Symposium on Consumer Electronics (ISCE)*, IEEE, pp. 1–2, 2015, June.

9. Peter, S. and Gopal, R.K., Multi-level authentication system for smart home-security analysis and implementation, in: *2016 International Conference on Inventive Computation Technologies (ICICT)*, vol. 2, IEEE, pp. 1–7, 2016, August.

10. Lin, H. and Bergmann, N.W., IoT privacy and security challenges for smart home environments. *Information*, 7, 3, 44, 2016.

11. Ashibani, Y., Kauling, D., Mahmoud, Q.H., A context-aware authentication framework for smart homes. *2017 IEEE 30th Canadian Conference on Electrical and Computer Engineering (CCECE)*, IEEE, pp. 1–5, 2017, April.

12. Wazid, M., Das, A.K., Odelu, V., Kumar, N., Susilo, W., Secure remote user authenticated key establishment protocol for smart home environment. *IEEE Trans. Dependable Secure Comput.*, 17, 2, 391–406, 2017.

13. Kumar, P., Braeken, A., Gurtov, A., Iinatti, J., Ha, P.H., Anonymous secure framework in connected smart home environments. *IEEE Trans. Inform. Forensics Secur.*, 12, 4, 968–979, 2017.

14. Pirbhulal, S., Zhang, H., Alahi, M.E.E., Ghayvat, H., Mukhopadhyay, S.C., Zhang, Y.T., Wu, W., A novel secure IoT-based smart home automation system using a wireless sensor network. *Sensors*, 17, 1, 69, 2017.

15. Ashibani, Y. and Mahmoud, Q.H., An efficient and secure scheme for smart home communication using identity-based signcryption, in: *2017 IEEE 36th International Performance Computing and Communications Conference (IPCCC)*, IEEE, pp. 1–7, 2017, December.

16. Chifor, B.C., Bica, I., Patriciu, V.V., Pop, F., A security authorization scheme for smart home Internet of Things devices. *Future Gener. Comput. Syst.*, 86, 740–749, 2018.

17. Baruah, B. and Dhal, S., A two-factor authentication scheme against FDM attack in IFTTT based Smart Home System. *Comput. Secur.*, 77, 21–35, 2018.

18. Alshahrani, M. and Traore, I., Secure mutual authentication and automated access control for IoT smart home using cumulative keyed-hash chain. *J. Inform. Secur. Appl.*, 45, 156–175, 2019.

19. Dey, S. and Hossain, A., Session-key establishment and authentication in a smart home network using public key cryptography. *IEEE Sens. Lett.*, 3, 4, 1–4, 2019.

20. Poh, G.S., Gope, P., Ning, J., Privhome: privacy-preserving authenticated communication in smart home environment. *IEEE Trans. Dependable Secur. Comput.*, 18, 3, 1095–1107, 2019.

21. Shuai, M., Yu, N., Wang, H., Xiong, L., Anonymous authentication scheme for smart home environment with provable security. *Comput. Secur.*, 86, 132–146, 2019.

22. Lyu, Q., Zheng, N., Liu, H., Gao, C., Chen, S., Liu, J., Remotely access "my" smart home in private: An anti-tracking authentication and key agreement scheme. *IEEE Access*, 7, 41835–41851, 2019.

23. Ashibani, Y., Kauling, D., Mahmoud, Q.H., Design and implementation of a contextual-based continuous authentication framework for smart homes. *Appl. Syst. Innov.*, 2, 1, 4, 2019.

24. Khalid, U., Asim, M., Baker, T., Hung, P.C., Tariq, M.A., Rafferty, L., A decentralized lightweight blockchain-based authentication mechanism for IoT systems. *Cluster Comput.*, 1, 1, 56–65, 2020.

25. Panda, P.K. and Chattopadhyay, S., A secure mutual authentication protocol for IoT environment. *J. Reliab. Intell. Environ.*, 1, 1, 23–35, 2020.

26. Fakroon, M., Alshahrani, M., Gebali, F., Traore, I., Secure remote Anonymous user authentication scheme for smart home environment. *Internet Things*, 9, 1, 100158, 2020.

14

Smart Sensing Technology

S. Palanivel Rajan and T. Abirami

Department of Electronics and Communication Engineering M. Kumarasamy College of Engineering, Karur, Tamil Nadu, India

Abstract

Smart sensing is an emerging technology that is used in various applications like healthcare monitoring and industrial applications. Smart sensor consists of the number of sensors that collects input from the physical environment to do a specific task based on the collected inputs. The process can be carried out before the data passed to it. The smart sensor includes transducer that is used to covert physical quantitatively into electrical quantity, an amplifier that is used to strengthen the original information, analog filter that is used to remove the unwanted signals, and finally compensator is used to compensate the process. Additional to that, some software-based functions are also processed like collecting, processing, and communicating with the device. Smart sensors can produce accurate data with the least amount of noise which is captured by the collected information. It can keep an eye on the entire process and then taking the necessary control action by itself. The different networks can be used to communicate the information like WPAN (802.15.1), Zigbee (802.15.4), GSM, and WLAN (802.11). Nowadays, Internet of Things plays a major role to access the data in anywhere at anytime.

Keywords: WPAN (Wireless Personal Area Networks), GSM (Global System for Mobile Communication), WLAN (Wireless Local Area Networks)

14.1 Introduction

14.1.1 Sensor

Our world is filled with sensors. The sensor is an instrument to measure the physical phenomenon like pressure, temperature, and humidity from

---

Corresponding author: drspalanivelrajan@gmail.com

C. Venkatesh, N. Rengarajan, P. Ponmurugan and S. Balamurugan (eds.) Smart Systems for Industrial Applications, (333–366) © 2022 Scrivener Publishing LLC

the atmosphere. Further, the sensed data are transferred to the external device for processing. Many automation tasks are done by using sensors. Before going to discuss in detail about the smart sensors, we will see the definition, types, and real-time example.

14.1.1.1 Real-Time Example of Sensor

Autopilot system in aircraft is a good example of the sensor. In the aircraft system, position, height, speed, location, and temperature are the parameters measured by sensors. The different types of sensor are needed for each parameter. It is also called automatic flight control system. The same features are used in all civilian and military applications. It is also called automatic flight control system as shown in Figure 14.1.

The sensed data is taken by the computer in order to process the information which is collected by sensors and the data is compared with pre-defined values [1]. To operate the plane in automatic mode, the devices like Minicomputers and Sensors are combined together in a single block.

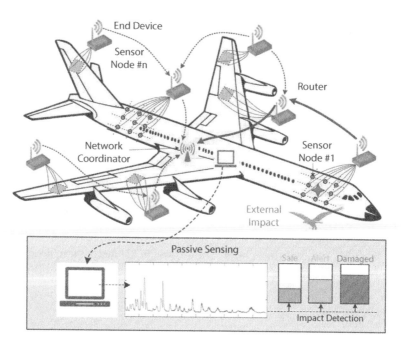

Figure 14.1 Block diagram of sensor [1].

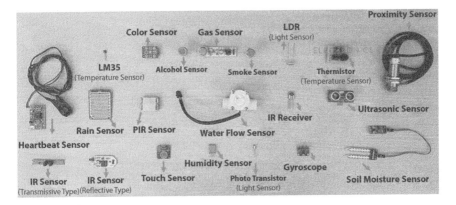

Figure 14.2 Classification of sensors [1].

14.1.1.2 Definition of Sensors

There are numerous definitions to explain the functions of sensors. The definition is given below, "Sensor is an input device to provide the output, which is equal to the input quantity". Another one is "Sensor is a device which is used to convert the signals from one form of energy to the equivalent electrical form".

In the above diagram, different types of sensors are shown, and it is used in many real-time applications. Very simple example is a Light Dependent Resistor (LDR) [2]. Depends on the variation of resistance, the intensity of the light can be measured. If the light falling on the sensor is more means, then the corresponding resistance will be less [3]. If the light on the sensor is less means, then the converted resistance value will be high. Hence, it is called as light sensors [4]. With this example, we will discuss the classification of sensors. We will discuss the classification of sensors as shown in Figure 14.2.

14.1.1.3 Characteristics of Sensors

The following characteristics are described about the sensor quality:

- High sensitivity
  Sensitivity is defined by how much output changes with respect to the changes in the input.
- Linearity
  If the output changes linearly with changes in the input.
- High resolution
  If a small change in the device can be predicted by this parameter.
- Less noise and disturbance
- Less power consumption

14.1.1.4   Classification of Sensors

The classification of the sensor is based on many factors. The classification of the sensor is based on many factors as shown in Figure 14.2. The factors are listed below.

- Based on an external power requirement
  Active or passive sensors
- Based on detection used in sensor
  Electric, biological, chemical, radioactive, etc.
- Based on conversion phenomenon
  Thermo-electric, electrochemical, electromagnetic, thermo-optic, etc.
- Based on the types of input and output
  Analog or digital sensors

14.1.1.5   Types of Sensors

The following sensors are commonly used in various applications [5]. Various physical parameter measuring sensors are mentioned below.

- Temperature sensor
- Proximity sensor
- Accelerometer
- IR sensor (infrared sensor)
- Pressure sensor
- Water quality sensor
- Chemical sensor
- Image sensors
- Motion detectors
- Gyroscope sensor
- Light sensor
- Smoke, gas, and alcohol sensor
- Humidity sensor
- Flow and level sensor

Let us discuss about temperature sensor in detailed manner because it is commonly used in all electronic applications to control and maintain the temperature of the system.

14.1.1.5.1   Temperature Sensor

In the environment, any change in the temperature will convert into the corresponding change in the resistance or voltage. The best example of the temperature sensor is LM35 - temperature sensor IC, Thermistor, thermocouple, and RTD (Resistive Temperature Devices).

This sensor is used in all computers, mobile phones, automobile, air conditioning, and industries to maintain the temperature level.

14.1.1.5.2   Proximity Sensor

Proximity sensor is a one type of sensor which is used to detect the movement of the object or whether the object is present or not. There is no contact between the sensor and the objects. So, it is named as contactless sensor. This sensor is not affected by the environment changes such that this sensor is manufactured, and also it is used to measure the distance between the objects. There are many types of proximity sensors.

The types of sensors are given below as shown in Figure 14.3.

i.   Inductive Sensor
     It is also a contactless sensor. Metal objects are only detected by this type of sensor. This metal object detection is done by the principle of law of induction. Capacitive sensor. It comprises four types of component. The components are Oscillator, Schmitt Trigger, Coil, and output circuit.

ii. Capacitive Sensor
     This sensor includes the operation of inductive sensor and also nonmetallic, powders, granular, and liquid level. When the object is detected, the capacitive sensor is oscillating the

LM35 - Temperature Sensor IC   10KΩ NTC Thermistor

Figure 14.3 Temperature sensor [1].

values. There are used, one internal and one external plate. Additional to that, oscillator, output device, and Schmitt Trigger are the components of capacitive sensor.

iii.   Ultrasonic Sensor
The sensor used to detect the object by emitting the ultrasonic waveforms and the detected values are converted into electrical signals. It detects objects in solid, liquid, granular, or granular as well. It has only Ultrasonic Transmitter and receiver.

iv.   IR Sensor
It is used for short range of detecting objects. It can emit the beam of Infrared Light to the object to detect the objects. It consists of IR LED.

14.1.1.5.3   Accelerometer

It is sensor in which used to find the acceleration [24]. It senses the vibration in the systems, according to that it can produce the electrical signal.

14.1.1.5.4   IR Sensor

IR sensor used to detect infrared radiation in the surroundings. This sensor was introduced in 1800. It is invisible to the human eye and its wavelength is very much longer than visible light. The classification of IR sensor is an active and passive sensor [25]. Active sensor is working as a proximity sensor and it emits the infrared radiation from LED while the object crosses it. When the object is identified by the passive sensor, it does not emit the radiation from LED. This is the major difference between active and passive IR sensor.

14.1.1.5.5   Pressure Sensor

The physical parameter of pressure is detected by pressure sensor and the detected signals are converted into equivalent electrical quantity [26].

14.1.1.5.6   Water Quality Sensor

In our day-to-day life, water quality is not assured. This type of sensor is introduced for checking the quality of water [27]. The water checking parameters are pH level, conductivity, turbidity, and finally dissolved ions like calcium and nitrate, and low-power sensor is designed for validating the quality of water.

14.1.1.5.7   Chemical Sensor

It is also working like water quality sensor used to detect the quality level of chemical content. It is used in myriad related applications such as nano-technology, automotive, and medical fields. It needs only two components [28]. The components are receptors and transducers. The receptor is having the contact with the analyte. Transducers are responsible for converting the detected parameter into electrical quantity. Sometimes, the transducers are used to send the signal to the next device.

14.1.1.5.8   Image Sensors

It is categorized based on several parameters like chroma type and structure type. By using this type of sensors, the image parameters like pixel value, resolution factor, and sensitivity are used to further doing of applications with an image [29]. Every year, based on their needs, the sensor has been manufactured and satisfying the customer needs.

14.1.1.5.9   Motion Detectors

It is created for identifying intruder in home and also in industries. In order to avoid the theft this detectors are used. If the sensor is placed in the area means, then it will detect the unknown person and gives the signal to our control panel. From that, it helps us to monitor area. Immediate action needs to be taken to avoid this kind of theft activities [30]. Main components of the system are recoding camera. Our security system can record all our action when the motion takes place. The various types of motion detectors are Passive Infrared (PIR), Microwave (MW), and Dual Technology Motion Sensors.

14.1.1.5.10   Smoke, Gas, and Alcohol Sensors

This type is made to find the gas leakage or alcohol vapors in the environment [31]. The breathing problem of patient went outside the means, and many forms of chemical content are present. To avoid the breathing problem of a patient, this type of sensor has been introduced.

14.1.1.5.11   Humidity Sensor

It is a small device that predicts the water vapor in the air. It can provide accurate measurement based on the robust capasitive technology. The relative humidity and temperature are added together to achieve the accurate measurements. There are resistive and temperature-based humidity sensors.

14.1.1.5.12   Flow and Level Sensor

In level sensor is classified into point level and continuous level measurement. In point level measurement, the threshold value is fixed if the measured value is greater than the threshold value means, it will indicate the level [32]. This is called the point level measurement. Second one is continuous level measurement. In that level, it indicates whether it rises or falls into level, and capacitance and optical are the example for point level measurement. Ultrasonic and radar are the examples for continuous level measurement.

Flow sensors are being used all over the world; it uses to measure the flow of liquid. It can be applied in smart energy applications, industrial processes, HVAC, and medical field also. Like that, a large number of sensors are available to do the different parameter measurements [33]. For measuring the physical parameters, the sensor concepts are developed. Nowadays, without the sensor, even a small project is not available. That much role is playing in all the research area by the sensors.

14.1.2   IoT (Internet of Things)

14.1.2.1   Trends and Characteristics

Various types of sensors are being used in industries and organizations for developing many applications or projects. So, IoT is taken as a platform to perform multiple tasks in automatic mode. It is used to collect the data and send it via network of all connected devices. The collected information makes the system to work autonomously and smarter in every day.

IoT platform is connecting many devices with using unique Identifiers (UID) and enables the transformation of data from machine to machine or human to machine. IoT creates the physical world into system-based environment, resulting with improved efficiency, economically balanced, and finally to reduce human effort. Year by year, IoT usage is increased to 31%, and it is expected that there will be 30 billion devices by 2020.

14.1.2.2   Definition

IoT are referred as "simply the point in time when more 'things or objects' were connected to the Internet than people".

IoT was born between the year of 2008 and 2009. Working behind the IoT is MOSFET [6]. The expansion of MOSFET is Metal Oxide Semiconductor Field Effect Transistor otherwise called as MOS Transistor.

14.1.2.3 Flow Chart of IoT

14.1.2.3.1 What is MQTT Broker?

It is a server that receives all messages from the clients and then routes the messages to the appropriate destination clients. It is an end-to-end process to send or receive the information.

14.1.2.4 IoT Phases

There are five phases in IoT projects. Those phases are given below.

1. Collecting
2. Transportation
3. Storing
4. Analyzing
5. Archive

We will discuss the phases of IoT project in detail manner as shown in Figure 14.4.

1. Collecting phase:
   This is capturing date and making it transportable.

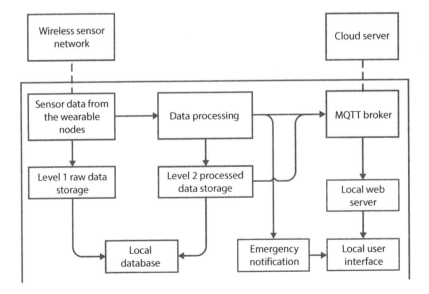

Figure 14.4 Flow chart of IoT [6].

2. Transportation phase:
The next phase is transportation which involves the reliable and secured data transmission from the machines or to the information center.
3. Storing phase:
The next to the transportation phase is storing phase which is used to entail the storing the data and always making it is available for data analysis.
4. Analyzing phase:
The fourth phase "analyze" comprises the analysis of the sensor data.
5. Archive phase:
The last phase is archive, which is about the less expensive recording of data that are possible to maintain for a long-term periods.

14.1.2.5 Phase Chart

The phase chart which includes various process of preparation, development, measuring the process to produce accurate values.

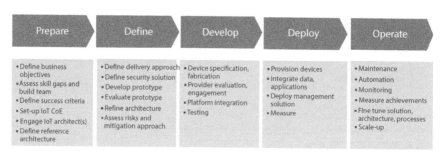

Figure 14.5 Phase chart [6].

14.1.2.6 IoT Protocol

The HTTP protocol is a distributed application protocol. All the users are able to communicate the shared, hypermedia information systems on the World Wide Web.

There are various protocol layers to perform operation of data communication as shown in Figure 14.5: first, the Things Layer; second, the Connectivity/Edge Computing Layer; third, the Global Infrastructure Layer; fourth, the Data Ingestion Layer; fifth, the Data Analysis Layer; sixth, the Application Layer; and the finally, the People and Process Layer.

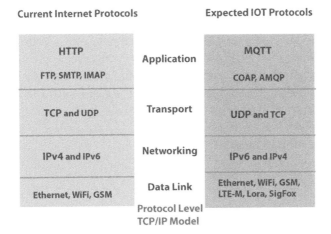

Figure 14.6 Internet protocol [6].

14.1.2.6.1 1 IoT Needs Internet

In order to operate the system, internet connection for all the time periods is required. By using the local server, the complete network can be controlled. An Internet Protocol (IP) is properly working without a web connection as shown in Figure 14.6. In agriculture, IoT plays major role to do work in automatic mode.

- Initially, soil moisture and nutrients are sensed by the sensors.
- The required amount of water is poured into the plants. According to the plant size, the water has been poured.
- Based on the soil chemistry, the choice of fertilizer is determined.
- Next important thing is harvesting time period.
- Report has been generated periodically with respect to the weather conditions.

14.1.3 WPAN

Wireless Personal Area Network is working based on the Bluetooth device. IEEE 802.15.1 standard was invented for WPAN in the year 2002 and it was approved by IEEE-SA Standards Board [35]. Every standard was reaffirmed within 5 years; otherwise, it will be withdrawn from the administrative committee.

14.1.3.1 IEEE 802.15.1 Overview

This is a standard used for portable personal devices to make short range RF-based connectivity. This standard deals with lower transport layers of the Bluetooth Technology. Further, v1.1 Foundation MAC is adapted with PHY layer (Radio). Next to that, normative annex is also specified which offers the Protocol Implementation Conformance Statement (PICS) proforma. Finally, it is integrated with ITU-T Z.100 arrangement and description language (SDL) model.

14.1.3.2 Bluetooth

A Bluetooth is designed for mainly low-power and high-speed technology, and it is designed for connecting mobile phones with portable another devices. It may be used to connect mobile to computers, computers with mobile phones over a short distance communication without using wires as shown in Figure 14.7. Typically, the distance is about 10 meters.

The transceivers are embedded in all electronic devices with low cost. Initially, it started with 2.45 GHz of frequency and the corresponding speed is 721 kbps. At the same time, there are possible eight devices to connect each other. Every device uses a different identifier number (UID). Unique identifier has a 48 bit address line, and it makes the connection between point to point or multiple points.

14.1.3.3 History of Bluetooth

Danish Viking and King, Harald Blatand, has named this technology as Bluetooth. This technology uses to connect two different devices with short

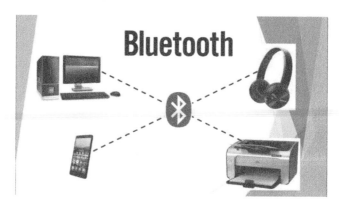

Figure 14.7 A Piconet [35].

range communication. The Ericsson Mobile Communications have taken charge to come out of Bluetooth technology in 1994 in order to find the alternative method of using cables for making connections between the devices. Next to that, in 1998, four companies are formed to publish the first version of Bluetooth Module in 1999. Initially, it is started with a speed about 1 Mbps. The next version is with a speed of 3 Mbps. Next, the speed has been increased up to 24 Mbps. The final version of Bluetooth technology is 4.0.

14.1.3.4   How Bluetooth Works

Bluetooth technology makes the devices with the network to connect, with minimum of two devices and maximum of eight devices. In this network, only one device is able to proceed as a master, and except master device, all are called as slaves in order to receive the information. Master device initiates the communication between the devices and slaves are used to respond the master device. Slave devices are synchronized with the master device. In addition to that, the master device may order the slaves to start the transmission. Time slot has been allotted to all slave devices to start the transmission.

Bluetooth devices use the frequency hopping sequence to allot the address of the master device. The first transmission starts with the master to send a radio signal to get a response from the particular device in the network. Then, the slave responded and it is synchronized with master device frequency. Two or more piconets are formed together to create scatternets.

14.1.3.5   Bluetooth Specifications

Bluetooth specifications are classified in two categories: core specifications and profile specifications. The core specification deals with stack protocol and also the requirement of qualification and testing. The profile specification defines the use of protocols for different applications.

14.1.3.5.1   Core Specification
It has five layers to specify the protocols. All the five layers are used to make from establishing the connection between the devices to transmit the information successfully. Each layer is having unique working process. Let us see the operation of each layers.

- Radio: In this layer, it deals with the basic needs of radio communication—such as choosing proper modulation techniques, assigning the frequency ranges, and power characteristics of the communication.
- Baseband Layer: In baseband layer, it defines the structure of connection between the devices and makes the logical link for data or voice communication. It particularly specifies the packet formats, timing, and channel control of the transmitter and receiver and the method used for spreading the frequency, and finally, it assigns the address of the device. The link details are specified in this layer. The packet length range can be fixed from 68 bits to 3,071 bits.
- Link Manager Protocol (LMP): before starting the communication, it needs to decide the number of device to be connected. After the proper connection establishment, the transmission will begin.
- Logical Link Control and Adaptation Protocol (L2CAP): this protocol is made to order from lower layer to the upper layer.
- Service Discovery Protocol (SDP): It can allow the device to enquiry about the entire task, providing QoS.

Bluetooth module can be explained by the first three protocols. The two protocols are together called as Host Controller Interface.

14.1.3.5.2   Profile Specification
It clearly mentions the usage of protocols for different types of applications. It can produce the detailed information about the models.

14.1.3.6   Advantages of Bluetooth Technology

- The interference problem can be solved by using speed frequency hopping. Totally, 79 channels can be used and each channel is allotted with different frequency range. Every channel is advised to use 625 microseconds. In every second the device can change the frequencies 1,600 times in every second.
  Transmitter can change the frequency at every 1,600 seconds. The frequency reuse concept is adapted successfully. By choosing various frequencies for different users, the interference can be removed.

- The power consumption is very low. The result of power consumption is based on the battery life.
- Very much secure communication between the devices. Secured communication is happened at bit level. The 128 bit key is used for authentication.
- Bluetooth makes use of voice as well as data communication with up to three voice channels.
- The line-of-sight problems are eliminated and make point-to-point communication between the devices.

14.1.3.7 Applications

The peripherals of all the Cordless Desktop are connected without using wires as shown in Figure 14.8. The connection is made within the range of 10 meters.

Ultimate headset: It allows one device to have a connection with numerous devices, including portable computers, stereos, and telephones as shown in Figure 14.9.

Figure 14.8 Portable desktop peripherals [35].

Figure 14.9 Headset [35].

The two devices are synchronized for starting the communication effectively which focus on the various applications of task that creates user awareness.

Multimedia Transfer: Using Bluetooth, the data exchange is increased such as songs, videos, and pictures.

14.1.4   Zigbee (IEEE 802.15.4)

14.1.4.1   Introduction

Zigbee is another network created for Personal Area Network with high speed and less power. It is developed for small level projects without wire connection. The IEEE standard was developed to make high-level communication protocols in Zigbee [7]. The physical coverage area of Zigbee is from 10 to 20 meters. Zigbee technology has been developed for simpler and less expensive when compared with all other Personal Area Networks such as Bluetooth Module as shown in Figure 14.10, Wi-Fi, and Wireless Light Switches, the power consumption restrictions to measure the transmission distance as from 10 to 100 meters. It is possible by passing the data from one device to the nearby device in which all the systems create Personal Area Network using mesh network topology. It provides long battery life and made the secure communication. It is having data rate of 250 kbps and used for intermittent data transmissions, for doing embedded projects, home automation, and industrial area as shown in Figure 14.11. This technology was developed in 1998, standardized in 2003, and, finally, it was revised in 2006.

Figure 14.10 Bluetooth module [35].

Figure 14.11 ZigBee technology [7].

14.1.4.2 Architecture of Zigbee

It consists of three devices to make the successful transmission. The devices are Zigbee coordinator, router, and end device as shown in Figure 14.12. Every network has only one Zigbee coordinator which is used to define the roots of the networks. While doing transmit and receive the information, the Zigbee coordinator is the sole responsible for storing and handling the information.

Router is only performing to pass the information to the next nearby nodes. End devices are permitted to make a converse only with coordinator. ZigBee technology supports any one from the tree, mesh, and star networks.

There are five layers of Zigbee protocol architecture. The layers are given as Application Framework, Application Support Sub-Layer, Network Layer, Medium Access Layer, and Physical Layer as shown in Figure 14.13.

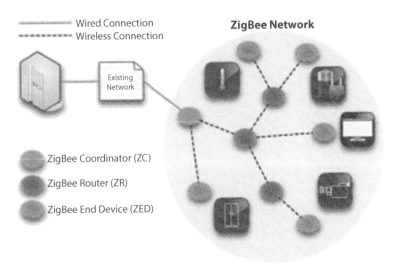

Figure 14.12 Zigbee architecture [7].

Application Layer (APL)
Application Framework
Application Support Sublayer
NETWORK LAYER
MEDIUM ACCESS
CONTROL LAYER (MAC)
PHYSICAL LAYER
Zigbee
Specification
IEEE
802.15.4

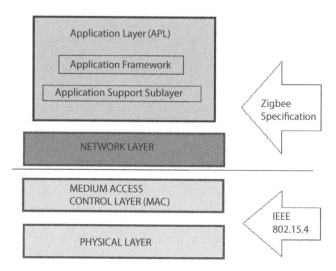

Figure 14.13 ZigBee protocol architecture [7].

- **Physical Layer**
  While transmitting the information, any of the modulation techniques could happened and vice versa as shown in Figure 14.14.
- **Medium Access Layer**
  The purpose of this layer is to give consistent transmission of information by means of dissimilar networks among CSMA-CA techniques. For synchronizing communication the beacon frames also be transmitted.
- **Network Layer**
  This layer will perform the network related operation like device configurations, routing, and network setup; it establishes the connection between the devices in the network, etc.

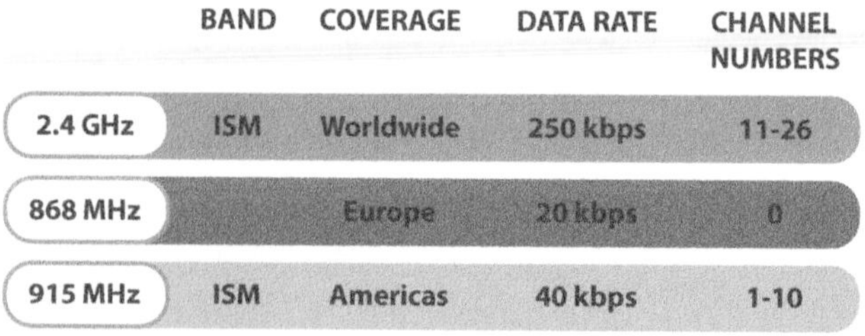

BAND
COVERAGE
DATA RATE
CHANNEL
NUMBERS
2.4 GHz
ISM
Worldwide
250 kbps
11-26
868 MHz
Europe
20 kbps
0
915 MHz
ISM
Americas
40 kbps
1-10

Figure 14.14 Physical layer of ZigBee [7].

- **Application Support Sublayer**
  This layer is used to enable the necessary service for Zigbee Device Object (ZBO) and it is connected with network layers for managing the data. According to the services and needs, the two devices can be perfectly matched.
- **Application Framework**
  Application framework is providing the key value pairs and generic message services. The structure of generic service is predefined by the programmer and the key value pair is receiving attributes with lends a hand of application objects. ZBO is providing a connection link between the APS layer and the application objects. It is used for initiating, detecting, and obligating the remaining devices to the network.

14.1.4.3   Zigbee Devices

Zigbee is having two devices as the FFD and RFD. Based on the working functions, it is classified into two types. FFD is having entire control of the device. But the RFD is having part of FFD to do particular tasks.

- Full-Function Devices or FFD
- Reduced-Function Devices or RFD

14.1.4.4   Operating Modes of Zigbee

Two modes are available in Zigbee. The operating modes of Zigbee are given below:

- Non-beacon Mode
- Beacon Mode
- Beacon Mode: This is the continuous monitoring of lively state of arriving data so that the power utilization is high. The node wakes up and communicates all the time. The overall power consumption is low because the nodes want to send or receive the data and that node can be alone in active state, and all the remaining nodes are in sleep mode.
- Non-Beacon Mode: In this mode, if there is no data transmission or reception, then the coordinator and router can go

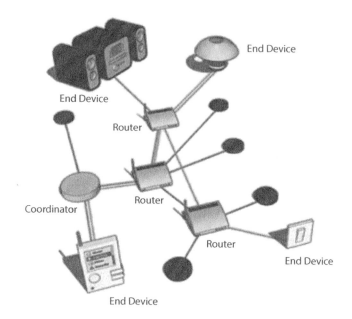

Figure 14.15 Zigbee communication operation [7].

to sleep mode. It is working based on need of transmission. Both modes are working periodically as shown in Figure 14.15.

14.1.4.5 Zigbee Topologies

Zigbee can support all the network that mainly focus on star, mesh, and tree topologies as shown in Figure 14.16.

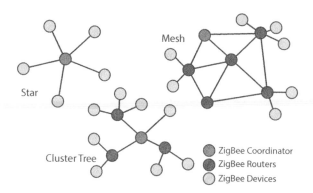

Figure 14.16 Zigbee topologies [7].

In all the above topologies, only one coordinator is available in the network. In star topology, managing and handling the data are done only by the coordinator. All the nodes are connected with the coordinator. The remaining two topologies are number of routers to decide the path of the network.

14.1.4.6 Applications of Zigbee Technology

Here, the Zigbee is used in tremendous applications like Smart Metering, Home Automation, Smart Grid monitoring, and Industrial Automation.

- Patient Monitoring System: Zigbee device is placed in the patient's body to gather the information about the blood pressure, heart rate, and temperature. The collected information are transmitted through the local server from the patient's house. Then, the local server sends the information to the corresponding clinic for further needs of treatment.
- Structural health monitoring System: The system is used to monitor the building condition for any natural disaster occurs [8]. During the period, major collapse of the building can be avoided. The status of the building should be periodically checked, where in case of any damage, building repair work can be started immediately. This system provides the public to lead the safe life during the natural disaster like earthquake and flood.

14.1.5 WLAN

14.1.5.1 Introduction

It is also called as Local Area Wireless Network. Without wire, the devices are connected to develop the networks. All the mobile phones are able to connect by using WLAN. IEEE 802.11 is the standard for wireless technology to create number of nodes in a single network. Ethernet protocol and CSMA-CA are used in WLAN for the purpose of encryption and path sharing. High bandwidth can be made in this communication with a low cost wiring. The connection can be made with large number of systems in a single block or building. A wireless LAN adapter is used to connect the personal computer.

In Figure 14.17, three systems are connected by using Ethernet. In the Ethernet, we have a router, a bridge that is used to connect the number of systems with the help of cables. WLAN is used to connect a number of devices and one end of the device is called as a station. Access Point (AP) is used to transmit and receive the information [36]. All the devices are connected to form a network using WLAN. In that network, every device is possible to communicate each other. It is called as basic service sets (BSSs). BSSs are classified into two types. First one is independent BSSs and the other one is infrastructure BSSs.

(i) Independent BSSs:
     Within BSSs, only two clients can communicate without using APs. This kind of network is called as peer to peer connection Ad Hoc WLANs.

(ii) Infrastructure BSSs:
     Here, using the APs, the station communicates with another station. Two stations are not in same BSSs.

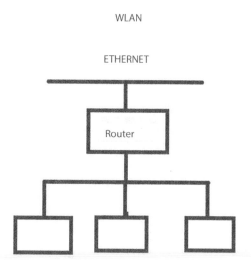

Figure 14.17 Wireless local area network [36].

14.1.5.2 Advantages of WLANs

- **Flexibility:** There is no restriction to communicate the devices within the radio coverage area. Radio waves can go through the walls, and senders and receivers can be located anywhere.
- **Planning:** In Ad Hoc Networks alone, there is no previous planning for starting communication. All other networks except Ad Hoc Networks are needed proper planning for making the communication.
- **Design:** Networks are advised to make the independent design for small devices. Before making the communication, the proper approval of designing is important.
- **Robustness:** During the disasters like flood and earthquakes, wireless networks can work. But in the wired networks, the connection will stop working in disasters.
- **Cost:** installation and maintenance cost of wireless networks is very less when compared with wired LAN.
  - After forming a network, the first user wants to connect via AP further adding users the cost will not be increased.
  - The installation is done by using a cable in wired LAN. But in wireless LAN, the cable is not there and labor cost for installing and making repair is also not allowed.
- **Ease to use:** The users are very much convenient in using wireless LAN. Everyone understands the procedure easily for using this network.

14.1.5.3 Drawbacks of WLAN

- **Proprietary solutions:** Many companies come up with proprietary solutions for developing features due to slow standardization measures.
- **Quality of services:** Quality of service of WLAN is always less than the wired networks. Lower bandwidth is the reason for the low quality of service. In order to have a limitations in radio transmission, error rate is high due to interference, timing for making error correction and detection is high, and delay is also high while in transmission.
- **Restrictions:** Restrictions are there with the frequencies to regulate the operation in several government sectors and private sectors like educational institutions and industries.

- **Global operation:** These products are buying from all the people in the world. So, frequency regulations of international and national have to be considered.
- **Less power: If the** networks are connected in wireless mode, then the power consumption is very high. This device can possible to work with the help of a battery.
- **License-free operation:** This network does not need the license to communicate with other devices. It is working in the license-free such as 2.4-GHz ISM band.
- **Robust transmission:** Wireless LAN transceivers cannot be accustomed for perfect transmission is a typical place of work or manufacture environment. The transmission made by the device in the network is robust.

14.1.6   GSM

14.1.6.1   Introduction

All the mobile users are using the Global System for Mobile Communication for communication purpose [20]. TDMA technology is used by the GSM. In the wireless technology, TDMA, CDMA, and GSM place a vital role for making communication between the devices [15]. This standard is developed in the year of 1987, and finally, it has been approved in the year of 1989 by the European Union (EU). This service is launched at first in Finland in the year 1991. The frequency band of GSM standard is increased from 900 MHz to 1800 MHz in the same year. Many countries are using this technology for developing their mobile technology.

14.1.6.2   Composition of GSM Networks

GSM technology is comprised of four components [21]. The components are Mobile Station, Base Station Subsystem (BSS) which is located in mobile device itself, Network Switching Subsystem, and Operation and Support Subsystem (OSS) [22].

- Mobile Node
  In mobile device, SIM card is providing the network connection about the network information of the mobile users.
- Base Station Subsystem

It manages the congestion between the mobile phone with NSS. In Base Station, Controller is having two components [16]. The base station controller (BSC) and the base transceiver station (BTS) are the components of BSS. BTS is having the control of getting and sending information to the mobile phones [23]. The BSC is used to intelligently control the number of Base Transceiver Station.

- Network Switching Subsystem
  Here, only the networks are decided and given to the mobile phone users. It is also called as core network, which is used to track the mobile phone. Connectivity, delivery, and receiving of the calls are happening by using the Network Switching Subsystem [17]. It consists of the home location register (HLN) and mobile switching center (MSC). Call management, SMS service, authenticating, and recording the calls via SIM cards are done only by these components of NSS.
- Operation and Support Subsystem
  The complete operation of GSM is supported by this system. Moral support is there for all the components of GSM as shown in Figure 14.18.

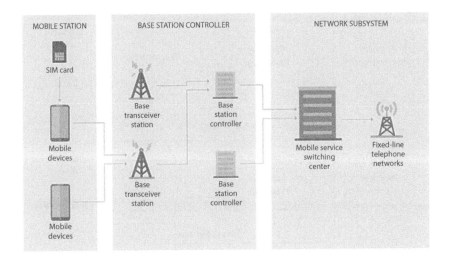

Figure 14.18 GSM network [20].

14.1.6.3 Security

The technology has to support with high security connection. Secure communication is performed by using the cryptographic technology [18]. Cryptography is nothing but the plain text (original information) which is created and having by the sender will be converted into cyber text. The cyber text will not be understandable by everyone. Only it can understand by the sender and receiver that who knows the secret key. Secret key may be private or public [19]. Two types of key are there in cryptography.

14.1.7 Smart Sensor

Senor is a sensing device which is used to detect the physical parameters like temperature, pressure, and strain, and the detected signals are transmitted to the next device. Traditional sensor is consists of sensing element and transmitter. In additional to that, transmitter has a data computing unit, signal processing unit, and communication unit, to enhance the functions of transmitter to be acting as a smart transmitter. Sensor is an important device in continuous monitoring and doing control action.

14.1.7.1 Development History of Smart Sensors

Many companies they started to manufacture the smart sensor in the mid of the year 1980's as shown in Figure 14.19. Finally, a Honeywell Company has

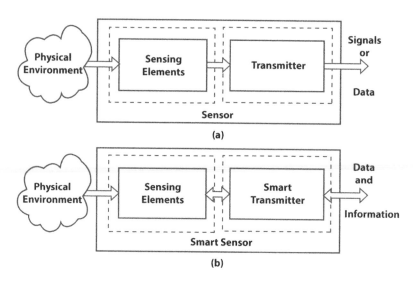

Figure 14.19 (a) Sensor. (b) Smart sensor [37].

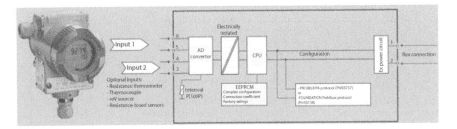

Figure 14.20 Siemens SITRAN TF functions diagram [37].

introduced the first commercial smart sensors in 1983. Measuring and monitoring the physical parameters such as temperature, pressure, flow, and level is done by the smart sensor. The smart sensor is having the sensing element along with that smart transmitter. A company smart transmitter includes analog-to-digital converters (ADCs), Central Processing Unit (CPU), Electrically Erasable Programmable Read Only Memory (EEPROM), and field bus communication functions as shown in Figure 14.20.

The main features of smart sensors are accuracy in measurement, self-diagnostic such as a short-circuit in sensing elements, self-configuration, self-calibration, and with wireless or wired communications. This devices are manufactured by the following leading companies like Rosemount, Siemens, and Honeywell. For instance, Siemens SITRANS TF provides high accurate value, as well as linearization, self-diagnostic, and functions. Honeywell product of SmartLine ST800 can produce the accuracy up to 0.0375% for stationary pressure measurement arranging within internal compensation [37]. The above device is an example for doing signal processing and analysis the process. The two processes are done in a smart transmitter. KROHN is introduced the OPTISWIRL 4070C flow meter which is also a smart sensor. This device is included with Intelligent Signal Processing (ISP) device. It can eliminate the unnecessary signal and exterior permutations so that the users get the stable output with the effect of pressure and temperature changes.

14.1.7.2 Internal Parts of Smart Transmitter

Smart Transmitter is used to make the decision of its own. It is made up of hardware and software components.

14.1.7.2.1 Hardware Components

The first block of the hardware components is Sensing Element Unit (SEU); here, the physical environment changes can be predicted and the signal is transferred into the next block which is illustrated in Figure 14.21.

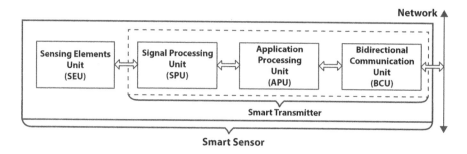

Figure 14.21 Internal parts of Smart Sensor [37].

The next block is Signal Processing Unit (SPU) and it is followed by Application Processing Unit (APU) and then the last block is Bidirectional Communication Unit (BCU).

- **Signal Processing Unit**

The signal received from sensing element is in the form of analog. The initial step of processing unit is converting analog signal into digital by using Analog-to-Digital Convertor (ADC). The output of the SPU is called the raw data which is in the forms of digital, and then, it is transferred to the next block. It includes some other functions like signal compensation, calibration, filters, and some transform functions.

- **Application Processing Unit**

It is embedded with many algorithms for performing different applications. Microcontroller Unit (MCU) is assigned APU to perform the complex algorithms. If we need to do multiple tasks simultaneously, then this means that the Real-Time Operating System (RTOS) is needed. The MCUs with RTOS are externally connected to APUs to carry out data analysis functions.

- **Bidirectional Communication Unit**

It acts as a communication bridge for APUs and External Network which is used to exchange the data from one device to another device. The data transformation is done by using appropriate networking protocols.

14.1.7.2.2   Software Components

It is coding part in smart sensor device. The programming language is dependent on the smart sensor. RTOS kernel's scheduler places a major role in the software side of the device. The scheduler is used to make the assignment of flow of work done by the device. To understand dissimilar application algorithms, programs can be assembled and allocated for each task. The every task can be elected as memory resources, independent loop, and the priorities. In a real time, algorithms and functions are to be prearranged flexibly.

14.1.7.3   Applications

- **Breathe Monitoring Systems**

Here, the microsensor is embedded with smart sensor to monitor, control, and transfer the condition of patient breathing issues. The modernized tool has been developed with small size and it can be used at home and also clinic [34]. The system is called as Smart Breathe Health Diagnostic Systems (SBHDS) and it is very compact, efficiently uses the energy, simple to use, capable of storing the data, and if it needs transfer the data to another place. The overall concept of SBHDS is very much simple and it can perform the diagnosis process and possible to give proper treatment within a span of time. It may offer very less expensive. To enhance the system capabilities, micro electromechanical systems (MEMS) or silicon processing is integrated with smart sensor. The advantage of MEMS is to reduce in size and weight, and it consumes low power.

The measured substances are having carbon monoxide, nitric oxide, and a multitude of volatile organic compounds. Exhaled breath condensate is nothing but the exhaled breath with aerosolized droplets. It is called as non-volatile compounds. People are really interested to do exercise. During exercise, any health issues related to breathing means this system

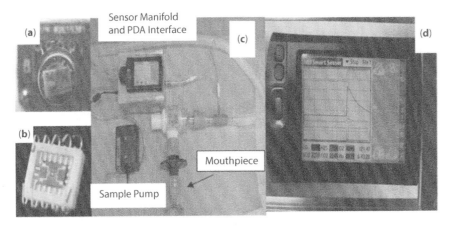

Figure 14.22 (a) Packaged CO_2 sensor. (b) Packaged O_2 sensor. (c) Overall exercise monitoring system. (d) User interface [34].

will identify that problem. That detected problem will be measured and it will be transferred to concern clinic to take necessary steps.

Initially, CO_2 and O_2 are measured to predict the abnormal health condition. The system is easily embedded with astronaut device and it gives reliable information for a long period of time without initial adjustments. The complete structure is shown in Figure 14.22. Mouthpiece helps us to get the breath component. The collected breath is analyzed by sensors which is integrated with Personal Digital Assistant (PDA). The analyzed data was displayed on the handheld device. The user interface is used to allow the device to connect with other device either with using wired or wireless transmission.

- **Flood and Water Level Monitoring System**
Various natural disasters happen all over the world in every year. So by using this technology easily, it is predictable and make some precautionary steps to save the people. But it is not possible to eliminate or eradicate the natural disaster [8]. Let us discuss how the disasters are focused and handling the critical situation. WSN technology has been used to handle the situation and taking necessary steps to overcome from this problem. Let us see the diagram of flood and the water level monitoring system shown in Figure 14.23. Here, flood switch sensors can be used and detect the level of water and pass the information to the Arduino UNO Microcontroller. For this to work, microcontroller needs power supply, externally providing the supply. Through GSM technology, the information is passed to the end user to make some necessary action to manage the situation.

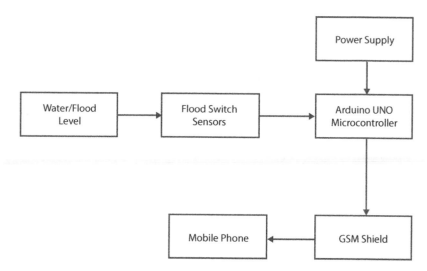

Figure 14.23 Flood monitoring systems [8].

Here, three sensors are used to indicate scenario. Table 14.1 will help us understand the nature of what is happening in the environment. The three sensors are placed in a different place to indicate whether the environment in safe condition or in a risky state.

If all the three sensors are in low level that indicates low water level, then it means a safe condition of nature (Risk-Free). If sensors 2 and 3 are getting the high value, this means that there will be a technical problem, hence immediately check with the sensors. In the next case, if the first sensor value alone is 1, then this means that early detection can be made via GSM Module to the public as well as the company sectors. When all the sensory level is high, it is considering the high level risk so rescue activities will be taken to manage the scenario. With the help of this system, major problem of the flood can be predicted and this gives the alert to the government as well as the public to ready for the situation.

Table 14.1 Sensor level indication via SMS.

Flood switch sensor				
Sensor 1	Sensor 2	Sensor 3	Conditions	SMS contents
0	0	0	Safe Condition (Risk-Free)	Safe Condition (No Flood Detection)
0	0	1	Technical Problem	Technical Problem (Check the Sensors)
0	1	0	Technical Problem	Technical Problem (Check the Sensors)
0	1	1	Technical Problem	Technical Problem (Check the Sensors)
1	0	0	ALERT! (LEVEL 1)	Alert Level (Early Detection and Alert)
1	0	1	Technical Problem	Technical Problem (Check the Sensors)
1	1	0	Moderate Risk! (LEVEL 2)	Moderate Risk Level (Respond to Alert)
1	1	1	HIGH RISK!!! (LEVEL 3)	High Risk Level (Rescue Activities)

- **Traffic Monitoring and Controlling**

Considering the present world is acquired with number of vehicles. Every home is having a minimum of 3 two wheeler and 1 or 2 four wheelers [9]. Because of this, congestion is happening. So, in the fast growing world, there is a possibility of has more accidents. To avoid such kind of things, traffic monitoring and controlling is needed everywhere [10].

In every four sides of the signal area, there will be one sensor array and IR sensor in order to measure the density of the vehicles [11]. So, the collected data from the sensors are given into analog-to-digital controller as shown in Figure 14.24. After converting the analog signal into digital, the data have been given to the controller [12]. The controller will pass the information to the server via wireless networks about the density of the vehicle [13]. Like that, four sides of information are collected to the server, comparing with all the data, which is having the highest density of vehicles decision can be made. The traffic signal opens in high density side of the traffic signals [14]. After the signal opened, that side may have a low density. Then, next highest value side will be considered for opening the signal. Like that, the decision can be taken by the system itself.

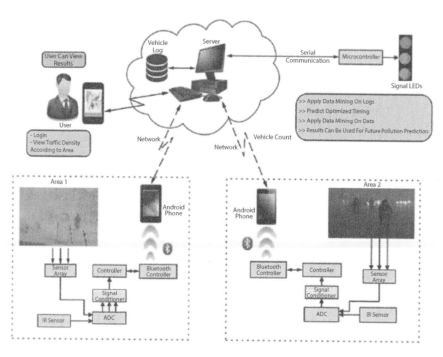

Figure 14.24 Traffic monitoring system [9].

14.1.8   Conclusion

In this chapter, we started with the definition and working principle of the sensor and its various types. The detected parameters are transferred by using different types of wireless networks. The different types of networks like WPAN, Zigbee, and WLAN are described in detailed manner. By using this, it is easily understood by everyone who want to study the concepts. Finally, it is illustrated about the smart sensor and it applications.

References

1. electronicshub.org, https://www.electronicshub.org/different-types-sensors/
2. electrical4u.com, https://www.electrical4u.com/sensor-types-of-sensor/
3. watelectronics.com, https://www.watelectronics.com/different-types-of-sensors-with-applications/
4. electricaltechnology.org, https://www.electricaltechnology.org/2018/11/types-sensors-applications.html
5. en.wikipedia.org, https://en.wikipedia.org/wiki/List_of_sensors
6. finoit.com, https://www.finoit.com/blog/top-15-sensor-types-used-iot/
7. elprocus.com, https://www.elprocus.com/what-is-zigbee-technology-architecture--and-its-applications/
8. researchgate.net, https://www.researchgate.net/publication/333538013_Flood_disaster_indicator_of_water_level_monitoring_system
9. Singh, L., Tripathi, S., Arora, H., Time optimization for traffic signal control using genetic algorithm. *Int. J. Recent Trends Eng.*, 2, 2, 4–6, 2009.
10. Milanes, V., Villagra, J., Godoy, J., Simo, J., Pérez, J., Onieva, E., An intelligent V2I-based traffic management system. *IEEE Trans. Intell. Transp. Syst.*, 13, 1, 49–58, 2012.
11. Pable, S.N., Welekar, A., Gaikwad-Patil, T., Implementation on Priority Based Signal Management in Traffic System. *Int. J. Eng. Res. Technol. (IJERT)*, 3, 5, 1679–1682, 2014.
12. Krishnan, S., Traffic Flow Optimization and Vehicle Safety in Smart Cities. *Int. J. Innov. Res. Sci., Eng. Technol.*, 5, 5, 7814–7820, 2016.
13. Li, Z., Shahidehpour, M., Bahramirad, S., Khodaei, A., Optimizing traffic signal settings in smart cities. *IEEE Trans. Smart Grid*, 8, 5, 2382–2393, 2017.
14. Janahan, S.K., Veeramanickam, M.R.M., Arun, S., Narayanan, K., Anandan, R., Parvez, S.J., IoT based smart traffic signal monitoring system using vehicles counts. *Int. J. Eng. Technol.*, 7, 309–312, 2018.
15. Sammarco, J.J., Paddock, R., Fries, E.F., Karra, V.K., *A technology review of smart sensors with wireless networks for applications in hazardous work environments*, National Institute for Occupational Safety and Health, NIOSH—Publications Dissemination, 2007.
16. Fernández-Montes, A., Gonzalez-Abril, L., Ortega, J.A., Morente, F.V., A Study on Saving Energy in Artificial Lighting by Making Smart Use of

Wireless Sensor Networks and Actuators. *IEEE netw.*, 23, 6, 16–20, 2009, University of Seville.

17. Smart Sensor Networks: Technologies and Applications for Green Growth, OECD, OECD Conference on "ICTs, the environment and climate, December2009. www.oecd.org/sti/ict/green-ict.

18. D.J. Cook and S.K. Das, John Wiley, LEWIS, F.L., Associate Director for Research Head, Advanced Controls, Sensors, and MEMS Group Automation and Robotics Research Institute, in Smart Environments: Technology, Protocols, and Applications, Chapter 2, The University of Texas at Arlington, *Wireless Sensor Networks*, New York, 2005.

19. Akyildiz, I.F., Su, W., Sankarasubramaniam, Y., Cayirci, E., Wireless Sensor Networks: A Survey. *Comput. Netw.*, 38, 393–422, 2002.

20. searchmobilecomputing.techtarget.com, https://searchmobilecomputing.techtarget.com/definition/GSM

21. tutorialspoint.com, https://www.tutorialspoint.com/gsm/gsm_overview.htm

22. electronics.howstuffworks.com, https://electronics.howstuffworks.com/question537.htm

23. mobilecomms-technology.com, http://www.mobilecomms-technology.com/projects/gsm/

24. learn.sparkfun.com, https://learn.sparkfun.com/tutorials/accelerometer-basics/all

25. fierceelectronics.com, https://www.fierceelectronics.com/sensors/what-ir-sensor

26. hbm.com, https://www.hbm.com/en/7646/what-is-a-pressure-sensor/

27. libelium.com, http://www.libelium.com/smart-water-sensors-to-monitor-water-quality-in-rivers-lakes-and-the-sea/

28. fierceelectronics, https://www.fierceelectronics.com/electronics/what-a-chemical-sensor

29. thinklucid.com, https://thinklucid.com/tech-briefs/understanding-digital-image-sensors/

30. safewise.com, https://www.safewise.com/resources/motion-sensor-guide/

31. electronicsforu.com, https://www.electronicsforu.com/electronics-projects/hardware-diy/smoke-alcohol-lpg-detection-alarm

32. realpars.com, https://realpars.com/level-sensor/

33. sensirion.com, https://www.sensirion.com/en/flow-sensors/

34. Hunter, G.W., Xu, J.C., Biaggi-Labiosa, A.M., Laskowski, D., Dutta, P.K., Mondal, S.P., Ward, B.J., Makel, D.B., Liu, C.C., Chang, C.W., Dweik, R.A., Smart sensor systems for human health breath monitoring applications. *J. Breath Res.*, 5, 3, 2011.

35. searchmobilecomputing.techtarget.com, https://searchmobilecomputing.techtarget.com/definition/WPAN

36. javatpoint.com, https://www.javatpoint.com/wireless-lan-introduction

37. He, A., Western Electronics Thesis and Disseratation Repository, *Design and Implementation of Smart Sensors with Capabilities of Process Fault Detection and Variable Prediction*, Western Electronic Thesis and Dissertation Repository, Western University Scholarship@Western, 2017.

Index

3D printing, 127–128

Accelerators, 241
Administrative and security
consistency, 122–123
Adulteration, 287
Agent, 142, 145, 149
Aggregator mobile device (AMD), 22
AI, 141–150, 269
AI in marketing, 126
AI in patient monitoring and wearable
health devices, 134
AI in surgery, 127
AI-assisted radiology and pathology,
228–229
Air bubble, 297
Airbnb, 141
AlphaFold method, 231–232
AlphaGo, 146, 148
Analog circuits, 93
Analog signals, 94
Analysis, 142, 144, 147, 149
Anchor nodes, 64, 70–72, 74–76, 78,
79, 88, 89
ANN, 272–273, 283
Anti-aliasing filter, 95
Apparatus, 297
Applications, 141–142, 144, 146, 148,
150
Applications of AI in pharma, 126
Approximate weighted total least
square algorithm, 249, 261
ARBIN battery tester, 262

Artificial, 141–142, 144, 146, 148
Artificial intelligence, 173
Artificial intelligence (AI),
driven augmented and virtual
reality, 25
driven body area networks, 13
driven communication technology,
6
driven IoT, 20
driven mHealth, 10
Artificial intelligence (AI) in
healthcare,
DL frameworks for identifying
disease, 240–241
healthcare system using ML, 228
primary examples of ML's
implementation in the healthcare,
228–232
proposed work, 241–242
reinforcement learning process,
227–228
related works, 232–240
results and discussions, 244–245
semi-supervised learning process,
227
supervised learning process,
226–227
unsupervised learning process, 227
Artificial intelligence in medical
imaging, 131
Artificial neural networks (ANN), 8–9,
11, 14, 183, 233–235
ASTM, 302

Also of Interest

Check out these published and forthcoming titles in the "Artificial Intelligence and Soft Computing for Industrial Transformation" series from Scrivener Publishing

The New Advanced Society
Artificial Intelligence and Industrial Internet of Things Paradigm
Edited by Sandeep Kumar Panda, Ramesh Kumar Mohapatra, Subhrakanta Panda and S. Balamurugan
Forthcoming 2022. ISBN 978-1-119-82447-3

Digitization of Healthcare Data using Blockchain
Edited by T. Poongodi, D. Sumathi, B. Balamurugan and K. S. Savita
Forthcoming 2022. ISBN 978-1-119-79185-0

Tele-Healthcare
Applications of Artificial Intelligence and Soft Computing Techniques
Edited by R. Nidhya, Manish Kumar and S. Balamurugan
Forthcoming 2020. ISBN 978-1-119-84176-0

Impact of Artificial Intelligence on Organizational Transformation
Edited by S. Balamurugan, Sonal Pathak, Anupriya Jain, Sachin Gupta, and Sachin Sharma and Sonia Duggal
Forthcoming 2022. ISBN 978-1-119-71017-2

Artificial Intelligence for Renewable Energy Systems
Edited by Ajay Kumar Vyas, S. Balamurugan, Kamal Kant Hiran Harsh S. Dhiman
Forthcoming 2022. ISBN 978-1-119-76169-3

Artificial Intelligence Techniques for Wireless Communication and Networking
Edited by Kanthavel R., K. Ananthajothi, S. Balamurugan and R. Karthik Ganesh
Forthcoming 2022. ISBN 978-1-119-82127 4

Advanced Healthcare Systems
Empowering Physicians with IoT-Enabled Technologies
Edited by Rohit Tanwar, S. Balamurugan, R. K. Saini, Vishal Bharti and Premkumar Chithaluru
Forthcoming 2022. ISBN 978-1-119-76886-9

Smart Systems for Industrial Applications
Edited by C. Venkatesh, N. Rengarajan, P. Ponmurugan and S. Balamurugan
Published 2022. ISBN 978-1-119-76200-3

Human Technology Communication
Internet of Robotic Things and Ubiquitous Computing
Edited by R. Anandan. G. Suseendran, S. Balamurugan, Ashish Mishra and D. Balaganesh
Published 2021. ISBN 978-1-119-75059-8

Nature-Inspired Algorithms Applications
Edited by S. Balamurugan, Anupriya Jain, Sachin Sharma, Dinesh Goyal, Sonia Duggal and Seema Sharma
Published 2021. ISBN 978-1-119-68174-8

Computation in Bioinformatics
Multidisciplinary Applications
Edited by S. Balamurugan, Anand Krishnan, Dinesh Goyal, Balakumar Chandrasekaran and Boomi Pandi
Published 2021. ISBN 978-1-119-65471-1

Fuzzy Intelligent Systems
Methodologies, Techniques, and Applications
Edited by E. Chandrasekaran, R. Anandan, G. Suseendran, S. Balamurugan and Hanaa Hachimi
Published 2021. ISBN 978-1-119-76045-0

Biomedical Data Mining for Information Retrieval
Methodologies, Techniques and Applications
Edited by Sujata Dash, Subhendu Kumar Pani, S. Balamurugan and Ajith Abraham
Published 2021. ISBN 978-1-119-71124-7

Design and Analysis of Security Protocols for Communication
Edited by Dinesh Goyal, S. Balamurugan, Sheng-Lung Peng and O.P. Verma
Published 2020. ISBN 978-1-119-55564-3

www.scrivenerpublishing.com

Printed and bound by CPI Group (UK) Ltd, Croydon, CR0 4YY